THE COMPLETE MAKING OF

INDIANA JONES™

THE COMPLETE MAKING OF

THE DEFINITIVE STORY BEHIND ALL FOUR FILMS

NEW INTERVIEWS BY LAURENT BOUZEREAU

WRITTEN BY J. W. RINZLER

DEL
REY

L. B.: To my offscreen heroes: my parents, Daniel and Micheline, sisters Cécile and Géraldine, and Markus Keith

J. W. R.: To Geneviève, with love

Page x: Concept art of the temple door by Miles Teves; graphics and coloring by Chris Kitisakkul.

A Del Rey Trade Paperback Original

Published in the United States by Del Rey Books, an imprint of The Random House Publishing Group, a division of Random House, Inc., New York.

Del Rey is a registered trademark and the Del Rey colophon is a trademark of Random House, Inc.

ISBN 978-0-345-50129-5

Printed in China through Palace Press International

www.indianajones.com

www.delreybooks.com

9 8 7 6 5 4 3 2 1

ACKNOWLEDGMENTS

At Lucasfilm: Once again much of this book could not have been completed without invaluable help from Lucasfilm's several archives. At Skywalker Ranch Research Library, huge thanks to: Jo Donaldson, Robyn Stanley, and Carol Moen Wing; at its physical Lucasfilm Archives, to Laela French, Dinah Houghtaling, and Christie Chappins; and last but far from least, at the Presidio's Image Archives, to Tina Mills, Stacey Leong, and Matthew Azeveda. At Lucas Licensing we owe a double debt to Howard Roffman for recovering the historically invaluable story conference transcript for *Raiders of the Lost Ark* and for guiding key elements of the book-making process; to Troy Alders for supervising the design with his usual aplomb and energy; to our publishing comrades for their support and advice, Carol Roeder, Sue Rostoni, Leland Chee, Frank Parisi, Mindy Goldberg, and Nancy Frisch; thanks to Lynne Hale and Steve Sansweet, in public relations; and Jim Ward, at LucasArts; in the legal department, to Lynn Bartsch, Chris Holm, Jann Moorehead, Elaine Mederer, and to Sarah Garcia for uncovering several key documents; and in the chairman's office, to Jane Bay—and to Anne Merrifield for finding George Lucas's handwritten story summary for *Raiders*; at Industrial Light & Magic, to John Knoll, for enabling us to take screen grabs of the films, and to Dennis Muren, for his key memories; to Miles Perkins and Greg Grusby; and finally a special thanks to Sarita Patel, at Park Way, for miraculously finding the PROFESSOR OF FLOPOLOGY baseball cap. And a special thanks to Rick McCallum.

At Amblin: A thousand thanks to Kristie Macosko, Samantha Becker, Marvin Levy, Kristin Stark, and Michelle Fandetti. This book would not have been possible without the enormous support, time, and help from Frank Marshall, Kathleen Kennedy, Harrison Ford, and the entire cast and crew from: *Raiders of the Lost Ark, Indiana Jones and the Temple of Doom, Indiana Jones and the Last Crusade* and, most particularly, the team of *Indiana Jones and the Kingdom of the Crystal Skull*.

Thanks to *Skull* unit publicist Deborah Wuliger, Martin Cohen, and Kay McCauley.

A special thanks to Derek Taylor for having recorded live and in words his impressions of the making of *Raiders of the Lost Ark* in his original book; and to the great teams at Paramount Pictures and Paramount Home Entertainment. To do-gooders at large, thanks to Hal Barwood, Amy Gary, Jenna Free, Jonathan Bresman, J. David Spurlock, and Arnaud Grunberg.

At Del Rey: Once again many, many thanks to the team—how many books have we done together?—editor Keith Clayton and production supervisor Erich Schoeneweiss, Scott Shannon and Dave Stevenson, and their support groups. One day we'll do a stress-free making-of book (and dogs will love cats).

At Palace Press: To Scott Erwert for taking the rough layouts and making them beautiful, and to Iain Morris for supervising that process with his usual expertise; and to Gabriel Ely and Donna Lee for eleventh-hour heroics; and to Raoul Goff, Michael Madden, Peter Beren, Mikayla Butchart, and Susan Ristow.

For key artworks and related information: A grateful thanks to Guy Hendrix Dyas and Jim Steranko.

A huge thank-you to the two men who started it all and who have been a huge help and inspiration throughout: Steven Spielberg and George W. Lucas…Jr.

CONTENTS

PREFACE

When I was a kid I loved watching the Saturday matinee serials at the local movie house. *Flash Gordon, Buck Rogers, Don Winslow of the Navy, Tim Tyler's Luck, Zorro*, and many others—they had lots of action and great cliff-hangers. The production standards were minimal at best, but who notices that when they're eight years old?

Years later I managed to persuade Twentieth Century-Fox to let me try my hand at re-creating those serials as an updated space-fantasy epic. As I was writing the first draft of what would become *Star Wars*, I watched again many of those two-reelers from the 1930s and 1940s—in a few the hero would try to track down a lost idol or a hidden tomb—and I realized that another type of character might work: an intrepid archaeologist-adventurer-professor-playboy-tomb-robber—an expert in the occult equipped with a bullwhip and a pistol. I wrote down a name I thought was pretty good: Indiana Smith.

Years after that a good friend of mine signed on as director: Steven Spielberg. I loved his work and I knew he understood instinctively the spirit of the adventures we would need to capture on film. He persuaded me to change Smith to Indiana Jones—and he suggested Harrison Ford as the perfect incarnation of our guy. During the 1980s the three of us went on to make *Raiders of the Lost Ark*, *Indiana Jones and the Temple of Doom*, and *Indiana Jones and the Last Crusade*. As I write these words in the twenty-first century, strangely enough, we're at work on our fourth: *Indiana Jones and the Kingdom of the Crystal Skull*. We may be getting older, but we've come up with our longest title yet.

Throughout the saga Kathy Kennedy and Frank Marshall have done a brilliant job of producing, helping Steven and me create a juggernaut production team. It's really been an ongoing extended family—which is now being enlarged by a new generation. But I still get a kick every time I see Harrison dressed up as the weather-beaten Indy; watching Steven and Harrison working their magical chemistry yet again is an absolute delight. Our goal is and has always been to take audiences on a unique thrill ride by combining images, rhythm, sound, and music into an unforgettable experience that you can have only at the movies. Like many fans out there, I can't wait to see this film.

Skywalker Ranch, Northern California
December 2007

FOREWORD

George and I have known each other forever it seems. We met at a backstage party after a student film festival and we just became friends. Years later, George had finished *Star Wars* and was planning to go on a trip that would take him far, far away from its opening weekend; so I joined him in Hawaii. We were just waiting for the grosses to come in; it was like waiting for election returns. As we all know, it turned out to be a landslide for George Lucas. George, at that point, just gushed a sigh of relief and then changed the subject from *Star Wars* to what I was doing next. He asked me, "What film would you like to make?" And I said, "Well, you know what I've always wanted to do? I've always wanted to direct a *James Bond* picture." And George said, "I got that beat." I asked, "What do you mean?" He replied, "I have *Raiders of the Lost Ark*"—and that was the beginning of our professional partnership.

In a sense, I ended up not wanting to imitate the James Bond series or even mimic it in any way. I think we all agreed that Indiana Jones had to be vulnerable. He had to be a real person. Part of him had to be the audience saying, " could be that guy."

Raiders is one of those films that I can look at with my kids and detach myself from how it was made, just watching it through the eyes of my children from start to finish. When I look back on *Temple of Doom*, I have to say that the best thing that came out of that experience was meeting Kate Capshaw, who went on from there to produce with me the greatest epic of all time … our family. And the most important thing about *Last Crusade*, the third *Indy* film, is that it doesn't end with a truck chase, or a climactic upheaval of special effects and ghosts and spirits; instead it concludes in a most personal way—more personal than any of the previous movies—with

Indy and his father finding common ground from which to start a great relationship. As we started making the fourth film, *Indiana Jones and the Kingdom of the Crystal Skull*, I wanted to continue in that vein; I wanted to have fun and to create more of that personal family dynamic. I want audiences to come to this movie and discover that their old friends haven't changed all that much—but also to make new ones.

Two decades later, I am thrilled to be back in business with George, Harrison Ford, Frank Marshall, Kathy Kennedy and … Karen Allen. While I miss many stalwarts of the old cast and crew—those retired, Dougie Slocombe, Robert Watts, Sean Connery; or no longer with us, David Tomblin, Denholm Elliott, and others—I'm happy to have with me now a new group for this one: Cate Blanchett, Shia LaBeouf, Ray Winstone, John Hurt, director of photography Janusz Kaminski, production designer Guy Hendrix Dyas, writer David Koepp, just to name a few. We've been working faster and more furiously than ever before.

As I write this, I am almost done editing the film with Michael Kahn and I can't wait to sit down on the recording stage—when John Williams will bring the baton down and a hundred orchestra members will start playing the *Indiana Jones* theme. I hope audiences around the globe have as much fun watching *Indiana Jones and the Kingdom of the Crystal Skull* as we had creating it.

Steven Spielberg

Hollywood, California
December 2007

INTRODUCTIONS

Laurent Bouzereau: I first saw *Raiders of the Lost Ark* in Paris where I grew up, with my feet off the ground for fear snakes might be crawling underneath my seat! Yet, on that day, I gave up my ambition of becoming James Bond—my new dream was to be Indy! It never happened but years later, in 2003, I got the unique opportunity of meeting the talented group of filmmakers that had stirred my imagination and forged my love for adventure films, when I was asked to produce retrospective documentaries for a DVD release of the *Indiana Jones Trilogy*. Four years later, I came on board to document the making of *Indy IV* and both experiences were, to say the least, amazing, educational, and unforgettable. Today, I am thrilled that my encounters and discussions on the making of all four films are available in book form, along with some fascinating text and facts dug up by Lucasfilm's in-house archaeologist Jonathan Rinzler.

I was on the set of the new *Indy* film for a large part of the production and it was quite touching to witness how everyone involved wanted to be part of the *Indiana Jones* history and legacy. On set, cast and crew truly believed that Harrison Ford was Indy. Everyone took their job extremely seriously and realized that every single moment, every single line of dialogue, every prop, set, costume, and camera angle had the potential of becoming iconic. I hope that the interviews and the text convey the spirit that lived on the set and that the archival material from the first three films pays equal tribute to Steven Spielberg, George Lucas, and the team that worked so hard with them in front of and behind the camera to make us all believe that Indiana Jones truly exists, that he is not just part of our imagination—Indy not only gave adventure films a new name, it gave cinema something worth writing about!

J. W. Rinzler: I'm fortunate enough to have been to two sneak previews that changed my life: *Star Wars*, at the Coronet in San Francisco, in 1977; and *Raiders of the Lost Ark*, in an SF theater on Van Ness, in 1981. Decades later I have been fortunate enough to be able to write *The Making of Star Wars* and now *The Complete Making of Indiana Jones*. For the latter, thanks to archival material and great new interviews by Laurent Bouzereau, we've been able to craft oral histories of all four *Indy* films told by the participants themselves.

This volume devotes the lion's share of its space to *Raiders* because that was the film that started it all. We even managed to get in highlights of the original story conference transcript for *Raiders*, thanks to president of Lucas Licensing Howard Roffman, who still had his copy.

The Complete Making of Indiana Jones also benefits from hundreds of never-seen-before photos uncovered in our Image Archives, while I scoured additional Lucasfilm Archives to bring to light some of its hidden treasures: artworks, storyboards, documents. In fact none of this would have been possible without the framework that George Lucas has created within Skywalker Ranch and without his support for this project. I'd also like to thank Steven Spielberg for greenlighting this book—and of course for directing some of the most thrilling scenes I've ever seen.

All in all I sincerely hope every reader enjoys the efforts of the many people who contributed to this book.

SELECTED WHO'S WHO

Karen Allen, Marion Ravenwood (RLA, KCS)

Vic Armstrong, stunt coordinator (RLA, TD, LC)

Cate Blanchett, Spalko (KCS)

Jeffrey Boam, screenwriter (LC)

Dan Bradley, second-unit director (KCS)

Ben Burtt, sound designer (RLA, TD, LC)

Kate Capshaw, Wilhelmina (Willie) Scott (TD)

Patricia Carr, production supervisor (RLA, TD, LC)

Sean Connery, Henry Jones Sr. (LC)

Alison Doody, Dr. Elsa Schneider (LC)

Guy Hendrix Dyas, production designer (KCS)

Richard Edlund, ILM visual effects supervisor (RLA)

Denholm Elliott, Marcus Brody (RLA, LC)

Deborah Fine, researcher (SAGA)

Harrison Ford, Indiana Jones (Henry Jones Jr.) (SAGA)

Pablo Helman, ILM visual effects supervisor (KCS)

Willard Huyck, screenwriter (TD)

Michael Kahn, editor (SAGA)

Janusz Kaminski, director of photography (KCS)

Lawrence Kasdan, screenwriter (RLA)

Gloria Katz, screenwriter (TD)

Howard Kazanjian, executive producer (RLA)

Kathleen Kennedy, associate to Mr. Spielberg (RLA); associate producer (TD); production executive, USA (LC); executive producer (KCS)

David Koepp, screenwriter (KCS)

Shia LaBeouf, Mutt (KCS)

George Lucas, executive producer/story (SAGA)

Frank Marshall, producer (RLA, KCS); executive producer (TD, LC)

Micheal McAlister, ILM visual effects supervisor (LC)

Michael (Mickey) Moore, second-unit director (RLA, TD, LC)

Dennis Muren, ILM visual effects supervisor (TD)

Lorne Peterson, ILM model shop supervisor (RLA, TD)

Anthony Powell, costume designer (TD, LC)

Gary Powell, stunt coordinator (KCS)

Glenn Randall, stunt coordinator (RLA, TD)

Norman Reynolds, production designer (RLA)

John Rhys-Davies, Sallah (RLA, LC)

Pat Roach, stuntman (RLA, TD, LC)

Elliot Scott, production designer (TD, LC)

Douglas Slocombe, director of photography (RLA, TD, LC)

Steven Spielberg, director (SAGA)

David Tomblin, first assistant director (RLA, TD, LC)

Robert Watts, producer (RLA, TD, LC)

John Williams, composer (SAGA)

THE COMPLETE MAKING OF

INDIANA JONES

CHAPTER 1
THE NAME IS INDIANA

1968 TO FEBRUARY 1980

"I met George Lucas for the first time backstage at Royce Hall at UCLA," Steven Spielberg says. "It was where his USC film *THX 1138 4EB* was being shown at a student film festival. I was going to school at Cal State Long Beach at the time, which didn't have a film department, so I didn't have a film to show. I was just a member of the audience; I wanted to see what the student films were all about."

Joining other college students and attendees on the evening of Friday, January 19, 1968, junior Steven Spielberg sat down in the 1,800-seat auditorium for the third annual National Student Film Festival, featuring the University of Southern California and the University of California at Los Angeles—at that time practically the only schools with cinema departments. Among the nine judges were directors Irvin Kershner and Norman Jewison, and writer Norman Corwin. Former USC graduate student George Lucas was probably seated near the front as his 16mm 17-minute-long experimental short was projected, along with those of his contemporaries John Milius, Walter Murch, Matthew Robbins, Randal Kleiser, Robert Dalva, Caleb Deschanel, Hal Barwood, Willard Huyck, and others. It was an exceptional group whose members would go on to help form American Zoetrope, revolutionize sound design, and make award-winning films. But at that time Lucas was intent on making a living as an editor and an avant-garde documentarian.

"I didn't know ahead of time about any of the films in the short-film category, so I anticipated nothing," Spielberg says. "I saw a number of shorts first—but when *THX* came on there was so much virtuosity in the craft and the vision and the emotion of that story that I... I couldn't believe it was a student film. I thought some Hollywood genius had slipped something

in—a ringer—and that it should have been disqualified for its sheer professionalism. It absolutely stopped the festival. You could have heard a pin drop in that theater. I just couldn't believe it! I was insanely jealous! Everything I had done before became irrelevant to me. George simply raised the bar higher than I thought I ever could reach at that time in my life."

The judges gave *THX 1138 4EB* the top prize; Lucas received honorable mentions in two other categories as well. Afterward Spielberg, who had made many 8mm movies while growing up, went backstage to meet some of the young filmmakers. "I think I may have seen him," Lucas says. "There were a lot of people afterward, but if we met it was definitely a handshake, hi, how are you."

"George was back there with Francis Coppola, who I didn't know either," Spielberg says. "That was the first time I actually laid eyes on George."

Coppola was not only a UCLA alumnus, but also a wunderkind of the student world for having broken into the professional film industry, an unprecedented feat. Ironically, he'd already become disillusioned with Hollywood and was about to embark on an independent film project with several friends, including Lucas—a road movie called *The Rain People* (1969), which they photographed during the spring and fall of 1968.

Such was the inspiration generated by that evening's experience, and such was his own drive, that Spielberg soon embarked on his own short subject, *Amblin'*, a 24-minute film he completed during the summer and fall of that same year.

"Steven came over to the USC cinema department, to try and find a cameraman to shoot it for him," Lucas says. "He was interviewing Caleb Deschanel, a good friend of mine and a great cameraman, who had worked

with me on lots of student films. It was through Caleb that I became aware that there was this kid who was trying to do a 35-millimeter film, which was a big deal at the time. That was when I first became aware of *Amblin'* and Steven."

Allen Daviau would shoot *Amblin'*, and that December it enabled Spielberg to sign a seven-year contract as a director in the television department at Universal Studios under the auspices of vice president of production Sidney J. Sheinberg.

"I think *Amblin'* was shown in some kind of film festival or something," Lucas says. "I saw it and it was good; it was professional. He knew what he was doing."

Lucas also made the professional directorial jump in 1968, when Coppola brokered a deal with Warner Bros. through American Zoetrope to expand *THX 1138 4EB* into a feature. But before Lucas began principal photography, he met Spielberg again in early 1969.

"I think Steven had seen an ad in *Variety* announcing *THX* and then decided to call Francis," Lucas says. "He said, 'I'm a young director working at Universal. I've just done my first TV shows, and I'd love to come over.' So he came over to Warner Bros. and had lunch with Francis and me. That was the first time I actually talked with Steven. He was the youngest director at Universal; I was the youngest director at Warner Bros. And he admired Francis, because Francis was this big success story. But I was already impressed. He was 22, directing TV shows. I hadn't directed anything yet, so I thought, *Oh my God, he's ahead of me.* I saw him as a contemporary up-and-comer."

"In meeting George I kept thinking about his filmmaking," Spielberg says, "so I really wasn't meeting George the person, I was meeting the man who had created this revelation for me that evening. So I was a little bit in awe of him, and George was, in those days, a little more guarded. George was this kind of maverick from Northern California, an independent filmmaker who was always extremely proud that he had very few attachments to Hollywood, and I was essentially a test-tube baby, incubated on the lot at Universal Studios, raised inside the establishment, and very proud of that. I think that difference attracted us to each other."

ENCOUNTER OF THE THIRD KIND

THX 1138 was released in March 1971, shortly after Spielberg's first television movie, *L.A. 2017*, an episode of *The Name of the Game*, was broadcast by NBC on January 15, 1971. In preparing it, Spielberg had

LEFT: Steven Spielberg directing Joan Crawford in "Eyes," an episode of the TV series *Night Gallery*, 1969.
BELOW RIGHT: George Lucas while directing *THX 1138 4EB* in 1967.

TOP LEFT: Lucas on the set of *THX 1138*, 1969. TOP RIGHT: At Park Way in Marin County, Hal Barwood, Lucas, Shar O' Donnell, and Lucas's assistant Jane Bay, circa 1978—with Lucas's Alaskan malamute: Indiana. ABOVE: Gary Kurtz, Steven Spielberg, and George Lucas, 1974.

worked with writer Philip Wylie and actor Gene Barry to create a vision of Los Angeles in the future.

"*L.A. 2017* was on television, and I saw it," Lucas says. "It was just kind of *THX*-y. It was a friendly homage in parts."

"I know George was curious because of a show Steve did called *2017*," says Hal Barwood, who also was introduced to Spielberg at around this time. "Matthew Robbins and I were working on *Star Dancing*, the movie Ralph McQuarrie illustrated. Our producer Larry Tucker was looking for a director and he heard about this young TV-movie hotshot at Universal, and arranged for us all to meet. Instant rapport and friendship, but, alas, no movie."

Spielberg would later remark that his first TV movie "opened a lot of doors for me." But his meeting with Robbins and Barwood in 1971 wouldn't bear fruit for several more years, after Spielberg had directed several more TV films—including *Duel*, which was broadcast on November 13, 1971, and which Lucas also happened to see.

"I was at a party at Francis's house, and I'd heard that Steven had directed his first movie of the week," Lucas says. "I thought, *Well, I'll watch 10 or 15 minutes to see what it is*. I remember very distinctly going upstairs during this party and I started watching—and I couldn't stop. It was so amazing. During a commercial break, I ran downstairs and said, 'Francis, you've got to come see this movie. This guy's *really* good.' But nobody came, so I ended up watching the whole thing by myself while the party was going on. I was very, very, very impressed with his work. Steven had taken a sliver of an idea and turned it into a compelling experience, with not a lot of story, dialogue, or character. It was all done very subtly and cinematically."

Shortly afterward the orbits of the two directors aligned again, early in 1972. "I was introduced to George by Matthew Robbins and Hal Barwood, friends of his," says Spielberg. "They were writing a script for me, which turned out to be the first feature film I ever directed—*The Sugarland Express*."

"I was actually doing the casting on *American Graffiti*, which took about five or six months," Lucas says. "So every week I'd come down from San Francisco to Los Angeles and stay at Matt Robbins's house in Benedict Canyon, because I didn't have any money and I was sleeping on his couch. Matt happened to be working with Steven on *The Sugarland Express*, so they'd still be around the kitchen table discussing their script, and we'd have dinner, talk, and hang out. That's where we really got to know each other. I was already very admiring of his work, and we respected each other a lot."

Two years older than Spielberg, Lucas was born in 1944 and grew up in Modesto, at that time a small rural town in central California, where he worked on cars and cruised the main street. Born in Cincinnati, Ohio, Spielberg grew up primarily in the suburbs of Phoenix, Arizona, spending much of his time making movies in and around his house with friends and family. Spielberg was raised in a Jewish household, Lucas in a Methodist one. Differences aside, they shared one overriding interest: cinema. What they had in common—and what, it could be argued, binds much of America together—was movies. They loved and studied *Casablanca*, *King Kong*, *Frankenstein*, *The Adventures of Don Juan*, *The Treasure of the Sierra Madre*, *The Searchers*, and a hundred other classics.

"We were of the same era," Spielberg says. "We were the movie brats who got together a long time ago and decided to talk about how hard it is to make movies. I mean, we're constant complainers. We love complaining to each other."

ABOVE: The Italian poster for Spielberg's TV movie *Duel* (1971), which was released theatrically in Europe, promotional artwork for Lucas's *THX 1138* (1971), and a British quad for Spielberg's *The Sugarland Express* (1974). LEFT: Spielberg behind the camera.

FROM THE ASHES OF SERIALS

As the two cinephiles became better acquainted over the years, Lucas's thinking was also developing. Interested in anthropology, science fiction, fantasy, comic books, and history, he made films that explored these subjects in different forms: *THX 1138* is a Flash Gordon–esque character in a dystopic future that parodies 1960s mainstream and counterculture, punishing citizens for *not* taking drugs; *American Graffiti* takes an anthropological look at cruising and music circa 1962, just before America would be forever changed by waging war in Vietnam.

Neither film, however, pleased the studio that paid for it. And in the spring of 1973, several months before *Graffiti* was released in August, Lucas was literally borrowing money to survive. Because he had the remnants of a deal for a sci-fi film at United Artists,

he sidelined his ideas for a dark Vietnam satire called *Apocalypse Now*, which he was having enormous difficulty selling to a studio, and wrote a treatment for a film that would combine mythology, anthropology, popular culture, and speed called *The Star Wars*.

After United Artists and Universal passed on the project, Twentieth Century-Fox agreed to pay for a first-draft script in June 1973. But as Lucas continued to write in the small alcove on the second floor of his house in San Anselmo—a petite Marin County town just north of San Francisco—his mind would often wander. Although his task was to invent an epic for a space-fantasy hero, another action-serial persona kept popping up—an archaeologist-adventurer-academic-playboy.

"Whenever I sit at a desk for eight hours a day, I can't help but think about things other than what I'm supposed to be thinking about," Lucas says. "Around April or May of 1973, I started researching, looking at serials. One that I really liked besides *Flash Gordon* was *Don Winslow of the Navy*. And I began thinking it'd be a good idea to have an archaeologist in a 1930s-style serial—the big shift would be that he was a grave robber who actually finds supernatural artifacts. I thought it would be a commercial idea, and I was in dire straits financially. Comics influenced me, too, but I was really

motivated by things like *Tim Tyler's Luck*, because he was always looking for the lost graveyard of the elephants or the golden eye of some idol. I thought, *Well, gee, what if you actually made it realistic?* I was interested in updating the genre so that it made sense, but so it still had all the fun and adventure, which I was also trying to do with *The Star Wars*.

"So I'd make little notes about what it would be, who his character was, and how all that would work out. That's how I came up with the idea of Indiana Smith."

Some of Indiana Smith actually snuck into early ideas for *The Star Wars*. In Lucas's rough draft of May 1974, the adventures of General Luke Skywalker on a jungle planet lead him to Owen Lars of Bestine, "an aged and scruffy looking anthropologist." In Lucas's second draft, dated January 1975, Luke Starkiller "picks up some small stones and begins to toss them at a large boulder. A chip in the boulder reveals a small shiny fossil. Luke spots it and goes over to study it. He takes a small camera out of his bag and photographs it, making some accompanying notations in a small book." A few pages later, when he finds himself duty-bound to rescue his brother, he protests: "But my catalog on the ancients. I haven't nearly completed it…"

"*Star Wars* and Indiana Smith are both based on the serial matinees I loved when I was a kid," Lucas says. "Action movies about adventurers set in exotic locales, with a cliff-hanger every second. I wondered why they didn't make movies like that anymore. I still wanted to see them."

Indiana Smith thus had many antecedents—*Spy Smasher*, *Tailspin Tommy*, *Masked Marvel*, *Commando Cody*, *Green Lantern*, and *Batman*, along with Don Winslow, a serviceman who traveled the world fighting Nazis—but the single visual inspiration came from an old lobby card of Zorro jumping from a horse to a truck. Lucas borrowed the name Indiana from his dog, an Alaskan malamute (who, around the same time, was also being metamorphosed into a furry Wookiee named Chewbacca).

"Indiana was this big, huge malamute, who would sit next to me in the car," Lucas says, "a giant bear of a dog. And so I named the character after my dog."

"I was very lucky when I was growing up in Phoenix, Arizona, because there was a revival house called the Kiva Theater in Scottsdale," Spielberg says. "The Kiva was a small art house that showed the current new-wave cinema, but on Saturdays they would have an old-fashioned movie showing. Sandwiched between two features would be a newsreel, ten cartoons, five previews, and Chapter 15 of *Spy Smasher*."

Lucas took a little time off from *The Star Wars* for Indiana Smith in the latter half of 1974. "I was trying to get people to do it," he says. "At one point Phil Kaufman was having a difficult time with his career. This was after *The White Dawn* [1974] and he was having a hard time getting another picture off the ground, so I said, 'I've got this great movie. C'mon, let's do this picture, and we'll get Francis or somebody to get us a deal somewhere.' And I told him the story, which at that point was Indiana Smith on the hunt for some kind of supernatural artifact. I knew it was set in the 1930s and that the Nazis were in it, because I knew the Nazis had also searched for supernatural artifacts. That's when Phil told me about the Ark of the Covenant."

"We were good friends with George and Marcia [Lucas]," Philip Kaufman says. "It was after George did *Graffiti*, and I remember him talking about *Star Wars* while we would take long walks. There was an old

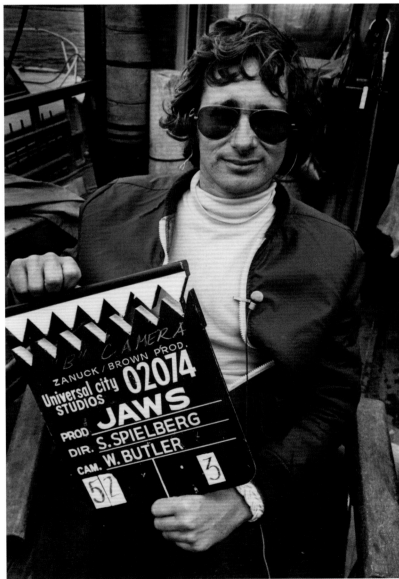

OPPOSITE: Lobby cards, posters, and comic-book covers from some of the serials and publications of the 1930s and 1940s that inspired Lucas in his creation of Indiana Smith. Leaping from his horse to a truck is Zorro—the key image that stuck in the mind of Lucas.

TOP LEFT: Lucas while making *American Graffiti* (1973) in 1972. LEFT: Spielberg while making *Jaws* (1975) in 1974.

ABOVE: The poster art for *Close Encounters of the Third Kind* (1977) and (RIGHT) Spielberg while making that movie.

dentist I went to in Chicago who was obsessed with the lost Ark's legendary powers."

"I also had at that point a little character backstory," Lucas says, "which had come out of the questions: Why didn't Indiana Smith become a regular archaeologist? Why did he become a thief? It was hard to figure out in my mind why a professor, who can live very modestly, would go out and do all this tomb-raider business and then sell the artifacts to museums. The answer was that he had a habit: the good life. He did it because he had a lavish lifestyle to support—he was addicted to being a playboy."

"We worked on it, I don't know, a couple of weeks," Kaufman says. "But I was totally broke, and I got an offer to do *Josey Wales*. I needed to work, so I wrote that script."

"We had about half a dozen story conferences over a period of about three weeks," Lucas says. "But then he got an offer to do a Clint Eastwood movie, *The Outlaw Josey Wales* [1976]."

Kaufman departed. Still, Indiana Smith now had a title for his first adventure: *Raiders of the Lost Ark*.

SANDCASTLES AND STORIES

Lucas had hit pay dirt in the summer of 1973, when *American Graffiti* became one of the most successful films ever. Following *The Sugarland Express*, Spielberg did likewise with *Jaws* in 1975. Although plagued by an unruly sea and an uncooperative mechanical shark, Spielberg prevailed in creating a box-office titan that soon became the number one film of all time.

Not pausing to take a breath, the director went from postproduction on *Jaws* to preproduction on *Close Encounters of the Third Kind*, which also turned out to be a long, grueling shoot. By the summer of 1976 Lucas, too, was having his own nerve-racking experience filming *The Star Wars*. Through their several difficult scenarios, the two directors would keep in touch, trying to boost each other's morale.

"When he was doing *Jaws*, we'd hang out together whenever I'd have to go down to LA," Lucas says. "That's when I went over to Universal and saw the shark, and I'd hear all the horror stories about location shooting in Martha's Vineyard. We knew what was going on with each other. We stayed friends. Actually, when I finished shooting *Star Wars*, I went to Mobile, Alabama, and hung out on his *Close Encounters* set for a while before coming home."

"When he wrapped at Elstree in England he came straight to my set in Mobile, where I was shooting *Close Encounters*, and he was so depressed," Spielberg says. "He brought a whole bunch of stills—the sandcrawler and the Jawas—and I was just amazed, but George was so depressed. He was really upset."

About ten months later, after Lucas had finished postproduction on his film and before Spielberg started post on his, the two took a brief break with their respective partners in Hawaii. Lucas arrived on the island first, just two days after *Star Wars* was released in 32 theaters on May 25, 1977.

"George was on vacation in Hawaii because *Star Wars* was opening in Los Angeles and he didn't want to be around for it," Spielberg says. "George felt that a five-and-a-half-hour airplane ride was a safe distance between himself and the opening of the picture."

In fact, Lucas was determined to stop directing. His last film had been a health-endangering experience, so he was retiring.

The two men compared notes, discussing films and their respective futures. "At dinner one night, when George got the news that *Star Wars* was a hit, he was suddenly laughing again and he told me he wanted to make a series of *Raiders* films," Spielberg says. "So I asked, 'What's a *Raiders* film?' And he said, 'Well, the first one's called *Raiders of the Lost Ark*.' He didn't know the titles for the other two, but every film was *Raiders of This* or *of That*."

The conversation continued the next day. "We were on the beach building a sandcastle at the Mauna Kea hotel after we'd heard that every single seat of the 9:30 AM shows across the country—the limited-release theaters—was filled," Spielberg says, "so we just began talking about other movies, other ideas, other possibilities, and George asked me, 'What do you want to do next?' And I said, 'You know, I've always wanted to direct a Bond picture starring Sean Connery.' We were fantasizing about movies we'd always wanted to make—George had a plan to make nine *Star Wars* films and he told me some of those stories—so I told George I'd always wanted to make a James Bond film, but much more like *Dr. No* as opposed to the later, more technological Bond films.

"But George said, 'I've got something you might like as much as Bond.' And while we continued to build the sandcastle—which stood against thirty minutes of tide—George told me the whole story of *Raiders of the Lost Ark*."

"After *Star Wars* came out," Lucas says, "I was with Steven and I said, 'I've got this great idea but I can't get anybody interested in it.' So I told him the story and he got very interested in it. I told him that the essence of *Raiders* is that it's a throwback to an older kind of film, a high-adventure movie vaguely in the mode of the old Saturday-afternoon serials."

"George said, 'Look, this is a B-movie,'" Spielberg says. "'They used to make four of them a week, at each studio, for fifteen years from the 1930s into the '40s.' He said *Raiders* was part of a series of sagas following the exploits of an adventurer-archaeologist, not unlike the *Tarzan* series or, by the same token, not unlike the serials of the '50s. The difference would be that our leading character would be involved in mortal adventures *and* in

otherworldly events. George said, 'We'll keep it in the '30s, but we'll update it and make it modern, and still keep it old.' It was great."

"One of my inspirations was a picture of Zorro jumping on a truck, which was easy shorthand for explaining the idea," Lucas says. "So I said, 'Indiana gets on his horse and he jumps from his horse to the truck.' Steven knew all that genre, so he said, 'Oh, yeah, I know that, the '30s serials. Oh, that would be fantastic.' I said I was basically backdating James Bond,

ABOVE: A poster for *Star Wars* (1977). ABOVE LEFT: On the Hoth set for the sequel, *The Empire Strikes Back* (1980), are screenwriter Lawrence Kasdan, Lucas, and Mark Hamill, circa 1979. Kasdan would also write *Raiders*.

film of all time. Although they'd agreed in theory to do *Raiders*, they still had many details to work out both contractually and story-wise, so neither neglected their new project.

"I think a couple of months later George called me up and said, 'If you're still interested, I'd like you to direct this when you get a chance,'" Spielberg says. "And it was kind of hard, because I was right in the middle of postproduction on *Close Encounters* and had already committed to directing *1941* for Columbia."

Spielberg took time out, however, to type up his conditions for directing on August 16, 1977, which included "Final Cut; sequels and remakes to be negotiated as they arise…"

Close Encounters debuted in November 1977 and was an enormous success, in some cases the first film to displace *Star Wars* from theaters in which it'd been playing nonstop since June. On December 19, 1977, Lucas had his lawyer Tom Pollock send a deal memo based on the director's proposal to Spielberg's lawyer, Bruce Ramer. (Such was Spielberg's appreciation of his representative's predator-like qualities that he'd nicknamed the mechanical shark in *Jaws* "Bruce.") A copy was also sent to Spielberg's agent, Guy McElwaine at International Creative Management. Ramer sent his comments back to Pollock on January 30, 1978, discussing numerous details for a film at that time budgeted at $6 million. Negotiations continued.

On a roll in terms of hiring directors, Lucas talked Irvin Kershner (who ten years before had been one of the judges at the National Student Film Festival) into helming what came to be called *The Empire Strikes Back*, also employing Leigh Brackett to write its first draft based on Lucas's story. In early 1978 Spielberg began work on *1941*, a comedy based on the exaggerated eccentricities of Americans and Japanese at the outbreak of World War II, as the former prepare to defend, and the latter to attack, the Los Angeles area.

A writer was also needed to turn Lucas's story ideas for *Raiders* into a full-blown screenplay. Lawrence Kasdan had come to Spielberg's attention in late 1977 via his script *Continental Divide* (1981). "There was a bidding war for it," Kasdan says, "and the producer that bought it was Steven Spielberg. After he bought it, I met him on the back lot at Universal, where he was producing *I Want to Hold Your Hand* (which was Bob Zemeckis's first feature). He told me how much he liked *Continental Divide* and he said, 'I showed this script to George Lucas and we're going to do a movie together.'"

"I found Larry when I read a script of his that I had Universal buy for me called *Continental Divide*," says Spielberg. "Then I introduced Larry to George, suggesting to George that I wanted Larry to be the screenwriter on *Raiders*."

What initially attracted both Spielberg and Lucas to Kasdan was his ability to channel a certain 1930s and '40s sensibility,

revealing the source behind him, 'cause James Bond goes from close shave to close shave—and I think that inspired Steven."

"George didn't have the whole story but he had the premise pretty complete," Spielberg says. "He had a really good profile of a kind of Fred C. Dobbs character [Humphrey Bogart in *The Treasure of the Sierra Madre*, 1948]. He had that character very formed. So after he told me the story, I said, 'That's terrific, George. It's something I'd like to do.' George knew I was interested in that sort of film. He knew that when he told me the story."

"Steven said, 'I'd love to do that,'" says Lucas. "And that's really how it got started."

"George said, 'Well, I've retired. I'm not directing anymore, so it's yours,'" Spielberg says. "We shook hands that day, and began to develop *Raiders of the Lost Ark*."

SUPERNATURAL TALES

Their vacations over, both filmmakers returned to the mainland. Spielberg had to finish *Close Encounters*, while Lucas began the process of making a sequel to *Star Wars*, which soon replaced *Jaws* as the number one box-office

OPPOSITE: An enlargement of the *Zorro* lobby card, which used to hang in the halls of Industrial Light & Magic; this particular photocopy was sent to artist Jim Steranko in 1979 to guide him in his early conceptual illustrations of Indiana Jones (see page 34). LEFT: Humphrey Bogart publicity photo for *The Treasure of the Sierra Madre* (1948); his look and attire partially inspired those of Indiana Jones. BELOW: Original title page for the *Raiders* story conference transcript.

"RAIDERS OF THE LOST ARK"

Story Conference Transcript

January 23, 1978 thru January 27, 1978

George Lucas, Steven Spielberg, Larry Kasden

à la Howard Hawks, whose films *Only Angels Have Wings* (1939), *His Girl Friday* (1940), and *To Have and Have Not* (1944) epitomized the kind of verbal and physical action they wanted for *Raiders*. But it wouldn't be a done deal until Kasdan met Lucas, who as executive producer would decide if the trio would work well together.

At the same time, Spielberg was looking for a producer. He suggested that Lucas meet with Frank Marshall, who was known primarily as Peter Bogdanovich's associate producer on several films, including *Paper Moon* (1973).

"So there I was in my apartment at UCLA," Marshall says, "and I got a phone call from Jane Bay [Lucas's assistant], who asked me if I was the producer that worked with Peter Bogdanovich. I said, 'Yes, I am.' And she asked, 'Would you be willing to come have an interview with George Lucas?' I said, 'Let me see if I can work that into my schedule.' I didn't have a schedule, so it was very easy to do that."

After flying down to Los Angeles from his home in San Anselmo, Lucas talked with Marshall. "I went in to meet with George in some trailers on the side of the Universal lot," Marshall says. "We started talking about the movies I had made with Peter. He told me that he had two producers for his two movies at that time, *More American Graffiti* and *The Empire Strikes Back*, and that he was looking for a third producer for his next film, which was a movie that he was putting together with Steven Spielberg, and that Steven had mentioned he would like to have me working on the project and would I be interested in something like that? After I recovered from the question, I said, 'Yes, of course I would. I'd certainly love to be considered.'

"So George said, 'Well, great, and thanks for coming in.' I was about to leave when he said, 'Why don't you wait a minute? Steven's coming back and you can say hi.' Now, I had only met Steven once five years before that," Marshall adds. "So I thought, *Well, okay, great, I'll stay and see Steven and then I'll go on my way. I'll wait to hear and I'll probably never hear anything, and that'll be it.*"

Spielberg arrived with Lawrence Kasdan in tow. "I met with Steven, Frank Marshall, and George—that was the first time I met him," Kasdan says. "He was in a little office on the Universal lot. George said, 'You know, we're going to do this adventure movie, and the hero is named after my dog, Indiana, and he carries a whip. It's like the old-time serials. That's the feeling of it. And Phil Kaufman's lost Ark of the Covenant is going to be the MacGuffin [a plot device that keeps the action moving].' Then he said, 'Do you want to write it?' And I said, 'Of course.'"

"Steven came in and he had this other young guy with him," Marshall says. "So George was introducing everybody. He said, 'This is Steven, of course you know Steven, and this is Larry Kasdan and he's the writer,' and everybody shook hands, and then he said, 'And this is Frank Marshall, he's the producer.' And that was it."

"We stood up after twenty minutes," Kasdan says, "and George said 'Let's shake hands, maybe this is a historic moment'—which is very unusual for George to be ceremonial, but he was that day. And we shook hands."

"Afterward I went home to my little room and wondered, *Did that just happen?*" Marshall says. "I wanted to pinch myself. *Was it some misunderstanding? Did I not get what was going on?* But sure enough, somebody from Lucasfilm called the next day and wanted to make a deal. I was just stunned."

"Frank and I walked out together," Kasdan says. "And he said, 'Did we just get that job?' I said, 'You got me, I have no idea.' And we said good-bye. But I got home and they had already called my agent and said, 'We want you to do *Raiders of the Lost Ark*.'"

"George knows what he wants," Marshall sums up. "He goes with his instincts, and he has this great way of making everybody feel comfortable. I think that he just wanted to make sure I didn't have three heads or something.

"Then began a series of meetings in which George outlined the story."

THE JUGGERNAUT TRIO

Kasdan, Lucas, and Spielberg met to brainstorm several times from January 23 to 27, 1978, the idea being that Kasdan would then take the transcripts of their taped conversations and turn them into a first-draft screenplay.

"George, Steve, and I got together in a little house in Sherman Oaks that belonged to Jane Bay, George's assistant," Kasdan says. "We went up to her house for a week, just the three of us, and we recorded all the conversations. But George already had the elements."

"Larry, Steven, and I worked together on it, but basically when I laid out the story it was fairly articulate," Lucas says. "Every scene was described. They changed and personalized it a lot, but essentially the concept remained the same. I enjoyed that part."

"We had a tape recorder going and George essentially guided the story process," Spielberg says. "The three of us pitched the entire movie in about five days. Most of the time we were trying to outshout each other with ideas. George, Larry, and I sat in a room and contrived a very structured story that is 80 percent of what the script turned out to be."

"It was my first job writing for someone else," Kasdan notes. "My first real job. I was daunted maybe for the first hour—you know, *Oh my God, I can't believe I'm in this room with these two guys.* But the problem of constructing a story and making things work and all the difficulties of actually writing is a great equalizer. It's a real democracy as soon as there's the problem of creating something. All the intimidation goes away very quickly, because the three of you have exactly the same goal: *How do you make this work?*"

The answer was to revisit scenes, sequences, characters, and plot many times during the course of their talks, each time approaching something they all liked. The result is a fascinating transcription in which Lucas tells his story and then the three of them come up with tweaks, new ideas, logic questions, budget concerns, and character development. Lucas begins by describing the female lead as a German double agent, but she ends up as a tough expatriate who's had an affair with Indy and is now stranded in Nepal. Clues that lead to the Ark start out as maps, turn into stone tablets, and wind up as a two-part medallion. The bad guy changes nationalities, they conjure up a monkey who can do the Nazi salute, and so on.

Spielberg came up with several ideas, including a dangerously fast-rolling boulder, Indy's fear of snakes, and the booby traps in the opening sequence. "The ball was my idea during the story conference, when we were knocking out set pieces and making suggestions," Spielberg says. "I don't even know where I came up with it—it might have been deeply in my subconscious from something I saw when I was a kid—but I just said, 'You know, at some point some huge boulder should start chasing Indy, and it almost squashes him three or four times until he gets out of the cave.'"

Not only did *Raiders* come alive during that week, but the trio was so creative that they conceived of many more ideas than could fit into one film.

"George would always be the first who backed out," Spielberg says. "He would always protect a friendship. Several times I wanted to back down first, because I wanted to be the person to show him that I was protecting the friendship, too. But he would always say, 'Okay, Steven, it's your movie.' It would always be like that, which was his way of saying, *I've got a better idea. If you're too dumb to listen to me, it's your movie!* And that always worked, believe me! Every time he'd come up with that attitude, I'd say, 'Okay, George, what's the idea again?' And there would be a compromise."

"The three of us came up with all the missing details, all the progression," Kasdan adds. "I made up some of the names. We talked about what we liked, the kind of things we wanted to see, and then how that could fit into the story."

"After sitting with him for many, many hours, for several days, I realized that George is tough on himself and he's tough on the people who collaborate with him," Spielberg says. "The story needs to make sense; he loves logic. And sometimes you lose your vision, because it's often swallowed up by his own. You've got to fight for your bit when you collaborate with George. But once George respects your vision and if he likes your ideas more than his, he will back down and let you go ahead and shoot your movie. But George is a bit like Disney: He does put a vision out there that's so attractive, you would be a fool or a slave to your own ego if you denied it just because it didn't come from you."

At one point Kasdan asked Lucas why he didn't direct *Raiders* himself. "Because then I'd never get to see it," Lucas replied.

"You sit back and wonder, *Why don't they make this kind of movie anymore?*" he says. "And I'm in a position now to do it. So I'm really doing it more than anything else so that I can enjoy it—I just want to see this movie."

ALL FOR ONE AND ONE FOR ALL

After the intense idea sessions and a twenty-minute talk with Phil Kaufman, Kasdan went off to write the first draft. As aids he had a story treatment by Lucas, typed up on January 25, 1978, along with their transcribed conversations. Lucas's 19-page summary (23 handwritten) combined all of their approved concepts and included a few new names, such as one for the hero, Indiana Jones—a 38-year-old "bachelor playboy, with a fondness for the good life; fancy night clubs, champagne, and especially beautiful women… He is a terrible shot with a pistol, but a master with the bullwhip." His Arab friend is called Digger.

"Originally the name was Indiana Smith," Lucas says. "But when I told the story to Steven on the beach, he'd said, 'There's only one thing I don't like. I don't like the name. It's too much like *Nevada Smith*' [a 1966 Steve McQueen film]. Later I said, 'Well, all right, what if we call him Indiana Jones?' It was the cultural aspect of the very American generic name that I was interested in, not the actual name itself."

"I left there feeling, *I'm in pretty good shape*," Kasdan says, "and then I sat down and realized, *Uh-oh, this is going to be hard*."

On February 6, 1978, Kasdan signed a deal memo with Lucasfilm. A letter dated March 20, 1978, from Tom Pollock to agent Michael Ovitz confirmed Frank Marshall as producer. "Steven found he could do *Raiders* after *1941*," Marshall says. "I was working on another project that was postponed, so I started on *Raiders*, too."

BELOW: The cover to Lucas's story treatment for *Raiders of the Lost Ark*.

Raiders of the Lost Ark

Story Treatment by
George W. Lucas, Jr.
January 25, 1978

BELOW, LEFT TO RIGHT: Spielberg's sketch for the façade of the Chachapoyan temple, followed by sketches by Dryden and Ron Cobb (FAR RIGHT) with final art by Dryden (RIGHT). "I do the thumbnails myself, which are often impossible to interpret, so I need to stand over the artist to explain which side is up," Spielberg says. "These shots are all subject to change, and I usually don't shoot every one. I always overdraw."

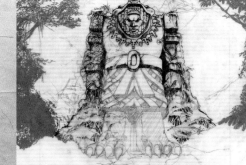

While Kasdan was writing the first and subsequent drafts, Lucasfilm librarian Debbie Fine did voluminous research on whatever was necessary: facts about the Ark, World War II history, what kind of newspapers were read in the 1930s. Her notes to Kasdan dated April 5, 1978, outline the political situation between Britain and Egypt in 1936.

"During the six months that I was writing *Raiders*, I never met with George Lucas or Steven Spielberg," Kasdan says, "except for occasionally checking in with them to say that my script was coming along. Steven was working on *1941* and George was preparing *The Empire Strikes Back*, so they left me totally alone. I had always hated doing research, but I was introduced to Debbie Fine. She brought me research about the era, about South America at that time, about Egypt, about Hitler's interest in the occult."

In a now well-known story, when Kasdan hand-delivered his first draft dated June 15, 1978, to Lucas at his Park Way office not far from his home in San Anselmo, Lucas offered Kasdan the job of writing the third draft of *The Empire Strikes Back*. Sadly, Brackett had died of cancer after completing her first draft, so Lucas had written the second draft, which he felt needed more work.

"The day I arrived, George said, 'Let's go out to lunch,'" Kasdan remembers. "He hadn't read the script, because I had just given it to him, but he said, 'I need someone to write *Empire*.' I said, 'Well, maybe you'd like to read *Raiders* first.' He said, 'If I hate *Raiders*, I'll renege on this offer tomorrow. But basically I've got a feeling about people.'"

"The next day after I'd read the script," Lucas says, "I remember calling Steven and saying, 'It's fantastic. We've got to cut it down quite a bit, but other than that…' It was funny and exciting—it was everything that was in the story conference, just better." (See sidebar, page 30.)

Lucas telephoned Kasdan the following day to confirm his offer, which the writer accepted. "He was very, very happy with *Raiders*," he says.

After Spielberg had a chance to go through the script, he had a notably different reaction: "I read it and wept, because it just looked like too much work."

Like many first drafts, Kasdan's had several and probably too many set pieces as well as expensive, complex chase scenes. It also had some one-dimensional characters, notably archaeologists Calvin Stansbury and Jules Spencer, as well as Sallah's son, Abu. Stansbury serves as a plot device, debriefing the government men about the Ark; Spencer puts Indy back on track after Marion's death, and deciphers the riddle of the medallion. Abu provides comic relief, but three archaeologists was definitely a crowd.

Kasdan also developed the major characters and assigned names. The heroine was Marion Ravenwood. "Marion, I thought, was a pretty name," Kasdan says. "It was my wife's grandmother's name. My wife and I drove up Beverly Glen Boulevard, and there's a street there called Ravenwood Court. I wanted them to be romantic, old-timey names."

Somewhat less than romantic is Indiana himself, who in this draft is a quasi-philanderer and flirts unabashedly with his students. Indeed, all of the script's characters are shadier than their serial counterparts, modernized and more complex—Marion has had to prostitute herself to survive—while the violence is more visceral and the danger more realistic.

ATTACK OF THE DEAL

With a first draft in hand and the key components in place—Spielberg as director, Kasdan as writer, and Marshall as producer—Lucas was ready to

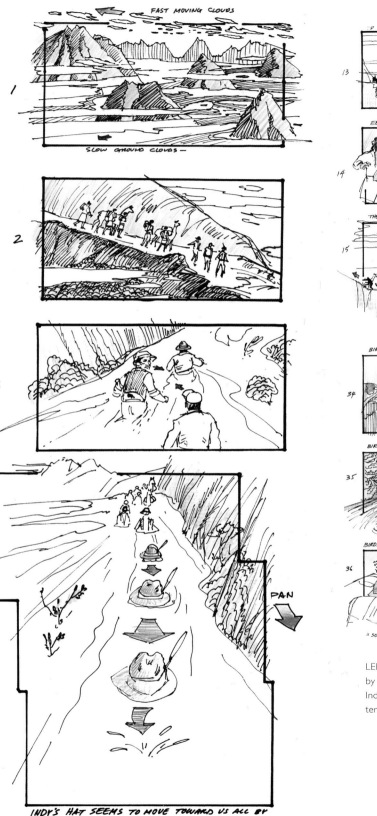

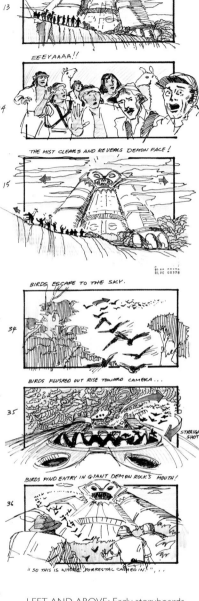

LEFT AND ABOVE: Early storyboards by Dave Negron show initial ideas for Indy's approach to the Peruvian cave temple.

"RAIDERS OF THE LOST ARK"
STORY CONFERENCE TRANSCRIPT EXCERPTS

GEORGE LUCAS, STEVEN SPIELBERG, LAWRENCE KASDAN • JANUARY 23 THRU JANUARY 27, 1978

[Note: The original transcribed tapes ran 117 pages.]

GEORGE LUCAS: I'll go through the story's specifics. Then we'll actually start talking scenes. Then we'll figure out how fast the movie is going to move.

It's basically an action piece. One of the main ideas was to have, either every ten or twenty minutes, a cliff-hanger situation. If it's every ten minutes we do it twelve times. I think that may be a little much. Six times is plenty.

STEVEN SPIELBERG: And each cliff-hanger is better than the one before.

LUCAS: The fact is, he is slightly scruffy: khaki pants, leather jacket, felt hat, a pistol and holster with a World War I flap. The other thing we've added to him, which may be fun, is a bullwhip. That's really his trademark. Maybe he came from Montana… I thought he'd carry it rolled up. It's like a samurai sword. He carries it back there, and you don't even notice it. It's just there whenever he wants it.

LAWRENCE KASDAN: How do you see this guy?

LUCAS: Someone like Harrison Ford, Paul Le Mat. A young Steve McQueen. It would be ideal if we could find a stuntman who could act. [Later, however, Spielberg would have to champion Ford, as Lucas didn't want to cast actors who had already appeared in his films—see page 46 and following.]

SPIELBERG: What's he afraid of? He's got to be afraid of something.

LUCAS: If we don't make him vulnerable, he's got no problems.

SPIELBERG: It would be funny if, somewhere early in the movie, we somehow implied that he was not afraid of snakes. Later you realize that this is one of his big fears.

LUCAS: Maybe it's better if you see early, maybe in the beginning, that he's afraid of them: "Oh God, I hate those snakes." It should be slightly amusing that he hates snakes, and then he opens the tomb: "I can't go down there. Why did it have to be snakes? Anything but snakes." You can play it for comedy.

KASDAN: I wonder what their reaction to light is…? Do you have a name for this person?

SPIELBERG: I hate this, but go ahead.

LUCAS: Indiana Smith. It has to be unique. It has character. Very Americana square. He was born in Indiana.

KASDAN: What do [they] call him, Indy?

LUCAS: That's what I was thinking. Or Jones. Then people can call him Jones.

BOOBY TRAPS AND A BOULDER

LUCAS: The film starts in the jungle, South America. We get one of these great shots with the pack animals going up the mist-covered hills, very exotic jungles. He goes into a cave.

He has a couple of native bearers, and you have two guys who are the locals. They speak English. They're going up this hill and they come into a clearing and you see the temple across the way. The pressure builds and one of the natives cracks, throws down his bundle and scurries off. Pretty soon, when they get right to the clearing, right in front of the temple, it's just three guys.

One of the guys tries to kill him and take the map, shoot him in the back. That's when you first see him with the bullwhip. He kills this one guy and the other guy backs off and says he didn't have anything to do with it.

So the hero and the other guy go into the temple. You know the guy's going to shoot him in the back eventually. We get to a point in the tomb where a light shaft is coming down. It's a very narrow shaft. He tosses a stick into it, and these giant spikes come out…

SPIELBERG: When the spikes come out, there should be skeletal remains skewered on some of them, victims that have been there before. It's like one of those rides at Disneyland.

KASDAN: Why are we letting the second guy get away? Why can't we sacrifice him to the temple?

LUCAS: We can. I just did it to build the pressure, but we can keep him in. We'll follow this scene through, and then we'll see where you want to dispose of him.

SPIELBERG: There could be wall mashers…I would just love to see our guys walking in, and there's a whole pile of skeletons—but they're like cardboard, completely flattened. They know that something around there is going to squish them.

LUCAS: They get into the main throne room and they see an idol, a voodoo idol. By this time we're afraid of sunlight and those kinds of things, so he moves in there very carefully.

SPIELBERG: He knows it's a trap.

LUCAS: Poison sticks are in the walls. If you spring something, they shoot out.

SPIELBERG: That's a great idea. More like little projectiles.

LUCAS: Yeah, little darts. He looks up and realizes that the whole place is perforated with them. They go off if an air current is broken, or some kind of thing. We don't have to fully understand…

Then the idea is he does something elaborate as he lifts the idol off its pedestal. There's a weighted trap. Then he turns and trips something, he steps into a light, or however we do it… Maybe it was the weight of the idol, a delayed thing.

But he takes one step and turns, then all of a sudden he hears some giant mechanism…

SPIELBERG: You know what it could be—I have a great idea. When he goes into the cave, it's not level: the whole thing is on an incline. So he grabs the idol, comes to a corridor—and there is a sixty-five-foot boulder that's form-fitted to only roll down the corridor, coming right at him. And it's a race. He gets to outrun the boulder. It then comes to rest and blocks the entrance of the cave. Nobody will ever come in again. This boulder is the size of a house.

LUCAS: It mashes the partner.

SPIELBERG: Right. The guy can't run fast enough. It's like merging in traffic on the freeway with a truck behind you. You have to run in front of the boulder and get out of the cave before it gets you. The reason the boulder is coming down is not to kill him, it's to seal off the cave.

Raiders of the Lost Ark.
Story treatment by George Lucas.
1-25-78

Indiana Jones is a PhD archeologist and an anthropologist. He is a professor at a small Eastern college and is a respected authority in his field although he is only thirty eight years old. He is a quiet man on campus, with rugged good looks under his horn rimmed glasses. He is the heart-throb for all the young co-eds, a situation that he has helped to foster, and isn't reluctant to take advantage of.

He is a bachelor - playboy, with a fondness for the good life; fancy nite clubs, champagne, and especially beautiful women. His nite-life is a sharp contrast to his quiet days on a college professor. In his tuxedo (and without his glasses) he is the proto-type of the eastern playboy of the 1930's. He plays polo and pool and is quite a gambler. He lives in a large 30's style house, and also has an penthouse apartment in manhattan.

He can afford the good life because of his second occupation. He is a soldier of fortune and a procurer of rare antiquities. A bounty hunter hired by museums and private collectors to find ancient artifacts and bring them back no questions asked. He is a tomb robber, but

but draws the line at stealing from cultures or museums. He has a keen interest in the occult, and specializes in religious objects by current etc. He is a terrible shot, protected with the bullwhip that he always carries with. He is a good fighter.

The film opens in a misty, peruvian jungle. A long train of natives and animals wind their way up the side of a steep mountain pass. Jones, the other two are three men. One is Indy. They are indigs partners are south american. As they reach the top of the mountain, interpt etc. with a dark and sinister temple ruin on the far side. Other natives get restless and start to split. Indys partners tell him that the natives are afraid of the curse of the temple. He tells them they can probibly make it the rest of the way on own. The two partners look a little worried, follow Indy toward the temple.

Indy stops in front of the entrance to the temple. He takes off his back packs and sets, his two partners. We get a hint that the two partners are trying to do him in. standing behind his back, the south americans talk about the whole thing, and talk about how dangerous it is, and

ABOVE: Early concepts for the *Raiders* logo, and the final version, which would adorn everything from letterheads to posters.

RAIDERS of the LOST ARK

move into deal mode. On July 20, 1978, Lucasfilm incorporated a subsidiary, appropriately named the Raiders Company, to handle the film's legalities and negotiations. Lucas had similarly created The Star Wars Corporation for that film, while his two other subsidiaries, Medway and Black Falcon, handled additional company projects.

"I've found myself getting much more involved in business affairs," Lucas says, "trying to stabilize and ensure the continued growth of what we've gotten so far. The big jump was deciding to make a company in order to get my freedom. I felt that was necessary. The one real difference with Lucasfilm is that most companies generate movies to make money—while the whole concept behind our company is to generate money to make movies."

Indeed, following the leapfrogging mega-hits *American Graffiti*, *Star Wars*, *Jaws*, and *Close Encounters*, Spielberg and Lucas were in a position to make the kind of studio deal that hadn't been seen since the days of silent films.

"I hate to talk like a mercenary," Spielberg says, "but George came over to my house when we decided to make the picture and he said, 'Let's make the best deal they've ever made in Hollywood.' We presented that to our agencies and said, 'This is the deal we want. Now, fellas, go try to make it.'"

The two who shared most of the responsibility for fulfilling those unique terms were Lucasfilm's president Charlie Weber and lawyer Tom Pollock. The latter had started with Lucasfilm pre-*Graffiti*, circa 1971, while Weber had joined in 1977 after the release of *Star Wars*.

"About a year before we were ready to show the script to anybody, Michael Eisner at Paramount called me up and said, 'Can we have lunch together?' So Tom Pollock and I went to see him," Weber recalls. "At lunch he said, 'Would you please show me this and don't make a deal with anybody else till you do?' We said we would show it to him first but we couldn't guarantee the deal."

"The [terms of the deal] were made fairly early on," Pollock says, "because George had the ability to realize a vision. But the idea of a filmmaker owning his own films and thereby controlling how they were exploited has been a dream of filmmakers since the industry started. United Artists was started by Mary Pickford, Douglas Fairbanks, Charlie Chaplin, and D. W. Griffith. They wanted to own their movies instead of those terrible people who owned the nickelodeons, who put up the money and then did whatever they wanted. So the idea of a filmmaker owning his own film is not a new idea—ever since there have been filmmakers, they've always wanted to own their films."

INDIANA JIM

Lucas made very few notes on his copy of the first draft, though he did delete dialogue about Hitler's real-life search for the Spear of Destiny. Because he was writing the third draft for *Empire* and working on his own film, *Body Heat*, Kasdan turned in the second draft for *Raiders* 10 months after the first. Lucas probably wasn't overly concerned, because he was busy with preproduction on *Empire* and Spielberg would be deep into principal photography on *1941* for some time. Lucas had also purchased 2,500 acres in September 1978 and needed to get work started on what would eventually become Skywalker Ranch.

"The first draft that I handed to George was long," Kasdan says, "but I had wanted to get in everything we had talked about in the story conferences. And the reaction was great. But when we got over that hump, George and Steven said to me, 'We're in good shape here. Now I want you to go back and get it down to 100 pages.' And I thought it was impossible."

Dated March 1979, Kasdan's second draft is not substantially different from his first, but it is much shorter: 106 pages instead of 144, the scenes in Cairo having been curtailed, combined, and reordered. Sallah's son and Jules Spencer have been absorbed by the character of Sallah, who is now very much enamored of American slang and baseball; Indy's race to rescue Marion is on foot; he goes to the bar after her "death," instead of before, where he

SIDE PANEL FOR ARK,
CARVED WOOD FINISH IN BAS RELIEF
ANTIQUE GUILDED + AGED

END PANEL FOR ARK
CARVED WOOD IN BAS RELIEF
ANTIQUE GUILDED + AGED.

SIDE PANEL FOR ARK
CARVED WOOD FINISH IN BAS RELIEF
ANTIQUE GUILDED + AGED,

LEFT AND ABOVE: Initial concepts for the exterior of the Ark of the Covenant by an unknown artist (possibly Roy Carnon) in the style of William Blake (1757–1827). One features a concept for the Ark's end panel (ABOVE)—"carved wood in bas relief, antique guilded [sic] + aged"—of the seated figure of Moses; the two others depict side panels. The serpent is a reference to the rod-and-serpent Moses created in the desert.

encounters Emile Belloq—the revised name for his nemesis; a new scene has Sallah's nine children extract Indy from Belloq's clutches. Later on, Indy chases the truck with the Ark astride "a magnificent Arabian stallion."

Otherwise all the set pieces and major action are the same. "That was probably my favorite draft of the film," Kasdan says, "because it moved very fast and it was very funny, which I thought was important for the movie."

Just before Kasdan handed in his second draft, Lucas initiated discussions with famed illustrator and comic-book artist Jim Steranko. As he had with concept artist Ralph McQuarrie for *Star Wars*, Lucas hired Steranko to establish the visual style of *Raiders* and the look of Indiana Jones in particular. Toward that end, on February 9, 1979, Carol Wikarska Titelman, director of publishing and creative properties at Lucasfilm, wrote a letter to Steranko, following up on a telephone conversation by outlining the terms: Lucas would commission four production paintings. To help Steranko begin, Lucas would also "elaborate the mood and general character of the production paintings."

"That was really born out of the *Star Wars* paintings by Ralph," Lucas says. "Steven and I said, 'Let's get a few paintings for this one, too.' I'd seen

"RAIDERS OF THE LOST ARK"

FIRST-DRAFT SUMMARY

JUNE 15, 1978

Lawrence Kasdan's first draft names the rich wilderness of the film's opening the Eyebrow of the Jungle. It contains an enormous structure: the 2,000-year-old temple of the Chachapoyan warriors. One of Indiana's companions, Satipo, translates the porters' whispering: "They say they have never been so near the House of Death." When Indy's second companion, Barranca, pulls a gun on the archaeologist, Indy uses his whip to make Barranca shoot himself.

Inside the temple's secret sanctuary, Indy places a lead weight on the pedestal to replace the idol, but as he and Satipo flee a giant boulder, Jones loses his hat, which is crushed. Outside again, the double-crossing Satipo is killed by Hovitos Indians, who remain hidden throughout their pursuit of Indy as he escapes to his waiting pilot and plane.

In the National Museum in Washington, DC, Indy and Marcus Brody admire the idol, and Indy has a "new felt hat…The jeweled figurine from Peru is on a small pedestal before him…"

INDY: If it's not the right one, I can always return it.

BRODY: It's even more beautiful than I imagined.

Brody takes Jones to meet with Musgrove, Eaton, and Davona—the "important people" who have come to discuss Hitler and his occult obsessions—and they discuss the Spear of Destiny. Hitler is planning to annex Austria to get it. Indy then leads them to the museum basement, where Calvin Stansbury debriefs them on the Ark of the Covenant. He explains that the medallion of the Staff of Ra, which enables one to locate the Ark's hiding place in the map room, is broken into two pieces, one of which can be found in Shanghai.

STANSBURY: There's one other thing that Hitler undoubtedly believes about the Ark—It's said that the Lost Ark will be recovered at the time of the coming of the True Messiah.

At three o'clock the following morning a sleeping Indy is awakened by the government trio, who cajole him into

pursuing the Ark by revealing that a Frenchman named Victor Lovar, Indy's nemesis, is already in Egypt hot on the trail. Indy takes the job.

In Shanghai, his first stop, American Buzz Kehoe and Chinese Bang Chow help Indy outrace and outsmart the Nazis who have come for the same piece of the medallion, which is housed in the museum of a warlord named Tengtu Hok. To retrieve it, Indy battles two samurai and then escapes Hok and the Germans, who are blasting machine guns at him, by hiding behind a rolling gong and crashing through a window. Kehoe and Bang then drive him to a plane bound for New Delhi; Indy can go from there to Nepal and locate the other piece of the medallion.

But the plane is ditched by its passengers and pilot, so Indy wraps himself in an inflatable life raft and jumps out, inflating the raft in midair and careering down snowy slopes and through a Sherpa village where a Shaman stands before the people.

Indy whizzes by on his raft. He waves once. The Shaman looks wearily... and decides not to mention it...

In Patan, Nepal, at the Raven saloon, the character of Marion is introduced as she breaks up a fight between an Australian and a Nepalese. Marion's hard life after the death of her father, Abner Ravenwood, is described in more detail—it's insinuated that she had to prostitute herself, which has left her determined not to return to the United States until she can do so in style. Like Indy, she is somewhat mercenary. After Indy's fight in the saloon with a Nazi named Belzig and his cronies, Marion runs back into the burning bar to retrieve the second part of the medallion.

In Cairo, Egypt, Indy meets with Sallah and pays a visit to the Tavern of the Crocodiles, intending to obtain more money from a US government agent for Marion's payoff—since Indy's first payment was burned up in the fire in her saloon. There he bumps into Lovar for the first time.

LOVAR: Funny, isn't it, our meeting in Cairo?

INDY: Just looking for a little sun.

LOVAR: You should have come directly. There is more sun here than in Nepal.

Jones then finds that his government contact, Stanton, has been murdered with three daggers in the back. Shortly afterward, Indy pursues on camel the Nazis who have kidnapped Marion in a brown Chevy. Jones believes that she is switched to a waiting Ford and killed after he shoots at the vehicle, which plunges off a cliff.

At this point Sallah recruits Indiana's college roommate, a more serious and more learned archaeologist named Jules Spencer, who talks Indy out of giving up. "Her death will be meaningless if you just concede to these people," Jules says. The poisoning of the dates takes place at Spencer's, and it is Spencer who figures out that the Nazis and Lovar are digging in the wrong place, after deciphering the clues on the medallion.

After their several adventures, Indy and Marion spot the Flying Wing landing on a secret strip; it's being refueled when the action begins. Indy chases the truck with the Ark on a motorcycle. Bad Nazi Belzig is killed when his car goes through a dust cloud and over a cliff.

When Indy meets Katanga, the captain of the *Bantu Wind* is friendly to Indy because of a mutual friend named Petrovich—"the Bloody Vulture"—and his legendary adventure with Indy in the "islands." In their cabin Jones reflects:

INDY: Looks like the whole damn world will be fighting soon.

MARION: That won't be much of a change for you.

INDY: Yes it will. I hate crowds.

The following day ten German wolf-pack submarines surround them; a short but tense scene ensues in which the German captain debates with the Nazi Schliemann whether or not to blow the *Bantu Wind* out of the water, ultimately deciding, "Nothing is to be gained." After Indy swims over to the Nazi U-boat, the *Wurrfler*, and lashes himself to the periscope, we see a number of quick scenes—morning, evening, night, morning, et cetera—that depict him barely surviving as the U-boat travels to its island hideout.

There Indy follows the Ark, which is taken through a railway tunnel to the Tabernacle, housed in a natural cavern. Just as Lovar emerges in robes to speak the appropriate invocation before opening the Ark, Indy arrives and threatens to blow it up with a bazooka—but Nazis come up from behind and subdue him. Because Lovar has forbidden them to kill Indy in the presence of the Ark, the Nazis hold him in the Command Center. Outside, Lovar opens the Ark—and he along with all the surrounding Nazis are instantly killed by searing arcs of light and a sound like "the whisper of God."

Indy takes advantage of the subsequent havoc, subduing his captors, then locating and rescuing Marion. They escape in the chaos caused by the fire started by the Ark, but also manage to load it onto a mine car. Schliemann and others jump into a second car... and the race is on.

The explosion of munitions kills the pursuing Nazis, but Indy and Marion outdistance it, going off the end of the tracks and plunging into the bay just as most of the island is blown to bits.

The "cast credits roll over" the tranquil bay, with no sign of Indy or Marion. They then pop up in the bay, as does the Ark. Cut to the Pentagon, where Marion receives a cash settlement and her new start in the States, while Jones tries to find out from Davona what's happened to the Ark, but leaves unsatisfied. "As they do, crew credits roll."

MARION: Just put your mind on something else.

INDY: Yeah, like what?

Marion makes a face, then puts her arms around his neck and plants a humdinger of a kiss on his mouth.

It goes on a while. Finally they break.

INDY: It's not the Ark... but it'll have to do.

The "end credits roll" as the Ark is encased in a wooden crate and filed away among thousands of similar crates in a top-secret government warehouse.

23

52   CONTINUED   52

Marion has the glimmer of a smile as she picks up the pile of money and taps it into a neat stack, eyeing the crowd.

                    MARION
All right, you no-good bums, get the hell out of here. I'm sick of seeing your ugly mugs.

Loo sallá harú nyan barra niska. (All right you no-good bums, get the hell out of here.)

But harú li harrdha harrdha thaken. (I'm sick and tired of seeing you ghosts.)

Cǎam Dǎam chianá? (Don't you have any work?)

No one moves, they're all intent on Marion's final shot glass. She knows it and laughs slyly as she swoops it up and tosses it down like her first nip of the night. Again the crowd ROARS.

                    MARION
Mohan, clear 'em out. Everybody out! We're closed.

Mohan in harruli necála. (Mohan get them out.)

Loo súbjana niska. (Everybody out.)

Dhōkan bundbhayō. (We're closed.)

As the place clears, Marion takes her stack of money and slips it into a small wooden box on a shelf under the bar. Then she slips through a doorway and heads across the back room to a door. For the first time, the effect of all that booze is apparent. She's woozy.

52-A   EXT. "THE RAVEN" - IN BACK - NIGHT   52-A

Marion comes out unsteadily. She walks over to a snowbank and forms a snowball in each hand. Then, slowly, as though she's done it a hundred times before, she presses a snowball to each of her temples.

52-B   INT. "THE RAVEN" - NIGHT   52-B

Marion walks in behind the bar. She looks marvelously sober. Mohan, a big ax-handle in

Jim Steranko's work, and it was very much what I thought *Raiders* should be. I think Charlie Lippincott [Lucasfilm vice president of marketing and merchandising] was actually involved in that; I think he knew Jim Steranko [as did Ed Summer, who helped introduce the two]. So I said, 'Get him.'"

On March 6, 1979, Jane Bay forwarded Lucas's notes for the four paintings to Steranko, with reference images: stills from old films showing actors wearing felt hats with their brims turned down; a photo of the Flying Wing; and the shot of Zorro jumping from his horse onto a motorized truck. (This image in particular reveals one of the central themes in Lucas's stories: the often adversarial relationship between the natural world and the technological one. A man on a horse throws himself quite literally from his living steed against a mechanized transport—much like Luke Skywalker's rejection of his targeting computer in favor of the mystical Force just before he obliterates the technical horror known as the Death Star.)

"I found images that were what I thought the essence of the adventurer would look like, then I worked with the artist and got the real thing," Lucas says.

On March 14, 1979, Lucas sent additional notes in response to Steranko's first sketches (see sidebar, page 34). On June 30, Steranko delivered the first painting and a letter in which he began by excusing himself for the delays. Part of the problem, he wrote, was changing the format of his vertical compositions to horizontal, to cinematic proportions. "Instead of using a full-figure shot of the hero, I pulled him closer to us, so that we may read his character more clearly, both in his face and in the detail of his attire."

He further explained that he'd painted and then deleted a squadron of airplanes in the sky, and asked for more information about the film so that he might better understand the character. "I've somehow conjured up an idea that the hero is a kind of cross between Doc Savage and Bogart in the ultimate pulp adventure [...] I'll close by saying that I'm very pleased to be working with you on this project, and hope I can make some small contribution to its eventual outcome."

On August 6, 1979, Steranko's final four paintings arrived at Lucasfilm. A letter from Titelman's secretary Kathy Wippert to Steranko dated September 14, 1979, sealed the deal. At this point casting hadn't even begun for Indiana Jones—but his visual persona had been fixed.

FEAR AMONG THE TITANS

In the summer of 1979, deal negotiations began in earnest between Lucasfilm and the studios, while Frank Marshall started to organize the shoot. On July 25 he wrote to Lutz Hengst of Bavaria Studios in Germany, on a tip from Mike Ovitz, about the possibility of acquiring a full-scale U-boat he'd heard they'd constructed for *Das Boot*, a German television show (later turned into a film by Wolfgang Petersen and released in the U.S. as *The Boat* in 1982).

On August 15 Lucasfilm president Charlie Weber wrote to Ted Ashley, chairman of the board at Warner Bros., sending him via messenger two copies of the screenplay. That same day he also sent copies of the third-draft script to Michael Eisner at Paramount and to Mike Medavoy at Orion Pictures Company.

ABOVE AND OPPOSITE: Two early conceptual paintings for the Well of Souls by Michael Lloyd, 1978.

"The script went to [several studios, including] Universal and Warners, who really wanted to get back into doing business with George, ever since the *THX* days of fallout," Weber says, referring to the very bad feelings created by the studio's recutting of Lucas's first feature. "Michael Eisner was outta town in Europe with Barry Diller, so Warners jumped all over it."

Kasdan's third draft, dated August 1979, had only a few changes. To introduce the villain earlier in the film, Belloq is now waiting outside the Peruvian temple to take the idol away from Jones, and archaeologist Stansbury has been eliminated. But nearly all the action was the same.

August 15 was also the day the world learned in *Weekly Variety* that Steven Spielberg would direct *Raiders of the Lost Ark*, even though negotiations continued between Lucasfilm and Spielberg's representatives. In fact the studios viewed Spielberg's participation as a mixed blessing, particularly because his *1941* production had gone long over schedule. Although the director undeniably had super-clout, Hollywood was and is notoriously fickle, with many executives more than ready to jealously predict a star's downfall.

"We took the deal everywhere, and pretty much everybody said no, because the terms were too difficult," Lucas says. "We said the budget was around X million. They said with Steven Spielberg directing, that will never happen. They were very worried about it. One of the studios said, 'We'll do it without Spielberg,' and I said, 'No. I've already made a deal with him. He's the director, and he's going to do it on time and on budget.' I believed very deeply that Steven could do it, because I knew he could do it—he had already done it in television.

"If we went over budget, a lot of penalties would be involved for both Steven and I," Lucas adds. "But I'd talked with Steven about it, and explained that we really needed to do this like a TV show: really quick and dirty, using old-fashioned tricks. Steven said, 'Great, that's the way I want to make it.' Part of it was, I think, the challenge of saying, 'Look, I can make a movie for half the price you can make a movie. Now, do you want to prove me wrong? Here's your chance.' And he said, 'I can do that.'"

"I said, 'Look, you want to make it for $17 million?'" Spielberg says. "'I'll give you a $17 million movie. You want to make it for $20 million? You'll get a $20 million movie, George. What do you want to make it for?' He said, 'Seventeen million.' I said, 'Okay, the $17 million movie is coming your way.'"

Studio negotiations approached an end with Warner Bros. in the pole position. "Tom Pollock and I spent a weekend, day and night, with Warner president Frank Wells making the deal," Weber says, "and we thought, including George, that we were gonna make the deal at Warners. We were a handshake away."

However, Frank Wells, a lawyer by trade, continued to scrutinize the unprecedented terms without committing to them, according to Weber, "which allowed us to continue our negotiations with Paramount. The deal was so tough, with huge advances, no distribution fee, and everything else."

"We were about to close a deal with Warner Bros., but they were negotiating really hard, and I didn't particularly want to do that," Lucas says. "Charlie was saying, 'We'll have to give up this, we're going to have to give up that.' I said, 'I don't want to give up that stuff.' And then Paramount came back and said, 'We'll do it.' And Warners said, 'You're going to destroy the industry because you're giving them everything!'"

THE FANTASTIC FOUR

In his notes to Jim Steranko, George Lucas requested four paintings along the following lines, as transmitted by Jane Bay (all paintings were delivered on August 6, 1979):

TOP LEFT: "Painting #1 should be similar to example 1A [OPPOSITE RIGHT]—should be inside an Inca-type temple with snakes on the floor and spiders on the walls. Our hero should be dressed more like guy in 1B [OPPOSITE LEFT], khaki pants, gun belt, leather jacket (brown like the one George wears), felt hat with brim turned down. He will have a bullwhip attached to the back of his belt…" ("If I could be a dream figure," Lucas says, "I'd be Indy. It's not just that I'm interested in archaeology or anthropology; a lot of that got into Star Wars, too. It's that Indy can do anything. He's a lot of different 1930s heroes put together.")

TOP RIGHT: "Painting 2—to be desert location with Arabs, with some Nazi trucks and tanks. (George suggests you get an old picture of Humphrey Bogart from The Treasure of Sierra Madre for the right look of our hero.)"

ABOVE LEFT: "Painting 3—a Nazi pilot… our hero… under the wing of a Flying Wing Air Plane having a fist fight on the ground very close to the propeller where one of them is going to get chewed up."

ABOVE RIGHT: "Painting 4—with our hero on horse leaping onto Nazi Army truck with canvas cover on the back of truck, circa 1936 before the war." ("It came from the serials," Kasdan says. "In fact, George showed me this picture while I was helping him hang these giant enlargements of photos around ILM, and one of them is a guy jumping from a horse onto a truck. He said that that image had been the heart of Raiders.")

"I prefer the tension of the moment just before the explosion," Steranko wrote in his June 30, 1979, letter to Lucas.

"I flew to the West Coast to meet with Steven and discuss his approach and inspirations," Steranko says. "He was busy editing 1941 at a Burbank facility at the time, but we chatted for a while, then he suggested we have dinner and continue the conversation. We piled in his car to drive to a nearby restaurant and his Indy inspirations became immediately apparent: the back seat was stacked with film cans of Spy Smasher and Zorro's Fighting Legion, the serial reference George had mentioned during our initial phone call. 'Raiders was not,' he explained, 'a suspense film.' The characters were larger than life; the locations were exotic, at times, bordering on the fantastic; and the set pieces were to be evocative of their period. Action was the keynote, and the plot was to feature enough cliff-hangers to stock a serial—which accounted for the homework in Steven's car. But I never saw a script; the key scenes I painted were all described in conversations with the guys."

ABOVE LEFT: George Lucas wrote his Indiana Jones comments to Jim Steranko on two pieces of the latter's artwork. An arrow indicates "bullwhip instead of gun"; "1940s felt hat similar to H. Bogart in *Treasure of Sierra Madre*"; "straight pants"; and, in place of the tents, "Nazi truck and tank." ABOVE RIGHT: Lucas's note reads, "Ins de temple (Inca type) spiders on walls and many snakes around floor."

Both images originally appeared in a 1976 issue of *Lone Star Fictioneer*, number 4. The magazine was devoted to the works of writer Robert E. Howard, and these illustrations were for a story entitled "Three-Bladed Doom," about a globetrotting Texas gunfighter named Francis Xavier Gordon, who is captured during his adventures in the Middle East during World War I; the locals call him El Borak. (Both images above are copyright © Jim Steranko ARR.)

Given an opening, Paramount pounced. On November 7, 1979, senior vice president of the feature division Richard Zimbert returned a signed deal memo to Tom Pollock—and on November 27, the Raiders Company, Lucasfilm, and Paramount signed the Assignment for Security of Motion Picture Rights and Copyright, which was also referred to in the correspondence as the "pay-or-play" agreement, a 58-page document.

Three days after the signatures, on November 30, 1979, *Variety* announced the deal. Underneath the headline screaming across the banner, Dale Pollock wrote: "Confirming one of the most talked-about deals in Hollywood, Paramount Pictures will finance and distribute worldwide the Lucasfilm production of *Raiders of the Lost Ark*, along with four sequels to the property. Steven Spielberg will direct *Raiders*, which Frank Marshall will produce, and on which George Lucas will act as exec producer."

Pollock reported that Eisner refused to divulge details, though Eisner insisted several times that it was a good deal for Paramount, which procured the contract thanks to its aggressive distribution. "We're not only ecstatic to get this," he said, "we would have gone even further to get it [. . .] You don't make standard deals with these kinds of people."

The article went on to talk about a budget of less than $20 million, and, Dale Pollock wrote, "As for industry scuttlebutt that Paramount accepted a deal turned down by other studios who considered it 'insulting' and 'suicidal for the business,' to quote one high-placed exec, Eisner had but one answer: 'If we got shafted on this arrangement, we would like to be shafted two or three times a year in this way.'"

FORTUNE AND GLORY

Even as Hollywood digested the news, Lucasfilm and Paramount lawyers corresponded by mail on December 3, 7, 12, and 20, debating the finer points. "The beginning of the deal took a week," Weber says. "Fighting over every line that they wanted to take back probably took another two or three months."

Ultimately they decided that gross receipts, after Paramount had recouped its investment, would be split 60–40 in the studio's favor up to "breakeven-plus $35 million" at which time the split became 50–50. All sequel rights were Raiders', with Paramount given the right to "first negotiation/last refusal." All merchandising rights also belonged to the Raiders Company.

SS-OBERSTURMBANNFÜHRER TOHT

On December 13, 1979, *1941* was released to disappointing results critically and at the box office, but Spielberg was well on the way to his next picture, signing his Director's Employment Agreement with Lucasfilm on January 21, 1980—two and a half years after his handshake on the beach with Lucas.

The signed agreement was forwarded the next day to Weber for Lucasfilm's signature, accompanied by a transmittal letter from Bruce Ramer: "Personally and on behalf of Guy [McElwaine], I want to thank you, Charlie, and the other representatives of your client, for the patience and understanding demonstrated throughout some rather protracted and difficult negotiations. Good faith has been demonstrated in abundance on both sides of the table, and, in fact, as you know, in a number of areas Steven is relying on the good faith of George and his companies as he and George have directly discussed."

Lucas had indeed been carefully guiding both processes as necessary: the deals with Spielberg and with Paramount. "George was informed every

OPPOSITE: Concepts are roughed out for the Nazi Belzig (BOTTOM RIGHT), who, early on, was equipped with a mechanical arm and a radio antenna that hooked into his head; artist Ron Cobb's notes read, "Hears songs that he hates…" TOP LEFT: He was later renamed Toht, and his arm was shown to double as a machine gun; Cobb noted that the arm would've featured a "banana clip, ejection slot & breech, gloved hand." BOTTOM LEFT: Another Toht illustration by Cobb resembles actor Christopher Lee (who was playing a Nazi at this time in Spielberg's *1941*).

Storyboards dated 1979 by Edward Verreaux show Toht's arm in action during the truck chase (LEFT) and in the Raven saloon (ABOVE). "I called Frank Marshall, introduced myself, and asked for a job," Verreaux says. "Although I got an interview I didn't get the job right away. They hired another person. But three weeks later I got another call, this time to come in and meet Steven. After that meeting and four test sketches to prove that I could draw, I began work."

night," Weber says. "He knew when we were turning left versus right, and why and how, and he had a participation in all of that. George is an excellent businessman."

Perhaps because of nagging worries about the genre and the characterization of Indy, along with the long wait, Spielberg was ambivalent about finally signing on. "I'm happy I'm making it, but essentially if George had approached me with this project just last year, I would have said no," Spielberg says, "because actually, more than a year ago, I was ready to explore other kinds of films. But because George and I essentially had agreed to do this movie together in the early part of 1977, I wasn't about to turn my back on it two and a half years later."

Other signatures followed that January. To sew up any legal entanglements created by his early involvement, Philip Kaufman signed a "certificate of authorship" on January 29, 1980, specifying that he had collaborated on the "original unpublished story" of *Raiders of the Lost Ark* and

that his employer (Walrus & Associates) owned the copyright. Lucas signed a similar document the day after. Both signatures cleared the way to the overall agreement with Paramount, as they then transferred their rights to the Raiders Company, which was signatory to the production distribution contract.

On February 7, 1980, the firm of Ferguson, Hoffman, Henn, Mandel & Heil (Doug Ferguson was Lucas's personal attorney) informed Richard Zimbert that the following had taken place: the signing of the production agreement; Paramount's approval of the budget; the signing of the agreement by Steven Spielberg to direct the film; and the signing by the Raiders Company of a Security Agreement, a Laboratory Pledgeholder Agreement, and a Power of Attorney agreement. The lawyers' letter thus ended: "Pursuant to such paragraph… Paramount is to advance the sum of $2 million" to the Raiders Company.

At last *Raiders of the Lost Ark* was a go.

BELOW: Storyboards from 1979 by Dave Negron of Indy's adventures in a Cairo bazaar show his fight with a scimitar-wielding foe and his discovery of an arms cache.

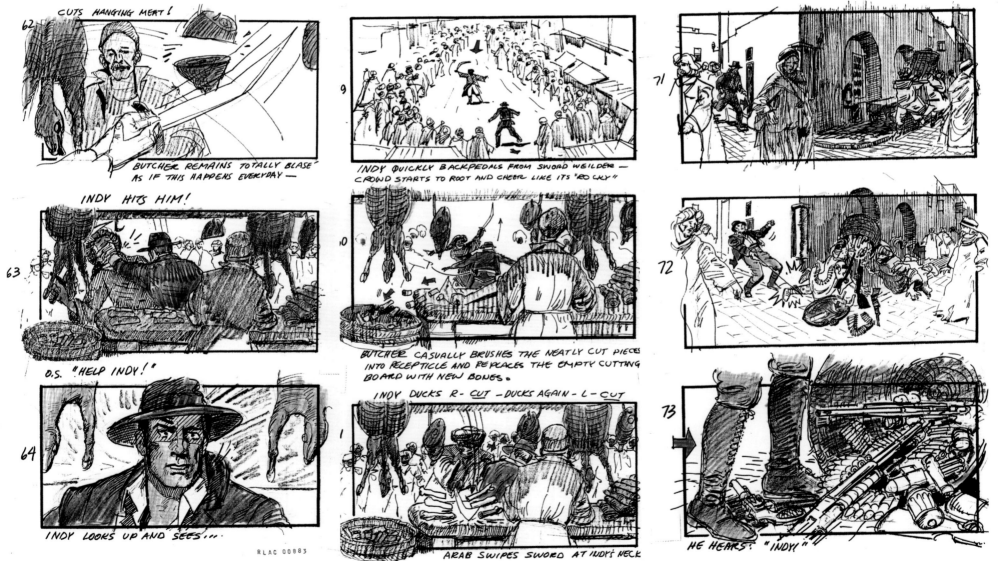

shall not otherwise be given any legal effect.

15. Entire Agreement; No Other Representations, Construction of this Agreement; California Law Controls. This Agreement contains the full and complete understanding between the parties with reference to the within subject matter, and supersedes all prior agreements and understandings whether written or oral pertaining thereto. Lucas acknowledges that no representations or promise not expressly contained in this Agreement has been made by Raiders or any of its agents, employees, or representatives with respect to the subject matter of this Agreement. This Agreement in all respects shall be construed under and shall be subject to the laws of the State of California.

IN WITNESS WHEREOF, the parties hereto have executed this Agreement as of the day and year first above written.

RAIDERS COMPANY

By _____

Title: V.P.

GEORGE W. LUCAS, JR

NOVEMBER 27, 1979

EXECUTED

RAIDERS

Paramount Pictures Corporation
5451 Marathon Street
Los Angeles, California 90038

Attention: Mr. Richard Zimbert

Re: "RAIDERS OF THE LOST ARK"

Gentlemen:

This letter (the "agreement") will serve as a deal memorandum memorializing the agreement between Paramount Pictures Corporation ("Paramount") and Raiders Company ("Raiders"), a California corporation and a wholly owned subsidiary of Lucasfilm, Ltd. ("Lucasfilm"), with respect to a proposed theatrical feature-length motion picture currently entitled "RAIDERS OF THE LOST ARK" (the "Picture"), as follows:

1. Paramount's and Raiders' Respective Obligations Regarding the Picture.

The Picture shall be a theatrical feature-length motion picture to be based upon the screenplay for the Picture (the "Screenplay") which has been written by Lawrence Kasdan and previously submitted to and Paramount. Raiders

LEFT: The last and first pages of the resultant distribution contract, with Lucas's signature. BELOW: The headline of the November 30, 1979, edition of *Daily Variety* announced in dramatic fashion Lucasfilm's deal with Paramount for *Raiders of the Lost Ark*.

DAILY VARIETY DAILY

35 Cents

Hollywood, California-90028, Friday, N

VOL. 185 No. 62   40 Pages

PAR FLOATING LUCASFILM'S 'ARK'

Will Finance And Distribute Original Feature, Well As Planned Quartet Of Sequels

By DALE POLLOCK

Confirming one of the most talked-about deals in Hollywood, Paramount Pictures will finance and distribute worldwide the Lucasfilm production of "Raiders Of The Lost Ark," along with four sequels to the property. Steven Spielberg will direct "Raiders," which Frank Marshall will produce, and on which George Lucas will act as exec producer.

The period action-adventure pic is due to begin production next May on a budget of under $20,000,000 at Elstree Studios outside of London, with Par to distrib "Raiders" as its major summer release in 1981 on a wide multiple break in 1981.

Mucho speculation has centered on the financial deal agreed to by Par, with published reports claiming the studio was waiving its standard distribution fee in what would have been an unprecedented action. But Par prexy and chief operating officer Michael D. Eisner

Italian Government Hasn't Ruled Out The Possibility Of Restricting U.S. Pic Imports

By STEPHEN KLAIN

New York, Nov. 29 — Looking to effect some kind of "balance" between the dominance of the Italian film marketplace by U.S. features and the "virtually nonexistent" presence of Italo features here, the Italian government has not ruled out the possibility of legislation to regulate the number of imported Yank films.

According to Italian entertainment and tourism minister

sor, Anica, Italo counterpart to the Motion Picture Association of America), D'Arezzo trotted out statistics indicating that by the end of the year, U.S. features

(Continued on Page 35, Column 4)

Court Stays FCC Decision On Net Time For Carter

Washington, Nov. 29 — Wast U.S. Court of

NBC-TV MID-SEASON SERIES STATUS: ADDS TWO AND CUTS TWO

NBC-TV has drafted a tentative midseason primetime schedule in which only two new series will be added and two dropped.

Pencilled in are a half-hour sitcom starring Redd Foxx, and a 90-minute Nick Vanoff-produced variety series. Erased from the new NBC blueprint are "Kate Loves A Mystery," and "A Man Called Sloane," latter having made its debut last September.

A wholesale sweep had been expected from NBC at midterm because it is running third in the ratings race.

Not in the midterm lineup are a number of series on which firm commitments had been made, starring Karl

1979 Banner Year For Dick Clark: Grosses $25 Mil

By DAVE KAUFMAN

A banner year, with an approximate $25,000,000 gross, has been recorded by Dick Clark, which more than

(Continued on Page 35, Column 4)

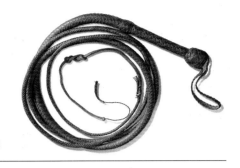

CHAPTER 2
THE FILM WITH A THOUSAND PARTS

FEBRUARY TO MAY 1980

With the key contracts signed and a start date of May 1980 for principal photography, preproduction began its multifaceted fast-forward march. Back on December 11, 1979, storyboard artist Edward Verreaux had signed his one-page deal memo. "I had Dave Negron and Ed Verreaux early on storyboarding," Spielberg says. "And I had Michael Lloyd, who did 20-inch oil paintings for us—concept visions in a kind of high-tech gloss."

On December 17, associate to the director Kathleen Kennedy signed on with a start date of December 31. "I was working with John Milius," she says. "I would answer the phones. But I had met Steven during the course of making *1941*, which John Milius had produced. One day Steven asked me to come work for him on *Raiders*; he put the script down in front of me and said, 'Here, read this. But don't tell anyone about it.' I read it in one sitting; I couldn't put it down. After I finished, I went running in and told him I thought it was fantastic."

As *Variety* had reported, Lucas had made the decision to shoot at Elstree Studios in London, England, because of the savings and because of the good relationship between Lucasfilm and the Elstree staff—a relationship that had started with *Star Wars* and which had continued during the shoot of *Empire* the previous summer. To take care of business abroad, another subsidiary was formed in England, Lost Ark Productions.

THE SECRET EGG COMPANY

Because Lucas was being spread so thin, with several Lucasfilm productions happening at once in different parts of the world, he appointed Howard Kazanjian to be his surrogate for *Raiders* and the liaison between his company and Paramount. Kazanjian's office was in Lucasfilm's corporate headquarters, known as the Egg Company, an old brick building at 3855 Lankershim Boulevard, North Hollywood, across the street from Universal Studios.

"We didn't want to call it the *Star Wars* building, we didn't want to advertise this was Lucasfilm," Kazanjian says.

"George had bought the property, an old egg warehouse, and

converted it into this very beautiful, kind of rustic office space," says associate legal counsel Howard Roffman (now president of Lucas Licensing). "The administrative offices of the company were located down there, the finance, accounting, business affairs, licensing, and marketing departments were all situated down there. The only thing that existed up in Marin County was George's office and the various production facilities of ILM and Sprocket Systems [today Skywalker Sound]."

"*Star Wars* and *Empire* were both done at EMI [Elstree] Studios," Kazanjian says, "with nearly the same crew. They're very good crew. They know the way George Lucas works, they know the way the company works. And *Raiders* is a bridge between *Empire* and the third *Star Wars* picture. So as soon as we're finished, these people will go on vacation and come back to the next picture, which is very good continuity. Also we wanted to maintain secrecy and that was certainly more easily done in England. Suddenly it'll happen that everyone in the States knows what the story is about, and then you see your story on television before you get your movie out."

Classmates at USC, Kazanjian and Lucas had met back in 1964. He had since worked as an assistant director for Alfred Hitchcock and Billy Wilder. Lucas had hired Kazanjian to produce *More American Graffiti* in 1977. Ten months later he was Lucasfilm's vice president of production; as such, one of his main tasks was keeping an eye on costs.

"We did a budget for the United Kingdom and another for the US," Kazanjian says. "The UK was cheaper. When we did our budget and submitted it to Paramount for financing in November of 1979, the pound was $2.10. When Paramount accepted the budget, the pound was $2.19. But Paramount has been very good, and we have an agreement with them that we are not penalized for any overages caused by devaluation of the dollar. So if we're budgeted at $2.10 and we shoot the picture at $2.36, that would cause no penalty."

Along with the talents of several hundred technicians and crafts-people, shooting overseas meant taking advantage in particular of the services of associate producer Robert Watts and production designer Norman Reynolds, both of whom had worked on the two *Star Wars* films. Reynolds had actually started on *Raiders* in October 1979, scouting for locations in Tunisia. He departed with Watts for his second "recce" in 1980.

"In January we left England," Watts says, "and went first to LA for a week of meetings with George and Steven and company."

"Watts was a big help in particular because he knew the English crew so well," Lucas says. "Frank Marshall was the real producer. Howard was like a studio executive, which I needed for Lucasfilm to make sure that everything stayed on budget."

Production meeting notes in the Lucasfilm Archives dated January 22, 1980, listed the individuals of the meeting attended by Watts and Reynolds: George Lucas, Steven Spielberg, Frank Marshall, Howard Kazanjian, Kathy Kennedy, Leah Schmidt, and Lawrence Kasdan. Others would come to specific meetings depending on the subject. To facilitate his work, Spielberg had also taken an office in the Egg Company building.

"Steven Spielberg's office was right outside the *Star Wars* fan-club office," says Maureen Garrett. "I think he had a bird in there. And he had a game of *Asteroids* that you could play."

"George flew down that day from San Francisco to our offices at the Egg Company," Kazanjian says. "I met George at the back door and he asked, 'How's everything?' And I said, 'There's one thing I haven't been able to figure out and that's the Flying Wing. It's a million dollars and we have $750,000 to spend on it.'"

"There were prototype Flying Wings that were being developed in World War II, but there was only one left, and certainly it didn't fly and it wasn't big enough to accomplish what we wanted," Frank Marshall says. "So we had to design and build a real Wing. It didn't have to fly, but it had to look like it could fly, and it had to be designed in a way that it could move around."

After their quick huddle, Lucas and Kazanjian joined the others to discuss the film. They all agreed that there should be "one memorable moment in each scene" and that the "main production value scenes would be the Well of Souls, Peruvian jungle, opening of the Ark." They also came up with the following details:

• "Opening Movie… Mountains peeking out of fog…see Indy's hat dipping in and out of the fog…between them and the temple is a thick jungle—with a huge horrible statue at the entrance [with] two legs and an opening. Can't see the head—clouds cover—walking into the mouth of the creature… when the rock comes, it knocks out the teeth; build head and feet in location jungle—rest on stage…

• "Peruvian temple: Whole set 100 ft. high at least…100 tarantulas—some real and some made…

BELOW: Another Well of Souls concept painting by Michael Lloyd. 1979.

• "Hok's palace: build, get gong scene to work; palace in middle of busy part of town; Ext. 2nd Unit—Macao? Penang (Malaysia)?

• "Saloon: light & shadows, stark stylized (e.g., *House of Frankenstein*); as fire spreads, shadows multiply—looks like 25 men though only four. Toht—no mechanical arm…

• "Digs: Should be action in the background during all shots in the dig area…

• "Well of Souls: Should be logical entrance from the hole above… Snakes should cover the ground. Four statues. Need a definite claustrophobic feeling. Scariest moment should be the run through the dead bodies…

• "Island: Need a logical path for sub—from Egypt to Germany… Indy hanging on—not too long a trip…change island from jungle to more barren—better for a miniature and sky effects…

• "Flying wing: Decrease size of wing—drop two engines and bring propellers closer to ground…No experimental jet. No longer in script."

"We had a bunch of models and a bunch of ideas because this was a production meeting to take it to the next step," Kazanjian says. "We had a model of the Flying Wing. And George picked up the four-engine Flying Wing with his two fingers and he said, 'This is beautiful'—and just broke off the two outer engines, leaving one engine on each wing. Steven's reaction

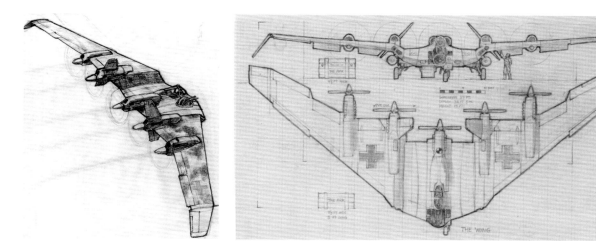

OPPOSITE: Ron Cobb's 1979 concept illustration for the "experimental jet," which was cut from the film in January 1980.

LEFT: Ron Cobb's early sketch and diagram drawing of the four-engine Flying Wing; he included an Ark for size comparisons.
BELOW: Concept painting of same by Joe Johnston.

was something like, 'What are you doing?' And George said, 'Looks good this way. How much can we save, Howard?' I said, 'Probably a quarter of a million dollars.' And he said, 'Do it this way.' Everybody, including myself, was shocked. But that was George's way of coming up with an answer. There were a number of times when he would do something like that."

Immediately after the meeting, Watts and Reynolds left on their worldwide recce, heading for Hawaii in search of a single site that could pass for a South American jungle and a Chinese street location. Earlier trips had taken Marshall, Reynolds, and Watts to Puerto Rico, Guatemala, and Mexico.

"We couldn't find Chinese streets in Hawaii," Watts says, "so we went on to Hong Kong via Tokyo." They weren't able to find anything suitable in Hong Kong, which had been built up and modernized, so they tried Macao,

which became a possibility for streets but had no jungle. They continued to Malaysia.

"We went to the island of Penang, where we found great Chinese streets and great jungle," Watts reports. "So we had South America and Shanghai within forty-five minutes of each other and that's where we decided to shoot."

After initiating work on the set, the two traveled home via Bangkok, Thailand, and Bahrein in the Persian Gulf.

"Steven, George, Robert Watts, and I have gotten together," Marshall says. "The planning on the movie has been hectic and in a short period of time, but it has been done in such a fashion that we are really organized."

THE TALE OF INDY AND MARION

Beyond budget considerations, casting the film's two major roles became the biggest challenge of the first half of 1980. "Steven did a very interesting thing," Kazanjian says. "He would first meet and talk with the actors in this very large, beautiful kitchen we had in the Egg Company. To put them at ease, Steven decided to have the actors help make cookies or cake or whatever. Sometimes he would have them add the ingredients. And there were other people standing around—sometimes myself; Frank Marshall; associate to the director Kathy Kennedy—and somebody would pick up a camera and take a few shots of the actor. No one was given the script."

"I was cooking with the actors and actresses," Spielberg says. "I just got real tired of having actors with their eight-by-ten glossies, model layouts, and all their credits in their head coming into an office and sitting across from me, a casting director, the producer, and some other people, and playing the game of let's-see-who's-the-most-intimidated. It was no fun. I never looked forward to waking up and casting a movie. But because of the design of the Egg Company, there was a fantastic, modern kitchen that was real conducive for cooking and talking, so I thought, *Well, great.*"

"Steven took over the kitchen at the Egg Company," Lucasfilm marketing president Bob Greber says. "And he brought in this singing parrot, so every once in a while you'd hear this operatic aria."

"I had moved on January 1, and made a lot of changes in my lifestyle," Spielberg says. "I really wanted to learn how to cook. So all the actors from 9 AM to 1 PM helped cook. We made everything from Charlotte au Chocolat to homemade pumpkin bread. Then all the actors who came in from two to seven helped eat. And word spread. I think Army Archerd and some of the columnists carried a few of the stories in their papers, so actors were calling their agents saying, 'I only want to come in after two.' Everyone wanted to eat. Nobody wanted to work."

"I would think it must be a little difficult for somebody coming in to meet Steven Spielberg," Kazanjian says. "He is very famous, after all—they were meeting almost a legend. So this was a good way to relax people. Of course, sometimes the interviews were done in an office."

Thanks to a series of memos preserved on Radio Pictures Inc. paper (another subsidiary acting as "part of the Lucasfilm family"), from Kennedy

OPPOSITE: Tanis Digs concept painting with the entrance to the Well of Souls by Michael Lloyd, 1979.

TOP RIGHT: Spielberg checks for camera angles and shot possibilities on a miniature of the Tanis Digs location. Several maquettes were made of sets for Spielberg's approval before they were built on soundstages at Elstree Studios or on location: a "proposed Int. of Imam's house" at half an inch per foot (TOP LEFT); part of the Peruvian temple that they were considering building (MIDDLE LEFT); and the interior of the Well of Souls (BOTTOM LEFT).

TEMPLE OF THE CHACHAPOYAN WARRIORS (PRELIMINARY.) THE SANCTUARY.

to Spielberg, it's possible to reestablish much of the casting chronology. On Thursday, January 24, 1980, Spielberg met with 12 actors, including Jane Seymour and Paul Le Mat. On Friday morning, he interviewed 15 people, including Lisa Eilbacher, Christopher Guest, and Jane Seymour (for a second time). Debra Winger and Mark Harmon tried out together at 2 PM. That following Monday, January 28, eight candidates came to the Egg Company, including Mary Steenburgen, Michael Biehn, Sam Shepard, and Valerie Bertinelli. On Tuesday, the number totaled eleven, with Winger reappearing.

"It worked well because it disarmed nearly everyone," Spielberg says. "In fact, with the exception of perhaps a half dozen who complained to their agents after the meetings, the 300 to 400 we saw, who came through that kitchen and helped us cook, had just a great time. A month and a half into casting our reputation had spread so far they would come in with ingredients and recipes that they had prepared the week before.

"Actors who were normally shy came out of themselves. Then I'd have them back a second time, and hopefully they'd be a little looser and a little more open to talking about the part."

On Wednesday, January 30, videotape sessions began with eight pairs, including Bruce Boxleitner with Debra Winger, and Michael Sullivan with Barbara Hershey. During their story conferences, when Kasdan had asked what actor he had in mind for Indiana, Lucas had immediately replied, "Harrison Ford"—but his name is notably absent from all the early casting lists.

"Harrison came up way early on, and Steven was all for it," Lucas says. "He wanted him in the beginning when we talked. He said, 'Harrison would be great for it.' I said, 'He'd be great for it, but I don't want to use him.' I hadn't been able to get Harrison to sign a contract for the three *Star Wars* movies, and I didn't think I could get him to sign a contract for the three *Indiana Jones* films. I also didn't want it to be a Bobby De Niro/Marty Scorsese thing. So I said, 'Let's get somebody new,' and Steven agreed."

On Friday, February 1, Spielberg was ready to introduce the front-runners to Lucas at 3:30 PM in the screening room. Instructions were that no actor was to see another, so the following people arrived at 20-minute intervals: Barbara Hershey, Sam Elliott, Lisa Eilbacher, Barry Bostwick, and Debra Winger.

No immediate decision was forthcoming, however, so casting continued through Friday, February 8, with more than 30 further tests, including newcomers Dee Wallace, Linda Purl, Patti d'Arbanville, and John Calvin, as well as repeaters Debra Winger and Barbara Hershey. A February 11 morning session included Eddie Benton and Michelle Pfeiffer.

"When you're meeting twenty-five people daily, all the people who come in between three and seven o'clock shouldn't bother," Spielberg says, as casting went on. "We totally phase out by then. Come between nine and lunchtime: We're hot, anxious to cast the movie, eager."

A memo from Kathy Kennedy to Spielberg on Wednesday, February 13, 1980, listed those 44 actors who had been turned away, including Jonathan Segal, Don Johnson, Jenny Agutter, Christopher Guest, and Dee Wallace. It also listed the 12 contenders for the role of Marion, such as Debra Winger, Barbara Hershey, Lisa Eilbacher, and Jane Seymour. Among the 11 possibilities for Indiana Jones were David Hasselhoff, Mark Harmon, and Paul Le Mat.

"Other casting sessions were out in the courtyard," Kazanjian says, "where they were either standing or sitting, and Steven would just talk to them or they'd read a scene, not necessarily from the movie but a scene. And this went on for weeks with women and men—but we couldn't find the young actors."

"Because George and I wanted to discover somebody new, we never thought of the established actors," Spielberg says. "We were looking for the guy who might be doing a Camel cigarette ad on television and hasn't had a break yet. So we went through the files and met everybody, from good off-off-Broadway actors to male models, and it was very discouraging."

THE DESERTS OF WAR

At some point in early 1980 Spielberg and Frank Marshall found the time to travel to New York City, where they met more stage actors and actresses, and Karen Allen was fortunate enough to see them during the morning hours. "Nobody measured up after that," Spielberg says. "'Not as good as Karen,' we kept saying."

Karen Allen had been cast for a supporting role in *Cruising* (1980) with Al Pacino, and had costarred in the very successful *Animal House* (1978), but Spielberg had been impressed after seeing her in *A Small Circle of Friends* (released on March 12, 1980, though Spielberg most likely saw a preview).

"They asked me to come to Los Angeles and read for it," Karen Allen says.

Allen thus joined the ranks for reading tests on Wednesday, February 20, at 3:30 PM. The next two days was more of the same—but Friday showcased a new frontrunner: Sean Young, who was flown out from New York and lodged at the Sheraton Universal. Young had only one film credit to her name—*Jane Austen in Manhattan*—but must have had something special, because Lucas was flown down to meet her the following Monday, February 25.

More readings with additional Marions and Indys took place that Friday, but nothing was settled. Spielberg thus took a break from casting and turned to location work. By this time they had fixed on La Rochelle, France, as the location for the submarine pen and the shots at sea. "We needed a World War II German U-boat and found one that had been built for a German film and TV series *Das Boot*," Watts says. "It was lying in La Rochelle in France. I had imagined something that could be dismantled, crated, and sent anywhere. But when we saw it, we realized it couldn't be transferred. So we had to do those scenes in La Rochelle, which added France to our schedule.

"The submarine was in a former Nazi sub pen that had been built during World War II," he adds, "an enormous concrete edifice that was too solid to pull down. So we decided that we would also use the interior of the submarine pen, and make it the Nazi interior base. It was a bona fide German construction. It even had German graffiti from the war."

Visiting another location possibility, probably during the month of March, Spielberg traveled to Tunisia to join Watts, Reynolds, and mechanical effects supervisor Kit West. Reynolds and Watts knew the terrain well from their *Star Wars* location shooting.

"I noticed palm trees sticking up and thought it had possibilities," Reynolds says of a particular site suitable for the Tanis Digs, "so we went with Steven and walked through a series of sticks and pegs showing where things would go."

"Steven decided that Tunisia it was, and work began," Watts says. "He was only in and out very quickly because he had a lot of other irons in the fire, shooting extra footage for the special edition of *Close Encounters* [released on July 31, 1980] and completing another movie of which he was executive producer [*Used Cars*, July 11, 1980]."

Spielberg had also just formed his own company, Amblin Entertainment (named after his short film), to handle his expanding work and business load. Because of that incorporation, a modified Director's Employment Agreement, known as the Amblin Agreement, was ratified on April 1, 1980. A letter of the same date from the Raiders Company to Spielberg's agent, Guy McElwaine, explained that Spielberg was now

OPPOSITE ABOVE: A "preliminary" set sketch of the "sanctuary" within the "temple of the Chachapoyan warriors" by production designer Norman Reynolds, February 1980. OPPOSITE BELOW: Construction manager Bill Welch, Reynolds, and associate producer Robert Watts.

LEFT: A publicity photo of Karen Allen. ABOVE: Allen's screen test with Tim Matheson, circa April 1, 1980.

considered an employee of Amblin Enterprises, Inc., which would receive 80 percent of his salary. All of his sequel and TV rights were also transferred to Amblin.

The following day screen tests recommenced, this time with actors in full makeup and wardrobe. "Steven would occasionally write up a small scene and have two people play against each other," Kazanjian says. "As we got down to our final choices, we filmed the actors."

After arriving half an hour early to get into their costumes, the following pairs went before the cameras: Mark Harmon and Patti d'Arbanville; Sean Young and Paul Le Mat.

"We'd been looking for a leading man for over six months," Spielberg says. "We'd wanted an unknown originally, a total unknown, but we couldn't find Johnny the Construction Worker in Malibu, so we began looking at more substantial people in the film industry. Of course, the bigger the name, the less likely they'd agree to do more than one *Raiders of the Lost Ark*. And George wanted a guarantee of at least three movies from someone."

"Later they asked me to come and do some screen tests," Karen Allen says. "They gave me the scene where Marion and Indiana Jones first meet. I did several different ones with different actors. Each of the screen tests took two or three hours, and just in the course of doing the tests Steven and I really got somewhere putting our heads together with the character, finding ways to put dimensions into it, which was wonderful."

The daughter of an FBI man, Karen Allen was by this time starring in ABC's TV miniseries based on John Steinbeck's *East of Eden* (1981). "I was working about 12 or 13 hours every day," she says, "so that did put a different perspective on it. I was really interested in the part, but I wasn't waiting for a phone call. I hadn't read the screenplay so I was going on a small amount of information plus a lot of admiration for Steven's work."

Another pair who went before the cameras on April 2 was Sean Young and Tom Selleck. Although he may have done readings before, no dates for

them exist in the archives—he seems to have surged up rapidly to become everyone's favorite.

"We did a screen test with Tom Selleck and Sean Young, and it came out really, really well," Spielberg says. "I showed George the screen test, and George said, 'Yes, he looks just like that Steranko art.' And he was a damn good actor."

"Originally everybody thought that the part of Indiana Jones should go to Tom Selleck," Kazanjian says. "Steven and George wanted him because he was the ideal character."

UNIVERSAL SUFFRAGE

On or around April 16, 1980, Selleck was offered the part of Indiana Jones. For Marion, Spielberg had four possibilities, including Debra Winger and Maureen Teefy, who had appeared in *Fame*.

"We'd seen screen tests back and forth, back and forth, and it was real hard for everyone to decide, so we did have a show of hands to see who was for what actress at the Egg Company," Lucas says. "It was the casting director, Steven, myself, and just all the people who are involved in that process. I thought Karen had a spunky personality that was very winning."

Karen Allen won the vote. On April 16 her Authorization for Engagement of Artist was issued to Lucas and Spielberg. After Allen accepted, the *Raiders* script arrived in her hands, at least temporarily.

"It was all very mysterious," Karen says. "I was working on *East of Eden* when a messenger came up with it. Every page was marked. He took back each page after I read it. But I fell in love with Marion; she's Indiana Jones's match. It's a sexy part."

BELOW LEFT: A production sketch of the "Ext. Raven" by Reynolds, November 1979. At one point in the drafts, Indy entered town riding a mule. BELOW RIGHT: "Int. Raven" also by Reynolds, November 1979.

EXT 'RAVEN'.

REYNOLDS. N

'INT' RAVEN'   REYNOLDS. NOV 79

Things didn't go as smoothly for the part of Indy. "We made the offer to Tom Selleck after an exhaustive search for a leading man," Spielberg says. "Of all the people we looked at, over 250 male actors, he was the best. But Tom Selleck had a deal with CBS for a series called *Magnum P.I.* that was inactive, and once they heard that George and I wanted to star him in the series, especially that the director of *Star Wars* wanted to take Tom Selleck away, CBS put the series into production and preempted our using him."

"When we came along and said we were going to hire him to do a feature, they suddenly said, 'Oh, we'd better use him or we'll lose him,'" Lucas says. "We prompted them to make a decision that they'd been delaying."

ISLAND OF THE ARK

"Steven was very helpful," Karen Allen says. "We spent a lot of time talking in the beginning, because when I first read the script there seemed to be some inconsistencies in the character. So we sat down and went through it piece by piece, and he then went to the writer and they had conversations. Changes begin to take place almost immediately when a certain person is cast in a role."

"Larry had disappeared after he finished writing the [fourth] draft, way back in November of 1979," Spielberg says. "He was getting his own movie off the ground, *Body Heat*. He was writing that and eventually he was able to direct it. But he did rewrite a few scenes for me late in April, just before he became too busy to do any more work, even too busy to come to London to visit the location and the sets."

The fifth draft was accompanied by a memo from Kasdan to Lucas, Spielberg, Marshall, and Kazanjian, dated April 25, 1980: "In addition to reflecting all the changes we discussed, this new draft also includes, as per Steven's request, more *banter* between Indy and Marion throughout the script."

Among the changes "discussed" were the addition of the drinking contest in the Raven saloon and the elimination of two major set pieces: Shanghai and the rail chase. (A small temporary change occurred when the villainous Frenchman became, for just this one draft, Chartiere.)

"We all wanted it to be more realistic, just a little bit over the edge of believability," Kasdan says, "but a lot of the adventures we had cooked up in our discussions were much farther over the edge than that, so we found ourselves drawing back. The part where Indy and Marion get away, and the island blows up and all the Nazis are killed—I always hated that, because to me every *Bond* film ended that way. I'd told them that right from the beginning. But finally, after I think the [fourth] draft, Steven, too, became uncomfortable with it, and George at the same time, so we came up with this other idea, which is very different. It's this explosive ending out of the Ark, which I was much more comfortable with."

"The ending has evolved a little bit," Lucas says. "It was always that when they opened the Ark, an event took place. But in the process of rewriting the script, the event has become much grander, because it's now the actual climax of the film, whereas before there was a big chase after this. But we cut that out, realizing that the Ark was really what the movie was about and that the climax should be with the Ark and not just another chase in a series of chases."

Of course budget considerations were also involved in their decision. "I was ready for reformation," Spielberg says. "I was ready to turn to George

LEFT: Tom Selleck's April 2, 1980, screen test with Sean Young.

ABOVE: Set construction of the Well of Souls on Stage 5 of Elstree Studios, early 1980. The major sets at Elstree took "a team of almost 200 designers, plasterers, carpenters, riggers, painters, electricians, and special effects men nearly six months to build," according to a Paramount press release. BELOW: Construction of the Flying Wing at Elstree; the plane would later be taken apart, shipped to Tunisia, and reassembled in the desert.

and say, 'Reverend, show me the light. How can I get my budgets and schedules down?' And George gave me a great piece of advice. He just said, 'I promise you, if you're tough on yourself, and you throw out your first or second ideas 'cause they cost too much money, I bet you anything your compromises are better.' And he was right. We had a whole roller-coaster chase, and it was impossible to shoot it because it was too expensive. So I threw it out. George really taught me the art of the compromise."

"The Chinese location was cut from the script," Watts says. "So that was the end of that. It was also the end of Penang. We didn't need to go to the Far East for jungle. We had that in Hawaii, so Hawaii came back into the scene."

Also around this time, in addition to asking Kasdan to spice up Indy's relationship with Marion, Spielberg debated with Lucas the character of Indy. "On the one hand, Indiana Jones is a college professor of archaeology and anthropology," Lucas says. "On the other, he's a soldier of fortune. He's a sleazy character right on the edge of legality; Indiana is also a 1930s playboy. He has nights on the town and spends lots of money. But Steven wasn't enamored with some of Indiana's traits; he just felt it got too complicated and it wasn't essential to this particular story."

SCRAMBLE BEFORE SHOOTING

"I made my movie debut in a thing called *Dead Heat on a Merry-Go-Round*," Harrison Ford says of the 1966 film. "It was not an uplifting experience. I did tons of television—*Gunsmoke*, *The Virginian*, *The FBI*—always playing the same part: 'the guy who didn't do it.'"

"Harrison was my idea," Spielberg says. "We had three weeks to cast the part, with nobody close. But then I saw a rough cut of *The Empire Strikes Back* [circa late April 1980], and Harrison was just real good in *Empire*. So I called George, and I said, 'He's right under our nose.' And George said, 'I know who you're going to say.' And I said, 'Who?' He said, 'Harrison Ford.' I said, 'Right.'"

"Steven is the one who said Harrison would be great, right after Selleck," Lucas says. "He literally was, 'Okay, we've got the bad news. The good news is that now Harrison could do it.' I said, 'Well, I don't think he'll do three pictures.' 'Well, why don't you find out?' And I said, 'Okay. I'll send him the script, but I'll send it to him saying he'll have to sign for three pictures.'"

"George called me and told me what I had heard for a long time before—that they were making this film," Ford says. "I'd assumed they had someone for the part, so I was surprised when George called me and said he would like me to do Steven Spielberg's next film if Steven and I got along. I had met Steven once, casually. And George told me right away that there would be three of these films, but only if the first film was successful.

"So I went over to Steven's house with Melissa [Mathison, Ford's wife] and Willard [Huyck, a friend]," Ford adds. "Willard played pinball machines and video games, and Steven and I talked. Steven was bubbly and enthusiastic, and seemed like he might be fun to work with. Then I read the script, and I was enthusiastic about

Indiana

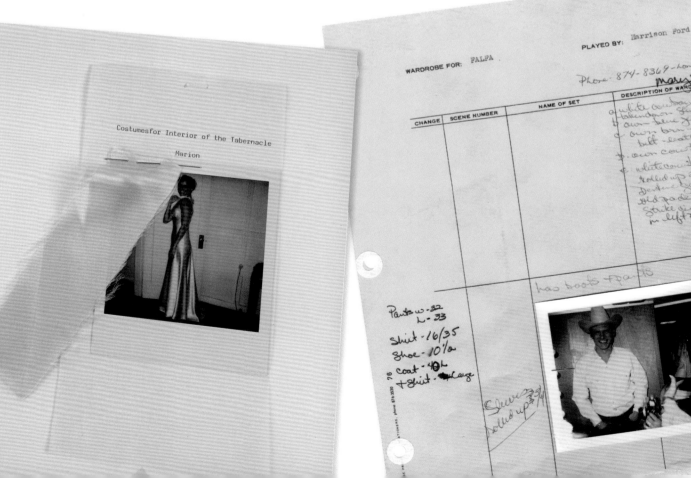

Costumes for Interior of the Tabernacle
Marion

WARDROBE FOR: FALFA.   PLAYED BY: Harrison Ford

LEFT: Original costume reference sheet from 1972 for Harrison Ford (Falfa) in *American Graffiti*; he also played Han Solo in *Star Wars*, so Lucas was reluctant to cast him in another Lucasfilm production. FAR LEFT AND ABOVE: Costume fabric swatches pinned to Polaroids of Karen Allen, in her interior tabernacle outfit, and to the costume sketch by Kelly Kimball of the still-to-be-cast Indiana, circa mid-April 1980.

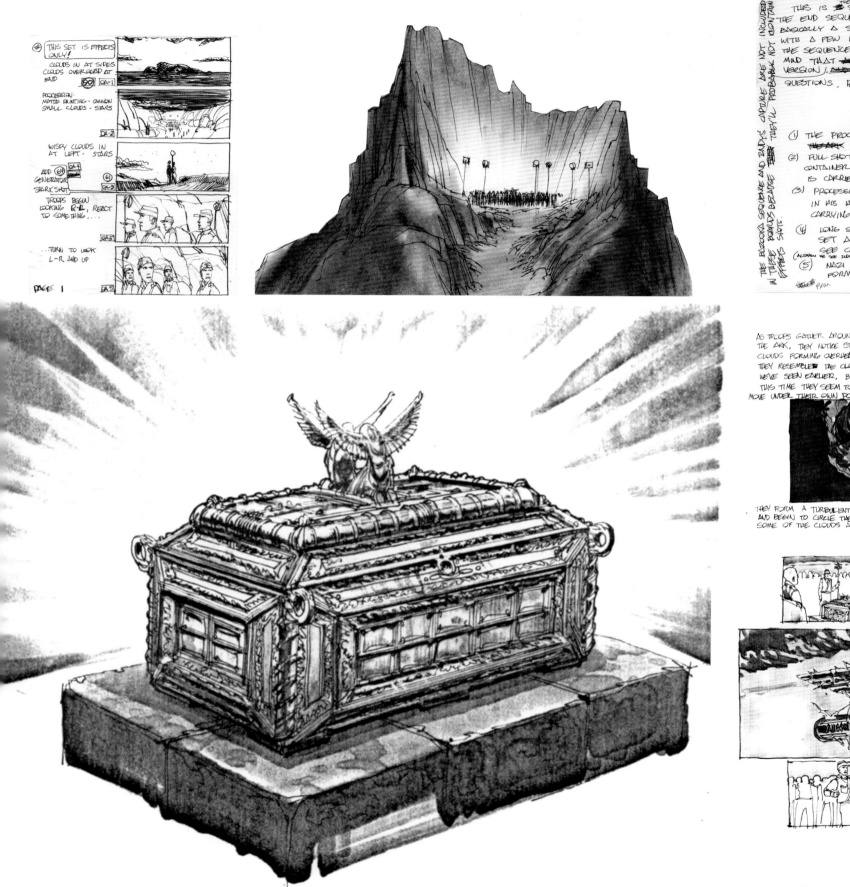

TO CAMPBELL BLACK.

THIS IS ~~THE~~ THE REVISED SECOND-DRAFT ~~OF~~ STORYBOARD OF THE END SEQUENCE OF "RAIDERS". ~~MOSTLY~~ IT IS BASICALLY A SERIES OF SPECIAL EFFECTS SHOTS WITH A FEW LIVE ACTION SHOTS THROWN IN TO MAKE THE SEQUENCE UNDERSTANDABLE. BEAR IN MIND THAT ~~ALL THESE~~ THIS IS NOT A FINAL VERSION ~~AND THAT~~. IF YOU HAVE ANY QUESTIONS, PLEASE CALL ME AT (415) 459-0220.

THANKS,

Joe Johnson

① THE PROCESSION INTO THE BOX CANYON ~~THE ARK~~

② FULL SHOT - THE ARK IN ITS PROTECTIVE CONTAINER, IS EMBLAZONED WITH SWASTIKAS, IS CARRIED ~~BY~~ CAMERA

③ PROCESSION WITH NAZI FILM CREW. BELLOQ IN HIS HEBREW PRIEST OUTFIT, NAZI TROOPER CARRYING STANDARD OF THE THIRD REICH.

④ LONG SHOT OF CANYON SET-UP. NAZI TROOPS SET ARK ON RAISED ROCKY AREA. WE CAN SEE CAMERA CREW FILMING PREPARATIONS. (ALTHOUGH WE SEE INDY AND MARION, IN THIS SHOT PROBABLY WOULD REQUIRE SECOND/CAPTURE.

⑤ NAZI TROOPS NOTICE WEIRD CLOUDS FORMING OVERHEAD.

(text running vertically along left of note): THE BAZOOKA SEQUENCE AND INDY'S CAPTURE ARE NOT INCLUDED IN THESE BOX-STAGE SHOTS BECAUSE THEY'LL PROBABLY NOT KEEP THEM

CLOUDS IN AT SIDES CLOUDS OVERHEAD AT END GA-1

PROCESSION: MATTE PAINTING - CANYON SMALL CLOUDS - STARS GA-2

WISPY CLOUDS IN AT LEFT - STARS
ADD GENERATOR SPARK SHOT GA-3

TROOPS BEGIN LOOKING R-L, REACT TO SOMETHING....

...TURN TO LOOK L-R AND UP

PAGE 1

AS TROOPS GATHER AROUND THE ARK, THEY NOTICE STRANGE CLOUDS FORMING OVERHEAD... THEY RESEMBLE THE CLOUDS WE'VE SEEN EARLIER, BUT THIS TIME THEY SEEM TO MOVE UNDER THEIR OWN POWER...

THEY FORM A TURBULENT "HALO" AND BEGIN TO CIRCLE THE ISLAND. SOME OF THE CLOUDS APPEAR TO BE LIT FROM WITHIN

BELLOQ BEGINS HIS INCANTATIONS... SUDDENLY, TINY SPARKS BEGIN TO DANCE ACROSS THE NAZI STANDARD...

both of them: the script and the director. I was convinced enough of the talent of the people involved to believe that the first one was going to be a good film. A good start, right?"

A note dated May 1, 1980, from Ford's agent Patricia McQueeney to Kazanjian makes clear that an agreement had been made by that date between Lucasfilm and Harrison Ford: "Harrison was very pleased with the deal and so was I," she writes.

"Harrison said, 'Hey, I love the script, it's fantastic, and I'll sign on for three pictures,'" Lucas says. "So I said, 'Wow, I would never have expected that.'"

"George was happy that we got Harrison for several reasons," Spielberg says. "Harrison liked the script enough based on the character to commit to more than one movie should the first film warrant sequels. I was very confident in Harrison, and Harrison was very confident in himself as this character, but it was a scary debut for both of us."

MYSTERIES WITHIN

A May 15, 1980, memo from Debbie Fine to Steven Spielberg went over the legalities of the fifth draft. To avoid confusion with real people, she requested that production change Belloq's first name from Emile to René. Colonel Schliemann becomes Colonel Dietrich. The *Bantu Wind* checked out as a name, but the National Museum in Washington had to become "a large museum in Washington." Moreover, actors would always have to say "Marcus Brody" or "Marcus," but never "Brody," as there was already a real museum administrator with the surname Brody. She also suggests hiring a rabbi in London "to act as a technical advisor for scene 144, Belloq's Hebrew incantations and other rituals concerning the Ark."

Other May events included the release of *The Empire Strikes Back* on the twenty-first of the month. While that film had come in way over budget, a cost of $20,590,643 was fixed by this time for *Raiders*, which meant it would break even with revenues of around $45 million at the box office, after all other costs had been added on (marketing, distribution, and so forth). Lucas and Spielberg had also proposed an 88-day shoot, which Paramount execs had okayed—but they privately planned to finish the film in 73 days, to save money, to test themselves and their crew, and perhaps even to exorcise a few demons from their systems.

"The studio puts so much pressure on you; they panic and they meddle, so this way you could always say, 'Hey, we're ahead of schedule,'" Lucas says. "Then they'd say, 'Oh my God, these guys are great.'"

To prepare for the imminent shoot, Spielberg traveled to London to see how sets were progressing. "Going from England to France to Tunisia, you have to have customs lists and ship things days and days ahead of time," Marshall says. "You have language barriers, vaccinations, passports, hotel reservations, the transportation of equipment and construction teams. All those things have to be considered. Right now we are spread thin because we have construction crews in three countries and it's hard for the production designer and director to get around and see everything."

Throughout preproduction the storyboard artists and Lucas's special effects house, Industrial Light & Magic (ILM), had been working out the

OPPOSITE: Early sketches and storyboards by Joe Johnston reveal concepts for the end sequence, circa May 1980. Johnston's notes, addressed to Campbell Black, the author of the film novelization, outline ideas for events linked to the opening of the Ark (LEFT), for which ILM would create the visual effects.

details of *Raiders*. Edward Verreaux and David Negron tackled primarily the action scenes; ILM, the optical effects storyboards. While *Raiders* was consistently touted as a B-movie, Spielberg and Lucas wanted certain A-moments, and one of them—the most important of them—was now the opening of the Ark.

Founded by Lucas for the first *Star Wars*, ILM had moved from Van Nuys in Southern California to San Rafael in Northern California, where it was easier for Lucas to supervise its work on *Empire*. Lucas then turned them toward *Raiders*, which had far fewer effects shots but a few surprises,

as it turned out. Special effects photographer Richard Edlund remembers that Lucas gave him a script early on: "George said, 'Read the end sequence.' At that time all it said was, 'They open the box and all hell breaks loose,' and the next shot was Indy embracing Marion. The sequence had not been at all laid out or defined as it was later. George, Steven, and I discussed it, and George said, 'Do me a rough storyboard of the end sequence.'"

Ultimately several artists worked on the ILM storyboards, but the first to tackle it was Joe Johnston, and several ideas were kicked around. Before they left for principal photography, Lucas and Spielberg had a key special effects meeting at ILM on May 27, 1980.

THE GHASTLY GAUL

"There's an actor coming in today who I think is great for the part of Belloq," Spielberg said toward the end of the ILM meeting. "He's a very soft-spoken Englishman, but we'll make him French. He's a real adult; he's a real rival for Indy; he's got good looks. His name is Paul Freeman and he was in *Death of a Princess* [a 1980 TV movie]. I can just see him sitting across from Indy and being a real threat."

Lucas agreed, and Freeman was hired to play Belloq. "When I was sitting in the office in LA reading it and I got to the bit with the monkey, I thought, *This is wonderful, it's a really witty adventure story*," Freeman says.

Other final casting included Alfred Molina as Satipo, and Denholm Elliott as Marcus Brody.

"I had always been a big Denholm Elliott fan," Spielberg says. "He had been around a long time and was part of the British cinema firmament. I believe he was my first choice to play Marcus Brody. He lent a kind of paternal warmth to the character. He's the voice of reason, the voice of caution; he's more paranoid than Indy could ever be."

Ronald Lacey was cast as Major Arnold Toht, even though the actor, Spielberg would tell him, "came at 4:30 PM. You looked nothing like the character, but you had a photograph with you in a play you'd done, where you looked like a cross between Vincent Price and Peter Lorre. That was what I wanted. The picture did it."

For the part of Sallah, Spielberg had wanted Danny DeVito, who was starring in the TV show *Taxi*. But he was too expensive, according to

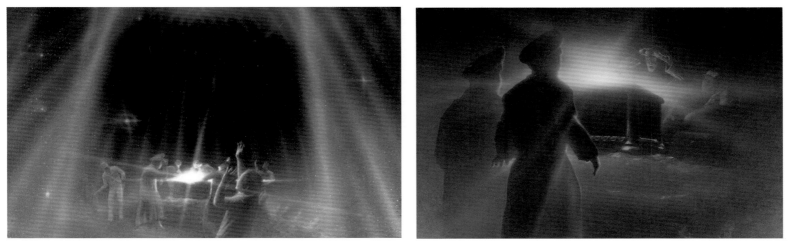

OPPOSITE, LEFT AND BELOW:
Airbrushed concept illustrations by Michael Lloyd of the opening of the Ark, early 1980.

Kazanjian. English actor John Rhys-Davies had just appeared in *Shogun*, which Spielberg had seen and liked, so he was cast instead.

"I went to Steven and said, 'Sallah is described as a five-foot-two, skinny Egyptian digger. Now, what do you propose? Surgery?'" Rhys-Davies says. "And he said, 'No, no, no, I want a cross between the character you played in *Shogun* and Falstaff.' I thought, *Oh, that's interesting.*"

"British Equity would let me bring only one American," Spielberg says, "so we had to go over the head of the Equity people to British immigration just to get Karen Allen in the country. They were insisting that we interview English actresses and change the part to an English girl, which we all somewhat resented and fought. The funny thing was that it really wasn't British Equity. It was a small group of Americans who had formed a society to keep themselves working and keep out other Americans, and those were the people who were protesting."

Already in England, first assistant director David Tomblin helped prepare the schedule for the shoot, which caused him some doubts: "I thought, with Steven's reputation, because I had never met him, plus the film's difficulty, that it was highly unlikely that we would do *Raiders* in 73 days. I expressed my concern to George, who said, 'Well, I think Steven has made up his mind, and he's going to go for it.'"

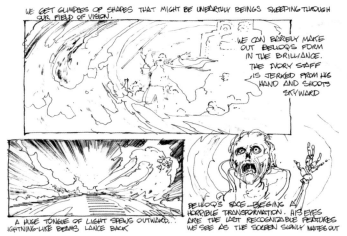

WE GET GLIMPSES OF SHAPES THAT MIGHT BE UNEARTHLY BEINGS SWEEPING THROUGH OUR FIELD OF VISION.

WE CAN BARELY MAKE OUT BELLOQ'S FORM IN THE BRILLIANCE. THE IVORY STAFF IS JERKED FROM HIS HAND AND SHOOTS SKYWARD

A HUGE TONGUE OF LIGHT SPEWS OUTWARD. LIGHTNING-LIKE BEAMS LANCE BACK

BELLOQ'S FACE BEGINS A HORRIBLE TRANSFORMATION. HIS EYES ARE THE LAST RECOGNIZABLE FEATURES WE SEE AS THE SCREEN SLOWLY WHITES OUT

ELAPSED TIME: 2 SEC.

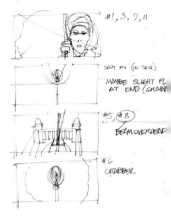

#1, 3, 9, 11

SECT 04 (IN SER)

MAYBE SLIGHT FL
AT END (GRABB

#5, #8

BEAM OVERHEAD

#6
GRABBER

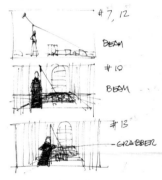

#7, 12

BEAM

#10

BEAM

#13

GRABBER

ABOVE: Early map room
storyboards.

OPPOSITE AND LEFT. More Joe
Johnston concept sketches of the
power of the Ark, and early concepts
of its vengeful angels.

⑦

— 15 hats

BASIC OUTFIT WORN & FAUD'EIT THRUOUT MOVIE

10-12 pants
25 shirts
10 leather jackets

5 pr. boots

④ DIGS SC. 82 —

③ CAIRO SC. 59-76

INDIANA

© L.F.L. 1981

LEFT AND RIGHT PAGES: Costume concept sketches by Kelly Kimball, early 1980. LEFT: Notes were made on the sketch of Jones before Ford had been hired: "Wilson's House of Suede, for style until character cast." Another note specifies that this is the "basic outfit worn off and on thruout movie." Because filming can take quite a toll on costumes, it is customary to have several versions of a single wardrobe, in case of tears, stains, or different needs. For that reason, the sketch bears several quantitative notations: "15 hats, 10-12 pants, 25 shirts, 10 leather jackets, 5 pr. boots."

MARION

"THE RAVEN SALOON"
SC 52-56

① MARION

NEW
STYLE

BLACK
NOT
USED

TENT
SC 95-
WELL OF
SOULS-
DIGS-
112

CHAPTER 3

MAKING IT UP

Alfred Molina may have been the first actor to arrive at Elstree Studios (EMI) in England, because he was scheduled for a body mold—necessary for the demise of his character—on June 3. Wolf Kahler (Colonel Dietrich), Vic Tablian (Monkey Man), and Tony Chin (Mohan) had makeup, wardrobe, and hair tests on June 9.

Ford signed his contract on June 15, 1980, committing to two sequels. "I was cast late—like two weeks before the cameras were scheduled to roll," Ford says. "That proved to be both a liability and an asset. Because I came in at the last minute, I made many of my own decisions about alterations in the costuming; everybody else was too busy to start nitpicking, and I stayed within George's general specifications. I worked with Deborah Nadoolman before we ever went over there, after she had already done a lot of work."

"Indiana Jones's costume was basically designed before anybody was hired," Spielberg says. "But our costume designer Deborah Nadoolman really refined it, made it more lived in and more honest to who Harrison Ford was."

Ford also picked up *The People's Book of Chronology.* "I went to 1936 and read back through 35 years, so I knew what the conditions of my character's life might be."

On Wednesday, June 18, Harrison Ford, Steven Spielberg, Karen Allen, George and Marcia Lucas, and Kathy Kennedy took off for the United Kingdom.

"Overall I felt very good about the script they went off to shoot," Kasdan says. "But it was always going to be a problem to hold the character."

"Steven always knew what he wanted out of the material, but I had questions and suggestions," says Ford. "We flew overseas together, took out the script, and spent ten solid hours discussing it on the plane. By the time we disembarked, we had a working rapport."

"Once Harrison came on the scene, he brought a personality to the role," Spielberg says. "I'd always envisioned the character of Indiana Jones as a real throwback movie hero, a lover and a cad and a two-fisted hellion. What Harrison and I did to his character was to take him out of the James Bond mold. After he's teaching school at an eastern university, the moment he puts on his fighting clothes, he suddenly has half an inch of dust and gristle and dirt around the cheeks and under the nails. He becomes a netherworld hero/villain."

"We worked on how to keep character in a fight and not let the fight just become a whirlwind of energy, but make it always Indiana Jones's fight," Ford says. "And we added some jokes. But it almost always arrived from practical problem solving. It was the first time we had a really good, long meeting about the script; as we talked about it, Steven thought of a number of changes that he wanted to accomplish, ways that we thought would help clarify the story and move it along faster."

"Harrison had a lot to do with shaping Indy's personality," Lucas says.

AH, LA ROCHELLE

On Thursday, June 19, having arrived in London, Harrison Ford and Karen Allen traveled to Elstree for wardrobe fittings. Another actor came

OPPOSITE (FROM LEFT): On location in La Rochelle, France, June 23–26, 1980: Spielberg, Harrison Ford (Indiana Jones), Karen Allen (Marion Ravenwood), and George Harris (Katanga).

ABOVE: Allen, Spielberg, Ford, and John Rhys-Davies (Sallah) pose with a typewriter as they pretend to rewrite the script in a joke photo destined to be sent to screenwriter Lawrence Kasdan (who appreciated the humor).

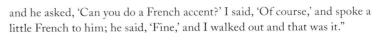

in for a belated test. "The funny thing was that Steven hadn't asked me if I could do a French accent [the first time we met]," says Paul Freeman. "I think he just assumed I could. But Steven had suddenly gotten worried. By now he was at Elstree Studios, and he wanted me to come in and do a French accent for him. I got rather nervous at that point, thinking, *Oh my God, having gotten the part, I'm going to be tested for it*. So I went into Steven's office,

and he asked, 'Can you do a French accent?' I said, 'Of course,' and spoke a little French to him; he said, 'Fine,' and I walked out and that was it."

On Saturday, all necessary cast and crew left for La Rochelle, France, where production had readied the location after about five days of prep. The *Bantu Wind*, whose real name was the *Abeer Delta*, had sailed from Newhaven on June 18, and it arrived in La Rochelle the same day as production, June 21.

"The *Bantu Wind* was found in Belfast," Reynolds says. "It was rusty and really, really beaten up, so it seemed to fit the part. As filming approached, I decided to go back and just check it out—to my horror, I discovered that the whole boat had been repainted. With very little time left, I had to actually send our paint team over to put it back in its previous condition. It finally worked out, but it was a very nerve-racking experience, to say the least."

The main crew stayed at the Hotel Le Yachtman on 23 Quai Vallin (others were housed at Hotel Terminus, Hotel Rupella, Hotel de Paris, et cetera). "When Steven arrived in La Rochelle, he got up to the passport man in customs," Marshall says. "The guy looked at Steven's passport, got real excited, and started jumping up and down, shouting, 'Steven Spielberg—Jaws of the Third Kind!'"

The next day Lucas, Spielberg, and key personnel went on a recce to inspect the *Bantu Wind* while makeup tests continued in the hotel conference room.

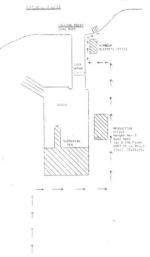

ABOVE: A map was attached to Call Sheets of the Port de la Pallice at La Rochelle, showing the "loading point" for the crew boat; the submarine pen; and the production office in Hangar 3.

TOP AND RIGHT: Filming the submarine scenes in the pen built by the Germans during World War II.

FAR LEFT: Harrison Ford dries off between shots. LEFT: George Lucas perhaps stricken by seasickness. BELOW: Images from the film: The moment when a Nazi soldier throws his cigarette butt into the air vent (TOP) and the cheering crew (BOTTOM) were improvised on their respective shoot days.

REPORT NOS. 1–5: MONDAY, JUNE 23–FRIDAY, JUNE 27, 1980
CALL: 08.00 (LEAVE HOTELS); LA ROCHELLE, FRANCE
EXT./INT. NAZI SUPPLY BASE (SUBMARINE PEN); EXT./INT. *BANTU WIND*; EXT. CAIRO NIGHT

On Day 1, the first day of principal photography, 59 extras were hired for a total of 17,000 francs. On the Progress Report prepared by Douglas Twiddy, the projected finish date was October 17, 1980. Making use of the Wurrfler submarine, Spielberg shot scene number 137, in which the Nazis unload the Ark in the sub pen, finishing at 7:30 PM after seven setups. First-day notes on props included: "Created Ark with long poles, Indy's holster, gun, and bullwhip; rope for tying Marion's hands…"

Whereas productions often schedule unchallenging scenes for the first couple of days, Spielberg had to choose between scenes with more than 60 people or scenes played out on the high seas, depending on the weather. Still, he and Lucas were making use of a seasoned, mostly English crew with tremendous experience and confidence in one another.

"It's a big advantage to have the same crew who've worked together on other productions," Lucas says. "They know each other, they know what to expect and how to deal with it. Because it's hard to put together a crew, have them all meet the first day, and make a picture. But over the years we've had the advantage of developing a good crew by keeping the people who work out very well and getting new people if this or that person isn't doing that well."

"George has a fully staffed company of great people, the kind of people you'd like to take home to dinner and be friends with for the rest of your life," says Spielberg. "It was like changing schools, which I did frequently as a kid; I felt like I'd moved into George Lucas's eighth-grade class."

"To start a film on location with a new crew and all that, you usually have to work all the bugs out and nobody really knows each other," Kathy Kennedy says. "They weren't really sure what Steven was like, because they hadn't spent any time with him. I think most everyone assumed that we'd get

off to a rocky start, that we'd probably go a little bit over and make it up once we got to the soundstages."

Spielberg and Lucas would also have to balance their long friendship with their relatively shorter professional collaboration through a breakneck shoot. Lucas would not be on location or on set all the time, however; he planned to look in only at the beginnings and endings of things.

"I think that friendship can go beyond a film unless there's a real difference of opinion," Lucas says. "It has more to do with ego than with anything else. If you don't let your ego get in the way there's usually no problem."

"The important thing to me," Spielberg says, "working with George Lucas, is that George and I have been friends a lot longer than we've been working together. George and I have been working together now for only a year. We've been friends for eleven."

On the second day, the first day's rushes were sent back to London, where Spielberg's editor Michael Kahn immediately began working on a rough assembly. That same day Norman Reynolds departed for Tunisia to start advance work on the set building. Unfortunately, "Karen Allen sustained a blow to her face" during a scene in which she struggled with Nazis extras on the *Bantu Wind*; after an ice pack was applied, she was deemed okay by the on-set doctor. Again, due to intemperate sea conditions, production confined its work to the submarine pen.

"Shooting at sea is always risky," Watts says. "The contract with the Germans who owned the sub said that we could take the submarine out to sea only if the waves were less than a meter high. So we had the engineer who built the submarine come from Munich, because I insisted that we have somebody with the authority to say that we could or couldn't go. It was a very valuable piece of equipment, and I'm no expert on the sea."

To complicate matters, the weather services in France went on strike, so it was up to Frank Marshall to get up at 4 AM and check sea conditions at the jetty with boat crews and captains—and this after staying up till 2 AM at least once, exploring La Rochelle's nightlife with Kathy Kennedy and Karen Allen.

"We needed three days of filming on the ocean, and finally that's all we had

RIGHT AND BELOW:
Spielberg discusses the farewell
scene with John Rhys-Davies (Sallah)
during a night shoot on the dock,
the last day of shooting in
La Rochelle: Friday, June 26, 1980.
Parts of this scene were improvised,
and dialogue was added.

left there," Marshall says. "And, like a miracle, on the third day it was calm."

On Wednesday cast and crew took to the ocean for the first time, shooting scenes on deck of the *Bantu Wind*. A note on the Call Sheet read, "Would all crewmembers please note that whilst working at sea, the weather may be very cold and windy. Therefore please bring warm and waterproof clothing." The team was divided into small boats. The *Aiglon II* was Spielberg's; *Venus des Iles* was the crew boat, while a tugboat, a safety boat, a dory, and two vedettes were also employed.

"The third day, it was calm when we went out and we shot all day," Watts says. They shot all day Thursday, too, but it "developed into a rough day. We managed to get through, even though I was worried that the waves were getting too high." The dory was in fact damaged due to a large swell that caused it to run into another boat, and several people became ill. Lucas got a very bad case of seasickness, as did Kazanjian, who spent two days in his hotel room, according to Kennedy.

Shooting day-for-night for part of that day, Spielberg seems to have ad-libbed a couple of shots not described in the shooting script: the *Bantu Wind* crew cheering when they spot Indy clinging to the periscope of the German sub, and a Nazi flinging his cigarette down the air chute in which Indy is hiding.

On Friday work was completed for the La Rochelle location, with an expanded scene 119. The Progress Report read, "Additional dialogue today increased page count," for Spielberg must have felt that more words were needed as Indy and Marion say good-bye to Sallah on the docks. The script had them play it mutely and certainly without the dance that Rhys-Davies improvised.

"On Friday we had some night shooting to do on the dock," Watts says. "We actually finished La Rochelle fifteen minutes ahead of schedule. That had been a great concern to me because dealing with sea shots, you can go many days over just because of bad weather."

Given his previously exasperating experience on the seas while shooting *Jaws*, leaving on time and on budget must have been particularly satisfying to Spielberg.

SETUPS COMP: 51; SCS. COMP: 7; SCREEN TIME: 9m42s.

On Friday, George and Marcia Lucas traveled from La Rochelle to Paris, arriving in London on Sunday, June 29. On Saturday, Spielberg, Kazanjian, Marshall, Watts, and Kennedy took a charter flight from La Rochelle to London's Gatwick Airport. By Monday, cast and crew had reconvened in the small town of Borehamwood, not far from London, where Elstree Studios is located and where it was raining and cold.

Around this time journalist and former Beatles press agent Derek Taylor arrived to observe the action; he'd been hired to write a book about the making of *Raiders of the Lost Ark*. In this work he'd often accompany Phil Schuman and his documentary team while they captured material for a making-of film, sometimes conducting the interviews himself. "Lost Ark Productions was clearly the studio's ranking tenant," Taylor wrote. "Even though the offices were very small and basically bare and dull in design, their appearance belied the activity taking place within. In the production office an extraordinary load of work rested on two young women: assistant production manager Pat Carr and production assistant Gill Case.

"A few feet down the corridor was the corner suite with three very simple rooms, built around a central secretarial area, occupied and controlled with great practical calm by Barbara Harley, secretary to producer Frank Marshall. Steven did have an office but rarely used it. George and Steven used a general-purpose table in what became known as Kazanjian's office. Howard's place tended to be a leisure room, especially since it had a very addictive electronic *Asteroids* game glittering and whizzing in a far corner. I never saw Howard use it, but it was a powerful magnet for Barbara and her other neighbor, Kathy Kennedy. Frank Marshall and Steven joined them when they had a moment free."

Elstree consisted of nine soundstages, eight of which were taken up by sets; the ninth was used as a construction and storage site. The *Raiders*

BELOW LEFT: Spielberg stands before the popular *Asteroids* arcade game in Elstree Studios' production office, with executive producer Howard Kazanjian sitting at the "general purpose" table.
BELOW RIGHT: Robert Watts, Harrison Ford, George Lucas, Kazanjian, Spielberg, and producer Frank Marshall relax for a moment on a soundstage at Elstree. "I think of myself as the person whose job it is to get the movie made, organizing the entire shooting period, and then delivering the finished product for the release date," Marshall says. "I'm also responsible for making the movie for a certain amount of money. It's partly business and partly creative."

CLOCKWISE FROM TOP LEFT: Alfred Molina (Satipo) with tarantulas; Ford in the Peruvian temple; Spielberg directs little person Kiran Shah, Tutte Lemkow (the Imam). and Molina. An English vine called old-man's beard was used to dress the Peruvian temple interior. Reynolds planned to use it later on the temple exterior in Hawaii for the sake of continuity.

OPPOSITE TOP: First assistant director David Tomblin (at far left) and director of photography Douglas Slocombe (center) watch Ford. BELOW LEFT: Ford, Slocombe, and Spielberg. "The idol in the opening sequence was very much based on a real Inca fertility figure," says Norman Reynolds. "But I modified it so that it could fit better in one's hand. I thought the head should really be the point of interest, so I made the lower body small and sculpted a large head."

production also used a mobile dressing room, while catering prepared meals the first week for 65 to 70 people, a number that grew steadily during their stay.

The first scene shot was in the Imam's house located on Stage 7, with Ford, Rhys-Davies, a little person named Kiran Shah (a circus entertainer), and Tutte Lemkow as the Imam. The latter suffered that day from a bit of stage fright, according to Kennedy, and couldn't stop his hands from shaking while holding the medallion.

Although these scenes had originally been scheduled for two days as a fail-safe, in case they'd gone over in La Rochelle, Spielberg sped through them in a single day. "If you start out like that on location with the crew pretty hyped up, it's a nice place to be," Kennedy says. "You come back ready to go right into shooting again—I mean, people were pretty pumped up and obviously liked one another. Steven had been introduced to most everyone by then, and so the fact that we hit our first day in England on stage by going again under schedule got things off to a nice start."

"We were back to England and the studio," Watts says. "Sometimes you think the pace will lessen when you leave location and get back, but it didn't. It kept up. Steven was pushing very hard."

"I've had to scale down my thinking, and then I had to break a stigma attached to me, which is that when I walk onto a soundstage everything's going to slow down because I'm a perfectionist," Spielberg says. "Sure enough, when I got onto the soundstage, the crews weren't expecting to get more than two or three setups a day. So I came in there and cracked the whip with 'please' after every harsh shout of, 'Get out of the set! We're ready to shoot! Out! Out! Out! Please.'"

Director of photography (DP) Douglas Slocombe had hoped on *Raiders* to have "lots and lots of time. I thought, *Well, this is wonderful—Steven Spielberg—here is my chance to do a picture as with David Lean*, who goes for almost forever and always gets the most magnificent results. But of course, not so."

After working together for about a week in Bombay, India, on the director's special edition of *Close Encounters*, Spielberg had chosen Slocombe again because he was personable; because he was a vastly experienced DP, having photographed more than 60 films, including *Kind Hearts and Coronets* (1949), *The Man in the White Suit* (1951), and *A High Wind in Jamaica* (1965); and because he had a firsthand stylistic sense of the 1930s.

RUN FOR YOUR LIFE

On the first of seven days in the Peruvian temple set on Stage 4, animal handler Mike Culling was standing by with live spiders and "maggots for dummy Forrestal" (the archaeologist who had evidently failed to extract the idol from the booby-trapped temple). The first note of many concerning the interaction of humans and nonhumans appeared on the Tuesday Progress Report: While shootings scenes 3 and 4, Alfred Molina "suffered slight irritation on his neck due to tarantula fur. The standby nurse administered medication."

"They were walking, actually walking on his neck," Marshall says. "I don't know how he did it."

"The tarantulas didn't bother me much," Ford says, "but Alfred Molina had to be covered with them on his first day of shooting and he wasn't too happy."

"Alfred commented to me, 'Is this what a career in front of a camera's gonna be, because, if it is, I prefer to be in British theater,'" Spielberg says.

"I was covered with at least a couple of dozen spiders," Molina remembers, "but they're not moving. I hear Steven say something like, 'Why aren't they moving? They look fake.' And the spider wrangler says, 'Because they're all males, you see? We have to put a female in there, then they'll

ABOVE: The Peruvian temple seen from the outside on Stage 4, where production filmed in early July 1980. The giant boulder can be seen on the right.

fight.' So he puts the female on me—and suddenly all hell breaks loose. These spiders were running, dropping, and fighting—they were running over my face, and Steven is going, 'Shoot, shoot, shoot! Alfred, look scared, look scared!' Trust me, I was scared."

"I promised the crew we would fence in the area by the actor's feet, so that when the tarantulas fell off they would fall in a small area," Spielberg says.

But again, after a couple of takes, the director felt the spiders were "too lethargic" and had fans trained on them to wake them up—whereupon the tarantulas were off and running. "Nobody realized they could hop and climb Plexiglas until then," Spielberg explains. "A lot of them took off after the crew. I'm talking about people running for their lives…"

In fact, more creepy-crawlies—bats and beetles—were standing by, but never used.

The scenes in the temple were complicated, with a variety of physical and special effects. The boulder in particular necessitated perhaps the first overage, according to Kazanjian, when an extra 60 feet of film of the giant rock bearing down on Ford cost $60,000; ultimately that scene was shot 10 times.

"That was one of those things that I thought we'd never get to work,"

CLOCKWISE FROM TOP LEFT: The
pre-paved path down which the boulder
rolled; Spielberg and the Satipo dummy,
the plaster mold for which had been
taken of the actor back on June 3; Ford
and his stunt double Martin Grace as
Indy escaping the temple.

Marshall says. "It was this huge boulder crashing down through this chute. And we had to make it so it could roll, but also so it could be controlled; we had to be able to take it back right away so we could do it again. Actually, we couldn't do it again very quickly, because we had to put in more stalactites each time, because they got broken off as it rolled. But the boulder was free-spinning on this contraption that was like a hidden arm, which came down on a weight on a track."

"Even though it was made of fiberglass, it was still very heavy and could actually do a lot of damage," Reynolds says. "But the construction manager assured me it would stop when needed. I'd shown it to Steven—who got very excited and immediately asked me to make it bigger!"

"I didn't know it was gonna look as good as it did until the day Norman Reynolds showed me that he had actually made a boulder that was something like 22 feet in circumference," Spielberg says. "So I didn't have Harrison step in the shot until I was completely convinced it was safe. Once we'd rehearsed it several times with a stuntman, Harrison did every shot himself."

Another tricky effect involved the blow darts. "I used to do photographic special effects," special effects supervisor Kit West says, "so I would know immediately when I saw a movie if the arrows had been added, printed in. So I wanted to have a go at doing them mechanically. With the arrows there, Harrison really was dodging them. I think he repaid the expense and effort [of having real darts] in giving that sort of reaction. It was a tough one with the arrows whizzing out of the holes—a couple bounced off his arm, but they were rubber-tipped, of course."

"The first time we did it, the arrows went so fast that Steven was horrified," Kennedy says. "Here we'd rigged both walls to show these arrows flying out, but you couldn't even see them. Looking at dailies was a little more comforting, because it ended up looking a little better than anybody had thought."

For insurance, however, Spielberg added to the shot list a few second-unit close-ups of the darts shooting out of the wall openings, along with puffs of smoke.

By now Harrison Ford was coming to appreciate that he'd taken on one of the more physical roles in the history of cinema. Of course his character was an expert with a bullwhip, so Ford took advantage of breaks in filming to learn how to use one, under the supervision of Glenn Randall, who, as stunt coordinator, was one of the busiest heads of department.

"I busted my wrist when I was a carpenter," Ford says. "I fell off

RIGHT: Set painters touch up the map room on Stage 5.

OPPOSITE: Ford dressed in Arab garb in the map room sequence on July 10–11.

a ladder at Valerie Harper's house, and my wrist has never quite come back—and when I started bullwhipping I realized how important a wrist is. But I had very little instruction. Glenn Randall showed me how not to whip the hell out of myself, but half an hour later he'd finished, because it's really something you have to learn yourself."

His first notable injury was reported the evening of July 3: Ford complained of a bruised right shoulder, where he'd received a blow during filming in the temple earlier that day. "I haven't been fit for about thirteen years," Ford says. "I don't work out. I don't jog. But I have to say I do have a good constitution."

On Saturday, July 5, Lucas returned to the States. "George did a wonderful shot before he left, of dates," Spielberg says, "little dates with wonderful backlight and a little red bottle of poison. It's great to see George running around with his director's hat on, chasing a second unit around, setting up shots and shooting them."

On Tuesday, July 9, Spielberg completed the Peruvian temple scenes, taking two days longer than anticipated, though overall the production was still on target. "We worked so well the first week in the temple that I was getting two shots for every one sketch," Spielberg notes. "I was getting the sketch and a bonus, so the sequences are much richer because of that."

SETUPS COMP: 150; SCS. COMP: 14/117; SCREEN TIME: 18m52s/120m.

REPORT NOS. 14-25: THURSDAY, JULY 10-FRIDAY, JULY 25, 1980; STAGE 5: INT. MAP ROOM; STAGE 3: INT. WELL OF SOULS

"Another complicated thing for Norman Reynolds is that he has to jump around and have these things ready when we get there," Marshall says. "If

ABOVE: Frank Marshall and others observe some of the snakes. TOP: Ford and Karen Allen among the thousands of snakes in the Well of Souls on Stage 3.

we get ahead, then he has to finish things ahead. The Well of Souls wasn't finished yet, but the map room was finished, so we went to the map room."

"The Norman Reynoldses and the Bill Welches of England don't exist in America," Kennedy says. "That old-style craftsmanship is a hangover from the history of apprenticeships in England, where kids at 13 or 14 years old could get a job as an apprentice. So you have these people working on your crew—the plaster mold maker has been doing it for 25 years—and they're the best. Norman's sets are unsurpassed, and our construction manager Bill Welch can build anything."

"The technicians and craftsmen are wonderful here," Spielberg says, "especially the guys who construct the sets. They're all artists, Norman Reynolds and art director Les Dilley, and all the people working under them. It's an art, not a business for them. But it's also a responsible art, within the budget and within the schedule."

All of the worries about sun logistics expressed during the early story conferences had evaporated in the shooting script, and Spielberg shot the scenes in the map room without overt astrophysical explanations on Thursday and Friday, July 10 and 11. To inspire his players, he placed a small cassette player onstage near the actors. Depending on the tenor of the scene, Spielberg would often play different music.

"Music just makes it easier," Spielberg says. "You let the beats and measures of the score or the classical piece tell you how to feel. And it just so happened we found a couple of wonderful numbers for the interior map room sequence, as if written for *Raiders*. Harrison just went with it, and everything happened. The sweat, the tears, all came from the music."

Friday was also the day on which the second unit used the VistaVision camera for the last shot of the film, on Stage 5. Following auditions held on July 3, the warehouseman part had been won and was played by Fred Gambia, with two additional warehousemen listed as "A. N. Others" (standard nomenclature for unnamed extras).

GAUNTLET OF THE SERPENTS

On Monday, July 14, production moved from Stage 5 to Stage 3, where the vast and impressive Well of Souls had been constructed by Bill Welch and his crew.

"One of the most exciting moments for me is usually at the end of the day when you're going to work up the setups for the next day," Spielberg says. "When you get to the set, you see things that you couldn't think up behind a desk in California. On the set, you're living those characters' lives, you're living the story. Because of that, things are going to change for the better. But I'm trying very hard, so that when I change something, it replaces something I originally planned as opposed to adding to it."

"At least a day, if not two days before going to a set," Kennedy says, "we would all sit down right after shooting—Steven, Frank, script supervisor Pamela Mann, David Tomblin, Norman, Robert Watts, and I—and we would have all the storyboards put up on a bulletin board, and we would all do a walk-through. Steven always at that point edited and would say, 'I've decided not to do this scene,' or 'I'm going to change this.'

"But he would get criticized for changing his mind," she adds. "And I would hear this among the crew, too, which I always found ironic. I would hear complaints: 'Well, Steven's not shooting the sketches.' Well, in basic theory he was shooting the sketches. But once you get into a scene and it's suddenly right there in front of you, I only think that it can be better if changes are made then."

While the director and main unit hunkered down for what were going to be difficult scenes with thousands of reptile extras, Robert Watts and Norman Reynolds left, again, to oversee preparation for the location shoot in Tunisia. Reynolds had long ago taken care of the most essential props for the Well of Souls set: "We had to think in terms of real snakes, which meant an animal handler," he says. "He suggested we order snakes three or four months in advance so he could arrange for them to be hatched. We did do that, and when the snakes hatched they were earmarked for EMI Studios."

Of course the presence on set of a few hundred snakes, emptied out of bins and crates by nervous crew, made most people rather cautious. It was the duty of Kit West and second assistant director Patrick Cadell to corral the reptiles—a task the snakes made difficult. Monday's particular scenes called for the snakes to be afraid of fire, but nobody had consulted the snakes beforehand.

"George, Larry, and I didn't know that snakes love fire," Spielberg says. "Cold-blooded, they warm to it. So we'll have to find something else that they hate: a smell, a pesticide. I'll have to have the insert team come and get little groups of them to move away. They could slow us down a couple of days. This will be the most aggravating sequence in the film, because I'm aggravated already, and it's my first day."

Spielberg took it in stride, however, despite the approximately $100,000-per-day budget on set and location, and Phil Schuman was able to film the director complaining to one of his uncooperative reptiles: "Why do you like fire? You're ruining my movie!"

Another major problem was that the number of snakes—boa constrictors, pythons, grass snakes, and more—turned out to be too few. "We had I think three thousand snakes and they hardly covered the set," Spielberg says. "So I couldn't get wide shots. I said, 'We need seven thousand more snakes to make the scene work.'"

Marshall took on the quest. "I said, 'Seven thousand more snakes? Absolutely, Steven.' And I rushed to the phone and we called all over Europe…"

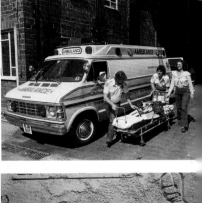

LEFT, TOP TO BOTTOM: Ford and Rhys-Davies; Rhys-Davies and Spielberg; Ford with a sheet of glass between him and the cobra. RIGHT, TOP TO BOTTOM: The on-call ambulance in case anyone was bitten by the cobra; R2-D2 and C-3PO sculpted on the wall of the Well of Souls; the package from Thailand in which extra snakes were sent. "Artoo shaking hands with See-Threepio is going to be one of those little-known facts in the movie you'll be able to see if you know where it is," Kathleen Kennedy says. "Norman Reynolds did that for George."

COBRA TERROR

The next day the crew was already becoming used to the snakes. Ford was essentially fine with them, safely ensconced in his durable wardrobe. "Harrison has his big boots, his big gloves, and his leather clothes—I have naked arms, nothing on my legs, and bare feet," Karen Allen says. "In the beginning that was tougher than it is now because I just couldn't bear to have the snakes on my feet. But I've gotten used to them."

On Wednesday first assistant director David Tomblin was bitten by a nonvenomous reticulated python. "David just stood there with the python not letting go and some blood was coming down his hand," Spielberg says. "David stared at it and said, 'Hey, somebody grab the tail and give it a snap.' Somebody grabbed the tail of that python and the shock wave went up to the head and the head let go. The snake was fine. David got some medical attention and he was fine."

On Thursday, Spielberg shot the scene in which Marion and Indy are imprisoned by Belloq and the Nazis. On Friday, the ten live cobras arrived.

"Everybody had gotten used to the snakes," Marshall says. "The tension had gone. Well, it came back with the cobras. A python—the one that's been trying to bite people—bit the cobra. The cobra killed the python.

"Friday morning we were supposed to shoot with the cobras," he adds, "but we had to call it off because the one serum man in the country didn't come through with the stuff. We'd ordered the snake serum two months ahead of time, but it didn't arrive on the day we needed it. We sent to a hospital, but their stuff there was out of date.

"So I went to the set, told Steven, and we decided that it was absolutely too dangerous to go ahead without having the serum on the set. We'd had the shot set up. Steven was ready. The cage was ready for the cobra. But Steven, being flexible, changed the shot, tore everything up, and we continued to shoot the other nonpoisonous snakes."

Despite the setback, midway through the day Spielberg was feeling good about the way things were going. "Of course, we're only on the twentieth day of shooting," he says. "I don't know what it's going to be like on the seventy-third day of shooting, whether that will be the end of the schedule or only three-quarters of the way through. Anything can happen along the way, but right now I'm kind of happy that there is a forward momentum, which I think was created in La Rochelle when we got out of there on schedule."

Spielberg was starting to enjoy himself and his crew replied in kind, though in a mischievous way. "They played jokes on him constantly," Kennedy says, "pinning little things to him, putting signs on his back that he didn't know about. He'd walk around all day with something absurd written on his back and have no idea, and they'd just get a big kick out of that. I've never seen him as relaxed and comfortable."

Marshall, meanwhile, was desperately trying to locate some antivenin. "We had heard there was serum in France," he says, "but then we found that there might not be any there, either. They couldn't tell us because of some technicality. They suggested we call someone in England and gave us a number—but it turned out to be the same guy who had been letting us down in England. Oh God…

"So we called the American embassy, got hold of the air force hospital and then the naval hospital to get them to lend us some serum just in case everything else failed."

On Saturday serum arrived from France and from farther afield, and was stored in the refrigerator in the Accounts Office, Room 115. "The antivenin we had on hand turned out to be two years outdated," Spielberg says. "So we had to fly in special serum from India."

FORGING AHEAD

After the weekend, shooting recommenced with the snakes and now the cobras. In case of emergency, on-set physician Felicity Hodder, two male nurses, and an ambulance were on standby. "We started to film today, Monday, and what do you know? The cobra hooded first shot," says Glenn Randall, who was pleasantly surprised. (As stunt coordinator on 1979's *The Black Stallion*, he and the crew had waited for two days before their cobra hooded in the right spot.)

"You can see a reflection on the sheet of glass that was between myself and the cobra," Ford says. "They took some elaborate precautions on that occasion."

"At one point the cobra hooded and whipped its head off to the side and literally threw venom all over the glass," Kennedy says. "That was something that caused everybody to sit up and recognize this was not something to play around with."

Into their second week Ford and Allen had passed many hours standing among the snakes, which now numbered between 6,500 to 7,200, more having been shipped in from several countries, including Denmark.

"Karen had read the script and liked the part," Spielberg says. "But we'd essentially talked about Marion's background, her father, her involvement with Indiana Jones ten years prior. Karen never brought up for discussion the sequence where she is dropped into the Well of the Souls amidst 10,000 live snakes. She just wasn't aware of that. Karen has never done an action picture before, so she came very prepared to play Marion, but very unprepared to fight the bad guys, beat back the snakes, and hang from the jaw of a 45-foot statue of a jackal god."

"I wasn't there when they shot the snakes," Lucas says. "And that's one of the reasons why Steven directed the movie and I didn't. I didn't want to sit on a soundstage with snakes, trying to get that sequence right."

The Well of Souls shoot continued to ebb and flow. As they lifted the Ark, music provided by Spielberg helped inspire Harrison Ford and John Rhys-Davies. But the reptile tedium wore on, and the gigantic set took a lot of time to prepare for each setup.

"It's very lonely when Dougie is on the stage with a director and everything is hovering around the lighting of a particular shot," says Reynolds. "The pressures are enormous for the cameraman at that particular moment."

Some of that pressure was relieved thanks to his two-person crew—camera operator Chic Waterson and assistant camera operator

OPPOSITE: On the Well of Souls set, time drags for Allen (TOP), Rhys-Davies and Ford (BELOW LEFT), and Spielberg (BELOW RIGHT).

ABOVE LEFT: Outside at Elstree, Ford practices with the bullwhip. ABOVE, TOP TO BOTTOM: Spielberg plays a little baseball and consults with Norman Reynolds; in the catacombs, whose cadavers were created by makeup artist Tom Smith. To ensure that his skeletons were accurate, Smith sent to the London College of Surgeons for real skulls, which he used as models.

Robin Vidgeon—who were intensely loyal and intensely synchronized after working together for many years.

"Dougie never took longer than two hours to light anything," Spielberg says. "But I would keep my adrenaline going just by pacing and worrying and thinking about Tunisia and about my next movie. My big problem, especially on an action picture, is that I'm trying to turn the page before I finish the shot. I've already shot that thing in my head. That's done, that's a print, but it takes an hour and a half to light it. Because of that, it's very frustrating to sit around the set and watch any cameraman, whether they're fast or slow."

"Steven is amazing," Kennedy says, "because his head is always ten shots ahead of what he's shooting at that time."

On Thursday, July 24, 1980, a Paramount press release touted *Raiders'* progress, highlighting the production's creation of specially built autos and trucks, and its work with the British aerospace firm of Vickers to build a full-sized 72-foot-span Flying Wing—all of which were about to be shipped to Tunisia. The press release noted that Spielberg was living in an apartment in a London hotel, next door to his editor Michael Kahn, who was well into a first assembly of the film.

"I've never allowed anybody to cut any of my movies while I'm on location before," Spielberg says. "I allowed Michael, starting on *Close Encounters*, to cut behind me. So while I was shooting the second week of the Well of the Souls, Michael already had an assemblage of the first week's

work. I was able to see everything I shot and was able to make corrections or additions the second week. It was an amazing visual aid."

Despite the glowing press release, things were not actually rosy at Paramount. Lucasfilm president Charlie Weber says, "It turns out that while we were in production, Michael Eisner's boss [Barry Diller] in New York would call him every Sunday and say, 'I'm sure I'm gonna fire you when this movie opens—'cause there's no way we can make any money on it!'"

SETUPS COMP: 298; SCS. COMP: 25/116; SCREEN TIME: 31m07s/120m.

REPORT NOS. 26–36: MONDAY, JULY 28–MONDAY, AUGUST 11, 1980; STAGE 3: INT. CATACOMBS; STAGE 2: INT. RAVEN BAR

"London was the first experience I had working on the Continent," Spielberg says, "and just the living conditions and the country and the fresh air and all the restaurants—the hot spots and all the places to go—took my mind off the movie and were a real godsend. Through the course of developing *Raiders*, I had also developed three screenplays, two of which I'll produce and one I'll direct, so I had writers down there constantly. I would shoot *Raiders* all day, and all evening I would work on my future projects with the writers. It was great to be able to go every night to a different restaurant and take long, long think-walks in Hyde Park. It was a really nice place to climb back inside oneself."

TOP: First AD David Tomblin with Karen Allen (ABOVE AND RIGHT), who performs with Ford in the Raven saloon sequences. Props for the Raven were listed as: "Stuffed Raven, money belt, $5,000 (in notes); medallion and chain (and burnt medallion); drinks, glasses, assorted money, small wooden axe handle, bar stools, whiskey bottle; two submachine guns; poker; Beretta pistol; Indy whip; Indy .45; Luger; spittoon; Toht's Luger; remains of box and money; Mauser pistol; dummy axe handles; Tibetan bells; breakaway furniture; bundles; sticks; snow shoes, pipes, cigars, ropes."

Screenings were also held nearly every night for cast and crew; among the films shown were *Tess*, *Jaws*, *Fame*, *Brubaker*, *Alien*, *Used Cars*, *Duel*, *Urban Cowboy*, *The Blue Lagoon*, and even a short by Les Dilley (art director on *Raiders*) called *Black Angel*. Catering was now for 105 people.

FEMME FATALE OF NEPAL

On Wednesday, July 30, production moved into the Raven saloon. Although Spielberg started with Marion's dialogue scenes—and not the subsequent shoot-out and fire—injuries occurred the first day: Slocombe was "burned accidentally by a special fx bee smoker," and electrician Roy Furness had a large plug fall from the rigging onto his head. Both men were treated by Dr. Hodder and continued working. There was also a Nepalese-language expert on set, sixty extras for the drinking contest, and a standby fireman; Stage 3 had recently burned down while Stanley Kubrick was filming *The Shining*, and no one wanted a repeat performance (that event had also effected the *Raiders'* production schedule, making them start in La Rochelle instead of on set).

Special effects supervisor Kit West had plotted with Norman Reynolds on just how to construct and then burn down the Raven saloon in a controlled manner. "We had to have certain sections built in the design for concealed pipes," West says. "And we needed a concrete floor."

Other special effects (fx) listed on the Progress Reports were: "practical fire; falling, burning beams; bullet fx on Ratty Nepalese (Malcolm Weaver), Second Nazi (Matthew Scurfield), and Giant Sherpa (Pat Roach); special poker; blank ammo; exploding bottles; breakaway bottles; breakaway window; smoke, wind, and snow fx."

"The Raven is going to be very complex stuff to shoot," says Karen Allen, referring not to the special effects but to her character's development arc. "To me it's the most exciting scene because there's a lot of real acting going on—a lot of pieces in the story develop and unfold. There are the complicated action sequences with the fight and the fire, which should be pretty tricky, but I think the real difficulty is continuing that character line through the rest of the film. Because she leaves the world of the Raven in which she's queen."

Facing Marion in the drinking contest was a mute character whom

the script refers to as the "Australian Climber," played by Patrick Dirkin. The script also describes them facing each other across the bar; the day of filming, however, Spielberg sat them at a table. He also cut down the dialogue for the scene, which Spielberg felt had been "force-fed" to Kasdan.

"It just bothered me that we were saying too much about these people so early in the movie," Spielberg says. "We weren't leaving enough to the imagination of the audience. I'm now finding a rhythm for *Raiders*—

TOP RIGHT: Stunt coordinator Glenn Randall shows Karen Allen how to throw a punch.

TOP LEFT: An early running joke in Kasdan's script had Indy constantly replacing guns that were damaged in some way. Here Ford holds Indy's .455 Smith & Wesson revolver (MIDDLE RIGHT, with production notes). MIDDLE LEFT: Ronald Lacey as Toht. ABOVE LEFT: Spielberg shows Malcolm Weaver (Ratty Nepalese) how to hold his gun. TOP RIGHT: Script continuity Pamela Mann sits on a table as Ford, David Tomblin, and others prepare a shot.

OPPOSITE: Ford and Pat Roach as the Giant Sherpa battle it out surrounded by flames in a more or less controlled burn.

watching the dailies and in each scene I shoot—and suddenly I reread the script a few weekends ago and I saw a rather lengthy 14-page sequence of pure character development. But so much of that information has been done in later scenes between the two actors, albeit out of continuity, in the form of free association, improvisation, and Harrison and Karen getting to know each other as their characters come to life.

"So I sat down over a weekend and took the more salient points of the scene, along with all of the character moments that Harrison was threshing out and Karen was beginning to discover, and did a highly concentrated version of the original lengthy scene."

"It was a highly charged day," Karen says. "Steven was great. He had rewritten the scene just several days before, and made it much stronger by taking out a lot of unnecessary background dialogue and picking up the rhythm of the scene, so that it was down to its most essential. As the day continued and we kept working and reworking the scene, I think we all got drawn into its tension, which became more and more alive for all of us, including Steven, probably Dougie, and everybody."

Part of the drama stemmed from the complex logistics of an involved Louma-crane shot, which Spielberg had designed to take in the whole drinking contest. (The director had grown fond of the Louma—a remote-controlled camera on the end of a boom arm, which rented for $700 per day—during his *1941* shoot.) "It was an actor's dream to be able to do that," Allen says, "to do a long, dramatic sequence that has a lot of movement and dialogue all in one piece. You get it alive and get that rhythm going, instead of depending on camera movement and cuts to create the tension. But it wasn't just the acting: It was being aware of what the camera was doing and being in the right light and the right place at the right moment, and not getting in each other's way. It was fascinating."

"I think the turning point in her character came in the Raven bar," Spielberg says. "We discussed it, we rehearsed it, then she came in. And I did the whole take in one shot, four or five minutes in one take, because I felt Karen, being a stage performer, could warm to the character and discover things within a five-minute take as opposed to a typical action movie, where everything is 15 seconds, cut, print, next shot. It worked great. Karen understood Marion Ravenwood on that day."

"There's a moment before it comes together in which you're both doing separate things," Ford says, "but when it comes together, that's the part that you're going to use, that's the part you want."

BLAZING GUNS AT THE RAVEN SALOON

As production moved on to the complex choreography of the fight scenes a couple of days later and the following week, the pace slowed noticeably. Consequently, the director began to feel bogged down again. "Not a good day," Spielberg says. "Things are taking too much time."

Taking advantage of the lulls, he would walk over to Stage 3 to check on Marshall, who was busy for several days with cameraman Paul Beeson supervising second-unit work with the snakes and the stunt doubles in the Well of Souls. In particular Spielberg watched over Indy's plunge on the head of a jackal through a wall. For this shot he also used a Louma crane.

"One of the jackal statues has to fall," Norman Reynolds says. "That means rams [hydraulic lifts] in the bottom of the legs of the beast. Then we have to prepare breakaway walls for the statue to fall through."

One of Ford's stunt doubles, Martin Grace (a veteran of several *James Bond* films), was set to do the stunt, which didn't go quite according to plan. "There's no rehearsal," he says. "If I had left my head in front, underneath the armpit, I would have smashed my face."

Back on the Raven set, people were successfully blasting away at one another. "Today I shot my first gunfight," Spielberg says. "My first real good-guy-versus-bad-guy shoot-'em-up, and it was just a lot of fun. When the scene started getting carried away, with Harrison moving too fast and not standing in any one spot where I could get a decent cut of him shooting and the bad guy falling, we began—which is something I've always wanted to do—we began to choreograph it like a dance, where each shot had a number associated with it and each squib effect had another number associated with it. I found the slower we played the gunfight for the camera, the faster and more directed the shots seemed to come out."

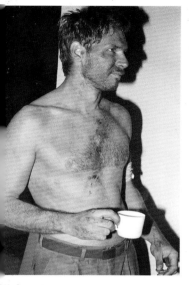

"I have to be a different director for each actor, moment to moment," Spielberg said at the time. "I've been as concerned about my actors as I've been about the visualization of my scripts. *Jaws* is a character study, not a shark fest. That film would not have been as scary without the empathetic performances of Roy Scheider, Robert Shaw, Richard Dreyfuss, and Lorraine Gary."

SETUPS COMP: 468; SCS. COMP: 31/116; SCREEN TIME: 50m18s/120m.

REPORT NOS. 37–49: TUESDAY, AUGUST 12–FRIDAY, AUGUST 29, 1980; STAGE 5: INT. SHIP'S CABIN; INDY'S HOUSE; STAGE 8: INT./EXT. TANIS DIGS (BLUE BACKING); STAGE 1: INT. MARION'S TENT, EXT. ALTAR; ROYAL MASONIC SCHOOL FOR GIRLS, RICKMANSWORTH: INT. ASSEMBLY HALL; INT. CLASSROOM; INT. WAR OFFICE

On Stage 5 Ford and Allen played out their action in the *Bantu Wind* cabin during the twelfth day of August. Most likely the result of their rehearsals, new pages were inserted into the shooting script for what was a difficult scene. The revised dialogue was shorter, with Ford's improvised line "It's not the years, it's the mileage" added for Indy. Whereas the film would end with Jones nodding off, in the script his "sleeping" was a ruse—the scene originally ended with Jones pulling Marion on top of him.

"I troll for the best ideas I possibly can," Spielberg says. "So I'm an audition man. I sit here and I say, 'That's good. We'll use that. I don't like that, don't like that. That's terrific.' And Harrison Ford is actually a very good writer, a closet writer; he comes out of the closet every once in a while when he's having trouble with dialogue, and thinks of some wonderful, zesty one-liners. A lot of those are in the picture."

"The script provided a very good framework," Ford says, "but it's inevitable that there'll be some rewriting. We did rewriting in most cases to cut down parts. Or circumstances come up where something has to be clarified, there is another point that we want to make, or Steven wants to emphasize something."

"The fire got a little out of control, and the firemen had to come in," Marshall says. "I looked up, and the flames were licking the top of the stage. The rafters had caught on fire. The problem was that if it caught on to the fake snow outside, Styrofoam, then it would've been a disaster."

August 11 was the last day filming in the Raven saloon, and Karen Allen burned her arm. Following the day's work she was spotted hanging out at the *Asteroids* machine in Steven's office, still dressed in rugged "Nepalese bar" style, while Watts and Kazanjian left for Honolulu to prepare the Hawaii locations.

On August 13 relevant cast and crew, numbering 150, traveled in four caravans and a "crowd coach" to the Royal Masonic School for Girls, Chorleywood Road, Rickmansworth, Herts, for two days of location work. Founded in 1788, the school would serve for many of the scenes in and around Indy's college, as well as the interior of the "war office" in the US government building seen at the end of the film.

"David Tomblin came over to me the morning we shot the classroom scene and said, 'I had an idea last night. Why don't you have one of the girls write LOVE YOU on her lids and when she closes her eyes, Indy sees the words?'" Spielberg says. "I loved it. That was such a juicy idea. So we changed the camera position, and picked a girl who had nice big lids!"

Shortened on July 25, the scene of Brody and Indy speaking about his adventures in Peru had the latter trying to find time for an attractive student named Susan (Pola Churchill). "I shot that in one take," Spielberg says, "basically because I didn't have time to shoot coverage. I had to get out of there in two days."

The sequence in which Indiana Jones meets with Brody and the government people was long on dialogue, so Ford had rehearsed with Elliott (Brody), Don Fellows (Musgrove), and Bill Hootkins (Eaton) the day before. Spielberg was able to move through those shots quickly as well.

Back at Elstree, Spielberg shot another scene (which would later be cut) with Indy and Pola Churchill, this time in his house: The libidinous professor is seen lounging with his student when Brody arrives.

Derek Taylor was on the scene that day and he happened to notice, on Stage 5, people talking quietly in small groups. Spotting Frank Marshall, he asked, "What's happening?"

"We'll have to walk as I talk if you don't mind," Marshall responded as they moved on. "Robert Watts has been taken to the hospital with appendicitis. And there is a problem in Tunisia. Things aren't getting through customs. Robert was to have gone. Now he can't, so I'll have to."

"How bad is Robert?"

"Well, he won't die. But he's not that good. We've lost him for a few weeks."

Watts had just returned the day before from Hawaii. "Barbara [Harley] has arranged transportation from here to Heathrow, then a good flight to Tunis," Marshall continues. "We have all the customs documentation done, everything is complete—still they won't let it through. Now I have to go and threaten—in a nice way, of course."

That evening Robert Watts underwent an emergency appendectomy.

STRANGE MINUTES

The next day Spielberg used the VistaVision camera for shots of the Tanis Digs with "blue backing"—primarily Indiana and others standing over the Well of Souls—so that suitably dramatic skies could be added later. To make

OPPOSITE: Ford and Allen in the cabin scene, filmed on Stage 5, August 12, 1980.

ABOVE LEFT: Ford, Spielberg, Bill Hootkins (Eaton), Denholm Elliott (Marcus Brody), and Don Fellows (Musgrove) at Rickmansworth on August 13–14. TOP RIGHT: Elliott and Spielberg; Ford, Pola Churchill (Susan), and Elliott, in a scene that would be cut where Indy tries to find time for one of his students; Indy is bewildered by another female student who has written LOVE YOU on her eyelids—a Tomblin idea embraced by Spielberg.

sure that what was shot on stage would meld with ILM's effects work, visual effects supervisor Richard Edlund was on hand, having arrived on Sunday.

On Wednesday, August 20, Spielberg filmed scene 103, in which Belloq gives Marion a dress in his tent. This scene, too, had been rewritten, with new pages arriving six days before, and it would later undergo even more additions. "In the studio early on in the shoot I had terrible problems," Freeman (Belloq) says. "I was saying, 'Steven, my accent doesn't sound French. It sounds Spanish, it sounds Mexican,' and he was saying, 'Oh, it doesn't matter. We'll redo it when we get to Los Angeles.'"

Starting this day and continuing the next few days, the Progress Reports recorded increased comings and goings as key personnel shuttled between London and Tunis. In short, Spielberg and company were moving so fast—now six days ahead of schedule—that production was preparing to make the jump to Tunisia earlier than planned. Thus set construction and hundreds of other details had to be completed.

On Thursday, in Degache, Tunisia, Frank Marshall succeeded in clearing their equipment through customs, so vital second-unit work, supervised by Micky Moore, was able to start on the truck chase.

From August 21 through 28 the principals were on Stage 1 for the opening of the Ark. Thirty extras were on hand, and a rabbi was on stage as Hebrew-language adviser to Belloq. Ultimately Freeman spoke a prayer in Aramaic that is recited in Jewish synagogues every week upon opening the Ark of the Torah:

Not in human do I trust
And not on any child of God do I rely
In him [who] God is true
And whose Torah is true
In him I will trust
And to his name holy precious praise

"Norman Reynolds built this incredible set for the opening of the Ark and we did the long shots there," Richard Edlund says. "Then I went around with Norman and said, 'Let's take this section and that section,' and I picked a bunch of pieces of the set; they were shipped over to ILM in

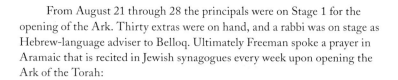

OPPOSITE, TOP LEFT: Slocombe, Lucas, Spielberg, Watts, and Reynolds on the altar set on Stage 1, circa August 25. TOP RIGHT: The slate is held for Take 2 of scene 100J, in which Indy discovers the entrance to the Well of Souls, shot on August 19 with the VistaVision camera so ILM would be able to add necessary visual effects in postproduction. BELOW: Allen and Ford tied to a pole on the altar set with bluescreen; scenes from this sequence were shot from mid- to late August 1980.

BELOW: Spielberg, Ford, and Allen. BOTTOM RIGHT: Douglas Slocombe, Spielberg, and David Tomblin.

Marin County, where we were going to do all the close-ups with local extras playing the Nazis.

"For the scene where the Nazi soldiers are hit by the bolt of light, I found these big flashbulbs that were used for high-speed photography," Edlund adds. "It was a flashbulb that was as bright as the sun, but only lasted two seconds. I then built rigs for the Nazis that went inside their shirts and over their shoulders like suspenders. They were plugged in through their leg, and then down their arm they had a little button where they would trigger their own flashbulb. The actual bolts were animated later at ILM."

On Sunday, August 24, Lucas had returned to the UK, and on August 28 he and Spielberg spoke about the last shot of the scene. "The sequence shouldn't last that long once they get the Ark up here," Spielberg says. "I've already got six angles, wider on Paul [Freeman], we've got the group listening, we've got Indy and Marion. We're fat."

"We'll have to race this afternoon," Lucas says.

"We always do it somehow."

"At least the bluescreen shot is the last shot," Lucas says. "We can always pick that up if we have to."

"It would just be nice to get a little wide here."

"Closer, yeah. That would be the sacrifice."

"The big climactic sequence in *Raiders* was my first experience with acting to nothing," Allen says. "Steven was over on the sidelines saying, 'And now the head is exploding!'"

Later that day, dailies from the second unit in North Africa were screened, their first glimpse of the truck chase. "Great, just fantastic," Spielberg says. "This is the desert. This is not shot on some back lot somewhere, that's for sure."

Dailies also revealed a surprise star.

"I'd gone to Tunisia to solve this customs problem," Marshall says. "So Richard Edlund did this shot of the rats with the crate, with the VistaVision camera, but the rats were totally uncontrollable. There was one crazy rat, which they named Vivian. It ran in circles like a crazy person."

"There was one deaf rat who performed strangely because it had no equilibrium," Kathy Kennedy says. "Patrick, Richard, and I were holding rats three at a time in our hands by the tails, while Richard took the VistaVision camera and turned it upside down on this little trolley. He had to almost stand on his head just to do the shot, which was ridiculous enough in itself, but we kept running over the rats. We'd have to stop because you'd hear this 'Eek! Eek!' And Richard would yell, 'Stop! Stop!'"

TOP LEFT: Visual effects supervisor Richard Edlund, Spielberg, and Lucas discuss the opening of the Ark. ABOVE LEFT: The deaf rat, Vivian, who became a "star" in the sequence where the Ark burns off the swastika from its crate. ABOVE RIGHT: Wolf Kahler (Colonel Dietrich), Spielberg, Paul Freeman (Belloq), and Ronald Lacey (Toht) discuss their reactions to the Ark's interior, which is then filmed (FAR RIGHT).

"Well, I've made more sacrifices on this picture than I ever made in my entire life with all my movies put together," Spielberg says. "But it's still a good movie."

Their conversation then turns humorous as they discuss what exactly they're going to show when the Ark is opened, and joke about having Charlton Heston—who starred in *The Ten Commandments*—jump out. "He comes out with his Moses beard, looks around, and says, 'What film is this?!'" Spielberg laughs.

"The problem for an actor with that final sequence was that you had to be talked through every moment," Freeman says. "We literally didn't know what was going on. They would say, 'Now there's a bolt of lightning coming from the right.' I spent quite a few takes screaming and screaming and screaming… I had no idea what was going to happen."

"Then once we went into dailies, Steven was so impressed with Viv that we discussed shipping her to the States to do special shots in front of the Ark," Kennedy adds. "So she became a star."

On August 29, after Ford and Allen finished shooting more footage of their cabin scenes at 11:50 AM, an early wrap, last preparations were made for production's voyage to Tunisia.

SETUPS COMP: 612; SCS. COMP: 44/116; SCREEN TIME: 78m59s/120m.

BELOW: Various on-set special effects were used during the end sequence, including lightbulbs placed within the clothing of the Nazi extras to simulate electricity shooting through them, which ILM would animate later on.

CHAPTER 4

DASH THROUGH THE DESERTS

AUGUST TO OCTOBER 1980

The main unit, including Spielberg, Lucas, and Ford, traveled by Monarch Airlines charter from Luton airport to Tozeur, Tunisia, on Saturday, August 30. On the plane, according to Taylor, who was traveling with them, "Many were wearing Sony Walkmans, a new craze that Spielberg had introduced to the crew."

They landed in the oasis town of Tozeur, a capital city in the area of Jerid, with a population at that time of 13,000 people—and 200,000 palm trees, key to the town's survival in the desert. The nearby town of Nefta would serve as headquarters for the full *Raiders* production team, having been prepared by the advance party led by Marshall. Nefta had 152 springs irrigating 400,000 palm trees. "Outside these oases, little survives except the Bedouin travelers and what they can carry or drive: their goats, sheep, cattle, and camels," Taylor wrote.

"It would be up to our security force to get Steven, George, Harrison, and everybody else out of the country," Marshall says. Their Tunisian liaison, Tarak Ben Ammar, was nephew to the president, but the Mideast political situation at the time, with American hostages being held by Iran, was volatile.

At the airport in Tozeur, travelers were met by second assistant director Patrick Cadell, who, "with adroit and very real courtesy," directed cast and crew to the awaiting vehicles. Depending on the color tags affixed to their luggage, crew went either to the Grand Hotel de l'Oasis or the Continental Hotel in Tozeur. Ford, Allen, Rhys-Davies, Freeman, Lacey, Lucas, and Spielberg were whisked away to the big hotel in Nefta, the Sahara Palace.

"God, it was hot out there," Taylor remarked.

As they settled into their new quarters, judgments concerning lodgings were made—the Sahara had a pool—and changes effected, to the extent that David Tomblin felt obliged to add a note to the first Call Sheet issued in Tunisia: "If you change your hotel room, please do not forget to advise Pat Carr in the production office."

On Sunday everyone unpacked, and Spielberg conducted a recce (a location scout) of the Tanis Digs location.

REPORT NOS. 50-60: MONDAY, SEPTEMBER 1-FRIDAY, SEPTEMBER 12, 1980; SEDADA, NEAR TOZEUR, TUNISIA: EXT. TANIS DIGS; TOZEUR: EXT. TANIS AIRSTRIP; EXT. FLYING WING; INT. MARION'S TENT; EXT. CANYON; EXT. WELL OF SOULS

On Monday, September 1, Paramount issued another press release, which began by calling out that day's record heat: 130 degrees. As the days wore on, the 150 crew members would drink on average ten to fifteen pints of bottled water a day, plus soft drinks. The Call Sheet for each of those days noted: "It is strongly advised that a good deal of liquid is consumed by everyone during the course of the working day to ensure that dehydration does not set in."

In addition to the first and second units, the Tunisian crew numbered 80, while some 600 Arab and "Nazi" extras were added to the Tanis Digs locations—a 100-acre set that Reynolds and his team had been building for the last eight weeks, finishing just in time for production's early arrival (according to Kazanjian, a 200-acre set had been reduced to save around $750,000). The press release also noted that the three-mile road across the desert to the location had already been built by the *Star Wars* unit four years

BELOW: In the blazing desert, keeping hydrated was a priority: Lucas and Kazanjian; Kazanjian, Lucas, and Spielberg; a sign directing cast and crew on the road to the Tanis Digs location; the swimming pool at the Sahara Palace Hotel in Nefta. Directions to the Tanis Digs site were printed on Call Sheets: "From the Sahara Palace Hotel, go through Tozeur. From Tozeur, take the road to Degache (10km). Go straight through Degache. Approximately 4 kms after Degache, turn right (signposted to Kebili). Two kms further on, turn left opposite small hut. ('Raiders' signs start appearing here). Three kms down this dirt track is the location on the left hand side of the road. The total distance from Tozeur is approximately 20 kms."

before. This road was used to transport the film's 42 vehicles, which had been freighted across the Mediterranean to the port of Gabes, then driven 500 miles, while the eight specially made trucks and cars were brought in by "low-loaders." The wardrobe department had brought in 100 Nazi uniforms, while local labor was busy producing 500 "jelabahs": long Arabic robes.

Other modes of transport at the Tanis Digs location were: six camels and five horses, which were complemented by other livestock (donkeys, sheep, goats). Leaving at 7:30 AM, actors and crew were driven to the location in approximately 17 cars, three Winnebagos, and assorted vans and minibuses. Catering was for 200 people.

"The Flying Wing had to be broken up into six parts," Kazanjian says, "shipped by truck to the border, loaded on a boat, shipped across the Mediterranean, put on additional trucks and shipped all the way down to the site, then lifted [into position] by a crane that had to be brought down there. We had to assemble that particular plane in the desert in about 130-degree temperatures. We had a huge crew down there, we had hotels, food, paint; we had electrical wire going back and forth. All the sound equipment, all the camera equipment, everything had to go by truck and boat and airplane. It's very costly. It scares me when I think about it."

TUMULT

Much of the first day was dominated by stories of food and drink. "Fifty thousand flies can't be wrong," the joke went around per their catered food. By all accounts, it was healthy and fresh—but Spielberg was taking no chances. He'd brought all his own food from Britain in cans: spaghetti, beans, meat, fruit, macaroni and cheese.

Late that morning, however, a crisis was averted. While recording sound for the making-of documentary, David Wisnievitz notes that, "It began when the 600 Arab extras started asking urgently for water. They were very, very thirsty. We had been drinking water from those ice-cold bottles all morning. Well, they had had nothing.

"A fire truck was brought, and when the water started to come up there was much more going on the ground than they were able to drink; literally twice as much was being spilled. They were screaming and fighting for it. The water was almost too hot to touch anyway, out of a fire truck that had been out all day in that heat. It was a real bad scene. And strange, too, because the educated Arabs around didn't seem concerned. Steven was real angry. Steven said he doesn't care who they are or how they have been treated before, they are going to get proper food and drink."

HARMONY

By their fifty-first day working together, star and director had gotten to know each other.

"I've had two days off since we started," Ford says. "So it's been tough that way; but I've been having a good time working with Steven. The interplay of ideas has been exciting. I more or less create a character out of the physical circumstances that I find myself in, the people that I'm working with. You really don't have to create character, you just have to create behavior that defines character—and in that a director and actor work together."

"Harrison never does a scene or plays a moment without feeling justification for that moment," Spielberg says. "Harrison is giving the

BELOW: A panoramic shot of Spielberg on the Tanis Digs location, September 1980. Many of the film's German extras were actually European vacationers signed up in various places. They were brought to the location and paid 20 dinars a day, with food and drink thrown in.

"Harrison never burns out," Spielberg says. "He tapers off the fun of the first take. Doing anything for the first time is usually better than doing anything for the twentieth time. The biggest danger is that when you get it on one take, you can't believe you got it on one. So you stop trusting yourself. Harrison says, 'I must be able to do better. It couldn't have been that good.' And I say, 'I don't know. It was great but we got it the first time. That's kind of odd.' So we do it ten times more, and then I'll say, 'It was number one. Why'd we spend an hour doing ten takes? It was number one.'"

AN AILING CREW

By Thursday, September 4, a trend of injuries and sickness had invaded the production of *Raiders*. The day before, stand-in Jack Dearlove had collapsed from heat exhaustion, and at least five others had been treated by Dr. Hodder, who was being run ragged. Documentary filmmaker Phil Schuman was sick. John Rhys-Davies had been feeling ill on Tuesday, as had wardrobe mistress Rita Wakely.

"Many crew members are sick but are too numerous to list," the Progress Report read. Hodder was also dispensing hangover cures to those who were partying hard during the hot nights at the Continental Hotel.

"We were down at Nefta at the edge of the desert, which was very rustic," Ford says. "Except for our hotel, which was meant to be a fancy hotel but had never served any patron longer than overnight, because they were used to bringing tourists in on buses and taking them out the next day. But we were there for four or five weeks, so they didn't know quite how to deal with us. I mean, there's nothing wrong with those places. The only thing that's wrong was trying to make a movie there. When you're trying to run a highly technological event out of those circumstances, it's ridiculous. We didn't have that many problems, it's just that everybody was sick and finally crazed from the experience."

"I was one of the 15 or 20 people out of 150 that didn't get sick," Spielberg says. "I think essentially it was because I'd been sick coming back from the second recce in Tunisia in April, and I think that once you have that little microbe in your system, it stays with you. It doesn't cause immunity if you have food poisoning, but it certainly prevents the general malaise from hitting you harder than if you were just a real stranger coming to a foreign country."

Spielberg was feeling so alive to his film that he added scene A108 to the schedule. Perhaps wondering how Sallah escapes after being found digging with Indiana Jones—indeed, finding the Ark—Spielberg had shot a brief sequence that wowed all the spectators that day. According to Karen Allen, a German youth had been hired for a small part—a Nazi who was supposed to execute, but then spares Sallah. Apparently this student, Martin Kreitt, had come to Tunisia for a vacation, but found himself playing an intensely moving and emotional scene with screen and stage veteran Rhys-Davies.

ABOVE: Spielberg discusses with Rhys-Davies the other scenes shot that day, which included Sallah's various interactions with hungry and thirsty Nazis, and Indy's approach to the map room disguised as an Arab digger (TOP RIGHT).

OPPOSITE: Horsemaster R. Street was on hand Monday, September 1—the production's first shoot day in Tunisia—when Ford rode a horse out of a tent in scene 113.

performance of his life. At least up to now, this is the best I've ever seen him. He's just amazing, every day. It has to look effortless and it does."

"I've had a real good time," Ford says. "Steven has a lot of energy and enthusiasm, and he's a very facile filmmaker, seems born to the job. I feel a sense of collaboration with him, which I like; and I think we get along well together, which is very helpful. Also it's nice if you respect a person's work, and I do respect the work he's doing on the film a lot.

"For one of the first times on a film I'm watching dailies every day," Ford adds, "so I know what we are doing and I am very happy with it."

The irony was that by this time Rhys-Davies was so ill, he became sick during the day. "I have never been so ill on a film set… I had a temperature of 105 or something—I was dying," he says. "And Steven said to me, 'Can you bend down to give him a better eye line, and as I bent down I filled my jelabah in front of 200 people. And I didn't care."

TOXIC TRAP

By Friday, September 5, Karen Allen had joined the ranks of the unwell and had to be escorted from the location to her dressing room. "It wasn't unusual to just see someone on the crew, or one of the actors, just drop whatever they were holding and make a mad dash for a trailer at any given moment," she says. Ford was also ill. On the landing strip set, sitting by the Flying Wing on the tarmac, even Spielberg was beginning to suffer.

"Everyone's sick," he says. "George is looking more like Howard Hughes every day. He'll be arriving with his feet in Kleenex boxes soon. You can't miss him. He's the one with red ears. He is terribly sunburned."

Lucas may have therefore felt somewhat relieved to be leaving the next day in Tarak Ben Ammar's (production coordinator, Tunisia) private plane on the first leg of his trip back to California.

CRUSHED BY CHAOS

On Saturday, September 6, George and Marcia Lucas left for Paris. At lunch near the Flying Wing with Harrison Ford, Karen Allen, Paul Freeman, and others, Spielberg says, "I think George sees that this movie is about characters."

TOP LEFT: Indy (Ford) locates the spot to dig for the Well of Souls. Shots from the interior looking out of the Well had already been filmed at Elstree, but now Spielberg directs Rhys-Davies (ABOVE), as well as Ronald Lacey and Paul Freeman (RIGHT), from the outside looking in (using a fake hole). FAR RIGHT: Kazanjian, Lucas, Ford, and Spielberg share a meal.

"He does," Ford says.

"We gotta have those emotional moments," Spielberg says.

"Paul looks so healthy today," Karen says.

"I have a terrible hangover," Freeman says.

"It doesn't show."

"I can barely speak," Freeman insists. "I make my own head hurt when I speak. I think there's something odd about this heat."

Afterward Spielberg continued a struggle that would go on for several days with a Flying Wing that wasn't performing properly—and even ran

over Ford's leg in one instance, as he lay on the ground during a fight sequence. Fortunately the heat was so terrific that it had turned the plane's rubber wheel into a soft gooey substance, so it didn't shatter his bone.

"Everybody's ready and the take begins," Ford says. "I go down and start to roll away—and my foot slips, right under the rolling plane's tire. Everybody was yelling, 'Stop! *Stop!*' while the tire crawled up my leg. Luckily the brakes worked—inches before my knee was crushed—but I was pinned to the sand, which resulted in tearing a ligament in my left leg. Rather than submit to any local medical care, we just wrapped it up, put ice on it, and carried on."

Fortunately scene 109, Indiana in one of the film's bloodier brawls, was forming up well, given Spielberg's preparation and improvisation.

"I've been cutting a lot of the sequences in Tunisia in my head, camera cutting," Spielberg says. "There were 24 sketches of the Flying Wing sequence, but I set up 140 shots in four days, averaging close to 30 shots a day. The story began to tell itself. The fight, which I think will be the best in the movie, just began to write itself. I would ask, 'What if we do this?' And then Harrison would say, 'Yeah, and then after that we can do this.' And then Vic [Armstrong, stuntman] would jump up and say, 'And after that we'll do this.'"

"I remember walking out to the airstrip," Kennedy says. "There was nobody else around, and Steven's walking around the Flying Wing. He was really pondering, way off somewhere, so I asked, 'What are you thinking about?' And he said, 'I'm trying to think of how I'm going to edit together 120 shots for this fight sequence, and I'm about halfway through in my mind.' He was trying to piece together and edit in his head a whole choreographed sequence before shooting it. I don't know what that's going to look like, but it should be pretty incredible…"

That evening Derek Taylor visited the production office in Nefta, which was humming with activity as they planned and prepared for the next day's shooting. Wardrobe supervisor Rita Wakely worked with a Tunisian woman at the sewing machines on 100 German uniforms that had to be repaired constantly. Lamps hung over the tables and rugs hung on the walls; ceiling lights had green shades. Red trunks and cardboard boxes littered the floor.

Staffed by about 15 troubleshooters and craftspeople, the office had no fixed hours. A Tunisian typing pool worked on one side of the room. Ben Ammar was on the telephone, switching from one language to another, while Pat Carr manned another phone. Norman Reynolds had returned from Sousse and Kairouan, where he'd been preparing sets for the final leg of the location shoot; Spielberg was speaking with him about the Cairo street scene and bazaar, and about a "skeleton action unit" that they'd use in Sousse.

Late that night lights were extinguished and Spielberg returned to his hotel. "I had Sainsbury canned food, a month's supply of British canned food of every variety in a big, old steamer trunk in my room. I'd just open a can and eat lima beans dripping out of the spoon, watching *Bridge on the River Kwai* on my Betamax—anything to get my head out of where I was.

"When I'm making a film I sleep like a baby," he adds. "Except for the first week. Then I have terrible insomnia. But right in the middle of the picture, I'm so punch drunk by the end of the day that I sleep. The harder the picture, the better I sleep."

PERILS OF THE STUNTMEN

Having started back on August 21, by September 8 Micky Moore's second unit was into its fourth week shooting the truck fight and chase.

"I worked with Micky very early on in LA," Spielberg says, "when we storyboarded the whole sequence. I think we had something like 200 individual drawings of the chase, which I did with Ed [Verreaux]. Then Micky came in and looked at it. When we came out to the Sahara, Micky expanded on it and asked, 'Do you mind if I change this? Do you mind if I do this? I can make this more exciting, if you let me.' And I said, 'Go. Make it as exciting as you can.'"

"When we laid this sequence out, it was originally in the mountains," Moore says. "When I got down here, I explained to Steven that I didn't think it could be done in the mountains. So we went and found locations in the oasis and through the short part of the mountains."

While Spielberg worked with the main unit at the Tanis Digs and then with the Flying Wing, Taylor would occasionally visit the second unit— after "quite a drive"—at one of its locations: "gully"; "oasis" on Paradise road; near Metlaoui; or on Rue du Paradis, Tozeur. He immediately noticed that this was a group "who were certainly unadorned by first-unit paraphernalia.

BELOW: A young German vacationer named Martin Kreitt ended up being directed by Spielberg in an emotional scene with veteran actor Rhys-Davies.

No caravans, few umbrellas, and not many of those people who make a location feel more human: wardrobe, makeup, family, friends. No, this was strictly action and support/supply systems. This was the front line."

This was the second unit: about fifty people, including stuntmen/ actors Vic Armstrong, Chuck Waters, Terry Leonard, and Peter Diamond (stunt coordinator of *Star Wars*); stunt coordinator Glenn Randall; second-unit cameraman Paul Beeson; assistant director Carlos Gill; and continuity Maggie Jones.

Back in August on its first day, Glenn Randall had "sustained a cut in his head whilst completing a stunt leap." Seven stitches. The next day electrician Mick O'Connell, who was traveling in the back of a truck, had been struck on the forehead when a piece of scaffolding had gone through the canvas. Paul Beeson was crossing a timber bridge while scouting a location when it collapsed under him. Minor abrasions.

"I first got involved with *Raiders* when I joined the crew halfway through their shoot in Tunisia," stuntman Vic Armstrong says. "I was in Mexico doing a movie with Ryan O'Neal [*Green Ice*, 1981], and I kept getting calls from Dave Tomblin, a great friend of mine, who said, 'Vic, you'd be a great double for this actor we've got on this movie. You've got to get out here.' So I flew out to Tunisia.

"On the second day I was on the set and it came to lunchtime, so we started wandering off to grab lunch. I heard somebody shouting, 'Harrison.' We kept walking, obviously. Walking, walking. And the guy kept calling, 'Harrison, Harrison!' In the end somebody grabbed me on the shoulder and spun me around, and I looked and it was Steven Spielberg. I introduced myself, and Steven called David Tomblin over and said, 'Look, Dave, this guy looks just like Harrison.' And Dave said, 'Yeah, well, this is the guy I kept talking about.' And that was my introduction."

On Day 12 stuntman Romo Gorrara was injured jumping out of a moving truck. But for each scar, bruise, and stitch, they were ticking off storyboarded shots, shooting numbers 29, 32, 37—six in all the first day—working from 6:30 AM to 2:25 PM, and generally quitting when it got dangerously hot.

"The less times I put them through it, the better," Micky Moore says. "Because it's always that third time. When you're doing a transfer or something on a rig or a wagon, by that time he's done it a couple times. He's tired, and nine times out of ten the horse shies away, and that's when you get into trouble."

"Micky and I have done a lot of films together," Terry Leonard says. "He is one of the grand great gentlemen of this business and I can't say enough for him. He is creative and he's knowledgeable; he knows stunts and the problems the guys have; he knows when he can put the pressure on and he knows when he can't. He never gets impatient when you are trying to set something up. [Serious] injuries can occur if preparation is poor, so Micky gives you all the time you need."

OPPOSITE ABOVE: Shooting on the Tanis Digs location. BELOW: Ford waits.

TOP: Ford and Spielberg discuss a shot. ABOVE LEFT: The crew takes a meal. ABOVE RIGHT: Karen Allen waits. LEFT: Spielberg confers with production designer Norman Reynolds.

THE TRUCK OF TORTURE

On Monday, September 8, they were all prepared to pay homage to one of cinema's classic maneuvers. Legendary stuntman Yakima Canutt had created—and survived—a feat in which he'd slid under the pounding hooves of a train of horses in John Ford's *Stagecoach*. That same year, 1939, he'd one-upped himself in *Zorro's Fighting Legions* by sliding underneath a coach—then climbing back up its rear.

Terry Leonard would be doubling for Ford in the sequence where Indy travels between the wheels of a truck. "Terry saw my storyboards and said, 'I wonder if I can talk you into doing something,'" Spielberg says. "'There's this stunt that was created by the famous stuntman Yakima Canutt...' He had tried to reproduce it in *The Lone Ranger* but had hurt himself, and this was eating him, so he really wanted to revisit that particular stunt. I said, 'My God, I wish I had thought of it. That's an amazing idea.'"

Preparation and prerequisites were many for this dangerous shot. Though the truck had been specially made, a long, narrow trench had to be dug on location because, as it turned out, the truck didn't have enough clearance. Because they'd worked together several times, Leonard would do the stunt, sliding along inside the trench, only if Randall was driving.

"I don't give Glenn one thought," Leonard says. "I've got confidence in him. I just eliminate that from my mind, because if I were going to concentrate on what I think he's doing then I'd have a split second under that truck where I am not paying attention to what I'm doing. But it is tough on Glenn when he's driving the vehicle. He can't go too fast because that would start a vacillating action underneath the truck. Once you start swinging back and forth, pretty soon you are totally out of control and those wheels will get you. And if you run over somebody there's no excuse in the world that's going to make you forget that it happened."

"Glenn is right with me," Moore says, "and let's face it, Glenn is a big factor in saying, 'I think we can do such and such that you want in a certain place,' where you've got a deep gully or things like that. Yes, he's a big factor. If you've got a good stunt coordinator, a lot of your directing is easier."

All went well that day, and they wrapped at 3:05 PM.

"Working with Micky has been great," Spielberg says, "but it's been rather estranged because he's been shooting in Nefta while I've been in Tozeur, and then he's been in Tozeur while I'm in Nefta. We never really get together except at dinner where he says, 'How was your day?' And I'll say, 'Fine. How was yours?' And he'll say, 'Great.'"

Back at *Raiders* HQ a memo was received that day from the second-unit assistant director for Hawaii, Louis Friedman, addressed to Marshall and Kazanjian, in which he clarified matters in the casting of Barranca: the best possibilities were Roger Bizley and Jacob Whitkin. Friedman also stated that he was confident they could cast 30 extras from the Honolulu area for the Hovitos. "I hope this clears matters and alleviates coronaries. Best alohas, Louis."

On the phone to Hawaii, Kazanjian talked about the plane they'd need: "Louis, I want you to call Dan in Hawaii and find out this following information. You know the Piper we looked at? That seems to be okay for us to use. Steven has okayed it, but he wants to add a lower wing. Now, I know when we were there Fred indicated that he could put another wing on without many problems, and then he threw out, 'But it would be shorter.' I'd like to know what that means. Most importantly I want to know the price..."

Preparations continued into the night. The following morning the desert heat once again stormed out of the east to engulf cast and crew.

KING OF THE EXPLOSIONS

As increasing numbers of crew were being sent home because of severe illness, animal handler Steve Edge arrived on Tuesday, September 9. "We had twin monkeys, Snuff and Puff, in Tunisia," Marshall says. "But Puff had a nervous breakdown when he got there, so he was in the mental ward of the pet hospital in Tozeur. Puff just started shaking, couldn't perform and wouldn't eat and wouldn't do anything, whereas Snuff did a couple of things that were real good on film."

The next day Spielberg added two scenes, 139 and 140, for inside Marion's tent, having decided to elaborate the scene on location. "It just was the evening before," Freeman says, "when Karen and I were sitting inside the tent talking about how we were going to do this scene, and we said, 'This should be fun, the two of us together. We could actually have a laugh about this. Why does it have to be so heavy?' Fortunately, Steven agreed with that and pushed us even further. And when we started shooting the scene, he allowed Karen all that enormous freedom to improvise and improvise, and we didn't stop. I don't think I've ever improvised for so long in a film. Whatever I was able to do was mainly sprung off Karen, who was so inventive that it was a great joy."

"It was born out of a problem," Karen Allen says. "And that was, there was no reason for my character to put on that dress. So Steven challenged me to find something. It was not difficult to enlist Paul and we went into the tent and just did a little improvisation together. We also thought it was beautiful to bring the drinking contest back into the story . . ."

"I think my playing of Belloq has changed how Steven sees it," Freeman adds. "I haven't spoken to him about this, but I think there's an understanding, because subsequently he's rewritten bits of the story to make sense of the fact that I'm a rather kinder, more civilized person than Belloq was in the original story."

On Wednesday, remarkably, Spielberg also shot scene 138 in the *Star Wars* canyon, where Jones holds up the Ark parade with a bazooka. By this time in the ongoing development of the story, Toht's life had been prolonged beyond the truck chase in which he'd originally died—Ronald Lacey was one of the party in the canyon. The scene had been rewritten as well since

the fifth draft: It now took place in the desert, not the jungle, and well before Belloq actually opened the Ark. Spielberg had also cut the dialogue down to the bone. Strangely, it rained that day, though it was turning out to be Tunisia's hottest summer in 29 years.

"The four-sketch sequence in the canyon became a 24-sketch sequence only because it was overcast," Spielberg says. "We didn't need any lights or reflectors, so I was able to pop around with almost a handheld camera and finish the sequence in a little under five and a half hours."

On Thursday they blew up the Flying Wing.

On the morning of the explosions, there was a great deal to do and things weren't going well. According to Taylor, Spielberg "was concerned about the light, and, therefore, the time. But the explosive connections were dealt with, Kit West spoke quietly and patiently to his men through the radio on his belt and to Spielberg in person, and, just in time, everything was okay. When the bangs came, even if the Wing wasn't thoroughly destroyed, it was close enough."

"While the fire department was putting out the plane, their hoses caught on fire," Marshall says. "The fire department had to put out its own hose. It was like a slapstick comedy. They were all falling down, and the hose was breaking and running out of water."

Another injury was duly noted in Friday's Progress Report: On September 12, Micky Moore "received a knock on his lower abdomen," but continued working. That same day, on the bus returning from the Digs

ABOVE: Spielberg works with stunt-man Pat Roach, a wrestler from Birmingham, England, who ran a gymnasium. Roach played not only the Giant Sherpa but also the German mechanic who fights Indy (RIGHT).

location, Spielberg was looking out his window when he noticed a particular location during sunset.

"Look at that. If David Lean were here he would get Freddie Young's camera on that so fast."

"Yes, Steven?" says David Tomblin, who was sitting in front of Spielberg.

"Look at that dust, that sand."

"Great."

"Let's get it right here tomorrow," Spielberg says. "Get the sunset right here."

"The sunset here tomorrow?"

"I think we need to be here earlier. The sunlight is too slanted now, it's coming straight into the camera."

"It's forty-two miles from that location to here, so we're going to have to leave pretty early to get here. Especially if we're to be here before this time."

"Yes. I want the sun higher than this. Look, see the smoke coming out of the wheels of that car. We have to do one. Those trees are real good, real good."

"Right," Tomblin says. "We'll work it out. We have to wrap at the first place to get here at, say, 5:30."

BELOW: Moving the Flying Wing took a team of men—so when it accidentally ran over Harrison Ford's leg it was slow-motion distress. Eventually, per the script, the Flying Wing was blown up (LEFT).

TOP LEFT: Spielberg, Frank Marshall, and Ford on the action-unit location. RIGHT: Spielberg re-creates the Zorro moment with Indiana Jones leaping from steed to truck. "This truck was built specially," art director Les Dilley explains, "based on an American GMC, 1943 model. There are the other vehicles as well, including a Mercedes staff car. We ended up having the Mercedes built by Classic Cars of Coventry, Jaguar specialists."

OPPOSITE: Another Zorro moment is re-created, with stuntman Terry Leonard doubling as Indy beneath the truck and Sergio Mont as the bulldog Nazi sergeant. "This is my fifteenth year," Leonard says. "I started on a picture called *El Dorado* [1966] with John Wayne, Bob Mitchum, and Jimmy Caan. There's been three guys become famous as doubling John Wayne: Yakima Canutt, of course, the first of the greats; Cliff Lyons; and the guy that started me in the business, Chuck Roberson."

"David Tomblin is among the best ADs I've worked with," Spielberg would say. "Physically, a good first AD will move a crowd of tens of thousands to where the director would like the crowd to be. He'll push the company along, he'll sense the pace the director would like to shoot the picture, and he'll encourage the company to work at that pace. He'll watch the lighting and he'll watch the director working with the actors, and he himself will place and direct the extras. Then he'll decide, when we're maybe ten, five minutes away from shooting, to start saying, 'Okay, ten minutes. Okay, five minutes. Okay, get ready, boys…'"

SETUPS COMP: 809; SCS. COMP: 63/116; SCREEN TIME: 110m29s/120m.

REPORT NOS. 61–69: SATURDAY, SEPTEMBER 13–WEDNESDAY, SEPTEMBER 24, 1980; METLAOUI, TUNISIA: EXT. ROAD; EXT. PHOSPHATE ROAD; KAIROUAN, TUNISIA: EXT. SALLAH'S DINING ROOM/TERRACE; EXT. ARAB BAR; INT. ARAB BAR; EXT. SMALL BAZAAR; EXT. OMAR'S SQUARE AND GARAGE; SOUSSE, TUNISIA: EXT. PERISCOPE AT SEA; EXT. DESERTED SQUARE AND ALLEYS

On the bus ride to join the second unit on location the next morning, Taylor asked Spielberg if he was happy. "I've always been happy," the director replied. "I've been happy when I've been up, I've been happy when I've been down. I've never not been content, basically content, about the things I've done."

On that Saturday, September 13, Ford and Spielberg joined what was also referred to as the "action" unit for the former's close-ups. "The rendezvous was at a desolate place called Metlaoui near a phosphate works where vast, long, irredeemably ugly conveyor belts bear phosphate away from jagged quarries," Taylor wrote.

"It's true, you can do a lot of stuff yourself," Ford says. "And I'm glad to if the stunt is coordinated so that there is an advantage for the film in my doing it. I don't want to do it for the glory. When I'm not too sore, I enjoy it, but sometimes I begin to feel more like a battered football player than a movie actor. You get a lot of bumps doing movie magic—even with stuntmen taking their share, a bump here and a bump there add up to a bruised and battered body."

Ford spent part of the day being towed behind the main truck via Indy's whip. Later he had to punch in the face his double, Terry Leonard, who was now subbing as the Nazi truck driver. Spielberg directed them: "Terry, I'm going to set this frame for you. I want to see how you're wrestling here. Okay, Terry, go ahead. I can still see you. That's good. Now you're blocking Harrison. That's good. Now you see obstacles. Perfect. That's a good place for you and a good place for Harrison."

"The stunt arranging was done by Vic Armstrong, Terry Leonard, and Glenn Randall, and they helped create some incredibly original physical moments," Ford says. "Steven and George both have a vivid imagination for these things, and it often is left to the arranger to figure out how to make it work. And, sometimes, a little bit is left over for me to wrestle with. But I had total confidence in the stunt guys. They thought through what was safe and what was not safe for themselves or for me. So it was just another day at the office."

Tomblin then wrapped the first unit early so they could catch the sun and trees on the airport road between Tozeur and Nefta, as Spielberg

had requested, while the second unit continued its setups, as described in continuity notes: "command car, front smashed, right-hand windscreen broken; truck, front smashed; truck, right side canvas ripped; truck, right-hand door missing; truck, front windscreen smashed."

But things didn't go well for the first unit as they tried to capture a mute moment in which two trucks arrive at the Tanis Digs. "Last night was one of those typical mad scenes of everything going wrong and nothing making sense," David Wisnievitz says. "A very minor scene in a way, but very complicated. You had so many elements, all the camels and sheep…"

"It makes it worth it when you get the shot," Spielberg says. "But I don't think we got the shot. First time, a truck stopped right in the middle of the sun. Second time, the truck stopped too far away from the sun, so I couldn't get the truck and the actors in the same shot. Third time, there were no camels in it. Fourth time, the sheep walked away, and the fifth time, the sun went down. Sunset shots are always a mad scramble because you're dealing with an hour hand that's moving as fast as a second hand in the last four minutes of sunset. I've never missed a sunset before so I was kind of crazy."

COLLAPSE

The next day—the day before he left the production—Taylor was sitting poolside with David Tomblin at the Sahara Palace. Although he'd been ill and injured, "Micky Moore came and set up a lounge opposite David. He said he was feeling better—but he didn't look better. As he lay on the lounge he began to shake very violently. David took charge, put a large towel over him, and had me call Dr. Hodder. Micky protested, apologized for making a fuss, but realized he was quite ill. Pat Carr in the production office immediately set about making elaborate and urgent arrangements…"

Moore was flown by light aircraft to Tunis and then by ambulance plane to Heathrow in London—and then to Los Angeles on September 15. Shortly afterward still others became acutely ill, even David Tomblin. One bit of good news was that Robert Watts had arrived three days earlier, having recovered from his appendectomy.

To cover for the sick Tomblin, Spielberg looked around and espied Kazanjian. "Howard was ready to go back to Los Angeles and see his baby and then go to Hawaii to prepare the Hawaiian week," Spielberg says. "But I remembered that he'd worked with Sam Peckinpah as an AD. I thought, *If anybody could work with Sam Peckinpah, they can sure work with me.* So I made Howard stay three more days to AD, and he was wonderful. He's more like me. He's a vocal pusher. Howard was running around the set saying, 'Okay, we ought to be ready now. We are ready now! Let's go! Let's go!' It took the pressure off me those three days."

NO-MAN'S-LAND

On Monday and Tuesday, September 15 and 16, now under the supervision of Frank Marshall, the second unit finished its last two days on the truck chase. Their final tally was about 23 days of shooting, 160 setups, and 105 storyboards, for approximately seven minutes of screen time.

On Tuesday the main unit transferred its base of operations from Tozeur to Sousse, and on September 17 it started several days of filming in Kairouan (which, appropriately, means "little Cairo"). Because the town had to look circa 1936, Tunisian location manager Habib Chaari spent the best part of a day organizing the removal of 350 television aerials from houses (apparently Robert Watts was so happy with his work that he kissed Chaari on both cheeks). Spielberg was then able to quickly shoot the panoramic scene on the balcony of Sallah's apartment.

"It's actually a real house in Kairouan," Marshall says, "but we built a terrace out on the roof of the place so you could see over the city."

On Thursday, September 18, the day Spielberg shot the sequence in the "Arab bar," Snuff burned his paw on a lamp and animal handler Steve Edge injured his leg while chasing the escaped monkey. Progress Reports continued to list those too sick to work among the increasingly decrepit crew.

Much of the fight in the small bazaar was improvised, including Indy's encounter with a scimitar-wielding bad guy played by Terry Richards ("sword Arab"). Despite the circa 2,700 storyboards—perhaps 80 percent of the film—Spielberg estimates that 60 percent went as planned and 40 percent was made up on the spot. Indeed, the fight was so complex that Friday's filming crossed over to Saturday, whose Report noted that Ford was treated for gastroenteritis but continued working.

"There was one morning when Steven Spielberg was not feeling well," Kazanjian says. "He had on his Walkman. He was on a six-foot riser with the cameraman, Doug Slocombe, and he was sitting hunched over on a chair, which is unusual for him. I went over to him and I said, 'Steven,' and I was talking about the scene we were setting up and asking him questions, but he wouldn't answer. I asked him again and he wouldn't answer. On the side Doug said, 'Something's bothering Steven. He won't even talk to me.'"

"I hate it here and I want to go home," Spielberg would say later. "I hate this desert; I love the Tunisians, but I'm not crazy about shooting in 110 degree heat every day. The crew is going crazy; they'd like to get out of here as much as I would. Kairouan has been probably one of my worst location experiences. Just the number of Tunisian assistants we've had to employ to get it through the heads of the crowd simply to stand back or press forward on a certain cue—no acting, just, 'Three steps back, three steps forward.'

"As a result, I've wanted to get out of here so bad that I've dropped half of my shots and I've just told the story. No style, no flair, no embellishments, because I really don't want to stay here another day."

"He was not feeling well that day," Kazanjian says. "But we started shooting Harrison fighting with the whip against this big guy, who pushes Harrison against a meat stand where a butcher is chopping meat. The Arab with the scimitar whips the blade down, Harrison moves, and it hits a piece of meat; before the second blow the butcher moves the meat over a little bit so the blade slices the meat again.

"Cut. Lunchtime. Steven's sitting at the table eating. I take my tray over and I sit next to him. And after a while, he says, 'Let's go home.' I say, 'Let's go home?' He says, 'Let's go home and come back tomorrow. We'll finish tomorrow.' I say, 'Steven, we can't do it. We'd lose a day.' He says, 'I really want to quit today and go home.' Just then Robert Watts comes over and Steven says the very same thing to Robert, and Robert explains it identical to what I just said, and walks away—but right after that, Harrison Ford comes over."

The two ailing men talked things over and came up with an idea to cut things short: Jones would simply shoot the scimitar-wielding bad guy. "We went back to lunch and Steven said, 'Let's try that,'" Kazanjian says.

"I'm much happier with the character of Indiana Jones than I was before," Spielberg would say, "and it's all due to Harrison's contribution. It's funnier, but it's not a send-up in any way. He brings a crass gentleness to whatever he does, an ingenuous anger to the character. In a way I think he was almost born to play Indiana Jones."

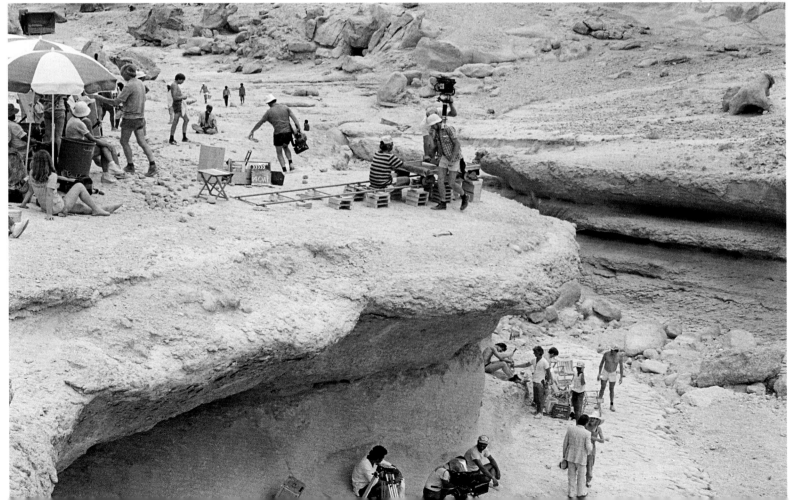

LEFT: In the *Star Wars* canyon, where Lucas had filmed R2-D2 many years before, Spielberg and company film Ford as he holds up the Ark train. ABOVE: Spielberg, sound boom operator George Rice, and Ford. Rice says that most of the crew had "a core of romanticism several inches in diameter."

THE AMAZING DR. FANTASY

Production's move to the port allowed them to shoot inserts of Ford strapped to the periscope cutting through the water, as well as more of the fight in the bazaar. Getting to the periscope, however, necessitated wading through some questionable water.

"The periscope goes on an underwater track," Spielberg says. "It leads to the rostrum where the camera will be, and Harrison is hanging from the periscope. And nothing is ready this morning as promised yesterday. There are little pockets of a urine-like substance that seems to be hanging on the surface, and we're having to swim through that to get out to the set every day."

Monday, September 22, was Karen Allen's last day. While she was free to vacation the next morning, Robert Watts had one more major task. "On Monday when I arrived in the streets of Kairouan," Watts says, "Steven came to me and said, 'I'm going to finish a day early.' That *sounds* great, except that we had a unit move from Tunisia to Hawaii, which is no easy thing. So that whole move had to be done one day earlier."

On Tuesday, September 23, Spielberg deleted scene 73, in which Indy knocks over a basket looking for Marion but finds instead a hidden cache

of contraband pistols. As production neared the end, however, things were getting humorous, at least in the production office. A note on the Call Sheet read, "Should anyone see Martin Evans [gaffer spark] biting his fingernails, would they slap his hand and growl."

The next day—the last day of principal photography in Tunisia—Spielberg deleted scene 79A, an establishing shot of the Imam's house, in which the Monkey Man was to emerge from the shadows and follow Indy. The second-to-last shot in Tunisia was part of scene 76 in which the truck supposedly carrying Marion banks sharply and falls over; the last shot would be the resulting explosion. Summing up perhaps the feelings of the entire cast and crew, Spielberg remarked to Glenn Randall during its preparation, "This is a good, symbolic get-me-out-of-Tunisia shot."

Although the stunt coordinator wasn't happy with the resultant take, the director knew it would work when cut into his sequence, and the truck was duly detonated.

The last Call Sheet for Tunisia implored everyone to return walkie-talkies, hailers, car keys, and documents. It also included an invitation: "Steven Spielberg would like to invite everybody to the cast & crew wrap party on Wednesday evening, September 24th, at the Hannibal Palace Hotel."

There was good reason to celebrate: The production was fourteen days under schedule. Drinks started at 8 PM in the Circular Garden; food and dancing began at 9 PM, while disco went from 1 to 4 AM in the Hannibal Disco. As an added attraction, "Dr. Fantasy will present his special wrap party show, 'Total Magic,' some time during the evening."

"I had developed over many years, as one of my thank-yous to the crew, a magic show that I would do at the wrap party; I was known as Dr. Fantasy," Marshall explains. "I'd had my magic trunk sent in and I did my full-blown show in Tunisia for the crew. George wasn't there, because he'd gone ahead of us, but Steven and Kathy were there and the rest of the crew.

"The finale of the show is that I have in front of the stage, where the band is playing and everybody's eating and dancing, a big cake that says, THANKS TO THE CREW, FROM STEVEN, GEORGE, FRANK, AND HARRISON. And as I'm taking my bow, I trip and fall into the cake."

The next day a second unit was scheduled to travel to Sidi Bou Said via boat to shoot establishing shots of the Nazi secret island, with the island of Zembra as the stand-in. But the boat that was supposed to take them "would a) not start and b) was not large enough to accommodate crew and equipment." The shot was abandoned, and ILM was slated to do a matte painting of the island instead.

SETUPS COMP: 964; SCS. COMP: 83/114;
SCREEN TIME: 132m37s/120m.

REPORT NOS. 70–73: TUESDAY, SEPTEMBER
30–FRIDAY, OCTOBER 3, 1980; HALEMANO
FALLS AT PUHI, KAUAI, HAWAII; EXT. POOL
& WATERFALL; EXT. PERU HIGH JUNGLE;
EXT. ENTRANCE TO PERUVIAN TEMPLE;
ALIOMANU ROAD: EXT. JUNGLE—INDY'S RUN;
THE RICE RANCH/HULEIA RIVER: EXT. THE
URUBAMBA RIVER; INT./EXT. JOCK'S PLANE

While director, principals, and stuntmen departed from Tunisia on September 25, stopping in either London or Los Angeles on their way to Hawaii, the main-unit location crew boarded several charter planes the next day for the same destination, no doubt relieved to be leaving the unrelenting heat—but the joys of intercontinental travel had another surprise for them. "The move out was made all the worse because the day the unit moved, the Canadian air-traffic controllers decided to have a one-day strike," Watts says. "So all the polar flights were held up. I was already in Hawaii but the bulk of the unit got stuck everywhere—and some took forty hours to reach Kauai.

"They eventually arrived about lunchtime on September 29. They were due to start shooting on Tuesday the thirtieth, so we sent them all to bed."

Indeed, for the last push everyone needed a little sleep. "Usually the last couple of days I have insomnia," Spielberg says, "because I'm sure I've missed the most important elements that would make the film either a hit or a miss."

LEFT: Indy is rescued by Sallah and his children. BELOW LEFT: Indy in the café-bar with Belloq; during this scene the latter makes it clear that he did not actually escape with the idol: "I was lucky to get away with my life. The Hovitos proved quite narrow-minded about the whole matter." (This line would not make it to the final cut.)

"Right before we started filming," says costume designer Deborah Nadoolman, "Harrison lent me his Swiss army knife, and, using a steel brush for cleaning rust off of car bumpers, I personally aged the ten jackets. I bought Red Wing work boots for him, which we aged and softened down. I had to have a hat that suited Harrison's face and yet allowed light to come in, so the brim couldn't be too wide. When I walked into Herbert Johnson, a famous hatter in London, I saw a hat I liked. With a couple of fittings, we got the hat right for Harrison, and then got ten of them and got them really dirty; I rolled them up, sat on them, had Harrison sit on them."

Perhaps the least jet-lagged of the lot, having arrived from Northern California on September 27, Lucas joined the 125 exhausted crew members on Tuesday, September 30, as they left the hotel at 7:30 AM in assorted buses, seven cars, and a minibus bound for Halemano Falls. The group included 24 "Peruvian" extras and Vic Tablian, the Monkey Man, who had been cast at the last moment in his second role as Barranca.

"All our stuff in Hawaii, every single location, was very difficult," Watts says. "The first one was down in a pit, like a mini canyon. There was a pool and a waterfall: a lovely-looking location, but very difficult to get

TOP RIGHT: Ford and Spielberg discuss Indy's duel with the scimitar-wielding bad guy, played by Terry Richards. The scene was shot two ways: as storyboarded (LEFT) and with a single gunshot (ABOVE). "More than anything else it's just having a good imagination," Spielberg says of directing. "You can develop a good eye, after all, if you have a good cameraman working with you over the years. If you have a good imagination and a good story sense, you like to tell stories, and you know a good story when you hear one; if you know what entertains you and if you think you can project it to a lot of other people, I think that's what makes a good director."

into. We had to build steps down an almost sheer cliff, and all the heavy equipment had to be put in with a crane from up above. And the thing was full of mosquitoes. We had to spray it every day and spray ourselves, but that didn't help much."

The location nurse was also equipped with mosquito repellent, while the location was sprayed at 7 AM and during lunch. Rubber-soled shoes were encouraged, because the newly built steps were slippery.

During those last days of photography, as Spielberg filmed Ford in the first scenes of the movie—a happy but important scheduling perk—both men had come to understand in their bones exactly who Indiana Jones was. Ford, of course, had already been playing Indy for months—and thanks to the three-plus weeks just spent in the harrowing deserts of Tunisia, he had achieved osmosis both physically and mentally with the death-defying archaeologist. The world-weary stare of Indiana Jones as his porters desert him and his "colleagues" betray him must have come quite naturally to the actor.

"The opening scene might lead you to believe that you're about to watch a film noir picture, because the jungles were so dense in Hawaii where we were shooting, it was very hard to get any light in," Spielberg says. "We were under a canopy of trees and everything suddenly got very dark on me. That pretty much suggested a dark opening for the movie, but the thing I kept saying to Dougie was, 'I want to see everybody's eyes. Let's just make

this look like an old-fashioned kind of an adventure movie.'"

"The reveal of Indiana Jones is teased," Ford says. "You're with him in the jungle for probably three or four minutes before you see his face, and it's all very mysterious at first. Then the dramatic reveal gives you a taste of who the character is and what he usually goes through in his adventures."

"Harrison is essentially a scavenger for all the human moments," Spielberg says. "He'll turn over the smallest rock to find one moment of identifiable behavior. That, together with my essential need to humanize *Raiders*, turned Indiana Jones into a very interesting man, a man with humor and with a great deal of self—without the loss of strength and Don Juan acrobatics and heroics."

The only other principal on this location was Paul Freeman, who finished his role as Belloq the next day. On that day Spielberg filmed Ford as Indy running for his life on the Aliomanu Road.

"The next location we could reach only by river," Watts says. The Call Sheet for October 2, their third day, read, "Unit will travel to location by boat leaving from the Nawiliwili small boat harbor at 7.20 hours." The ride up the Huleia River took 25 minutes.

On the last day of principal photography, October 3, the "Waco Plane crashed into the riverbank" while taxiing, necessitating postproduction second-unit shooting. Nevertheless the main unit finished its work that

LEFT: Ford clings to the specially rigged submarine scope (deleted from the film), while bearded mechanical effects supervisor Kit West watches from the water, and Spielberg stands with a bullhorn. BELOW: Spielberg shoots the truck falling over, then—in the last shot in Tunisia, on September 24, 1980—he films its explosion.

TOP: Kathy Kennedy, Lucas, Spielberg, and Kazanjian in Kauai, Hawaii, early October—their last stop during principal photography where, ironically, Ford was filmed in the first scenes of the film (ABOVE AND TOP RIGHT).

day, leaving 25 scenes incomplete, with ILM scheduled to finish approximately nine scenes. Others would be handled in pickups.

The last Progress Report noted several final statistics: total exposed film, 318,755 feet, with 192 rolls of sound; average screen time per day, 1 minute 59 seconds; 14 setups per day. The main unit wrapped 15 days early, 73 days of shooting on the 88-day schedule—way ahead of the official estimate, but exactly right for the secret schedule.

"Paramount was relieved, obviously," Lucas says.

"The crew is as much responsible for coming in this far under schedule as anybody," Spielberg says. "I think Dougie Slocombe and David Tomblin are major contributors, because David's pushed as I've pushed. And Dougie has never shot a film this fast in his entire life—he's not only doing a very fast job but he's photographing probably one of his prettiest movies ever."

"It has been unlike anything I have ever done before," Watts says. "The most interesting experience. I've never done a movie that's come in so much under schedule and been so busy. I've never shot in four countries with a first unit. Logistically a very, very complex film. And yet there has actually been nobody on this crew, nobody at all, that I don't want to work with again. It has been absolutely wonderful."

"Most everything I've done in the past has had problems on the production level," Spielberg says, "but this film was so smoothly organized by Robert Watts and Frank Marshall. The two of them together gave me everything I wanted within the budget, and I rewarded them and myself by giving them everything that I wanted under the budget and ahead of schedule.

"I have never enjoyed making a movie as much. I felt like I was playing a role. I was Indiana Jones behind the camera. I needed this picture to

exorcise myself from a kind of technological rut I was falling into, where I wouldn't walk away from a shot until it was 100 percent of what I intended. To be able to walk away and say, 'I think that was good enough for what we're trying to do here' was the most important film-school lesson a professional production has ever taught me."

"You know, it's funny, I have always envisioned George and Steven directing side by side," says Kennedy, "because I think there was a constant discussion that flowed back and forth between the two of them. Whenever George was on the set, Steven really wanted George's input."

The last Call Sheet noted: "The Wrap Luau will begin with cocktails… at 6:30 PM; dinner at 8 PM; be careful of Dr. Fantasy's famous punch!"

The wrap party again featured Dr. Fantasy's magic show, with a twist. "Word had filtered from Tunisia to Hawaii that I had done a cake dive," Marshall says. "And we were having a big luau for Marcia Lucas's birthday. We were sitting out there and they were bringing out this cake, when George said, 'Hey, jump in the cake!' But I said, 'George, I can't do it. This is not my party. It's not my thing.' 'You gotta go jump in the cake; it'll be really good.'

"George is egging me on, egging me on… I took the bait finally—and I came screaming out of the crowd and flew up on the stage and smashed into Marcia's real cake. George loved it. Marcia was a good sport, and we picked up the pieces and everybody had a little cake."

SETUPS COMP: 1,038; SCS. COMP: 89/114; SCREEN TIME: 145m18s/120m.

POSTPRODUCTION REPORT NOS. 1-4: SATURDAY, OCTOBER 4-THURSDAY, OCTOBER 9, 1980; KAUAI, HAWAII (HANALEI) LOCATION T.B.A.: EXT. PERU HIGH JUNGLE (TITLE SEQUENCE MONTAGE); THE HULEIA RIVER: EXT. THE URUBAMBA RIVER; EXT. JOCK'S PLANE

On Saturday, October 4, 1980, while most of the crew was in the process of leaving, second-unit director Frank Marshall, with Slocombe as cinematographer, took off for another logistically difficult destination—so difficult that the Call Sheet had no name for it, listing it as "TBA," for "to be announced." While repair work continued on the Waco plane, he used five extras for the shot of the title montage, with Will Welch as Indy, Joe Moranz for Satipo, and Stan Vienna as Barranca.

"One of the locations for the trek—we were doing the trek stuff for the credits—we could reach only by helicopter," Watts says. "We had to take everything in by helicopter, including two donkeys."

"Steven called me over and said he needed to find a mountain that looked like the Paramount logo," Marshall says. "So I drove around for a couple of days all over the island and I found this mountain. We scheduled to film it on our last days and I finally understood Steven's intention to dissolve from the Paramount logo to the mountain, and open the film that way. It was an idea he came up with while we were on location."

LEFT: Spielberg and Lucas pose for a photo with the Hovitos extras. ABOVE: Spielberg, wearing a *Jaws* T-shirt, directs Freeman, chats with Lucas, and clowns around in the river (without T-shirt).

Photos of The "Goose"
attached.

"When I was a kid, my first film company was called Playmount Productions," Spielberg says, "and I had a mountain as my logo, because Spielberg in German means 'play mountain.'"

On October 6, Marshall completed the title montage photography. Spielberg left the next day, while Harrison Ford and Fred Sorenson (Jock, the pilot) were able to start their scenes with the Waco plane on Wednesday, October 8. Unfortunately the weather closed in, making them shoot one more day on the Huleia River.

"At the end of the shoot in Hawaii, Steven was not there when we shot that airplane the second time, because he left after it crashed the first time," Ford says. "But when he got the film a week later and looked at it, he told me there was only one good take. I said, 'What do you mean? We got three good takes of the close-up and of the master.' He said, 'Well, there's only one good one, and the others are just you pounding on the plane telling him that he's stepping on your lines.' I said, 'What?' He said, 'Yeah, you're pounding on the side of the plane and screaming at him.' It turned out he couldn't hear any of the dialogue because—well, there wasn't any dialogue because they'd taken away the sound man. I said, 'Steven, that was it. That was the performance.'"

On October 9, at 6:30 PM, Harrison Ford completed his role, after 73 workdays. By October 12 Ford, Marshall, and the last of the crew had left the island.

"I remember this moment after *Raiders* was completed when George called Steven and told him that he had done a really good job," Kennedy says. "It was interesting to watch that because I think sometimes very successful, very creative people get to a point in their lives where, frankly, there aren't a lot of people left that can give them a pat on the back and make them feel like they did do a good job. And I think that meant a lot to Steven, when George called him and so genuinely felt not only that Steven had done a great job, but that he had gone beyond what George even imagined that the series could be. So that was a great compliment."

CHAPTER 5
BIRTH

OCTOBER 1980 TO JUNE 1981

"This film could very easily not be a hit," Lucas says. "All films are a risk. I mean, there's just no way to know. You can't predict a hit."

With a late June 1981 release date, *Raiders of the Lost Ark* now entered postproduction: editing, scoring, sound design, and visual effects.

Spielberg's editor Michael Kahn had of course returned to Los Angeles some time before, where he'd continued his work on the film. After meditating every morning, Kahn would cut fast—so fast that not long after principal photography wrapped, he had a fairly tight edit.

"Michael was only a day behind me," Spielberg says. "So I saw the entire movie assembled two weeks after we returned from Hawaii."

"When Steven sees a scene, he knows right away how he feels about it," Kahn says. "If he says to me, 'I don't know if it feels right,' we discuss it, I sense his input, and we communicate on that level. That's the way these filmmakers, these very creative, brilliant people function: on the feeling level."

As always in postproduction, advances toward the movie's completion took place on several fronts. As composer John Williams wrote the soundtrack music, Spielberg spoke with sound designer Ben Burtt. "I had a long conversation with Steven about what he wanted," Burtt says. "He spoke in terms of how he felt the things should be emotionally. He talked first about the Ark. He thought it might hum or make some kind of electronic sound. The opening of the Ark at that time was just a series of videomatics and storyboards, with a little bit of live action cut in, so we worked to come up with the sounds of the ghosts and things. Steve wanted the ghosts to be howling, spooky and scary."

"John [Williams] saw the movie and loved it, and went off to write the music," Spielberg says. "And then he called me one day and previewed all the themes on the piano. He'd actually written two *Raiders* themes. He played them and I think my only input was to ask, 'Can't you use both?' And he did: He made one the bridge and the other the main theme."

RIGHT AND OPPOSITE: In July 1980, months before principal photography wrapped, Joe Johnston, Nilo Rodis-Jamero, and others at ILM had already started storyboarding visual effects shots for *Raiders*—everything from map overlays and sky inserts to matte paintings and miniatures.

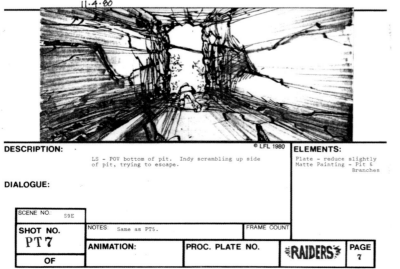

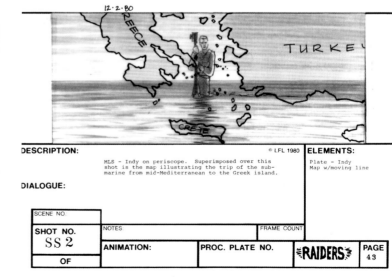

7.11.80

RIPTION: ELEMENTS:

11.17.80

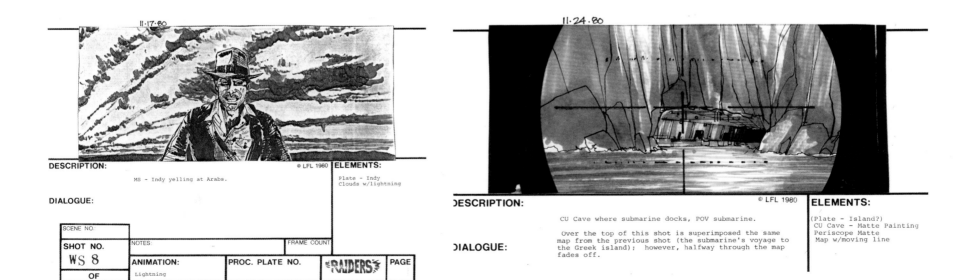

DESCRIPTION: © LFL 1980   ELEMENTS:

MS - Indy yelling at Arabs.   Plate - Indy
                                                             Clouds w/lightning

DIALOGUE:

SCENE NO.			
SHOT NO.	NOTES:		FRAME COUNT
WS 8	ANIMATION:	PROC. PLATE NO.	RAIDERS PAGE
OF	Lightning		

11.24.80

DESCRIPTION: © LFL 1980   ELEMENTS:

CU Cave where submarine docks, POV submarine.   (Plate - Island?)
                                                             CU Cave - Matte Painting
   Over the top of this shot is superimposed the same   Periscope Matte
DIALOGUE: map from the previous shot (the submarine's voyage to   Map w/moving line
   the Greek island); however, halfway through the map
   fades off.

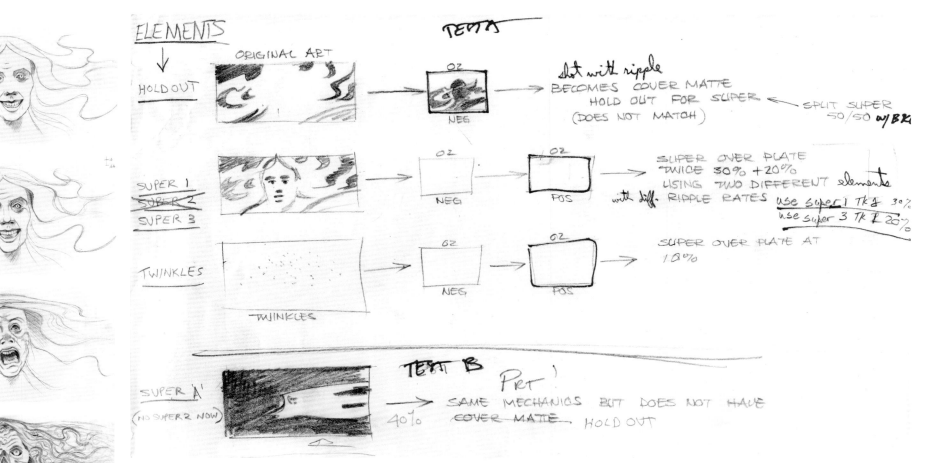

A GHOST OF A CHANCE

"*Raiders of the Lost Ark* was the very first outside project that we did," says ILM model shop foreman Lorne Peterson. "And it was a little bit of a twist, I remember, because when we'd been doing *Star Wars*, the feeling was we were competing against *Jaws*, which was the benchmark at the time. And while they were doing *Close Encounters*, I thought maybe Doug Trumbull and those guys [its visual effects team] would continue doing Spielberg projects, and we would be doing George's projects. But Douglas Trumbull didn't really want to become a permanent special effects person. He wanted to be directing his own projects, interactive games and films. So all of a sudden we got the project."

Although it had far fewer effects shots than either *Star Wars* film, *Raiders* did present a few significant challenges—more than first anticipated—and Lucas's worst fears about using animation for the Ark effects had already been realized. Between June 1 and September 27, 1980, ILM had spent $408,149 on art, camera, optical, film control, mattes—and animation—but had yet to crack the end shots.

"I don't think *Raiders* really made use of any of the *Star Wars* technology," artist Joe Johnston says. "The big challenge in *Raiders* was the sequence at the end of the movie, when Belloq opens the Ark and all the stuff comes out, the wrath of God. That was probably 90 percent of the work in the show—and we did not have a clue how to do it. We had storyboards and we knew that there were gonna be ghosts flying around and fire, but we were basically in a lot of trouble really late in the game.

"Richard Edlund had tried animation, just hand-drawn pencil animation for the ghosts," Johnston adds. "He'd hired a fairly well-known animator and set him up at ILM. And the guy worked for months."

"We have to show 'the wrath of God' in a way that's organic and biblical," Edlund says. "That means we have to manipulate what is accepted as being natural and real looking, to make it look different, but not weirdly different."

"We started wondering, 'Well, where's the ghost?'" Johnston says. "'Because if we're going to commit to doing it this way, we better get crackin'.' But when we finally saw it, it looked exactly like traditional cel animation—so it was a pretty dark day at ILM, because now we had almost no time left. It got to the point where we were asking ourselves, 'Are we gonna have to farm this out?' because we couldn't figure it out."

Given how intimately Lucas was involved with *Raiders*, there was no chance of the project going elsewhere. "I'd done *Star Wars*, for God's sakes," Lucas says. "I knew what real worry was." Instead his ILM production supervisor Tom Smith issued, on October 23, 1980, a budget titled "Special Effects for 'Raiders of the Lost Ark.'" Compiled by Laura Kaysen and Pam

LEFT: In November 1980 Spielberg and Ford reconvened at the Richmond Marina in Northern California for pickups of Indy boarding the Pan-American *China Clipper* (Dennis Muren as a Nazi spy wears the tan overcoat). Although filmed on land (BELOW), the boat-plane was later composited with a matte painting by Alan Maley and a plate of a dock in the water (FAR LEFT). The *China Clipper* was in reality the *Solent IV*, built by Howard Hughes and subsequently owned by Rick and Randle Grant.

ABOVE: Karen Allen in her Washington, DC, dress was filmed with Ford in January 1981—with Lucas and Richard Edlund in attendance—in the San Francisco City Hall. RIGHT: An insert shot of a book with an illustration (drawing by Ralph McQuarrie) showing the Ark's devastating power was also completed by ILM. "It was done as an etching by a fine-art printing press in Berkeley to give the page the feel and look of an old manuscript," Edward Verreaux says. "It's a very beautiful and detailed drawing. It doesn't look half as good on screen as it does holding it in your hand." BELOW RIGHT: The completed shot of Indy with map overlay as he flies to Nepal.

Traas, it reads somewhat like a justification, pointing out that more than 80 scenes included some kind of special effects: "Many of these effects are totally new in concept and were developed by ILM during a period of research and trial." At the same time, the report attempted to calm the waters, promising to "deliver the last composite shot by the end of April 1981."

The estimated cost to finish the bulk of photography, storyboards, compositing, and the approximately 20 matte paintings was $1,232,469.50 for 26,680 hours. On November 4, 1980, ILM issued its itemized budget for the seaplane matte and interior shots, which they shot at nearby Richmond Marina: the $80 round-trip airfare for Spielberg along with Ford's one-day fee of $11,000 brought the total to $18,915.

"Jim Kessler, my husband, was actually one of the extras that they used for the shoot over in Richmond," says administrative assistant Chrissie England (who later became president of ILM), "where they had the *China Clipper*. He was a steward."

Another extra was ILM visual effects photographer Dennis Muren, who had started on *Raiders* but then moved to another outside ILM project, *Dragonslayer* (1981, a Matthew Robbins and Hal Barwood film). "I did some of the initial tests for the ghosts," Muren says, "trying some sort of motion control to make the ghosts ethereal. Then *Dragonslayer* came along and I went to work on that instead, but I got cast by Steven to be a Nazi spy in one scene. It was a real surprise and a lot of fun to do. We shot it over in Richmond where one of the airplanes was docked. I don't even know if it could fly anymore. I was all dressed up as a Nazi with the glasses and the trench coat, and preceded Harrison Ford into the airplane. And then I got a close-up where I'm reading a *Life* magazine and I lower it down."

For his part Ford, who would be brought back for several pickups, was looking forward to opening day. "I have no fear they'll muck it up," he says. "The only anxiety I feel is like I'm waiting for Christmas. I want to see the finished film as much as anyone else. All I've seen so far are dailies."

"Gary Summers was recording sound effects with me," Burtt says, "so he spent a day on the set when they were filming Indy getting on board the *China Clipper*. Harrison had some time between shots and tried to show Gary how to crack the whip. And of course people started stopping and looking—and then realizing it was Harrison Ford cracking a whip."

By November 17, 1980, such was the worry level about ILM on the corporate side of Lucasfilm that Charlie Weber sent to Lucas, for approval and comments, a rough draft of an explanatory letter he'd written to Spielberg.

CUT TO THE QUICK

"Movie making is a collaboration and we had some wonderful collaborators on this movie," Frank Marshall says. "And that's what makes each sequence so exciting. The truck chase couldn't be the sequence that it became without the seamless cutting that Michael Kahn did, putting together all of the different elements."

"*Raiders* is just a tremendous action picture," Michael Kahn says. "I loved getting all the coverage. Steven always says that he shoots for the editing room, which he does, so I had a lot of footage. And Steven just went with it. It was a lot of fun. And it's good to know that it's not a motion picture until it's edited. You need to put all the pieces together, and there are a lot of devices used to influence an audience. Sometimes it just needs a little touch, or another beat. Or it's a beat too much. It's all very sensitive and it affects the audience psychologically."

"Michael's rhythm and timing are incredible," Spielberg says. "He just knows how to balance action with a love scene; how to create suspense, which invariably has to be slower. He knows when to cut on a breath, when not to cut on a breath. I don't know what I would do without him, frankly."

"Steven and I have this great working relationship where we respect each other," Lucas says. "So it's very easy for us to collaborate on things. And Steven gave me a chance to sit down with Michael Kahn, and I went through the whole picture. Ultimately I cut out one joke where, when Indy and Marion come out of the catacombs, an Arab is standing outside the tomb, who looks at them and faints. I just thought it was a little bit over the top."

"I have final cut," Spielberg says, "so I get to change it all back if I don't like what George is doing to the picture, but I have never not liked what George has done. George has always just put the right sort of objective eye to the movie in the editing room."

"Whenever we had a decision to make," Lucas says, "I would ultimately

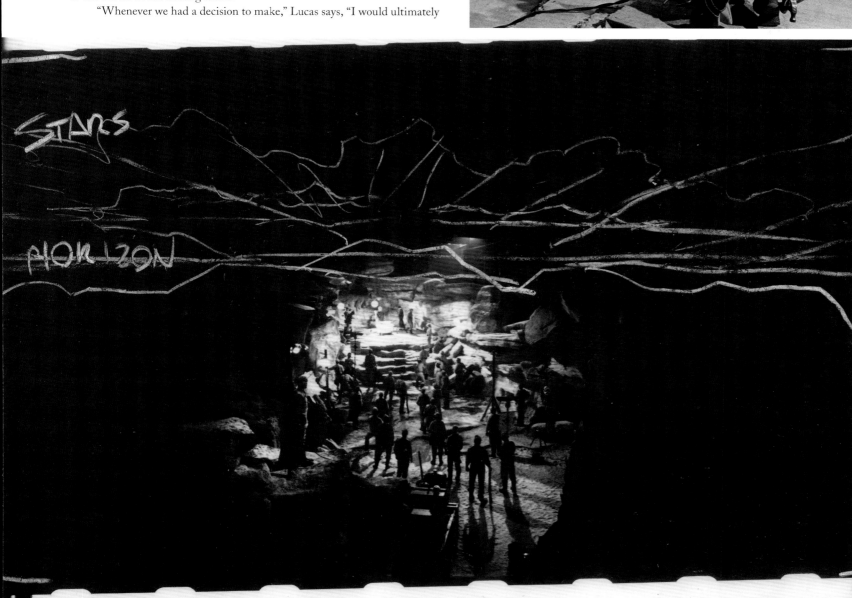

Under Spielberg and Lucas's supervision, ILM created several pieces for the end sequence that intercut with principal photography already completed at Elstree (LEFT). ABOVE LEFT: Part of the set was reconstructed with twenty Nazi extras and filmed by Richard Edlund, with stage technicians Peter Stolz and Bill Beck, in January 1981, for $3,516. ABOVE RIGHT: A miniature set was also created and populated with action figures (shown with model maker Paul Huston). "We were taking Ken dolls and dressing them up in Nazi outfits," model shop foreman Lorne Peterson says. "That was for the scene where the Nazis get blown into hell or something like that. With a camera facing up, we had somebody ready to light 'em up, because they had some kerosene on 'em. On the count of three, we all threw our Nazis up in the air, and that became the slow-motion sequence of Nazis spinning and flaming."

BOILING CLOUDS

ABOVE LEFT: As with *Star Wars*, ILM used the VistaVision wide-screen format to preserve film quality for its VFX shots. "VistaVision is a system that feeds through the camera horizontally, rather than vertically," Richard Edlund says, "so you end up with an image about twice the size of normal thirty-five millimeter. Since everything we do is duplicated once, we shoot on a bigger negative and then reduce." ABOVE RIGHT: The original film was blown up at ILM and then drawn on to plan out certain shots, such as the sky effects during the end sequence and digging at the Well of Souls (BELOW LEFT). BELOW MIDDLE: "We dropped colored fluids into a tank," says Edlund. "We already have some magnificent clouds and skies." Gary Platek manipulates a remote-controlled pneumatic arm to help produce the desired cloud formations in the water-filled glass tank.

say to Steven, 'You're the director. This is your movie. You do whatever you want.' Then he would say, 'Wait a minute—you're the producer. This is your movie. We'll do whatever you want.' And we'd come to a decision that seemed to be right for the movie, because it wasn't ever about Steven's idea, or my idea, or my side, or his side. We would just ask, 'What is best for the movie?'"

THE FATAL TRAILER

As the June 19, 1981, release date drew near, a letter from Warner Hollywood Studios to the Raiders Company noted that Kahn and his assistants would start editing on its premises on December 29, 1980, "for a period reasonably required to complete the postproduction of your motion picture." They would use the rooms designated "Formosa South 200, 201, 202, 203, 204, 205" at a cost of $620 per week.

Around this time the teaser trailer for *Raiders* needed to go into theaters. "George had an idea for the trailer," says Sid Ganis, Lucasfilm's director of marketing. "It was the Ark opening, looking inside, and seeing the title of the movie: COMING SOON: *RAIDERS OF THE LOST ARK*. And Paramount hated it. Barry Diller and Michael Eisner were the heads of the company, and Eisner, I think, agreed that we would run it at Grauman's Chinese Theatre and see how it played with a test audience. And we did; we took it to the theater one night and we showed it."

"There was a long time when people thought the title was wrong," Marshall says. "Hit movie titles aren't popular until they're hits. But with *Raiders of the Lost Ark*, they said, 'Well, what's an Ark? What's a Raider?' So we had trouble with the trailer. The first trailer that we ran at Grauman's

Chinese Theatre, people walked out because it was way too artistic."

"It was one minute long," Ganis adds. "And Barry Diller said, 'Over my dead body. We will never show that trailer anywhere in the world.' And we never did. We went out and made a new one."

By January 1981, ILM had rebuilt a section of the set for close-ups of extras during the Ark opening. "All the close-ups you see of them being wrapped by ghosts, for example, were shot at ILM," Edlund says. "Then everything was composited by Bruce Nicholson into the sequence. We also had Harrison and Karen come up here, and we shot them against a bluescreen and later added fire around them."

Ford returned for another pickup on January 24, 1981. A small crew shot the film's penultimate scene on the interior steps of the San Francisco City Hall, running up a tab of $5,352.63 below the line costs (including $3 for "bridge tolls"). Two days later a splinter unit shot missing footage of Indy's school on the University of the Pacific campus in Stockton, California, for $2,687.82, including $625 for antique-car rentals and $20.25 for coffee and doughnuts.

"It seemed like the start of a great friendship," Karen Allen says of Marion's last scene with Indy. "It's a *Casablanca* moment. I imagined that they were really back in each other's lives to stay."

THE BIG SCORE

On February 5, 1981, while going over publicity for the film, Spielberg mentioned that they'd finished the ADR (additional dialogue recording) not long before: "I lost my voice in the looping with Harrison the other

day, trying to do screams and yells for the movie. We were both at the microphone going, 'Aah! Ooh! Aah!'"

Not long afterward, on the other side of the ocean, John Williams and the London Symphony Orchestra checked into Anvil Abbey Road Screensound Ltd. Studios at 3 Abbey Road, London, to record the soundtrack on February 18, 19, 23, and March 2 and 3, with March 5 held in case it was needed.

"Music has always been an influence," Spielberg says. "When Johnny Williams and I met, we were a perfect couple because I really appreciate the music he writes. And although I have absolutely no talent in that direction whatsoever, I know enough about what I want that the two of us have very simple yet thorough conversations about the kind of music that's right for the movies I've been making for the past five years."

"He was so young when I met him," Williams says of their collaboration, which started in 1973. "In his twenties. His idea of dinner out was a hamburger. He had never seen a wine list. He did everything except hold it upside down. Without being ingenuous, he was a real treat. Having said that about him as a person, I should say he is also very talented musically. He plays clarinet, and it is not so much that he plays it very well but he plays it with such feeling. He is fascinated by music and has an instinctive understanding. He also has great recall and can sing me themes from films I made ten years ago. If I have an insecurity with something I'm trying to do, he can understand. If he has an anxiety, then I can help him. He is very nearly unique in my experience."

"I have about 300 hours of soundtrack music on cassette," Spielberg says, "and I play it all the time. I don't associate the music with the movie, but soundtracks have become one of the very few outlets for symphonic classical contemporary composition."

The composer's and director's ability to inspire each other had already worked wonders. Williams had won an Oscar for *Jaws* and been nominated for *Close Encounters*; he'd also nabbed an Academy Award after Spielberg introduced the composer to Lucas, who hired him for *Star Wars*.

"The way music editors cut the music into the film, I like to cut the film itself," Spielberg says. "I make quite certain that there is music in the background and scenes cut to music. Also, there are scenes that I edit with music in my head. When I am talking music to Johnny, I talk in rhythms, *yada yada yada, bumpa bumpa bump*—that kind of talk. Like a horse gallop, say. We talk in feet and measures."

Gathered on Abbey Road to listen to Williams's work were Spielberg, Lucas, Robert Watts, Howard Kazanjian, music supervisor Lionel Newman, Norman Reynolds, Pat Carr, and—on the floor of the number three studio— the LSO, playing to the scenes projected on the screen over their heads.

"Doing eighty minutes of music in eight, ten weeks, as I have, leaves little time for pleasure," Williams says. "It has almost to be done journalistically, until it is finished. Recording it with an orchestra is a pleasure; and there is still a kick, after all these years, when you see and hear it on the screen."

"We got to go to London and do the score," Lucas says, "and both Steven and I were like kids in a candy shop."

Matching the retro yet contemporary look and feel of the film provided Williams with a challenge—particularly given that the 110-minute film would have about 80 minutes of music. "To discern a '30s mood and express

TOP: Model maker Steve Gawley, Richard Edlund, and Paul Huston prepare the model submarine for its shots, which Huston (ABOVE) had helped modify. MIDDLE LEFT: "We actually borrowed a submarine from Steven Spielberg," says Gawley, "who had a twenty-five-foot Japanese submarine from *1941*. We brought it up here and turned it into a German submarine. We put a little remote-controlled figure of Indiana Jones on top of the conning tower and we shot this out in the Bay." "We fixed up the *1941* submarine and one early morning dragged it out to an island off San Rafael, where we shot that scene where Indiana Jones has hidden himself on its top," Lorne Peterson says. BELOW LEFT: Later the real island was replaced by a matte painting.

it isn't like doing a pastiche," Williams says. "A pastiche is not that difficult. What is not easy is taking it a stage further and doing the real thing, with some sincerity.

"The Ark: This is religious, orchestra and chorus, but using the two-as-one sound; you won't hear the chorus. Indiana Jones's theme, this is heroics. Marion's theme is a recurrent love theme. The baddies' theme, the Nazis, et cetera, is dark music. Those are the four main themes, which recur. It's difficult to come up with this sort of thing these days, to get the right feel, but I hope people will think we've succeeded."

Perhaps while they were in London, or at another time in early 1981, Spielberg, Lucas, Marshall, and company returned to Elstree to do some pickups. "We had a little bit of a street from the bazaar sequence built in the studio, on the stage," Lucas says. "We were shooting things like Marion looking out of the basket, things in that little marketplace during Marion's chase, but mostly it was a lot of monkey pickups."

"The prop man and the animal people had been working in England to get the monkey to do this salute," Marshall says. "So George asked to see it, and the animal trainer, who had a little stick, went over and tapped the monkey on the head and the monkey saluted; the *Heil, Hitler* was actually based on the monkey being hit on the head and trying to protect himself. So George said, 'No, no, no, you can't do that. What are you doing?!'" (See photos at left.)

"The trainers were being a little rough with the monkey, and we said, 'Wait, wait, wait, that isn't going to work,'" Lucas says. "But then it went on for days, and Steven would say, 'That will never work. That will never work,' because they kept trying tricks that failed."

"This little shot that we thought we'd run over and do in 20 minutes now became a big megillah because the monkey hadn't really been trained to do the proper salute," Marshall says. "The solution came in a bunch of grapes, which we hung on a little fish line just outside of the monkey's reach; the actual shot is the monkey reaching for a grape."

"We just kept shooting it," Lucas says. "He'd keep grabbing for the grape, and it barely cut together."

RISE OF THE PUPPETS

Meanwhile, several solutions had been found at ILM. "*Raiders* had this ghost sequence that was a challenge," model maker Steve Gawley says, "how to get the very fluid look that both Steven and George were looking for. I got to offer my two cents' worth on that one, which is what George always encouraged. Anyway, I came up with a fabric solution: a silk puppet, with a little bit of a head, for a ghost."

"There was that part where the ghosts come out and swirl around everybody," Lorne Peterson says. "And we were like, 'How are we gonna do that?' And we tried a couple of things that were just so-so. But then Steve Gawley came up with the idea of making a ghost out of silk."

"We had a big cloud tank, filled with water, and we had a camera looking into the window of the cloud tank," says Gawley, "and I was actually suspended above the water. So I would puppeteer a variety of these ghosts back and forth, upside down, you name it. Richard Edlund would have a film clip of the live-action set, and he would give me directions on which way to go and how long to do it and so forth. The puppets had this really neat flowing quality—you could not only make it move, but you could stop the ghost in the water and everything would catch up to it, which gave it a really great alive look. [Optical photography supervisor] Bruce Nicholson could then actually composite these into the live-action set."

"What was great about this was, we didn't have to shoot this a frame at a time," Johnston says. "We could basically roll the camera with a bluescreen on the other side of the tank. It was extremely simple, stuff that they could've done fifty years ago—but without that breakthrough, it would've been a disaster. We wouldn't have finished the movie."

The follow-up to the puppet was the ghost's facial transformation from human to screaming skull, which was shot live-action, because animation had proved untenable. "We took a woman that worked as a receptionist [Greta Hicks] to the main stage," Peterson says, "and she was dressed in a white outfit and lay flat on a big trapeze. Then we picked her up like a big swing and let her fall away from the camera, which made all the silk trail toward the

camera. When they ran the film backward, it looked like an object coming toward you with hands that were going out and drawing you forward."

"The scene when the beautiful angel comes up toward Belloq was shot with this Playboy model," Edlund says, "in a body pan, made up, and then with lots of diffusion and material on the lens to make her look fuzzy without being out of focus. When all of a sudden she turns into this skull, that was done in a water tank using a puppet.

"Belloq's exploding head was made out of the dental alginate, and was stuffed with pieces of meat, and liver," he adds. "We added a column of fire to tone down the gore."

As soon as these effects shots were completed by ILM, then approved by Spielberg and Lucas, they would be sent to Kahn and cut into the film. "When you get the shots, you might have to make some little adjustments," Kahn says. "But it's not as difficult as some people think. Dealing with ILM, you get some very good product. Every shot you put in looks better and better. So that was fun."

ROARING BOULDERS

"At that time, our [sound] editing room was right downtown at 321 San Anselmo Avenue," Ben Burtt says of Lucasfilm's studio in Marin County. Like the ILMers, Burtt had been searching for and ultimately finding responses to the film's needs.

"The giant boulder was a difficult prospect," he says, "because we wanted something that obviously sounded quite heavy—but it also had to accelerate in speed. We thought perhaps a bowling ball would be the solution, so we went to a bowling alley, but that sounded more like a bowling ball than anything else.

"So we came out to the Lucas ranch, which at that time was just a ranch, there were no buildings. But it was a great place to go late in the afternoon when the birds were quiet, and record outdoor sound effects. We came out several times, and eventually, after trying many things, we got frustrated. But late one afternoon after we'd finished a recording session,

we were coming down a steep dirt road filled with large stones [the size of a grapefruit] and I noticed there was an interesting sound in the car, a Honda Civic station wagon, so we turned the motor off and just coasted a bit down this narrow road filled with all these stones. And when the car would roll over them, it would grind all these stones together. It was a very interesting sound, so I hung out the back of the car and held a microphone near the back wheel as we coasted down the hill, going from a stop to a high enough speed where we were practically gonna turn over around the corners. And that turned out to be a great sound when slowed down a bit with the bass frequency boosted. That became the sound of the rolling boulder."

"We had Ben creating all these wild sounds for all of the unique situations that were in the movie," Marshall says. "A lot of the chases and a lot of the action scenes were filmed without sound, MOS [motor-only

TOP LEFT: Lorne Peterson poses the ghost puppet, brainchild of Steve Gawley (TOP MIDDLE), who performed its puppeteering in the tank. ABOVE LEFT: For some shots an actress (Greta Hicks,) was used or a life-sized sculpted death's-head (TOP RIGHT). ABOVE RIGHT: Spielberg works with editor Michael Kahn.

EVERYDAY SUPERNATURAL SOUNDS

BY BEN BURTT

"The **temple** in the opening sequence is basically very quiet, except when **mechanisms** begin to operate. Almost all of those sounds were recorded using the sounds from a mechanical garage door in San Anselmo, California.

"We started out recording real **snakes** but they don't really vocalize all that much and we had better luck with cheese casserole. My wife makes a cheese casserole and when it's in the dish and you just run your fingers through, it gives a real oily, mushy sound. If you record that and build it up in several layers, you can give a nice sense of slimy snakes. That was augmented with wet sponges being moved around on top of a skateboard.

"The end sequence begins with the lid being slid off the **Ark**; I experimented with a few different things but I found that sliding the toilet tank cover in my own home toilet was perfectly sufficient; if I recorded that in an echoey bathroom, it seemed to fit, although in a rather undignified way, the character of the Ark. Its humming, deep undulating tones were generated by a synthesizer. Once the **spirits** start flying around, those are animal screams and human vocalizations, as well as dolphin cries and sea lions (a lot of these sounds I developed for *Alien*, but Ridley Scott didn't use them).

"The third element in the end sequence is really the **lightning and the sparks** and all the destructive elements that destroy the Nazis. Those sounds were made from a set of recordings I'd made of the old gear that was used in the *Frankenstein* movies. When the **Ark closes**, once again we used the clanging sound of the toilet tank cover. I saved that cover, by the way. When we remodeled our bathroom, I saved the cover because I just couldn't throw away the lid of the Ark."

ABOVE: Sound designer Ben Burtt with Indiana. RIGHT: Ben Burtt created key sounds for *Raiders*, including its jungle scenes, and the opening—and closing—of the Ark (a toilet tank cover).

sync]. So these whole sequences had to be created on a Foley stage or up at the ranch. I think that was appreciated by sound editors and sound mixers because so much had to be created out of nothing, and it was so inventive."

"Richard Anderson and I were splitting up the duties of being the supervising sound editor," Burtt says. "He was responsible for doing the Foley for the film, which is where you go into the studio and perform sound effects while you watch the movie. Richard was engaged in doing the torches in the snake sequence, where Indy was walking around with a torch. He made up some mixture—I think it was benzene and rubber cement or something dangerous—without testing it ahead of time. And while he was doing the sound, it boiled over and dripped onto his pants and set his pants on fire. And of course the microphone was still running in the room and everybody's yelling and they throw a blanket on Richard, roll him around and spray him with a fire extinguisher, and his glasses fly off. I wasn't present at that session but I got the tape. I labeled it later RICHARD ANDERSON ON FIRE.

"We also brought different kinds of weapons and went to different spots all over the ranch," Burtt adds. "The *Indiana Jones* gunshot was recorded in a U-shaped canyon. We found this one beautiful sweet spot where you got a two-syllable slap of the gunshot; I was shooting a .30-30 Winchester at the time. There was a lot of old derelict farm equipment out here, as well as some old cars and rusty hulks. So we brought out the pyrotechnic people from ILM and we blew up a lot of these things with Primacor and dynamite.

"I can remember the first time I came out here with Sid Stembridge, from LA. He's a munitions expert who has licenses to handle machine guns and things. Sid was brought up here with a truckload of weapons and we did all kinds of machine guns with both live ammunition as well as blanks, to get ricochets and the various guns in *Raiders*. I can remember the first time we did it, that we actually forgot to tell the ranch personnel. And they came roaring out in their vehicle thinking that they were gonna meet up with some terrorists or something."

"During the course of making *Raiders*," says Steve Starkey, production assistant, "Ben would often come to me and say, 'Steve, come and listen to this sound effect. Is it too insane?' Or he'd play these four different bullwhip cracks and ask, 'Well, which one do you like?' He was always using me as a guinea pig. But he actually mixed these wild combinations where there'd be a spaceship sound to enhance a bullwhip crack."

"The first time I really flipped was because of something Ben did in the jungle scene," Spielberg says. "All of a sudden there was a sound made by a strange, otherworldly creature. I don't know where he got it, but it made that entire jungle scene so incredibly alien, just because of that one sound—I thought, *This is going to be a great adventure in sound.*"

"There were two other particular birds in that opening sequence," Burtt says. "One came from recordings of kookaburra birds at the Laboratory of Ornithology at Cornell, and there was another strange bird called a willow ptarmigan. We used that one when the two native guides see a dart in the tree and they are alerted to danger offscreen by this funny sound [see bottom left photo, opposite].

"We did the entire *Indiana Jones* fight sound library—body hits, punches, face socks," Burtt adds. "The *Indiana Jones* whip cracks and swishing were done out here. Gary Summers, under the tutelage of Harrison Ford, had learned to crack the whip, so we got one of Indy's whips from the

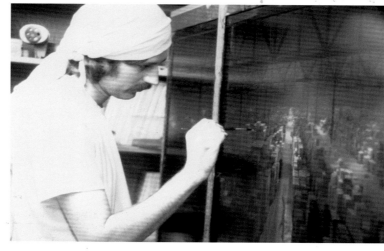

TOP LEFT: Michael Pangrazio works on the matte painting for the film's closing shot. MIDDLE LEFT: To help visualize the painting, miniature blocks were set up and examined by: camera assistant Jody Westheimer, Ed Hirsh, matte photographer Neil Krepela, his assistant Craig Barron, and Pangrazio. The painting was combined with the set at Elstree (ABOVE, a Polaroid of the crates taken for continuity purposes) to create the final shot (BELOW LEFT). "We actually built a very simple set, comprising boxes, all identical," Norman Reynolds says. "And we built it sufficiently high so that the boxes themselves follow the matte line. I think that has become a classic matte painting. I was really impressed with that. It was a wonderful way to end the film."
"I think it is the longest time a matte painting has ever been on screen," Spielberg says. "It was executed by a wonderful artist doing a somewhat impressionistic painting of all those boxes à la *Citizen Kane* [1939]."

prop department. I remember we kept the whip after that, hoping that no one would ever ask for it, and we used to keep it hanging on the wall in the sound department."

THE PREVIEW ACE

Spielberg and Lucas had one ongoing discussion about how a particular scene should play. The final decision came late on May 9, 1981, but the story, told by Kazanjian, begins with the first cut:

"So Steven Spielberg brings the film up for us to see. He's cut the film and George and I are looking at the film, and the version that Steven has shown us is the one where Harrison takes out his gun and shoots the Arab. The lights come on and it's quiet for a minute, and then George's comment is something like, 'Very good It works. But what happened to the scene where Harrison fights the Arab?' And Steven says, 'Well, I thought this worked better, this is funnier.' George says, 'I don't know.' Now Steven goes back to Hollywood and leaves his editor, Michael Kahn, for George to do his version. Two weeks later, Steven comes back up and sees George's version.

"So we look at the film and in this version we have the full fight. Lights come back up and Steven says, 'Boy, you really tightened the film.' Dead quiet. 'I like it. But, George, I think it works best with Harrison shooting the Arab.' And George says, 'Well, we're gonna test it with an audience. We'll test it two ways.'

RIGHT: Composer John Williams.
BELOW: Spielberg and Williams.

OPPOSITE: Artist Tom Jung created sixteen poster concepts for the *Raiders* one-sheet, one of which was approved to go to color.

"And what George has always done with his films is to test-screen them when they're finished, usually down at the Northpoint Theatre in San Francisco. He just gets different classifications of people into the theater, older people and whatnot, and then you get a reaction from them. Well, when we ran *Raiders*, we ran the Spielberg version of Harrison shooting the Arab—and the audience went crazy. It was the biggest laugh in the movie. George says, 'Well, I guess that works.' And that's the story of how Indiana Jones shoots the guy instead of fighting him."

SECRET SURPRISE

"I'm pretty numb in the preview," Spielberg says. "I usually pace. I never sit down. I stand by the back door. And if people get up and leave, I run over

to them and ask why they're leaving. With *Jaws*, I was standing up when a man ran out in the first twenty minutes and threw up at my feet, ran into the bathroom, and then ran right back to his seat and saw the rest of the movie. I usually see all that while I'm pacing. I don't often watch the audience watch the movie. I listen to the audience watching the film and record it on tape. Then I play the cassettes over and over in the car driving back and forth to the cutting room, making changes based on the preview."

Press previews were held on both coasts, with those for the New York critics on May 13 and 22. A June 2 Lucasfilm memo written by Tamara Rawitt summarized the reactions of the major news outlets: "Both *Newsweek* and *Time* saw the film and, based on their incredibly strong feelings for the film, *Newsweek* is giving us the cover on June 8 and *Time* is doing a three-page takeout in their June 8 issue." Apparently Janet Maslin of *The New York Times* had already seen the film three times; Pauline Kael of *The New Yorker*

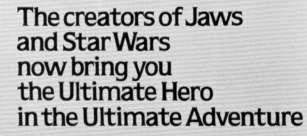

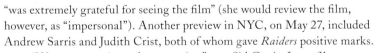

"was extremely grateful for seeing the film" (she would review the film, however, as "impersonal"). Another preview in NYC, on May 27, included Andrew Sarris and Judith Crist, both of whom gave *Raiders* positive marks.

"We were so quiet and so secretive," says Sid Ganis, Lucasfilm marketing executive. "I took the film to New York City to show to the critics just before it opened and I remember the critic for *The New York Times*, a man named Vincent Canby, was walking into the Criterion Theatre or the Loews State. I was standing in the lobby and he said, 'What is this movie? What's this all about?' He was saying something very revealing—that he, a movie critic who of course knew what was happening in the business, really and truly hadn't been aware of *Raiders of the Lost Ark*.

"So I told him a little bit about it, and he went into the theater and I remember him coming out of the theater joyous. Of course he gave us a great review—but part of the reason that he gave us a great review and was so amazed was because he had no anticipation whatsoever. *Empire Strikes Back*, the world had anticipation. But *Raiders*? People didn't know what the hell it was about. And then we had George's edict and Steven's as well, which was to refer to it as an updated version of the serials. And people had no idea what we were talking about."

"I've never had a lot of advance publicity on any picture I've ever done," Lucas says. "I've always tried to keep it fairly quiet and then orchestrate the publicity so it all comes out a month before the film comes out."

"We came on silently, stealth-like," Ganis says, "and then we actually benefited from the fact that we surprised everybody with this great, great story. Of course it was one of Steven's moments as a great director."

"Once the studio saw the film, there was no question that Steven was the hot guy of the moment," Lucas says. "Everybody was salivating and all was forgiven for everything."

Ad Age magazine confirmed that Paramount's and Lucasfilm's strategy was not to hype the film in advance, instead spending $7 million via the advertising agency Diener/Hauser/Bates to promote the film only a few weeks ahead of its release in 1,078 theaters, while also building on sneak-preview buzz. A one-page ad created by Richard Amsel was published in papers, while merchandising included books, a board game, trading cards, watches, clothing—but not toys, as the characters weren't deemed appropriate.

Part of that promotion included broadcasting on PBS a sixty-minute documentary on *The Making of Raiders of the Lost Ark*, which was executive-

OPPOSITE: Promotional artwork for *Raiders*.

TOP LEFT AND RIGHT: The two approved posters by artist Richard Amsel, several of which Spielberg signed for charity purposes (ABOVE).

produced by Sid Ganis and Howard Kazanjian, and edited by Steve Starkey from all the footage shot by Phil Schuman. The summation of months of work on the set and location, it won an Emmy.

"One of the great things that George introduced me to was documenting the making of the movie," Marshall says. "I think it became a very valuable tool all through the '80s for additional ways to promote the film, but the only person doing it at that time was George."

THE LIGHTNING-ROD FILM

In a strategic financial decision, Paramount decided to release *Raiders* on June 12, one week in advance of its original date, to get a jump on its main competition, Warner Bros.' *Superman II*, even though that schedule change entailed about $148,000 in overages.

On that day the reviews were overwhelmingly positive. "I don't know how strong is Paramount's percentage in the distribution of *Raiders of the Lost Ark*, but of one thing I'm certain—Lucas and Spielberg have just opened up another goldmine," Arthur Knight said in *The Hollywood Reporter*. Like his fellow critics, Knight recognized the film's serial roots, but he also asked, "Just how *did* Harrison Ford make it all the way to Gibraltar clinging to the conning tower of a German submarine anyway?"

"I don't give a damn how Indiana Jones could hang onto that Nazi sub's conning tower for 2,000 submerged international nautical miles," Harlan Ellison® wrote in his review, "because I love everything about *Raiders of the Lost Ark*. Like you, I go to movies to be dazzled, enriched, entertained, and uplifted; and to give myself over with the trust and innocence of a ten year old."

In *Rolling Stone*, Michael Sragow called *Raiders* "the ultimate Saturday action matinee—a film so funny and exciting it can be enjoyed *any* day of the week." Correctly identifying one of the film's inspirations, he added, "This movie has as many garish corpses as the most macabre EC comic book."

Negative reviews ran in a few papers, of course, some pointing out how silly the film was and how lacking in substance. "There's no exhilaration in this dumb, motor excitement," Nicholas Kenyon wrote in the June 15 *New Yorker*. David Denby gave it an overall positive review in *New York* magazine, but added, "There's a lot of fun and action, but nothing to chew on afterward."

"George and I decided to wait for the grosses on the Big Island of Hawaii just like we did with *Star Wars*," Spielberg says, "and we built our good-luck sand castle. This time the sand castle lasted a long time. It didn't get washed away right away, which is always our way of guessing if the film has legs. We have this weird superstition."

The first-weekend gross was $8.3 million, however—less than hoped for—and *Raiders* was only neck-and-neck with *Superman II* after its first couple of weeks. Given the stealth-like marketing strategy that had lulled reviewers, it's possible that the public was at first largely unaware of the film, too.

"I thought we had failed," Spielberg says. "Despite the amazingly good reviews, we didn't have a spectacular opening. Not that we're greedy, but everyone was hoping we would do something like $12 or $11 million."

Over the next few weeks and continuing over the summer, however, something unusual happened: Audiences actually grew as word spread, apparently thrilled by the film's consecutive cliff-hangers, which had nearly no match in the history of cinema.

"It was this offbeat movie, almost a Western," Lucas says. "Nobody knew what it was, or what to make of it. But the word spread very fast and excitement started to build. Once they saw it, they loved it. It was one of those films that after it was put together, it worked like crazy. You know it works."

"I was blown away by it when I saw it," Karen Allen says. "I had imagined a different movie in my head while we were making it. So when I went into the theater and sat down, I was like, *Wow!* I got it instantly. And suddenly I was in the most celebrated film of the year, and it did certainly, irrevocably change my life.

"I'd adore revisiting that character," she adds. "I'd be fascinated to see how that relationship continues: Whether we were married and divorced, or whether we were just old friends, or if some later adventure brings us back together…"

"You still never know what the mood of the audience is going to be when the film is released," Harrison Ford says. "So I was very pleased at the amount of success that we had with it."

As box-office receipts accumulated, early concerns about the film's cost disappeared. According to a consolidated budget dated August 13, 1981, in the Lucasfilm Archives, the final tally for

ADMIT ONE

LUCASFILM LTD. INVITES YOU TO A SCREENING OF

RAIDERS of the LOST ARK.

Paramount Studios
5451 Marathon Street
Los Angeles, CA
(Enter on Melrose at Windsor)
2 Lights East of Gower

June 4, 1981
8:00 pm

RAIDERS OF THE LOST ARK
Questionnaire
Northpoint Theater
May 9, 1981

1) ___ Male
   ___ Female   Under 10 11-15 16-20 21-25 26-35 36-45 46-55 56 &
2) List in order of preference your favorite scenes (number 1 is your favorite, number 2 is...
3) What did you especially like about the movie?
   Why?
4) Was there anything you disliked about the movie?
   Why?
5) What is your all-time favorite film?
6) How often do you go to the movies?

STEVEN SPIELBERG   c/o MGM STUDIOS
                          10202 N WASHINGTON BLVD.
                          CULVER CITY
                          LA 90230

DEAR STEVE
FROM ALL OF US ARCHEOLOGISTS YOU LEFT BEHIND IN LONDON.
GOOD LUCK ON OSCAR NIGHT. I HAVE A FEELING YOU'LL WIN.
REMEMBER BE CAREFUL, DON'T MAKE A FOOL OUT OF YOURSELF,
THERE WILL BE EIGHTY MILLION PEOPLE WATCHING.
BEST WISHES
G.L.

ILM   BEN BURTT   70 PARK WRL, SAN ANSELM
      RICHARD ANDERSON   CA 94960.

WITH YOUR TALENT AND DEDICATION THE ARK HAS BEEN FOUND.
CONGRATULATIONS ON WINNING SPECIAL AWARD FOR SOUND EFFECTS EDITING.
BEST - G.L.

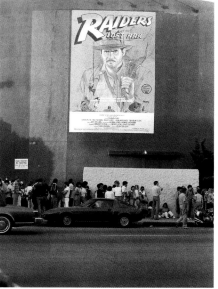

Academy Awards

Raiders was $22,778,581, or $2,187,963 over budget (a circa-1983 document puts the total slightly higher at $22,805,758). Notable overruns in special effects, set construction, location costs, and transportation had created overages totaling $2,336,812. Above-the-line costs, though—script, producer, director, and principal cast—actually came in $148,849 *under* budget.

"Having been a bloody veteran of the overinflated-budgets era," Spielberg says, "I can tell you there is really something good to be said for the era when there was healthy collaboration between producers and directors. I probably sound like the enemy, but there are some directors who definitely have to have a very strong hand working with them."

By summer's end *Raiders* had outstripped *Superman II* and all competitors with $125,254,773 in 88 days. By October 5 it had become Paramount's biggest film ever, surpassing *Grease* (1978), with more than $135 million—and it was still playing in 621 theaters. By April 7, 1982, *Raiders of the Lost Ark* had become the fourth-highest-grossing picture in the history of cinema, behind *Star Wars*, *Jaws*, and *The Empire Strikes Back*.

ABOVE LEFT: Lines in front of a theater featuring Amsel's artwork. "I have vivid memories of seeing *Raiders of the Lost Ark*," says future screenwriter David Koepp. "I was eighteen years old. I went in to Milwaukee to see some movie that was sold out, but they were having a sneak preview of *Raiders*, which I'd never heard of. We said, 'Let's see the movie with the funny title instead.'" ABOVE RIGHT: A page from the Lucasfilm 1982 yearbook features the film's Oscar winners. *Raiders of the Lost Ark* was nominated for best director (Spielberg), picture (Marshall), cinematography (Slocombe), and score (Williams). It won Academy Awards for art direction (Reynolds, Les Dilley, and Michael Ford), editing (Michael Kahn), sound (Bill Varney, Steve Maslow, Greg Landaker, Roy Charman), and a special achievement award for sound effects editing (Ben Burtt and Richard L. Anderson). Richard Edlund, Kit West, Bruce Nicholson, and Joe Johnston also won for best visual effects, beating out another ILM film—*Dragonslayer*.

LEFT: *Raiders* became a sensation, making the covers of several magazines; it was parodied, made into a comic book, and of course released all over the world: *Newsweek*, September 28, 1981; *MAD Magazine*, January 1982; *Rolling Stone*, June 25, 1981; the Marvel comic-book adaptation; and the Japanese poster for the film—a source of bemusement for Harrison Ford, as it focused on Spielberg and Lucas, such was their fame in that country. A letter from Howard Kazanjian to Lucasfilm marketing executive Sid Ganis, on October 21, 1981, requested that his department do a better job of keeping Ford in the loop.

CHAPTER 6

TEMPLE OF DEATH

BELOW: The lobby card for *Gunga Din* (1939), a major inspiration for *Indy II*.

OPPOSITE ABOVE: Another page from the 1982 Lucasfilm yearbook was titled "The Further Adventures of Indiana Jones," and featured yearbook-like photos of producer Frank Marshall, Robert Watts, *Indy II* screenwriters Gloria Katz and Willard Huyck, Spielberg, and Kathy Kennedy. BELOW: That same title would be used for an ongoing *Indiana Jones* comic book produced by Marvel, which kept fans of the new hero satisfied with monthly adventures for several years. Also shown is the stat and final color painting for an early story called "The Sentinel."

Looking back on *Raiders* it's clear that Lucas had gathered, in terms of American-Anglo cinema, an Olympian team—Spielberg, Ford, Williams, Slocombe, Marshall, Kennedy, Watts, Burtt, and many others—nearly all of whom would continue on *Indy II*.

"I can't even really speculate about Indy's next adventure," Kasdan says, "because *Raiders* doesn't have that many loose ends. My script left it open for Abner Ravenwood to return, but I recently learned that George Lucas thinks he might make the next two *Indiana Jones* pictures prequels."

"We had all signed on for three movies," Marshall says. "That's what I liked about it: We had already decided to make three movies when we were making *Raiders*. We didn't make the movie and then when it was successful say, 'Oh, we need to make a sequel.' We'd already said, 'We're committed and we're gonna make these three movies.'"

Ford's contract stated the terms for the next two films, while Spielberg's, as noted, gave him an option to direct both follow-ups. However, before work on the second *Indy* film could begin, Spielberg and Lucas had to attend to other projects. The latter continued work on what had begun simultaneously with *Raiders*: the third *Star Wars* film, *Return of the Jedi*. Lucas also consolidated his company's Northern California location by moving Lucasfilm corporate into buildings designated A and B on Kerner Boulevard in San Rafael, next to ILM, and oversaw continued construction on Skywalker Ranch.

For his part Spielberg had already dived straight into *E.T.*, seemingly impervious to the trials of *Raiders*. "On a film the people involved become his family," his sister Anne Spielberg says. "He loves them, and he hates for it to be done and to leave everyone. That's why he goes from one thing to the next."

"When George and I were in Hawaii, George said that if I directed the first one, I'd need to direct three of them," Spielberg says, "because he had three stories in mind. That was assuming the first warranted a second, and so on. So I shook his hand and promised to do three movies. Well, two months after *Raiders* opened we knew we were going to have to sit down in a room to figure out what *Raiders II* was going to be—but it turned out George did not have three stories in mind. We had to make up the subsequent stories."

"The original story was about a haunted castle in Scotland," Lucas says. "But Steven said, 'Aw, I just made *Poltergeist* [1982], I don't want to do that again.' And that's when we started working with Bill [Willard] Huyck and Gloria Katz."

Lucas had already worked with the couple on the shooting scripts for both *American Graffiti* and *Star Wars*, and they had concocted the story and script for a film still in development called *Radioland Murders*. After more conversations with Spielberg, Lucas transformed the Scottish haunted house into a demonic temple in India. Spielberg then joined Lucas, Huyck, and Katz for a four-day story meeting in the spring of 1982, about a year after the release of *Raiders*. For the second *Indy* film, in addition to new set pieces,

GUNGA DIN

INSPIRED BY RUDYARD KIPLING'S HEROIC LINES, starring

CARY GRANT · VICTOR McLAGLEN

DOUGLAS FAIRBANKS, JR.

SAM JAFFE · EDUARDO CIANNELLI · JOAN FONTAINE

PANDRO S. BERMAN IN CHARGE OF PRODUCTION
PRODUCED AND DIRECTED BY GEORGE STEVENS

Out of the stirring glory of Kipling's India they roar . . .
Three fighting, loving, swaggering sons of the British Battalions!

Robert Watts

Gloria Katz & Willard Huyck

Steven Spielberg

Kathy Kennedy

Frank Marshall

The Further Adventures of Indiana Jones

they would recycle many ideas from the initial brainstorming sessions for the first film.

"George told us that he and Steven wanted to set the next *Indy* film in India," Willard Huyck says. "And he knew of our interest in India. We had traveled there, we were collecting Indian art and so forth, and I think that's why he came to us."

"We were really looking at *Gunga Din*," Gloria Katz says of the 1939 film starring Cary Grant and Douglas Fairbanks Jr., who fight Thuggees on the subcontinent.

"George said that it was going to be a very dark film," Spielberg says. "The way *Empire Strikes Back* was the dark second act of the *Star Wars* trilogy. So George came up with this idea along with Gloria Katz and Willard Huyck that it was going to be about the Kali cult, with black magic and things that I personally find very spooky.

"In many ways the visual style of the film was conceived when George first told me the story," he adds, "which was a very rough sketch of the movie he wanted us to help him construct. I heard a couple of things—Thuggees, temple of death, voodoo,

and human sacrifices—so what came to mind immediately was torchlight, long shadows, and red lava light. I wanted to paint a dark picture of an inner sanctum."

"Steven was the most wonderful director to work for," Katz says, "because you could write up the most outlandish piece of action that you could ever imagine and he would say, 'Oh, this is great!'"

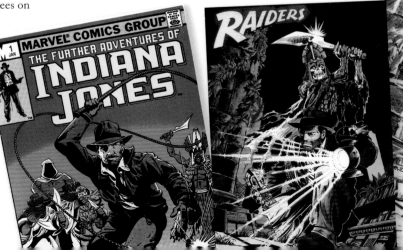

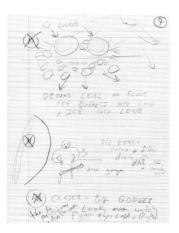

MYSTERY HOUNDS

As Kasdan had noted, the sequel would be a prequel, taking place a year before *Raiders*, in 1935. Following the four-day conference, as he had for the previous movie, Lucas wrote a story treatment based on their sessions. Titled *Indiana Jones and the Temple of Death*, it runs 20 typed pages and is dated May 30, 1982. In it Lucas lays out essentially what would become the film. Notable elements that were transposed from the first to the second *Indy* movie include a big brawl in Shanghai (enhanced by a dance number moved over from *Radioland Murders*); an inflatable-raft escape from an airplane; giant vats of water overturned to create a mini tsunami; and a mine-car race through narrow tunnels, which Spielberg specifically wanted to revive. Even its title, *Temple of Death*, can be traced back to the name of the hidden Peruvian temple, House of Death.

Another revived idea concerned an aspect of Indy that was more James Bond–like. "Originally there were three parts to his life," Kasdan says. "He was this tweedy academic and he was the leather-clad, whip-snapping adventurer. George also had this idea that he was a playboy at night, dressed in a tuxedo, and went to nightclubs. For *Raiders* we dropped the sophisticated part, his nightclub life. But these were ideas that eventually shook themselves out and showed up in the next two films."

"There was an homage to James Bond, in the conceit that the *Bond* movies often start with an action sequence from another story," Huyck says. "George wanted to open like that, and then go into a second story."

"George's idea was to start the movie with a musical number," Spielberg says. "He wanted to do a Busby Berkeley dance number where Willie Scott would come out singing. At all of our story meetings he would say, 'Hey, Steven, you always said you wanted to shoot musicals. You're a frustrated musical director.' So I thought, *Yeah, that could be fun.*"

The tale's MacGuffins were Sankara stones, which, according to ancient history, became magical when the Hindu god Shiva touched them. "We had a lot of incidents that were taken from the first script," Lucas says. "But for the life of me I couldn't think of another MacGuffin that I thought would work. Eventually we landed on the Sankara stones."

"We came up with this religious cult that had appropriated the stones and was doing evil things," Huyck says. "And then we asked ourselves, 'Well, what kind of evil things? Steven wants a mine, so who is working in the mines?'"

"What is, aside from the stones, the most valuable thing that the village could have?" Katz asks.

"And we said, 'Children,'" answers Huyck.

Continuing the theme, Indy was also supplied with his own 10-year-old sidekick, a Chinese orphan named Short Round. Arguably the hero of the second film, he drives the getaway car, defends Willie, figures out how

to cure Indy, and saves the Maharajah, who calls in the cavalry. He was also named after a pet, in the tradition started by Lucas, while Willie was named after Spielberg's cocker spaniel.

"Short Round was indeed the name of our dog," Katz says. "It was the name of a character in an old Samuel Fuller movie called *The Steel Helmet* [1951]."

Willard Huyck and Gloria Katz signed their contract on June 1, 1982. Dated August 1, 1982, their first draft followed Lucas's story treatment faithfully; their revised first draft, dated September 13, 1982, arrived shortly thereafter.

"There was this narrow window of opportunity where Steven could direct this movie," Huyck says. "George said, 'Guys, you've really got to write it fast.' So we wrote it very quickly and got it to Steven. He said, 'My God, it's done already?'"

Spielberg liked the script enough to commit, and contractual negotiations began in earnest. "There was a point there where Steven said, 'That was fun. Let's do it again,'" Lucas says.

Lucasfilm researcher Debbie Fine made several comments on her copy of the first draft. She noted that the Maharajah would not partake of monkey brain, and that the torture scenes were "violent." Indeed that remark would be repeated by others and would have consequences throughout the film's life.

"The story ended up being a lot darker than we intended it to be," Lucas says. "Part of it is that I was going through a divorce at the time, and I wasn't in a good mood; and part of it was just that we wanted to do something a little bit more edgy."

JUNGLE SHADOWS

E.T.: The Extra-Terrestrial was released in the summer of 1982 and rapidly became the most successful film of all time, leapfrogging *Star Wars*, but Spielberg by then had turned his attention to *Twilight Zone: The Movie*, which he was co-producing and for which he was directing one of the four segments.

In November 1982 Frank Marshall and Robert Watts went on a location-scouting trip. Both had moved up in rank, to executive producer and producer, respectively. "When we heard that it was going to be set in India," Marshall says, "we started making our treks there to look for locations and to start the process of getting permission to shoot."

They settled on a palace in Jaipur, for which they scheduled three days. "Originally the scenes were going to be shot in India at a fantastic palace," Marshall says. "They required us to give them a script, so we sent it over and we didn't think it was going to be a problem. But because of the voodoo element with Mola Ram and the Thuggees, the Indian government was a little bit hesitant to give us permission. They wanted us to do things like not use the term *Maharajah*, and they didn't want us to shoot in a particular

DAGGER MAGICALLY - SLOWLY RISES FROM SLEEVE TO HAND.

INDY TAPS MOLA RAM AND THEN DROPS THE STONES.

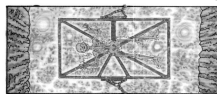

.... THE BURNING SKELETON OF CHATTER LAL .

temple that we had picked. The Indian government wanted changes in the script and final cut."

"I was beginning to get bogged down in a kind of bureaucracy that's extremely difficult when you're a filmmaker with limited time and flexibility," Watts says. "So I rang George and said, 'Look, the only thing we haven't got in Sri Lanka is the Maharajah's palace. How about a nice couple of matte shots and building the courtyard on the back lot?' He agreed, and then I took it to Steven. He agreed as well. The bigger problem was, *How are we going to do the rope bridge?*"

Other recces were taken, with production designer Elliot Scott joining the hunt, because Reynolds was busy with the third *Star Wars* film. Scott had actually helped budget the sets for the first *Star Wars*, so he had known Lucas since 1975. "Norman recommended Elliot, because Elliot was the one that had trained Norman and production designer John Barry," Lucas says. "He was like the grand old man."

"We started looking and we found Sri Lanka," Marshall continues. "Not many people had shot in Sri Lanka, but we were all very adventurous in those days and we loved the challenge of going to a place that nobody had ever been to before. And Elliot Scott found this little village…"

Marshall, Watts, and Scott recorded their findings on video, enabling Spielberg and Lucas to approve each location without leaving the United States. In fact, it turned out that Sri Lanka had a small local film industry that was producing between 30 and 35 films a year, which provided a talent pool for Marshall and Watts. "We found everything we needed," Marshall says, "including a jungle, a river, and a gorge, all in one spot—which is always your goal when scouting locations. And it's always easier when you work in a small country. There's less bureaucracy, and the government is more eager to help because they appreciate getting motion pictures."

Watts and company even found a team of British engineers who happened to be constructing a dam a few hundred yards downriver (the Balfour Beatty Nuttal Victoria project), and they were hired on the spot. "Building our bridge was a lark for them," Watts says.

Back in the States, Spielberg worked with Scott and his storyboard artists Andrew Probert and Phil Norwood; Joe Johnston and Stanley Fleming would again tackle the VFX (visual effects) boards. "I start with generic illustrations of principal master shots, which gives me a geographical floor plan of how to pace the sequences and break them down into cuts," Spielberg says. "I use that master shot to pick my angles. I had about ten master shots, and then Elliot Scott caught up with me by building these elaborate miniatures of all the sets. So rather than having to work from a flat piece of paper one-dimensionally, I could take my Nikon with a 50-millimeter macro lens, get right down into a 17-inch cardboard set with half-inch cardboard characters, and photograph angles."

THE TEMPLE QUEEN

At the outset of 1983 several pieces of the sequel puzzle came together in fairly rapid succession. On January 1, Paramount and Lucasfilm ratified the film's modified 106-page-long production-distribution contract. On February 1, Spielberg signed a Director's Employment Agreement between Amblin Enterprises and the studio. Lucas signed his executive producer contract the same day.

A newcomer to the production was costume designer Anthony Powell, a three-time Academy Award winner (*Travels with My Aunt*, *Death on the Nile*, and *Tess*). The search was on, too, for newcomers to play Willie Scott and Short Round. As before the casting process was exhaustive, and yet no one had been found—and time was running out.

Casting director Mike Fenton was complaining about just that fact one morning while jogging in Tarzana with William Morris agent Peter Meyers. Fenton had yet to find a female lead for *Indy II*, after at least 120 actresses had tried out for the part, so Meyers suggested a new client of his. According to a newspaper article at the time, when Kate Capshaw found out a few days later that Spielberg wanted to talk to her about the role, she put down the phone and started to scream. In reality she was more reserved.

"I got a phone call from my agent saying the sequel to *Raiders of the Lost Ark* was being cast and, 'They would love to meet you,'" Capshaw says. "But I was looking at foreign films and little art films, and being a very serious actor studying in Manhattan; I was not interested in doing a sequel. I expressed that to my agent, who, in hindsight, was very patient and tolerant of my judgment and arrogance. And so we set a time to meet Steven."

"I looked at a lot of possible *Indy* girls," Spielberg says. "I really wanted to bring back Marion but George and I discussed it and we ultimately decided there should be a different Indiana Jones lady in each of the three films."

Years earlier, after earning her master's, Capshaw had left a job teaching people with learning disabilities to pursue a modeling career in New York City. Her first break as an actress had occurred when she read for a small role in *A Little Sex* (1982): Director Bruce Paltrow decided to give her the lead role instead. Of course a starring role in the second *Indiana Jones* film could be another big break, and by the time Capshaw came in for her interview, she had changed her mind about the part. But her enthusiasm quickly turned to anxiety when she met Spielberg.

"I went into his office on the Warner Bros. lot," Capshaw says. "He was sitting with his back to me. When I came into view, he looked at me and said, 'Oh, you're not who I thought you were.' I thought, *Great!* Then I found myself thinking, *Maybe I can make this work for me…*"

Though she was asked to sit on a couch that faced him—"I felt like I was a mile away"—she moved to the edge of a marble fireplace that was

OPPOSITE LEFT: Spielberg's written notes and sketches related to the mine-car chase and new action in the nightclub, during which a large diamond becomes mixed up with spilled ice. OPPOSITE BOTTOM AND BELOW: Storyboards by Andrew G. Probert include a Mola Ram who uses a knife concealed in his sleeve.

INDY'S WAITING—   A BACK SWING AND FORWARD TO…

SB-33c

THUGEE #2 ANSWERS BY ELIMINATING INDY'S THREAT.

THUGEE SCRAMBLES UP HILL.

PAN UP TO REVEAL REINFORCEMENTS.   PULL BACK PAST INDY—HE TURNS…

INDIANA JONES AND THE TEMPLE OF DEATH

FIRST DRAFT AND REVISED FIRST-DRAFT SUMMARY

AUGUST 1 AND SEPTEMBER 13, 1982

[Note: This summary highlights the differences between the early drafts by Gloria Katz and Willard Huyck and the final film.]

The prequel begins in a nightclub named Shanghai Paradise with a ten-year-old Chinese "street urchin" named Short Round. He sneaks into the club, watches the dancers, and then leaves as a man in a tuxedo enters. It's Indiana Jones. In the fight that ensues, the ashes of Emperor Nurhachi are strewn in the face of Lao She, a crime lord. Dragged along by Indy, Willie Scott boards the plane only because Lao She's gunman opens fire on her with a Thompson machine gun; in the revised first draft she takes the plane because an extra ticket has become available thanks to the death of Wu Han, Indy's friend, in the club:

WILLIE: I'll take the extra ticket.
(grabbing it from Indy)
Where's this plane going anyway?

INDIANA: Siam.

WILLIE: Siam? But I'm not dressed for Siam....

Their transport is attacked by two biplanes in the service of Lao She. As the dogfight intensifies, Willie and Short Round struggle to wake up Jones, but the poison and the antidote have combined to make him sleep deeply. The plane's passengers bail out, along with the copilot; the pilot is shot dead by the biplanes. Short Round and Willie are bickering over the last parachute when the fighters attack again; a stray bullet hits a fire extinguisher, which sprays into Indy's face, waking him up. As he takes in the situation, Short Round manages to set up a machine gun on a tripod and, with Willie feeding him ammunition, shoots down one of the biplanes. He also swivels the gun around and destroys one of the DC-3's own engines—their engine.

Indy grabs the life raft for their escape, but Willie screams: "Are you crazy, a life raft?! We're not *sinking*, we're *crashing*!"

They end up in a wilderness and—after spotting a menacing "seven-hundred-pound Bengal tiger"—Indy notes

that they're in India. The tiger is driven away by a Shaman. On the way to Pankot Palace, Indy has a fight with a crocodile. As the trio gets to know one another, we learn that Short Round's parents were killed during the bombing of Shanghai.

WILLIE: When my nightclub career was run over by the Depression, some pinhead convinced me that "a girl could go places in the Orient..." So, look where I got.

As they approach the cursed palace, their guide makes an excuse and leaves to sell his elephants. Short Round, who has grown attached to a baby pachyderm, wipes a tear from his eye.

In Pankot Palace the roles of Captain Phillip Blumburtt (who would be played by Philip Stone) and Chattar Lal are larger than in the final film. The British captain is clearly at the palace to investigate. The power of the voodoo dolls—the "krtya"—is explained as giving one complete control over one's enemies. The role of the Maharajah is also larger, with Jones teaching him how to use the bullwhip. The Maharajah and Short Round vie for Indy's attention, actually fighting over the whip when...

The little Maharajah's eyes begin glowing yellow and he hisses softly in a strange voice. Nobody else sees or hears the bizarre transformation...

Indeed, anyone who has drunk the blood of Kali has yellow eyes off and on—including the assassin who attacks Indy in his room. Indy then goes into Willie's room when she screams because of a bug crawling up her arm. Noticing insects emerging from an opening in the wall, the trio finds a secret passageway. After several close calls, they discover a hidden temple. Following the ceremony, Indy investigates and is captured, but Willie escapes thanks to Short Round's fighting abilities.

Willie makes it back to the palace, where Chattar Lal makes light of her story so that Blumburtt doesn't believe her. Her case isn't helped when Indy returns, apparently unharmed.

The British troops ride away, with Blumburtt noting that his report will list nothing unusual at Pankot Palace. Even Willie thinks that Indy is okay—until they kiss and she sees that his eyes are glowing yellow.

He abducts her and all progresses as in the final film. When Indy confronts the slave overlord, he says:

INDIANA: Listen, I'm from the union and I'd like to talk about the working conditions here. Could you step inside a minute?

After a chase in the mine tunnels, when the giant water urn is overturned, they descend a waterslide that deposits them in a larger tunnel. At the climax the British return and face the zombie-like enemy on the opposite cliff:

Across the gorge, Kali fanatics have climbed up into the trees and are holding onto branches in crucifixion-like poses—while below them other guards bend the trees back with ropes—the trees bow backwards and become catapults! A Kali Ma priest yells and the ropes are released—the fanatics in the trees are catapulted through the air, hurtling across the gorge like human missiles.

When the trio returns to the Indian village, they are riding horses (though Lucas notes in his first draft that they should be in a car).

Short Round runs toward the sunset, toward the three elephants being brought back to the village. The baby elephant starts walking faster, as if he recognizes Short Round running out to meet him...

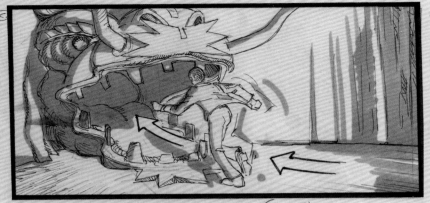

ROUND PAST CAM INTO DRAGONS MOUTH... (CUT TO)

CAM PANS THEM ROUND TILL THEY'RE DIRECTLY IN FRONT OF DRAGON FIRING INTO ITS MOUTH.

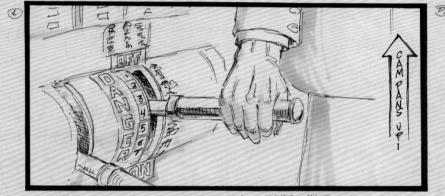

BACKSTAGE... ANGLE ON CONTROL PANEL... INDYS HAND IS GRASPING THE FLAME CONTROL LEVER... PAN UP TO SHOW...

SN-108A

SUDDENLY FLAME BURSTS FROM DRAGONS MOUTH... (CUT TO)

SN-109D

AE-21 A

AE-24

TOP AND RIGHT: Storyboards by Edward Verreaux show Indy fleeing into the mouth of the dragon in the Shanghai Paradise club and activating flames that roast his pursuers; the boards also show passengers parachuting out of a plane when it is attacked by fighters, which Short Round and Willie blast with a mounted machine gun. ABOVE: Lucas and Spielberg during the making of the latter's E.T., circa 1981.

WIDE CROSS S.H. AS SHORTROUND FIRES OUT OPEN DOOR... (CUT TO)

AE-65

AE-53

RIGHT: Concept sketches by production designer Elliot Scott for the Mayapore village, barren and rejuvenated (1981), and (BELOW) the Thuggee temple.

closer to the director. "I think there was something about my doing that that he liked. After talking for a while, Steven showed me how to play a new video game.

"I went home, and got a call immediately from my agent saying, 'He'd like for you to read some sides [script excerpts] and he'll put you on tape.' I was so nervous," Capshaw says, describing the next meeting. "I stood there talking away while Steven fiddled with a video camera in the corner, getting it ready. Finally I said, 'When do we start?' And he said, 'We've started. I've been taping you for 15 minutes.'"

"I took her tape from that reading, and I thought she was absolutely Willie," Spielberg says. "She wasn't that character in real life but she had the energy for that girl. I remember taking the tape over to Harrison's house that night and saying, 'Look I've got about 20 girls on tape. But I only want to show you one.' And I put Kate in, and he said, 'She's the one.'"

Spielberg cast Capshaw, with Lucas's blessing, and she signed her contract on March 1, 1983. "I remember the day I took the script home, after I found out I would do the film," Capshaw says. Apart from studying her role, she was looking for spots that would allow her time to come back to the United States from location—scenes she wasn't in—but she began to get antsy

because Willie was on every page. "I kept thinking, *Maybe she dies soon*."

To help her prepare for the role, Spielberg had Capshaw watch a number of films, including *The African Queen* (1951) with Katharine Hepburn and *A Guy Named Joe* (1943) with Irene Dunne (which Spielberg would later remake as *Always*, 1989).

The role of Indy's sidekick went to Ke Huy Quan, whom Spielberg found in Los Angeles, his metaphorical backyard, after talent scouts had scoured the world. Born in Saigon, and having lived there until he was six, Quan had spent the last six years in the United States. "Basically they had an open call in my elementary school," Quan says. "All the kids that fit the description were called into a room to meet this casting director, Mike Fenton. My brother went in, and I accompanied him."

"Ke actually didn't show up to do the interview," Kennedy says. "He brought his brother. But the entire time that he was trying to tell his brother what to do, we kept looking at him—until we finally said, 'Who *is* this kid?' and we asked him to audition. We then ran to the phone, called Steven, and said, 'We think we found him.'"

"After my brother's audition Mike wanted to see me as well," Quan says. "My English was horrible, but I read the lines from the sides and I thought I

LEFT: Recce photos taken in India of potential palace and nightclub locations. ABOVE: Research photos taken of a small derelict roller coaster, which would help the construction and design departments build tracks for the mine-car chase at Elstree Studios.

65c

BLACK SK[...]

Black Robe to
the ground

Ran up from
the ground

65d

as the
John Coveralled
(Indian) very spooked
a la RAM

APPLIQUÉ FOR BELT BUCKLE.

The sketch above was a suggestion
by Steven for Mola Ram. I
developed it into the sketch on the
right, but when the part was
finally cast the design was adapted
again to fit the actor.

AR[...]

PENDANT

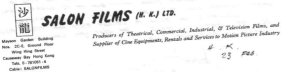

OHAN TROUGH WILL ALSO BE STRAIGHT — NO CORNERS.
IN THE SPADE'S BASE. SEE WHAT YOU CAN DO.
IDEALLY SOMETHING LIKE

12'   6'6"

M.R. LIES DOWN AND ROLLS AGAINST THE (SAY) BOT-
HURTS TRAP WHICH OPENS MORE THAN 90°. ALLOW-
HIM TO CONTINUE ACROSS AND DOWN OUT OF SIGH-
A CHUTE.   TEMPLE
THE WHOLE 'STAGE' ON THE SKETCHES SUGGEST
SIZE OF COVENT GARDEN. SEE IF YOU CAN W-
IT (MOAT TO STATUE) BY 3' N 4' WITHOUT LOS-
THE STUDIO TANK AREA. AND I DON'T WANT TO   THE
THE MOAT   MAYBE SLIGHTLY WIDEN IT.
SWING BRIDGE OUT. NO BRIDGE AT ALL. TH-
SIDE FLOOR MAY HAVE TO BE ADJUSTED NOW
HAS SHOTS LOOKING BACK AT IT.   BUT THIS
AFFECT THE SET GENERALLY.   AND THEY HAVE
2 ENTRANCES/EXITS

沙龍 SALON FILMS (H. K.) LTD.

Mayson Garden Building
Nos. 2C-E, Ground Floor
Wing Hing Street
Causeway Bay, Hong Kong
Tels. S-781051 - 4
Cable: SALONFILMS
Hong Kong
Telex: 76303 SALON HX

Producers of Theatrical, Commercial, Industrial, & Television Films, and
Supplier of Cine Equipments, Rentals and Services to Motion Picture Industry

H. K.
23 FEB.

DEAR ROGER,   ENCLOSE A FEW THOUGHTS

TO AUGMENT THE PHONE CONVERSATION I HAD WITH
ALAN.
        YOU WILL HAVE GATHERED THAT THE
MINE AREA IS THE MOST   AS FAR AS PRODUCTION
GO. STEVEN HAS NO CRITICISM OF THE PRESENT PET-
HE JUST WANTS MORE AND THIS WILL HAVE TO
AWAIT MY RETURN. BUT IT IS CLEAR FROM ABOUT
HIS SKETCHES THAT HE DOES HOPE FOR ABOUT
4 LINES OF CHILDREN ABOVE ONE ANOTHER WHEN
SEEN IN LONG SHOT. HE KNOWS THAT THEY WILL
MOSTLY BE WORKING ON INCLINED FACES — NOT
HORIZONTAL AS HIS SKETCHES. PLEASE DISCUSS THIS
WITH STEPHEN (WHO ALREADY HAS DONE A LOT TOWARDS
THE MODEL) TO SEE IF HE CAN

Mines (inc. Temple of Doom)
Thugee guards + children

not necessarily
same both
sides — can
be twisted.

dulled
blade.

HARDY

P.52

HARRISON FORD CUFFLINKS. (ANCIENT EGYPTIAN EYE OF
HORUS — AGAINST
EVIL EYE.)

27 MM.

VIEL

SARLAND + WHITE

BODICE

BRAIDING

SKIRT

was horrible. After that I didn't think much of it. At the time, I just wanted to learn English and be a doctor."

"I saw his videotape and the search stopped at that moment," Spielberg says. "Even though he didn't understand his English 100 percent, I just loved his personality. I thought he was like a 50-year-old man trapped in this 12-year-old's body. He had an old soul. He had ancient eyes and a beautiful smile and a great willingness to do it all."

"A few days later we got a call from Steven's office, asking me to go meet him," Quan says. "My mom dressed me up in a three-piece suit. But when I walked in, Steven took a look at me and said, 'We'd love for you to come back the next day, but when you do, be very casual.' So I went back in jeans and a shirt, and I auditioned with Harrison. Steven told me what he wanted, what the scene was about, and then he just let me say whatever I wanted. After that, he told me I got the part."

OPPOSITE ABOVE: The genesis of Mola Ram, from sketches by Spielberg to a 1983 concept sketch by costume designer Anthony Powell (his note on the second reads: "The sketch done was a suggestion by Steven for Mola Ram. I developed it into the sketch on the right, but when the part was finally cast, the design was adapted again to fit the actor"). MIDDLE: Following a phone conversation with Alan Casie, Frank Marshall wrote a letter (dated February 23, 1983) to art director Roger Cain discussing Mola Ram's secret getaway within the Temple of Death (Salon Films was part of the location shoot in Macao). BELOW: Costume sketches and concepts by Powell.

ABOVE LEFT: A reference photo of dancing girls. ABOVE: Costume sketches for Willie by Powell, along with fabric swatches—and a photo of Kate Capshaw in Willie's nightclub gown (LEFT). "I met with Anthony Powel about the costumes," Capshaw says. "And we really thought Willie should be a redhead—a flaming redhead. But George couldn't get his head around the redhead. He wanted her blond. So Steven and I went to the beauty parlor. It took hours and hours and hours, and he sat with me, with foils in my hair, and he was very patient—and I got very, very blond."

BELOW: Costume fabric reference for Short Round and Indiana Jones. "I found this wonderful 1937 book of photographs by Henri Cartier Bresson, which he took in Shanghai in 1937 when everybody was leaving the city," says Anthony Powell. "And my recollection is that I found a photograph of a little Chinese boy that gave me the idea for the way Short Round should look." RIGHT: A production maquette of the Pankot Palace exterior, which had to be constructed when India as a location proved unworkable.

OPPOSITE ABOVE: Reference photos of weapons to be used and an old vehicle with a California license plate for a chase through the streets of Shanghai. BELOW: Production designer Elliot Scott stands next to one of the mine cars to be used at Elstree; a blueprint for the temple interior statue.

Quan's legal papers—his contract and documents related to the fact that he was still a minor—were all signed in early April 1983. "I had never seen *Star Wars* or *Raiders*, never seen *Jaws*," he says. "So when I met Steven, Harrison, and George, I didn't know who they were. I guess it helped in a way."

Filling out the cast were two well-known Indian actors. For bad guy Mola Ram, Spielberg chose Amrish Puri, who at the time was working simultaneously on two movies, as actors often do in Bollywood, one in the morning and one in the afternoon. "We did have trouble working around his incredible schedule," Marshall says.

"At the time, I had come through a kind of second rebirth," says Roshan Seth, who would play corrupt minister Chattar Lal. "Years before, I had given up acting. I had gone back to India and was editing a journal. But Richard Attenborough pulled me out to do *Gandhi* [1982]. I did it, I went back to the journal. Then in 1982 David Hare, the great playwright, offered me a wonderful role I couldn't say no to. So I gave up the journal and returned to acting."

As casting was wrapped up, so was the rest of preproduction. The first storyboards had been finished circa February 1983. Sequences were revised by March 25; additional boards reveal that Short Round's machine-gun battle with the biplanes was deleted from the film on April 5. For their part Willard Huyck and Gloria Katz finished revisions on the shooting script dated March 1 and April 10. By the latter date, just eight days before the onset of principal photography, the title movie of the movie had been changed to *Indiana Jones and the Temple of Doom*.

SHORT ROUND

TEMPLE + MINE CAR (PRINCIPAL)

CAP + NAVY PEAK

SHIRT

TROUSER

INDY

MINE CAR (PRINCIPAL)

SHIRT

TRS.

THOMPSON SUB MACHINE GUN .45 CALIBRE AUTOMATIC
1ST USED BY CHINESE GANG LEADER WHO WAS SITTING IN PASSENGER
FRONT SEAT OF PURSUIT CAR

INDIANA JONES AND THE TEMPLE OF DOOM

SHOOTING SCRIPT SUMMARY

APRIL 10, 1983

Primarily the same as the first draft, this version by Katz and Huyck has a few notable changes: Short Round is now 12 years old; the escape on the life raft from the plane ends up in a river, which becomes white-water rapids. And as they head to Pankot Palace, Willie has a run-in with a boa constrictor while bathing in the river:

WILLIE: Indy! Help me!

INDIANA: Don't worry, I'm coming in! What is it?

WILLIE: A snake!

Indiana freezes and a strange look crosses his face—

INDIANA: A what…?

Willie suddenly screams as the boa constrictor wraps around her arm […]

INDIANA: Don't let it pull you deeper!

WILLIE: It's pulling me deeper!

INDIANA: Don't let it curl around you!

WILLIE: It's curling around me! Damn it, stop talking and do something!

From the sidelines, Indy manages to coach Willie into petting the snake on the head, inducing it to fall asleep and release her. She emerges from the water "and hauls off and punches him in the mouth."

WILLIE: Thanks for nothing! I hate snakes!

INDIANA: I know the feeling…

After the dinner at Pankot Palace, a new scene takes place in its gardens, where the men smoke cigars and Indy talks to Captain Blumburtt.

INDIANA: Even if they were trying to scare us away, a devout Hindu would never touch meat. (looking around)
Makes you wonder what these people are…

Later when Indy is under the spell, his attack on Willie in her room is much more violent:

…his face slowly comes toward the mosquito netting […] he starts hissing grotesquely, smoke billows out of his mouth and the mosquito netting burns open to expose his terrifying face. Willie screams!! She sees Indiana moving toward her ranting incoherently as he smashes a vase out of his way—

INDIANA: Kali knows!… [There have] been too many lies—there's not god's heaven—just—the

horror! I've seen it—life preying on life! […] rivers-destroying mountains—a comet in space—exploding! […] the hate—the greed—always greed! […] Don't you understand—Kali is freedom!

And now the script provides an explanation for how Short Round discovers that burning people can bring them out of the zombie-like trance: When he is a prisoner and digging with the other child slaves, they accidentally trigger a small lava flow, which spurts onto a guard's legs; when Short Round helps douse the flames, he notices that the burning has brought the guard back to his senses. "The pain—the pain makes him wake up!"

Finally, as Mola Ram and Indy are fighting on the collapsed bridge, when the burning Sankara stones touch Ram's flesh as they fall, he too exits the nightmare just before plummeting to his death.

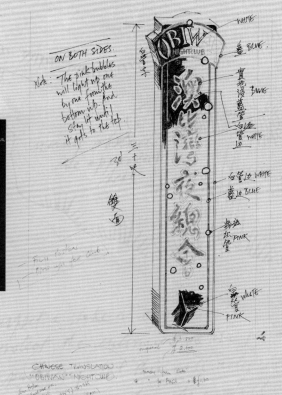

ADD 2 MORE BLINDS.

= CLUB WINDOW NOT SEEN.

INDY WILLIE GONG ETC
- OVER BALCONY ONTO BLIND
- ROLL ONTO SECOND BLIND

MAKE NEW ENTRANCE CANOPY
NEON SIGN ?

SHANGHAI
PARADISE

84

PARADISE

STREET

CAR ENTERS

Scott
NOV 82

IGHT CLUB
- SAN SAN HOTEL

TREE PLANTED SQUARE.

8'   8'

4'

TOP: Micky Moore (center) and his team on location in Macao for the second-unit shoot of the Shanghai chase and exteriors, mid-April 1983, as based on production sketches by Scott and his team of the façade, street dressing, and a neon sign with the Chinese translation of "Club Obi Wan," the club's new name (OPPOSITE RIGHT). OPPOSITE LEFT: A production painting by Elliot Scott shows Short Round in the Temple of Doom.

CHAPTER 7
DOOMRUNNERS

APRIL TO AUGUST 1983

REPORT NOS. 1–13: MONDAY, APRIL 18–MONDAY, MAY 2, 1983
KANDY, SRI LANKA (OODEWELLA TEA PLANTATION AND HANTANA
PLANTATION): EXT. MAYAPORE HILLS & VILLAGE, INT.
SHAMAN'S HUT, EXT. INDY'S HUT; UDAWATTA KALLE: EXT.
JUNGLE CLEARING; VICTORIA DAM: EXT. MAYAPORE HILLS

The majority of cast and crew left London at midday, April 13, on Air
Lanka flight UL512, and arrived in Colombo at 6:30 AM the next day.
They then boarded a coach to Kandy. Spielberg arrived in Colombo on
Saturday, April 16, with Frank Marshall, Kathy Kennedy, Harrison Ford,
Kate Capshaw, and Ke Huy Quan, who traveled with his mother, Mrs. Tran;
Tommy Phong, his cousin and translator; and Adrian Later, a California
state welfare worker (who sprained her foot on set the first day).

The film's snakes had to be flown into the country by animal handler
Mike Culling. Because they weren't exactly welcome, he had to book them
into hotel rooms under fake names. "The Sri Lankans aren't very partial
to snakes, funnily enough," production manager Patricia Carr says. "So we
booked the pythons into their own hotel room under the names Mr. and
Mrs. Longfellow."

That same Saturday, Spielberg led a group on a recce to the Sri Lanka
locations, including "Bo Derek's Lake"—nicknamed after the costar of
1981's *Tarzan, the Ape Man*, which was shot partially in Sri Lanka—where
scenes 36, spotting the Shaman, and 47, putting perfume on the elephant,
would be shot, among others. They also surveyed the rope bridge.

On Sunday, Ford, Capshaw, and others sat for makeup tests at the
Hotel Suisse, while crowd fittings—mine guards, village elders, and assorted
villagers—took place at the Hotel Hilltop. The location group grew when
the first unit was joined by the second unit, again headed by Micky Moore,
after it had completed six days of shooting in Macao. A new member of the
second unit was Ian Bryce, who had started out as a parking lot attendant
at the Lucasfilm offices in LA. After nine weeks he'd moved up to the
mailroom, and was now a second assistant director (today he is the producer
of such films as *Transformers*, 2007).

"We shot in Macao, across from Hong Kong," he says. "The Macao
unit did the rickshaw chase sequence with the Duesenberg. We'd hired

a Hong Kong first AD [Patty Chan] to communicate with the extras,
quite a number of whom had come from mainland China. They were all
dressed and wardrobed, and she starts talking with them about what the
photography was gonna be—but they were all looking at one another and
not answering—until she figures out that none of them understand a word
she's saying. So she has to go through and talk to them all in several dialects
to figure out who's from where. I think international filmmaking is full of
logistical and practical challenges like that."

DEMOLITION BRIDGE

On Day 1 of principal photography, Monday, April 18, Patricia Carr filed
her first Progress Report. Catering was for 100 cast and crew, who had a
finish date of August 26, a 93-day shoot. The first scenes shot were 174 and
175: the return of Indy, Willie, and Short Round to the Mayapore village.
An elephant was on standby, a Hindi adviser on set. The Indian village
had been constructed on the grounds of the Hantane Tea Estate, one of the
country's most popular tourist attractions. Spielberg was shooting the village
in reverse, first prosperous and then barren, because it was easier to defoliate
than to make it appear progressively more beautiful.

On Day 2 Spielberg slipped on a rock and sprained his foot, but
continued working.

On Day 3 production moved to the Kandy River for shots of the
exterior river scenes. "I'm with Harrison Ford in this little raft," Capshaw
says, "and Steven Spielberg is on the shore. We're a ways from him so he's
got one of those bullhorns. But we must have been on take eight—three of
those takes were not good because of the raft, but the others were because
of me—and Harrison says, 'Look, doll, you're making way too much of this.
You don't have to do anything. This is a B-movie. Just say your lines.' He
said it with warmth and respect—but he said exactly what I needed to hear."

On April 21, Day 4, George Lucas arrived from Kandy in a helicopter,
having flown from San Francisco via Amsterdam and Colombo. By Day
6 at least one of the extras was suffering from heatstroke. On Day 7, with
135 people now on location, Kate Capshaw was stung on the hand by an

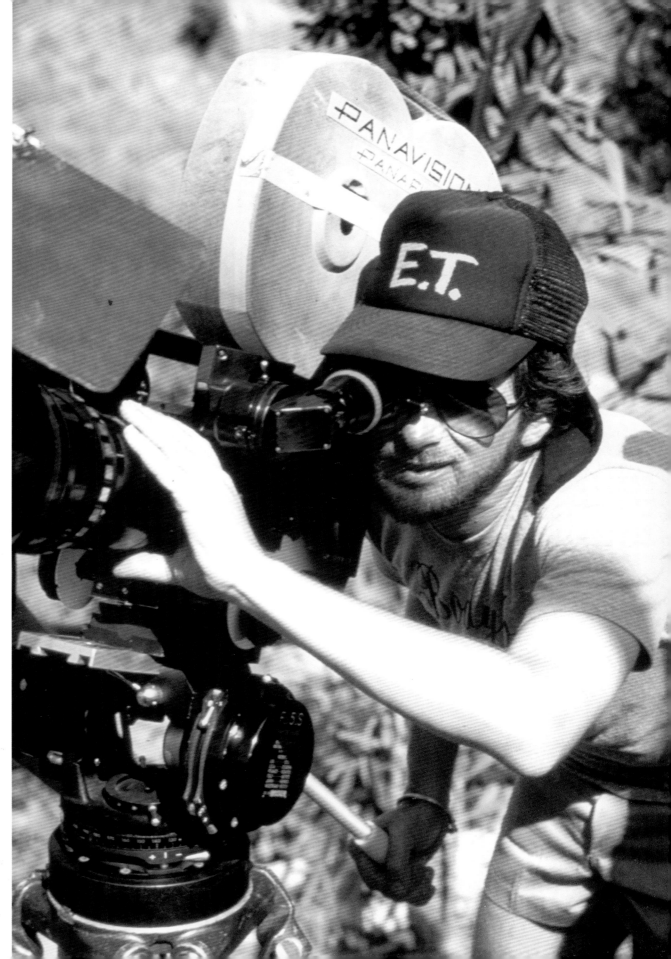

insect and an electrician twisted his ankle; Ford hurt his finger and Quan got a sore throat. Another crew member was diagnosed with a viral infection and sent home by on-set physician Dr. Ranasinghe.

"The first week we were filming, Harrison and I had to have our first screen kiss and I had a cold sore," Capshaw says. "I was mortified. It's every actress's nightmare. It's every director's nightmare; it's every makeup artist's nightmare. That scene we had to reschedule."

"The heat, the humidity, the food actually in Sri Lanka gave a lot of people stomach problems," Bryce says. "You have to be very careful about eating and drinking because you can get some fairly serious stomach problems, which I know happened to me and to plenty of other people."

In addition to the physical issues of his crew, Spielberg had to cope with emotional crises. By the time she had to do the boa scene, which had been rewritten on April 14, Kate Capshaw was in a panic. "I had started visiting the snakes," she says. "The animal trainer assured me I had nothing to worry about, and a lot of people came up and told me such snakes were harmless, but it didn't help; even looking at them was disturbing. I'd talked to Frank Marshall about it and it was suggested that we all go with Steven on our day off to the set and visit the snakes. So I went over and I put my hand on the snakes—and I lost it. I absolutely lost it. I just became hysterical. I started crying. And I was terrified my fear would somehow communicate itself to the snake, which would then turn dangerous."

"She was shaking," Spielberg says. "So I said, 'I'm not going to put you through this,' and I cut the whole scene out of the movie."

"I was so relieved," Capshaw says. "And he said, 'But you have got to do the bugs.' I went, 'The what?' And he said, 'The bugs. You know, the bugs,' and he tells me the scene. I'm not very good at reading a lot of the stage directions, so I'd missed all the snake stuff—and I'd missed the bug part!"

On April 27, Day 9, the rope bridge was blown. "For that big sequence, Steven wanted all the cameras he could get," Micky Moore says. "So naturally the second unit worked with him. George Lucas took over one of the cameras, and it was an exciting sequence."

"We had to work out how to cut inch-thick steel cables," mechanical effects supervisor George Gibbs says. "I'd been told about a company in Marseilles, France, that made explosive bolts for satellites, so I asked them if they could make special cable cutters that wouldn't be visible. They worked out a system for us—but we never had time to do any tests.

"There were also many discussions about who was going to make the dummies that were on the bridge when it collapsed," Gibbs continues. "We were ready to go to Sri Lanka in about six weeks' time, so I finally asked Frank about the dummies and he said, 'Why don't *you* make them?' So we worked out a way to mass-produce 14 mechanical dummies. We bought mannequins, and then we put into them crude mechanisms that worked off ordinary flat batteries. The day of the explosion we set up all the dummies, tied them to a switch—and when the ropes were cut and they fell away, flinging their arms and legs in the air, it was amazing."

"It was perfect," Robert Watts says. "Those moments are incredible because it's one go. If we'd blown it, we could never have re-rigged the bridge without rebuilding it."

On Thursday, April 28, Day 10, Spielberg and company returned to the Mayapore set, now barren, for scenes in the Shaman's hut. "We built the village around this huge, beautiful rock, right in the area where David Lean had shot many scenes from *The Bridge on the River Kwai* [1957]," Spielberg says. "In one of the scenes, we had an actor who I believe was Singhalese and didn't speak English at all [D. R. Nanayakkara]. So I had to speak the lines, and he copied my words right there as we filmed."

BELOW: D. R. Nanayakkara (Shaman) directs Kate Capshaw (Willie) and Ford (Jones) to his village (MIDDLE), after meeting them in a scene filmed on the Kandy River (BOTTOM LEFT, with Ke Huy Quan as Short Round). BOTTOM RIGHT: Capshaw, Spielberg, and Quan in the Mayapore village set built on a tea plantation.

"A translator translated the script for me," Quan says of his own trials with English. "The translator would also practice the lines with me and would tell me what they meant. But because films are shot in chunks, I didn't have to memorize a ton of lines, just bits and pieces. Steven would tell me what the shot was about, and then he would pretty much give me a lot of freedom to do whatever I wanted."

An extended shooting day had been planned for a dusk shot of the Indian village, but "torrential rain set in at approximately 6 PM, so the unit was dismissed for the day." "They would have almost monsoon-type rains sometimes," Bryce says. "It'd be absolutely gorgeous at one point in the day and then the rains would just come down and almost wash the set away."

"Sri Lanka was an amazing experience," Kathy Kennedy, now associate producer, says. "It was a very pristine place that really didn't have a lot of experience dealing with movie people, Hollywood people."

"We had a group of local production assistants," Bryce says. "One afternoon, the first AD is yelling down the radio at me, he's ready for something and why isn't something ready? So I'm running around trying to figure out what it is that's holding up the progress. I can't find any of my PAs, they're not answering the radio—until I find them asleep under a tree. They're all taking a nap at three o'clock in the afternoon. It was like, 'Guys! Let's go, time to go to work.'"

TOP LEFT: Ford. MIDDLE: First AD David Tomblin, Elliot Scott, Spielberg, Marshall, and Watts. BOTTOM: Lucas, Spielberg, and DP Douglas Slocombe. TOP RIGHT: Ford as Indy battles Thuggees. ABOVE: Continuity Polaroid shot during the same sequence. "Harrison really got into even better shape," Spielberg says, "because he had to have his shirt off for much of the time. He did a lot of weight training and aerobic training, and he got himself into peak condition."

TO RIDE AN ELEPHANT

By the end of the location shoot Kate Capshaw had gotten to know the man in the hat slightly better. "Harrison is very quiet, internalized, private," she says. "It was a new experience for me, because I'm such a jabbermouth. If someone doesn't jabber with me, I begin to think they hate me."

Physically the leading man was suffering, thanks to several days of elephant riding. "Sri Lanka had plenty of them," Marshall says. "Ours came from an elephant orphanage. They were trained and brought up to our location."

"Riding elephants looks like fun," Ford says, "but in fact you have to sit right astride the shoulder muscle, behind the back, which kind of pulls you apart."

"Harrison had back problems because he had to ride elephants for two weeks," Spielberg says. "Kate was having some pains as well. It's not easy to ride an elephant, I found out. We all did."

On April 29 Lucas returned home. On Monday, May 2, the first unit wrapped the Sri Lanka location on schedule. On the way back some of the team, including Frank Marshall, stopped in Colombo to visit Arthur C. Clarke,

TOP: Ford and Lucas. ABOVE: Amrish Puri (Mola Ram) and Lucas. RIGHT: A British team of engineers built a rope bridge for production while moonlighting. Spielberg and Lucas test it out.

author of *2001: A Space Odyssey* and many science-fiction classics. "It was kind of exciting," Marshall says. "His books covered three walls from floor to ceiling."

SETUPS COMP: 164; SCS. COMP: 13/174; SCREEN TIME: 20m49s/120m.

REPORT NOS. 14-33: FRIDAY, MAY 6-FRIDAY, JUNE 3, 1983
EMI STUDIOS, UK; STAGE 7: EXT. CAMPSITE; STAGE 3: INT.
PLEASURE PAVILION; STAGE 2: INT. TEMPLE ALTAR

Spielberg and company arrived back in London on May 3, with two days to rest before studio shooting began. Two days later the director had added pages to the script to compensate for the deleted boa. "On the plane back to London, he wrote that other scene where we're in a clearing and all those animals keep scaring me," Kate Capshaw says. "I'm afraid my fear of snakes must have cost Steven a couple of hundred thousand dollars shooting that new scene."

The new scene ratcheted up costs in particular for the costume department. On the second day at Elstree Studios, the Progress Report dutifully noted that Kate Capshaw's dress—which had been draped over a chair—was mangled by an elephant, "who proceeded to chew several holes in it. Insurers have been advised."

"Kate Capshaw had to wear this glamorous sequined dress, which I had wardrobe mistress Barbara Matera make in New York," Powell says. "It was very expensive and was made completely of original beads and sequins from the 1920s and 1930s, which Barbara had been collecting for years. But when we were shooting the scene with Harrison and Kate sitting by a little campfire, I saw an elephant calmly eating the whole back of the dress. So Barbara had to come to England and, using the few pots of beads and sequins that remained, she repaired the dress."

That scene also involved a lot of wild antics on the part of Willie, some of which were a challenge to the actress. "I didn't read the parts where Willie has to scream, either," Kate Capshaw says. "But I didn't know how to scream. So Steven taught me how to scream. Screaming is not as easy as it looks."

As with *Raiders*, *Temple* production sets occupied eight of the Elstree facility's nine stages, with the last used as a workroom. For studio shooting they switched from location film Eastmancolor 5247 to Eastmancolor 5293. Bill Welch once again directed construction, which the production notes say

BELOW LEFT: Indy prepares to cut the rope bridge, which was then blown (ABOVE) thanks to complex explosives and remote-controlled dummies overseen by mechanical effects supervisor George Gibbs. After the first unit departed, Micky Moore's second unit continued work at the Victoria Dam site, shooting scenes on either side of the blown bridge till Friday, May 6.

Steven Spielberg
sends his thanks to
SRI LANKA LOCATION SERVICES LTD.
and to the people and government
of Sri Lanka
for their wonderful cooperation and support
during the production of

and the

RIGHT: Spielberg directs Ford's ride on an elephant. FAR RIGHT: Production ran a page in *Variety* addressed to Sri Lanka, thanking everyone for their great location shoot.

OPPOSITE: Spielberg and Lucas duel with water pistols. ABOVE: Marshall, Quan, and Kennedy.

included 5,000 sheets of plywood, 700,000 feet of timber, 250 tons of plaster, and so on. Even though they were back home, some of the crew were still suffering from viruses caught on location, including typhus and hepatitis; at least one member had to visit the Tropical Diseases Hospital in London.

From the campsite Spielberg moved to the Pankot Palace interiors, the subject of several script revisions, on April 14 and May 9, including the deletion of the scene in which the Maharajah and Short Round fight over Indy's whip. The banquet scene was shot in mid-May on Stage 3.

"If you think of the Republic serials from the 1930s, they take themselves a little bit too seriously," Lucas says. "So we wanted to infuse into *Temple of Doom* the humor you find in the old *Abbott and Costello* movies or in the *Thin Man* series. The dinner scene where outrageous dishes are served was something that I'd always wanted to put in a movie. Steven has a sense of humor that fits right into that, so he went hog wild."

"I said, 'What about a meal of the worst stuff you would ever imagine as long as you live?'" Spielberg says. "Eels, bugs, monkey brains—this was a scene that really leaned toward gross-out comedy. But it was a lot of fun to shoot. It was a lot of laughs. We had rubber bugs with high-quality custard dessert inside; the monkey brains were custard with raspberry sauce; inside the soup were rubber eyes. The worst thing was the eels. Nobody liked the eels, especially Kate. When those eels came out of the fake rubber boa constrictor, I lost Kate for about an hour."

On the other side of the Atlantic, production designer Elliot Scott was in New York City working with choreographer Danny Daniels on the logistics for the nightclub set, while on May 12 John Williams recorded a group of singers in Boston for "chant playback for the interior Temple sequence." This choral music was delivered to production in England on the following day by John Withers, and production moved into the Temple of Doom toward the end of May.

"We had these scenes where Mola Ram was leading his chanting followers in the Temple of Doom," Marshall says. "And we had this chant that had been written by John Williams, but we had a lot of drummers and chanters that couldn't actually keep a beat and couldn't stay together. I have a musical background and I know Johnny very well, so I decided that in the role of a problem-solving producer, I would have to direct the chanters. So I went onto the stage and did some directing to get them into a fever pitch and also to keep them on the click track."

"The actual Temple was a huge set," Spielberg says. "When I walked on for the first day it looked like an opera hall. It was just one of the biggest sets that I had ever seen. Dougie did the most ingenious lighting for it. He lit the pit with a lot of lights with red gel on them, to give the effect of fire coming up."

"We often had to use the larger stage in the studio," Slocombe says. "And they did need an enormous amount of light. But Scott was very helpful. I would ask him if he could cut certain sections to enable me to hide lights, which enabled me to get the quality of illumination that I wanted in those big set pieces."

The weekend of May 14–15, Joe Johnston and visual effects cameraman Kim Marks arrived from ILM. "My big input into the second *Indy* film, other than some of the design stuff, was the sequence where the Kate Capshaw character is lowered into the lava pit," Johnston says. "We shot that on a big stage out at Elstree, and we were weeks on that sequence. It just went on and on and on. And Borehamwood is this run-down little town outside of London. My memory of it was that the sun never came out. We'd go to the line producer and say, 'You know, we're not gonna work today. Can we go to the hotel or go stand in the rain?' He'd say, 'No, you better stick around. Steven might want you to do something.'

"So we'd sit there for ten hours watching the crew work. We were like sixty feet in the air, 'cause we were shooting down on the lava pit, so we'd go up and we'd come down. Well, the stage was not heated, but with all the lights on and all the lava pit's practical effects, it was about ninety degrees

up on the catwalks—but it was like forty degrees on the floor. So our bodies were constantly trying to adjust to this fifty-degree change in temperature, as we were going up and down all day for several days in a row, and all of us got sick. We got completely wiped out, until we couldn't come to work. But somehow we got through it, as you always do. But it wasn't an awful lot of fun."

SETUPS COMP: 557; SCS. COMP: 38/174; SCREEN TIME: 48m47s/120m.

REPORT NOS. 34-63: MONDAY, JUNE 6-FRIDAY, JULY 15, 1983 EMI STUDIOS, UK; STAGE 9—INT. MOLA RAM'S CHAMBER, INT. BUG TUNNEL, INT. TUNNEL & SPIKE CHAMBER; STAGE 3—INT. PALACE HALL & WILLIE'S SUITE, INDY'S SUITE, INT. NIGHT CLUB (LIMBO); STAGE 6—INT. MINE QUARRY, INT. QUARRY CAVERN, INT. MINE TUNNELS, INT. HOLE BEHIND ALTAR, INT. PIT; STAGE 1—INT. OBI WAN NIGHT CLUB

Stage 9 became a chamber of horrors, otherwise known as "the bug tunnel," on June 8. "I'm a firm believer that in an adventure saga every sequence needs to have two or more activities happening simultaneously," Spielberg says. "Where Indiana is accusing the Maharajah and the palace authorities of stealing the Sankara stone, on the other side of the table unspeakable entrées are being served. With the sequence inside the crusher room as Indiana and Short Round are about to be crushed, Willie is having her own problem with tens of thousands of insects."

Frank Marshall, who again pulled second-unit duty with the nonhumans, estimated that they had around 50,000 cockroaches and 30,000 beetles, mostly purchased through a bug farm, and that each shot would use around two to three thousand insects—and the shooting went on for days.

"We had some giant hissing beetles," Marshall says. "We sent a guy down to South America during bug season. We had all sizes and varieties. I also found a bug wrangler in England and we created this really disgusting bug hotel where we kept them."

Like the snakes in *Raiders*, the insects didn't always cooperate; for one thing, they didn't like the hot lights on the stage and would run for the shade. "Finally I designed this box," Marshall says. "It was enclosed on the top and bottom, and we put this slippery stuff on the top of the lip, so they'd fall back down."

"I knew now that I had to do the bugs," Kate Capshaw says. "So I was asking people, 'Is there a pill I can take to keep myself from freaking out?' So I did take something like a relaxant. I came to the set, and I was like [dreamily], 'Hi, Steven.' He said, 'Hi, we're gonna do the bugs.' 'Ohhkay. Where will they be coming from?' 'We're going to pour buckets of them on you from above.' 'Ohhkay. And where will you be?' 'I'll be right next to you.' And that was how I was the whole day. There wasn't much to do except stand there and let bugs fall all over you."

"I had all sorts of shots planned showing the migration of bugs up and around Kate," Spielberg says. "But once I got on the set and saw how she was reacting to being around the bugs, I felt the best thing to do was throw out the storyboards and take one camera and hold Kate's side, with a second camera panning from the bugs up to her face. We were being as spontaneous as she was. The situation for her was very real, as it would have been for

OPPOSITE: Torrential downpours would often interrupt location filming in Sri Lanka.

TOP LEFT: Ford as Indy inspects a warning sign. LEFT: Quan and Spielberg. BELOW: Capshaw, Spielberg, Lucas, and Ford. "I'll never forget when George came to visit us and we were in between setups filming inside the hut," Capshaw says. "A still photographer came up, and there we were, Steven, George, Harrison, and I, having a great time."

anybody having a thousand creepy insects crawling all over her body."

"We went through about six or seven actresses trying to get them to stand in there," Marshall adds, referring to Willie's body doubles. "We'd have people that would go home and find the bugs in their hair, clothes, shoes…"

"The spike room was one of my favorite sets," Spielberg says. "That scene was my flagrant homage to the old Republic serials, and I wanted it in the story very early on. I had so much fun directing the scene because it was a race against time with the spikes coming down and Indy screaming at Willie to reverse the mechanism. I also liked the little coda that I added at the end after they finally come out, when Willie leans over and her butt hits another device and the whole thing starts over again—and they have to kind of throw their bodies through one of the doors that's quickly closing—and the last thing was Indy retrieving his hat. God forbid it should stay behind."

IRON FINGERS OF PAIN

From the next day onward, Progress Reports mentioned that Harrison Ford's back was causing him pain. Ford was immediately sent to see specialists, and

the film's insurers were advised. According to Marshall, Ford had experienced a slipped disk some time before, which had been aggravated by riding the elephants and other physical stunts.

On Thursday, June 16, Spielberg deleted scenes 129 and 132, in which the bewitched Jones returns to the palace and kidnaps Willie, while Ford's pain increased. "By that point my back problems had pretty much advanced," he says. "I had tried everything and nothing had helped. Then I woke up one morning and, after I stood up by the side of the bed, I realized I was unable either to move forward or to get back in bed."

"Steven called and said, 'Harrison is in really bad shape here and I don't know how much longer this is going to last,'" Lucas says. "So I immediately jumped on a plane and flew over there."

Lucas arrived on June 20. "Harrison was in really terrible pain," he says. "He was on the set lying on a gurney. They would lift him up and he'd walk through his scenes, and they'd get him back on the bed."

That same day Ford was filming his fight with the Thuggee assassin in Indy's suite on Stage 3. "Harrison had to roll backward on top of the guy," Spielberg says. "At that moment his back herniated and Harrison let out a call for help."

152/154 DIRTY COSTUME

Lucas said, "'We can't do this. If we have to shut the picture down, we'll shut the picture down. Let's get an airplane, let's fly Harrison to Los Angeles, let's have this operation happen as soon as possible,' so we did."

On June 21 Ford was transported by ambulance to Oswestry to see his specialist. He was then flown in the Warner Bros. jet, accompanied by his wife, Melissa Mathison, to Los Angeles for further examination on June 22. Thereafter, the Progress Report notes, he would be recuperating in his home.

Of course Spielberg had to make do. When he could, he shot around his injured star by using Ford's stunt double Vic Armstrong. "We had a very good double for him," David Tomblin says. "And I take my hat off to Spielberg, because we never stopped shooting—and it wasn't stuff that one would say, 'Oh, that's a double.'"

"I was left in London for three weeks with a stunt double," Spielberg says. "So I shot most of the fight scene on the stone crusher with Vic Armstrong. That scene was all made up; it wasn't storyboarded at all. I shot it like the Flying Wing scene in *Raiders*. But it was particularly difficult to pull off because by the time we got to the end of the take, I'd look at the crusher and say, 'Hey we aren't supposed to be anywhere near the crusher for another two pages. Get back.' The continuity was very hard."

"We shot the whole thing with me and Pat Roach," Armstrong says. "It was a great example of how you can interact with doubles and with artists, and still come out with a seamless piece of work."

"Harrison's absence was the big drama, one of the bigger dramas we've ever had," Lucas says. "But Steven stepped up and said, 'We can do these fights with his stunt double, and we'll cut to his close-ups later on.' He really got the whole situation under control and managed to shoot those seven weeks without Harrison. That's amazing. I don't know any other director who could do something like that. Literally. They would just throw their hands up and say, 'Well, no cast. I guess we're off for seven weeks.'"

On June 24 Robert Watts held a meeting with loss adjuster Bill Bolton and production supervisor John Davis "to discuss re-scheduling, due to current unavailability of Harrison Ford for shooting purposes." Lucas left England on June 25, no doubt after powwowing with Spielberg on a plan of action.

While dance rehearsals began on June 27, with seven dancers, Daniels, and assistant choreographer Caroline Hamilton on Stage 8, the director

OPPOSITE: Amrish Puri (Mola Ram) and Ford; the vast Temple of Doom set on Stage 2; Polaroids taken for continuity and for fun. TOP RIGHT: Mola Ram (Puri) holds the flaming heart of his victim. Mechanical effects supervisor George Gibbs explains: "When Mola Ram pulls the heart from a man's chest, we used a heart that had an electric motor inside that simulated the beating. Because the heart had to burst into flame while Mola Ram was holding it, we fitted the actor with a fake arm so it would be safe."

TOP LEFT: Indy helps the children escape over the lava pit (this scene would be cut). TOP RIGHT: Spielberg jokes with an imprisoned Kate Capshaw, with DP Douglas Slocombe in the background. LEFT: Spielberg.

TOP LEFT: Indy (Ford) and Short Round (Quan) in the spike room on Stage 9, where they also filmed the bugs on Willie (Capshaw). (TOP RIGHT). BOTTOM RIGHT: Two shots lit by Slocombe: "I witnessed Dougie's skill one day," Spielberg says, "when he was shooting little children, filthy and dirty, digging for the lost Sankara stone in the huge quarry cavern with very bizarre lighting. There were lights hidden under rocks shining up at their faces, lights out of little holes in the walls just giving them enough face light to accentuate their pathos. The very next day he shot the love tease and lit Kate Capshaw as James Wong Howe might have lit Marlene Dietrich. That to me is skill."

continued to shoot scenes that didn't require Ford, such as those with the approximately 100 child extras. Alas, Douglas Slocombe had also been added to the list of those sidelined on June 24, when he became feverish; he was subsequently put on sick leave until July 7.

As June rolled into July, the weather became very hot. On July 8 Kate Capshaw was at Anvil Abbey Road Studios under the musical direction of Ian McPherson. With a trio, she recorded the "song and dance number" from 9 AM to noon. That evening she returned for a half-hour session to re-record a backing track.

"Danny Daniels put together this crazy number based on Cole Porter's song 'Anything Goes,'" Spielberg says. "Kate had to learn the entire song in Mandarin, and then learn all the choreography, but luckily what I didn't know about Kate was she could also sing and dance. She has a great voice."

On July 11 Capshaw was the only principal on Stage 1 as Spielberg began shooting the scenes in the Obi Wan Nightclub (on that day he deleted scene 2, of Short Round in the club). While word came from Los Angeles that Harrison Ford would be able to return to work in London on Monday, August 8, production experienced yet another problem. "When I put on that beautiful red dress, it was so tight that I couldn't dance," Capshaw says. "So all the hard work I put into the musical number was for nothing."

With Lucas back on set, Spielberg soldiered on, filming the dance and gun battles using balloons and pigeons and extras, with the only problems being sprained ankles and a pigeon dropping that fell into one of the dancer's eyes on July 13.

A fake injury occurred when Dr. Fantasy made a surprise appearance at two-year-old Amanda Lucas's birthday party. "The cake dive had become a Lucasfilm tradition," Marshall says, "which we followed up on during the second *Indy* movie with Amanda's birthday. We had her party on the

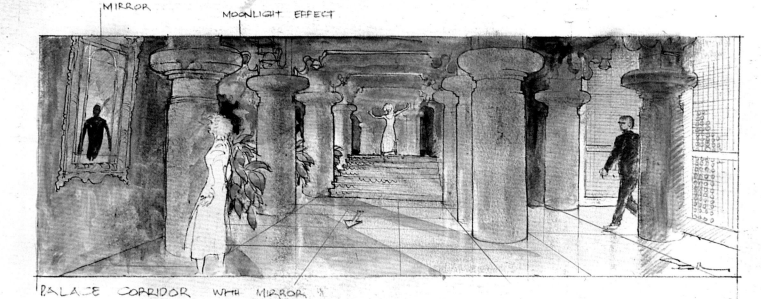

MIRROR

MOONLIGHT EFFECT

PALACE CORRIDOR WITH MIRROR

LEFT: Elliot Scott's production painting of the palace corridor and the set as Ford and Capshaw play their scene (BELOW). BOTTOM: A telex sent on July 18, 1983, by producer Robert Watts to production manager Patricia Carr concerning costume—and domestic—requests.

'Anything Goes' set. They brought out a little cake for her, and I fell into the cake—and Amanda burst into tears. So I was zero for two now."

Lucas headed back to the United States on July 14, along with editor Michael Kahn, who had been in England the whole time creating a rough assembly of the film. In fact, all of the production heads had to alter plans drastically at this point. The July 15 Progress Report read, "As agreed by insurance adjusters, shooting unit closes down today for a three-week hiatus period. Resumption of shooting will take place from Monday, August 8, 1983, which is the anticipated date of Harrison Ford's return to work."

SETUPS COMP: 1,192; SCS. COMP: 69/169; SCREEN TIME: 95m41s/120m.

DANGEROUS INTERLUDE

Spielberg, Lucas, Marshall, and key ILM personnel regrouped in Northern California to plot out their options. Their plan was to shoot whatever they could in the States before returning to England.

"We had some second-unit shooting about to go to Mammoth Mountain and Sonora," Marshall says, "so it was a large meeting, all production people, going over storyboards. Steven and George were there, and we were deep in discussion, but about midway through the meeting George got up and walked over to the door and said, 'Well, I'll see you guys later.' Steven asked, 'Where are you going?' and George says, 'I've got a guitar lesson.'"

While Lucas clearly remained relaxed, Marshall compiled a list of shots for several second units, which he sent to Spielberg on July 18, 1983. They had decided to shoot the raft escape, plummet, and slide down the mountain into the river—in what Progress Reports revealed to be a strenuous and breakneck period.

851897932"

LFL SRFL

8119756 EST 2001   JUL/18/1983

897932 STWARS G
7-18-83
LFL SRFL

TO   PAT CARR
FM   ROBERT WATTS

PLEASE SEE IF WARDROBE CAN SPARE ANOTHER INDIANA HAT FOR SHOOTING HERE. WE ARE CONCERNED THE ONE I BROUGHT MAY GET LOST. ALSO WE NEED A SPARE SHORT ROUND COSTUME FOR THE DUMMY. I WOULD OK ORDERING ANOTHER HAT IF THAT HELPS. IF AGREED PLEASE SEND BY QUICKEST ROUTE.

PLEASE ALSO CALL FOR ME THORN E.M.I. DOMESTIC ELECTRICAL APPLIANCE LTD. SERVICE DIVISION ON 903 3421. THEY WERE COMING ON JULY 20TH TO CHECK WASHING MACHINE AT HOME. PLEASE ASK THEM TO ARRANGE ALTERNATE DATE DURING WEEK COMMENCING AUGUST 8TH.

TALK TO YOU TOMORROW.
LOVE, ROBERT
LFL SRFL

 97932 STWARS GLLLLL
 12.1 MINS

From about July 19 to August 1 Glenn Randall supervised second-unit shooting in several locations, with Spielberg flying from one place to another to oversee their work. Other cast and crew included Dean Ferrandini doubling as Indy, Donna Keegan as Willie Scott, Felix Silla as Short Round, and longtime Spielberg collaborator Allen Daviau on camera.

Their first destination was California's Mammoth Mountain Crest's Ridge Run (and "Secret Spot") ski area, where they filmed the raft jump and landing. As head of the ski patrol, Cliff Mann would ski down the mountain holding the camera between his legs to photograph the plates they needed for the raft's bumpy ride. Because the raft ride was equivalent to a toboggan

run, quite a few reports made note of stunt people and doubles being thrown out of the raft, things being run over, and collisions.

They then built a ramp—basically the end of the toboggan run—which they used to launch the raft into the air before it splashed into a river. This was filmed on July 29 at Lumsden Bridge, Tuolumne River, Sonora County, California. Unfortunately Donna Keegan was injured during the jump off the bridge; she was replaced by Fred Washburn (and later "M. Gilman") in subsequent footage. Other units shot inserts in Stockton, Groveland, Pine Mountain, and Gnoss Field.

ABOVE AND RIGHT: Spielberg directs Ford in the fight that exacerbated the latter's back problems.

TOP LEFT: Capshaw as Willie emerges from the dragon's mouth in the dress that prevented her from doing the dance she'd rehearsed for days. LEFT: Spielberg with the Club Obi Wan dancers: Gaynor Martine, Sue Hadleigh, Marisa Campbell, Louise Dalgleish, Debbie Astell, Carol Bebbington, Deirdre Laird, Samantha Hughes, Julie Kirk, Lisa Mulidore, Nina McMahon, Sharon Boone, Andrea Chance, and Julia Marstand.

TOP LEFT: Lucas flew from the States to strategize with Spielberg, who somehow managed to carry on without Ford. RIGHT: The interior quarry cavern set on Stage 6 where Spielberg shot as much as possible without his ailing star. ABOVE AND BOTTOM RIGHT: Spielberg filmed much of the fight between Indy and the huge Thuggee foreman (Pat Roach) with stuntman Vic Armstrong, carefully concealing his face from view by shooting from behind or in shadows.

OPPOSITE ABOVE: While Ford recuperated from back surgery, second-unit work was done in the United States by several crews, one of which shot footage for the life raft's toboggan run down a snowy slope on California's Mammoth Mountain. Cliff Mann is on skis with a camera. OPPOSITE BELOW: The filming was perilous. One injury report, dated July 29, 1983, describes how Donna Keegan (Willie's body double) was hurt filming on the Tuolumne River.

With the frenetic work accomplished, Spielberg boarded a Concorde jet on August 6 and headed back to London.

REPORT NOS. 64–80: MONDAY, AUGUST 8–AUGUST 26, 1983
EMI STUDIOS, UK; BACK LOT: TUNNEL EXIT, TUNNEL
ENTRANCE, PALACE, EXT. PALACE COURTYARD, EXT. BRIDGE;
STAGE 4: INT. MINE TUNNELS & MINE CAR; STAGE 6: INT.
THE CHUTE/CELL/KIDS' ESCAPE; INT. MINE QUARRY AND
CONVEYOR BELT; STAGE 1: INT. OBI WAN NIGHTCLUB

Shooting in the United Kingdom resumed as planned on August 8 with scenes 56 and 58, the arrival at Pankot Palace, filmed on the back lot. Although he had returned, in itself an incredible feat, Harrison Ford was still in pain. "An experience like this is really an endurance test—a marathon, not a hundred-yard dash," Kate Capshaw says. "You have to pace yourself. You have to create a lifestyle that's nourishing."

"I had a remarkable recovery," Ford says, "pretty much based on the fact that I was in pretty good shape for the film to start with."

"Harrison had this very controversial papaya enzyme surgery performed on his back—thank God successfully and permanently," Spielberg says.

On August 10 the main unit moved to Stage 4 for the mine-car sequences. During breaks in that shooting they did close-ups for scenes shot in his absence, but Ford was injured again, this time "a swollen left eye sustained during fight scene on cliff. Ice pack applied by Unit Nurse." On the third day back, Slocombe, who had also rejoined the team, had his eye

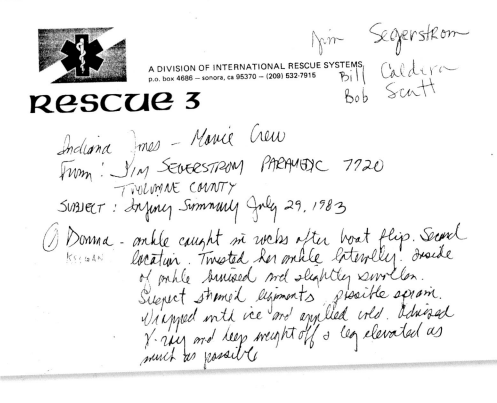

Jim Segerstrom
Bill Caldera
Bob Scutt

A DIVISION OF INTERNATIONAL RESCUE SYSTEMS
p.o. box 4686 — sonora, ca 95370 — (209) 532-7915

RESCUE 3

Indiana Jones – Movie Crew
From: Jim Segerstrom Paramedic 7720
Tuolumne County
Subject: Injury Summary July 29, 1983

① Donna
Keegan – ankle caught in rocks after boat flip. Second location. Twisted her ankle laterally. Inside of ankle bruised and slightly swollen. Suspect strained ligaments possible sprain. Wrapped with ice and applied cold. Advised X-ray and keep weight off & leg elevated as much as possible

94-119

ABOVE: On August 8, miraculously, Ford was back. During the next few weeks Spielberg shot the close-ups he needed for Indy's fight with the Thuggee (Pat Roach, FAR LEFT), and they began the mine-car shoot on the mini roller coaster constructed on Stage 4. LEFT: Continuity Polaroid of Ford.

injured by an exploding 10K lamp. Both men were able to continue working.

"I came back six weeks later and resumed shooting, plugging in close-ups of Harrison throughout the sequence I had done with Vic," Spielberg says. "Eighty percent of that scene was done with Vic and twenty percent with Harrison."

To avoid having too many process shots in the sequence, the mine-tunnel track set was a real roller coaster, designed by Elliot Scott and built by the art and construction departments. "It's on three levels," Spielberg says, "with two loops: the mine-train loop and the dolly-track loop. The photography on the first day of testing was almost unusable because the camera shook so much when it was in the mine car. Everyone said, 'Gee, this looks terrible.' I said, 'No, it looks absolutely realistic.'"

On the dolly-track loop, cameraman Chic Waterson was in his own mine car trying valiantly to keep the action in frame; ultimately he had to see the nurse due to abrasions on his nose caused by the constantly jolting camera.

"One day the actors accidentally went through a large lump of smoke," Spielberg says. "The effects man didn't take the B-smoke and properly paddle it evenly across the track. He created a cloud that hung in the air, so when the mine car hit the cloud, it created a contrail that flowed off the shoulder and hat of Harrison—and I just loved it. From then on I had the effects man lump his clouds in midair."

LEFT: A light affixed to a mine car illuminates Ford as Indiana Jones. BELOW: Quan and Ford (Capshaw is hidden behind Ford) in a mine car especially equipped with a camera.

In mid-August, Spielberg shot more scenes on the partial cliff and bridge set on the back lot. "I remember this one scene where Kate and I walk to the end of the cliff," Quan says. "We don't know if Indy is dead or alive. Then we see him and we had to laugh—because Harrison was off camera, just making funny faces to get that genuine laugh out of me. We would rehearse a couple of times, and then we'd do it, and every time we'd do it, it felt like a new experience for me."

"Ke was a real natural actor," Ford says. "He invested emotionally in what he did."

"For the collapse of the bridge where Mola Ram falls, knocks Indy off, and they both free-fall until Indy grabs on to a bit of rope," Vic Armstrong says, "we used a piece of equipment I'd invented a couple of years earlier called a Fan Descender [which would win a science and technology Academy Award in 2001]. It controlled our descent. I doubled for Harrison in that scene and my friend Frank Henson was Mola Ram. We shaved his head and painted him up. He was on the Fan Descender and I was about 15 feet below him, and he came whistling past me, hit me, and knocked me off. But as he came past me I thought, *God, he's going too fast*. The cable snapped and we both fell another 15 feet on my safety cable. It was quite scary."

On August 22 (production was now two days over schedule) photography began on Stage 1 for the nightclub scenes. With 14 dancing girls and Harrison Ford—still in pain—Spielberg began directing the complex action. On the first day Ford received a nick on the hand from cutlery and his back started acting up again. He was given a sonic massage, and work continued. The next day, crowd extras and four musicians were fitted—and a fire accidentally started when a lamp burned through some wooden steps on the set.

With Lucas in attendance, principal photography wrapped as originally planned on Friday, August 26, 1983; there were still 75 scenes to be completed by ILM and 15 days of live action to be shot in the United States. Given the complications that had besieged production up to this point, it's perhaps not surprising that the main-unit wrap party had been thrown discreetly a few days before, while the principals were still shooting. At this point Ford had worked 61 days, Ke Huy Quan 74, and Kate Capshaw 79 days.

SETUPS COMP: 1,511; SCS. COMP: 94/169; SCREEN TIME: 118m22s/120m.

ABOVE AND RIGHT: On the Elstree back lot a cliff and rope bridge were rigged to film the fight between Indy (Ford) and Mola Ram (Puri).

OPPOSITE: Ford takes a break, with first AD David Tomblin, Spielberg, and company. Earlier in his career Tomblin had—with Patrick McGoohan—helped create the cult TV series *The Prisoner*, writing several of its stories and directing two episodes.

OPPOSITE: Lucas was on hand as Spielberg shot Ford's scenes in Club Obi Wan, with Kate Capshaw and David Yip (Wu Han, ABOVE). Lorraine Doyle played the Cigarette Girl who gets famously slugged by Indiana (ABOVE RIGHT). Bill Reed was the fellow with the gong (TOP RIGHT).

CHAPTER 8

FORWARD ON ALL FRONTS

AUGUST 1983 TO JUNE 1984

O n August 27, at ILM, the "1st Unit American" began preparations for its share of the shoot. All the necessary principals and crew had already traveled to San Rafael, where prelighting was being set up supervised by Dennis Muren, production manager Robert L. Brown, and DP Allen Daviau.

Whereas ILM had struggled with aspects of *Raiders*, the financial results of that movie, the *Star Wars* sequels, *E.T.*, *Star Trek II: The Wrath of Kahn*, and *Poltergeist* had made its services very valuable—so sought after, in fact, that the company was having a hard time keeping pace with demand. "We were starting to get so many projects," model shop supervisor Lorne Peterson says. "The studios in LA were going, 'ILM is the key to the gold mine. If we can have this key, which they produce in Northern California, it will open us up to blockbusters.' So we were doing more and more projects, but with *Temple*, because it was George and Steven's project, there wasn't an option to say no or *How about next year?* It had to be a summer release."

While Muren, Peterson, Johnston, and others plotted out how they were going to complete ILM's visual effects to-do list in time for the May 1984 release, the live-action pickups began on Monday, August 29, 1983, with the interior of the trimotor cargo area. On hand with Ford, Capshaw, and Quan were Akio Mitamura (pilot) and Michael Yama (copilot). Together with Spielberg they finished scenes that had been rewritten at least twice and inserted into the script on June 21 and July 14, 1983 (script revisions had also been made to the interior Duesenberg and exterior airport scenes).

Although the biplane attack had been cut, now the pilots were charged with killing Indy themselves:

    The copilot picks up a large wrench and hefts it.
    He peeks out the door again at Indiana Jones—and looks
    worried. He puts the wrench down and pulls a knife out

OPPOSITE: Scenes in the airplane went through several iterations, including one in which the pilots are so impressed at how Jones, even sleeping, can catch an egg in his hand (BELOW, with drawing and mousetrap-like steps spelled out by Joe Johnston) that they pull a gun on him (BOTTOM RIGHT, with Akio Mitamura as the pilot with the pistol).

RIGHT: Matte painting storyboards by Stanley Fleming.

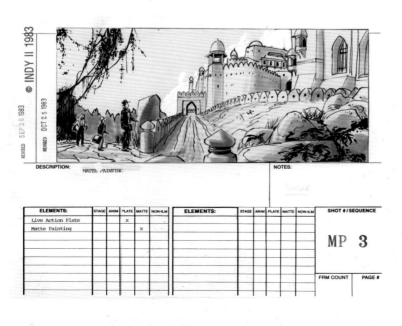

of his belt… The pilot angrily jabbers in Chinese and hands the copilot a .45 automatic.

Indiana is asleep. Above him a chicken lays an egg—the egg rolls and totters on the brink of the cage—and then falls. Without opening an eye, Indy's hand instinctively reaches out and catches the egg before it hits the ground!

Scared off by Indy's reflexes, the pilots decide to empty the gas tanks and bail out of the plane, without leaving parachutes. When the trio sees its predicament, Willie says, "I picked the wrong week to give up Valium." On August 30, Spielberg shot Shorty looking in vain for more parachutes; Ford came down with the stomach flu, but kept working.

After Spielberg filmed a few more pickups, he and his crew traveled to Hamilton Air Force Base in Novato (about 20 minutes north of ILM) on September 7 to shoot exteriors for the Nang-Tao Airfield and runway. In addition to cameos by Lucas, Marshall, and Watts, *Saturday Night Live* legend and Blues Brother Dan Aykroyd performed his small role as "Weber" for this night shoot, arriving at 6:45 PM and finishing at 3:40 AM. Weber's last line, addressed to Willie, was, "You give me a large charge, sweet mama!"

"Among the photographs of people fleeing Shanghai in the Bresson book were missionaries, wearing long black cassocks and tropical pith helmets," Powell says. "And for some reason they were carrying tennis rackets. I showed this to Steven, and with his usual openness of mind, he said, 'Yeah, that's great, let's go for it.' And then I said, 'We only need about a dozen people. Why don't all of us do that? George Lucas, Kathy Kennedy, and Frank Marshall.' And so we did."

Meanwhile, a possible solution to ILM's traffic gridlock had been found. According to Peterson, the main problem was that their pipeline involved several departments—model shop, animation, camera, et cetera—all of whose work converged in one place: the optical department, which became an inevitable bottleneck.

"Everything had to go through optical at ILM to be composited," Peterson says. "And those people were starting to work late into the night, sometimes six and seven days a week. Tom Rosseter would come on the intercom, because he hadn't seen his children, and he'd say something anguished like, 'It's eight o'clock and I imagine some of you are going home to see your children and your wives. Well, we're staying here! We'll be here till one o'clock!'

"So we were all getting together in groups and saying, 'Well, how can we do this? What are we gonna do? What are we gonna do?!' And I think it was Dennis who proposed an idea, saying, 'What if we can figure out some way to get this show done without going through the bottleneck of optical?'"

Muren also favored this technique because it would create shots that were more believable and realistic—it was difficult to successfully blend

CHICKEN, Ⓐ, LAYS EGG, WHICH ROLLS INTO EGG COLLECTION BASKET, Ⓑ WHICH IS UPSET BY BUNDLE OF BAMBOO PIPES, Ⓒ. EGG ROLLS THROUGH PIPE ONTO BOX OF CANNED GOODS, Ⓓ. PLANE LURCHES, SENDING EGG ROLLING DOWN SCYTHE BLADES, Ⓔ INTO PORCELAIN SINK, Ⓔ½. EGG ROLLS OUT DRAIN .....

THIS BASKET IS ONLY $35.

FOLDED RAFT—

|← 24" →|

... AND ONTO BUNDLE OF BROOMS, Ⓕ PLANE LURCHES, TILTING BROOMS AND LANDING EGG ON RACK OF BIKE TIRES, Ⓖ. EGG FALLS THROUGH SPOKES AND INTO INDY'S HAND. Ⓗ

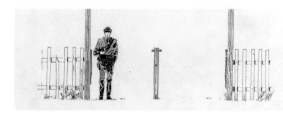

ABOVE LEFT: Recce Polaroids of Hamilton Air Force Base in Novato, California, which was transformed according to Joe Johnston's illustrations into a Shanghai airport (ABOVE RIGHT). RIGHT: Lucas is put into costume for his cameo, which—along with others—was featured in the 1984 Lucasfilm yearbook (OPPOSITE, BOTTOM RIGHT, many cameos were shot, but some were cut). FAR RIGHT: Lucas, Mitamura, and Spielberg. OPPOSITE: Spielberg and Ford at Hamilton, where (FAR RIGHT) Dan Aykroyd joined them for his cameo.

ON THE LOT

LFL UP ON DOCU PICS

Behind-the-Scenes.... under the glitter of Hollywood, examining those often overlooked moments of movie magic, is an off-shoot group of student bodies dedicated to the pursuit of filmmaking at its finest. Following the tradition of a young George Lucas, who followed the bohemian camp of Francis Coppola across the nation during the filming of "The Rain People," a discreet yet merciless duo of sleight of hand artists attempt to maintain the traditions of their forefathers....

Raiders of the Lost Ark, The Empire Strikes Back, E.T. and Jedi are just a few of the films our documentarians found had the subject matter which was worth photographing. Glimpses of the behind the scenes process were even captured during the making of the documentary on Poltergeist and can occasionally be seen at screenings in Ben Burtt's living room.

NANG TAO AIRPORT
PASSENGER TERMINAL-
CUSTOMS

LAO CHE
AIR FREIGHT

=LAO=HSEIH=AIR=CA=

LAO=HSEIH=AIR=CARGO

LAO HSEIH AIR CARGO

several images on the optical printer. "What that meant was doing as many shots as possible with all of the elements," Peterson explains. "Each shot would have to have the spinning lava, the smoke, the steam, the moving slave inside the cage—all that stuff would happen at once. What would get into the camera would be the completed shot rather than just one element. So that's what we worked out as well as we could—Dennis Muren, me, Joe Johnston, Nilo Rodis-Jamero, and a variety of other people. And eventually it started to look like, yes, there were all kinds of things that we could do—if they redesigned the shot in a certain way, we could get it done."

OVER THE FALLS

On Wednesday, September 7, Marshall traveled with a small contingent to the American River in the California Sierras to shoot more raft inserts in white-water rapids. On November 21–22 unit director Kevin Donnelly shot

ABOVE: Ford and Quan. RIGHT: Frank Marshall, with bullhorn, instructs Ford, Quan, and Capshaw during pickups filmed on the American River in California.

OPPOSITE: At ILM, on August 31, Spielberg directed the principals in their mine car, extras in the "redcoat mine car," and other live-action inserts shot against bluescreen.

additional footage of the raft (with dummies) going off a five-hundred-foot "bluff" at Snake River Canyon, Twin Falls, Idaho.

Approved shots were sent to Kahn, who inserted them into his rough cut. As they had with *Raiders*, Spielberg and his editor ran their version for Lucas when they were ready.

"After I showed the film to George," Spielberg says, "at an hour and 55 minutes, we looked at each other, and the first thing out of our mouths was, 'Too fast.' We needed to decelerate the action. So I actually did a few matte shots to slow it down. We reestablished the palace outside in a night shot before going back inside again. We made it a little bit slower, by putting breathing room back in so there'd be a two-hour oxygen supply for the audience."

"There's one funny thing," Kahn says. "On the second *Indy*, almost every other couple of cuts, George would say 'I wanna flop this [reverse the direction of the shot]; I want it the other way.' He made a lot of flop shots. So my assistant and I got him a cap that said PROFESSOR OF FLOPOLOGY. And we put the letters backward, too, so you could read it in the mirror. He laughed when I gave it to him."

SISYPHUS ON THE BACK LOT

December 5–9, 1983, Ford and Quan were again at ILM to do pickups: Indy's cell, on a hill above the Indian village, a mine quarry, a Shanghai street, and so on. They also finished the live-action portion of one of the matte shots Spielberg had added, on the palace balcony, with the director on hand.

"Steven came up, and we did the sequence at the end of the mine-car sequence, where they're being chased by the wave of water," optical photography supervisor Bruce Nicholson says.

"We did things out in the parking lot," says Peterson, "like where Indiana Jones and Willie run out of the rock face and put their backs against the wall, and then the water comes flying through the wall. Well, water you can only scale down so far; there's no way of making miniature water, so we made a big carved wall. After we'd painted it, we didn't have anywhere to put it inside, but it was wintertime, very cold, and it rained overnight. The paint hadn't had a chance to dry, so it just ran and was white again in the morning. So we repainted and touched it up—and then it rained again!"

The film's patchwork finale meant a flurry of further pickups. On January 11, 1984, Muren used Skywalker Ranch as a substitute for the hills above the Indian village in scene 175. On January 25 Marshall flew to Gatorland Zoo, in Kissimmee, Florida, to shoot inserts for scene 172, during

BELOW AND RIGHT: To create the shot of water cascading out of the cliffside, footage shot at Elstree was combined with matte paintings by Chris Evans and Caroleen Green, a backdrop painting by Green and Frank Ordaz, and a large-scale cliff wall built by the model shop in the parking lot of ILM.

174

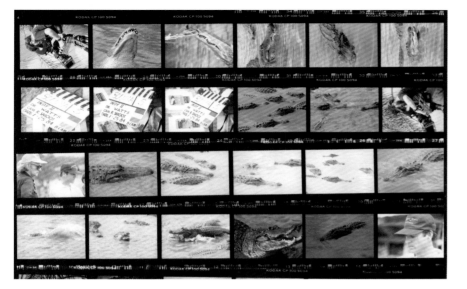

which dummies were dressed in costumes and thrown to the alligators. The next day he was at Alligator Farm in St. Augustine, Florida, for more insert shots. On January 27 pickups were completed at ILM—with 50,000 assorted insects and beetles—because Spielberg wanted a shot, according to Marshall, of a bug on Willie's shoulder crawling into her hair.

"We sent a crew to South America and they returned with giant centipedes and other unusual insects," Marshall says. "We shot the sequence with doubles at ILM." The stage was fumigated after wrap, according to the Progress Report, "after most insects had been returned to their boxes."

The film's very last image was photographed by VFX supervisor Dennis Muren, who returned to Skywalker Ranch on February 2, 1984, for scene 175's added matte shot of the village.

MINI MINE CARS

"We did build a section of parallel track in England for what we called the 'taffy pull' with Short Round between the two cars," Spielberg says. "But the high overhead shot of Short Round between the two cars going over the lava pit is a miniature."

"One of the best sequences, of course, was the mine-car chase," Tom Smith says. "We actually used a Nikon still camera to photograph it, and that worked out very well."

"The budget on that film was fairly tight," Muren says. "And the construction costs to build our miniature sets of the mine tunnels were based on how big the camera was. So I started thinking that if we had a smaller camera, we could build everything smaller. And I came up with the idea of taking the back off a Nikon still camera and putting a movie shuttle in there, and running movie film through it. The thing worked great—and because the camera was now much smaller, our mine tunnels could be built at a lower cost. In fact, we just bought a lot of aluminum foil, crumpled it up, painted it to look like rock, and for $1.98 we got some great sets."

"We had live action that we had to match with the mine cars," Bruce Nicholson says. "And then there were these miniature mine cars that we shot using puppets as subs for the actors. I thought it was a big breakthrough to be able to successfully incorporate those into the sequence. There was a lot of puppetry in that movie, which most people don't know."

"There were scenes when you actually saw the characters in the mine cars and they had to move," Muren says. "Those characters were animated by Tom St. Amand using stop-motion animation. For those shots, for every frame of film, Tom would go in there between frames and animate the puppets a little bit, step out of the way, and we'd shoot another frame, and so on."

"Steven invited us to come up with gags," visual effects cameraman Micheal McAlister says. "So as soon as we got storyboard pages from Steven, we built little sets and shot a version of the sequence using this little video camera and this funky set, just to see if it was going to play. On the basis of that, Steven was able to eliminate certain gags that he didn't think were going to pay off, and accept other ones: for instance, going over the lava flow and the ski jump."

ABOVE RIGHT: After returning from Elstree, Joe Johnston did several illustrations that were used as guides in creating the miniature set with "lava" at ILM (RIGHT, with Paul Huston). "For the sequence when a slave and then Willie get lowered down into the lava pit, we built a half-size model of Kate Capshaw and a half-size of the slave that were probably about three feet long or so," Dennis Muren says. "We put them in a half-size model of the cage, and lowered that down into our pretend lava." (FAR RIGHT)

BEN BURTT ON SOUNDS

"The **insects** were really a combination of two elements. One was our old standby, cheese casserole, and the other was the sound that you get as you pull the shell off a hard-boiled egg.

"The **mechanisms in the spike room** were derived from the same garage springs and counterweights that I'd recorded for the Peruvian temple in *Raiders*. The **spikes** coming down had an element that I produced on an autoharp, which I actually found broken in a trash can along the side of a road. But if you rubbed a piece of metal on the strings, you got a wonderful grating, high-pitched sound.

"The **mine-car chase** came from many sources. We set up a very interesting recording event at Disneyland. Gary Summers and I were allowed to go in at night when no one was there and ride all the different roller-coaster rides and record them without any music turned on. We also made loops of clicking sounds using a toy railroad car and moving it across the railroad tracks. The trick was to create the sensation that everything was going faster and faster and faster without the sounds necessarily rising in pitch."

SOUND DIMENSIONS

On yet another postproduction front Spielberg supervised ADR (additional dialogue recording) at Mayflower Recording Ltd. in London and at Warner Hollywood Studios. Meanwhile, in Marin County, Ben Burtt advanced the sound design for *Temple* as he had for *Raiders*.

"Each *Indy* film was a new challenge because they covered so much ground," Burtt says. "*Temple of Doom* suddenly had us running all around the world, so we really knew that we had to record a lot of new things—I didn't want to use some stock jungle sound from another movie. I wanted something unique to *Indy*."

John Williams also returned to compose and conduct the music for the soundtrack, this time at MGM with the Los Angeles Philharmonic Orchestra, finishing circa April 6, 1984—the first time a Lucasfilm production had recorded its music in Hollywood. *Temple of Doom* would also be the first film to play in theaters fully utilizing TAP, Lucasfilm's Theater Alignment Program, so that every cinema showing the film would adhere to high technological and presentation standards for picture and sound.

"One of the aspects in scoring a film like this is to try to find the right speed for these things," Williams says. "There's so much quick cutting in all

TOP LEFT: At ILM a miniature water tank and mine-car tracks were created for shots that could not be captured as live-action. LEFT: Barbara Gallucci models the walls of the mountain out of aluminum foil. TOP RIGHT: An internal invitation to an ILM party; crews were working on *Indy II* and on *Star Trek III: The Search for Spock* (1984); a VFX storyboard by Stanley Fleming and the resultant final image of the "taffy pull"; Dennis Muren (standing, with Joe Johnston) came up with a method that saved money and time on many of the miniatures shots.

DESCRIPTION: INT. CAVE

Indy, Willy & Shorty come toward camera at a
slight 3/4 angle.

NOTES:

DESCRIPTION: MATTE PAINTING

Exterior palace at sunset.

NOTES:

of the scenes, quick action, overlapping dialogue, sound design, and music, that we really feel like we're on this kind of roller coaster. So what I need to do is to get the speed of the music right. The challenge and fun for me is to make sure the music is always moving at the right pace with what we see and hear and feel."

"Johnny Williams saw the film and I think he reacted appropriately," Spielberg says. "His music is beautiful for Willie and Indy. I love the trek score where the elephants are going across India. That was some of the most beautiful trek music I'd ever heard. Then he got really dark and strange with the all-male chorus inside the Temple of Doom itself. John did an amazing score, which really brought the movie up in my eyes."

CONTROVERSY IN THE TEMPLE

Debbie Fine's early reactions to the violence in *Temple* proved to be prophetic. When the film was submitted for its rating to the Motion Picture

Association of America (MPAA), its members were surprised by the film's graphic depictions of organ removal and child slavery, and they were confused as to what they should do about it.

"The biggest and most controversial issue for *Temple of Doom* was about what the movie should be rated, in a day when the rating systems were simpler than they are now," says Sid Ganis, marketing president of Lucasfilm. "There was a G-rated movie, an R-rated movie, and an X-rated movie. There was no PG-13."

A controversy that had been brewing then erupted in the media about what level of violence was appropriate for younger children. Just days before the film's release, the MPAA decided on PG, but its chairman Richard Heffner was reportedly "delighted" that industry leaders were now favoring a new rating and "more explanation." Early ideas for the new rating were PG-2 or R-13, but after all the criticism, Spielberg called Jack Valenti, president of the MPAA, and suggested that it be either PG-13 or PG-14.

"*Temple of Doom* became the catalyst for the Motion Picture Association

OPPOSITE ABOVE: Matte painting storyboards by Stanley Fleming, from November–December 1983. OPPOSITE BELOW: Matte painting of the temple mountain interior by Frank Ordaz. Note that a joke caption has been inscribed: "*Jaws IV*" (*Jaws 3-D* had just been released in the summer of 1983).

BELOW: A Pankot Palace matte painting by Chris Evans and Michael Pangrazio.

INDIANA JONES

2 velox proofs
follow tissue for
stripping
background
artwork enclosed
for background
tint.

May 23rd

It adventure has a name...
it must be Indiana Jones

INDIANA JONES
and the
TEMPLE OF DOOM

C

Steven Spielberg,
George Lucas
and Harrison Ford
on location in
Sri Lanka, Hong Kong
and London filming the
greatest adventure
of all time...

INDIANA JONES
and the
TEMPLE OF DOOM
Coming Friday, May 25th, 1984.

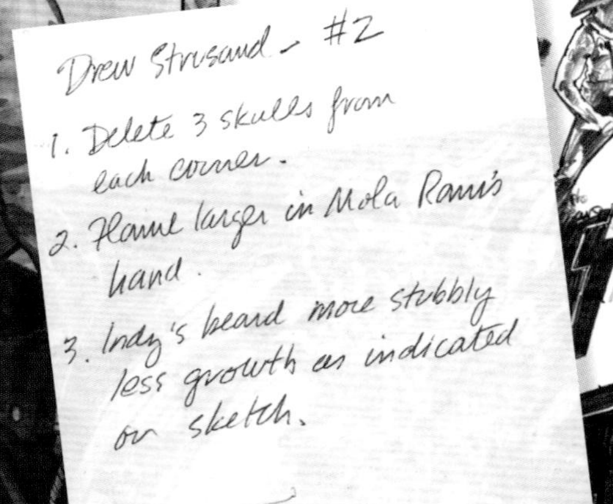

Drew Struzand — #2

1. Delete 3 skulls from each corner.

2. Flame larger in Mola Ram's hand.

3. Indy's beard more stubbly less growth as indicated on sketch.

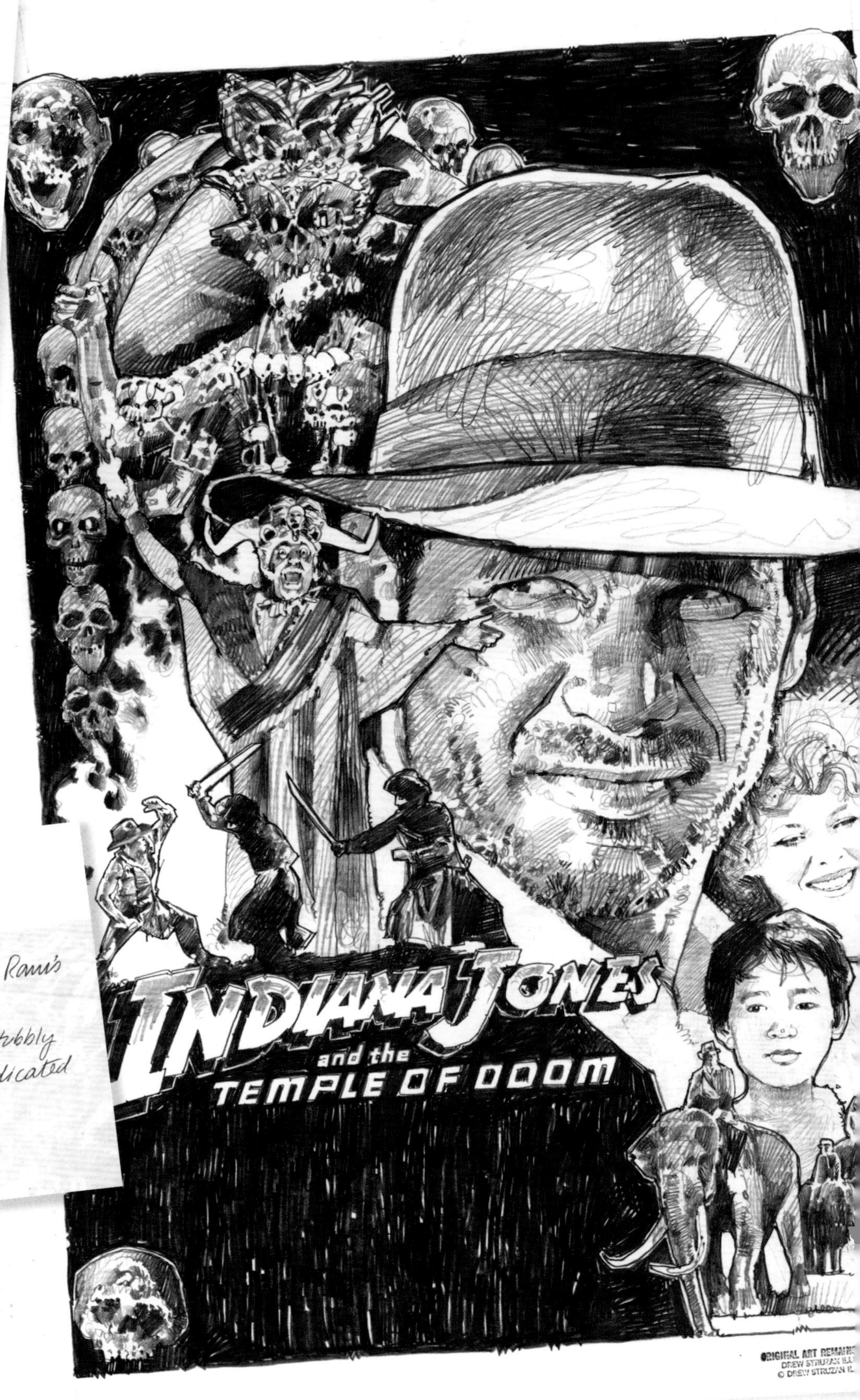

INDIANA JONES
and the
TEMPLE OF DOOM

ORIGINAL ART REMAINS
DREW STRUZAN
© DREW STRUZAN

DAILY VARIETY

VOL. 203 No. 60   12 Pages   Hollywood, California-90028, Wednesday, May 30, 1984   Newspaper Second Class P.O. Entry   50 Cents

'JONES' BUILDS A TEMPLE OF GOLD

Dingillian, Kroll, Ziegler, Boone-Isaacs Join In Exec Exodus From The Ladd Co.

Four more executives of The Ladd Co. are leaving the organization June 30 with no sign that they will be replaced.

They are Robert Dingillian, v.p., ad-publicity-promotion; Cheryl Boone-Isaacs, director of publicity and advertising; Leonard Kroll, v.p., production operations, and Randy Ziegler, director of special projects.

Only survivors are company president Alan Ladd Jr., v.p. Jay

He reportedly is a candidate to become production head of the recently formed Japan American Film Associates. It is understood that he and Kanter have indicated interest

(Continued on Page 8, Column 4)

Cineplex Plans Acquisition Of Odeon Chain

THEFT OF 419 FILMS DRAWS 9 FELONY COUNTS

By DAVE KAUFMAN

Merle Harlin, a film librarian with Hollywood major studios for years, yesterday was charged with nine felony counts involving the alleged theft of 419 motion pictures, most of them from Warner Bros., MGM and Columbia Pictures.

L.A. District Attorney Robert H. Philibosian filed the charges, which consist of three for grand theft, three for receiving stolen property and three for theft of found prop-

Six-Day Total Of $42 Mil Tops Mark Set By 'Jedi'; 2 Other Records Also Fall

By JAMES GREENBERG

As anticipated, Summer arrived with a bang at the national box-office in the form of Paramount's

'Jones' Shatters First-Week Mark In L.A. Launch

By RICHARD KLEIN

"Indiana Jones And The Temple

"Indiana Jones And The Temple Of Doom."

The Lucas/Spielberg sequel to "Raiders Of The Lost Ark" set industry records in a number of categories, surpassing high-water marks established this time last year by "Return Of The Jedi."

With $42,267,345 in six days at 1687 theaters, "Indiana Jones"

(Continued on Page 4, Column 1)

---

left counting the grosses for the first day—and we had this phenomenal weekend. It was just huge, the biggest ever."

Temple went on to earn $333 million internationally, easily outpacing its final budget of $28,175,356. To cover itself, Paramount had inserted a warning into its newspaper advertisements—"This film may be too intense for younger children"—but kids were not grossed out for the most part. A nine-year-old interviewed on *Hollywood Tonight* said, "It's not that scary. I think it's a great movie for the whole family." A young boy said, "I really think Steven Spielberg's movies are great, and I've seen a lot of them, such as *Poltergeist*, which was also supposed to be a scary movie." The consensus on that TV show was that kids under the age of eight should stay home.

While audiences enjoyed *Temple of Doom*, many reviewers did not, though it could be said that critics are often biased against films that are pre-sold. Leonard Maltin on *Entertainment Tonight* said, "Steven Spielberg is an extraordinarily talented filmmaker, and he's given action junkies the perfect fix. But for me, *Indiana Jones and the Temple of Doom* is an overdose."

In *Starlog*, Alan Dean Foster objected to, in his view, the film's abandonment of logic and physics: "What the audience will *not* accept is someone stepping out of an airplane with only an inflated rubber life raft to cushion his fall of several thousand feet… As the young audience at the showing I attended murmured sotto voce, 'Aw, come on!'"

"I was really unprepared for people's reaction to the film," Kate Capshaw says. "When I did interviews, people got very serious and some said they didn't like the portrayal of my character. They felt she was a caricature—but I have to admit, I couldn't have had more fun doing it. I felt

---

to change its rating system to include a PG-13," Ganis says, "because of what was called 'undue violence' in *Indy II*. That was a pretty big deal."

"*Temple of Doom* invented the PG-13 rating," Lucas says. "It was too gross to be PG, and it wasn't quite gross enough to be an R."

(The MPAA made PG-13 effective on July 1, 1984. The first film to come out with a PG-13 rating was John Milius's *Red Dawn*, on August 10.)

Indiana Jones and the Temple of Doom was then released on 1,685 screens in the United States and Canada on Friday, May 23, 1984. Just weeks before its opening, theater owners had become so excited by *Temple of Doom*'s potential earning power that they'd snatched up 500 additional screens. And they were right: The sequel recorded a one-day record of more than $9 million, followed by the largest one-week gross in the history of motion pictures: $45,709,328.

"It was a big, important movie for Paramount," Ganis says. "A lot was riding on it. As usual, opening day, George took off for Hawaii, so we were

---

OPPOSITE, LEFT: The teaser poster by Drew Struzan and a teaser concept sketch (TOP LEFT). TOP: Early pencil drawings by Struzan resulted in the choice of #2 (RIGHT), minus the skulls—as indicated in written instructions from Lucasfilm (MIDDLE).

ABOVE LEFT: Struzan's final one-sheet for the film. ABOVE RIGHT: The front page of the May 30, 1984, edition of *Variety* attests to *Temple of Doom*'s financial prowess.

Congratulations

Lucasfilm Ltd. congratulates
INDUSTRIAL LIGHT & MAGIC
on winning its 6th Academy Award.
BEST VISUAL EFFECTS
INDIANA JONES AND THE TEMPLE OF DOOM

George Gibbs,

Congratulations
Micheal McAllister, Dennis Muren,
and the entire team
at ILM.

Lorne Peterson,

© 1985 LUCASFILM LTD

TOP LEFT: Quan, Capshaw, Spielberg, and Lucas are introduced to Prince Charles and Princess Diana at the film's London premiere. ABOVE MIDDLE: Outside the Empire Theatre in London. ABOVE LEFT: Spielberg and Lucas sign their names in cement outside Grauman's Chinese Theatre on May 16, 1984. ABOVE RIGHT: Lucasfilm took out a page in *Variety* on Tuesday, April 2, 1985, to thank the winners of the Best Visual Effects Academy Award: George Gibbs, Micheal McAlister, Dennis Muren, Lorne Peterson, and the "entire team at ILM."

OPPOSITE LEFT: The Marvel comic-book adaptation contained scenes from the script that were cut from the film: Short Round's discovery that searing pain caused by burning snaps people out of their zombie-like trances; and Willie's encounter with the boa. BELOW: An Asian language poster for the film. RIGHT: Promotional artwork for the film.

that the signature of the film, starting with the poster, was, *Fasten your seatbelt, you're in for a ride*. As opposed to, *We're making a statement*. We weren't."

In July, *Temple* broke records in Australia; it would later break records in Japan, becoming that country's most popular film of 1984.

"I think one of the things that we were able to do in the *Indiana Jones* movies is set a level of expectation for the audience that they would see certain elements," Marshall says. "They loved the world of *Raiders* and now they were coming in to see Indiana Jones's next set of adventures. There was a lot of word-of-mouth that this movie was just as good as the first one, but there was also a new element: *Temple of Doom* was a little darker than the first movie."

"I think we went darker than any of us really wanted to go," Lucas says. "But when you're in the middle of filming it, you do a little dark thing here, and then you do a light thing, then another little dark thing, and so on. And pretty soon you put it together and you realize, *Uh-oh, it's darker than it is light. This stuff is stronger than we thought*. But I don't mind the film. We definitely wanted to make a different movie from *Raiders*. We didn't want to just do the same movie over again."

"I was fairly well pleased with the final result," Ford says. "It certainly was a darker story, but worth it. It was a little bit more challenging than I think what people anticipated."

On July 6, 1984, paperwork was completed at the behest of Lucas, who had decided to give point percentages of Lucasfilm's net profits to Quan, Capshaw, and Williams, in addition to their fees. In a letter to Quan's financial caretaker, Howard Roffman wrote that the bonus was "in recognition of Ke's wonderful contribution to the film."

"I didn't get to see the movie until the premiere at Grauman's Chinese Theatre," Quan says. "It was amazing, because when you're shooting it, it's all

bits and pieces. To see it put together like that with the sound effects, I loved it. I had never thought of acting, but after seeing the film, I thought, *I want to do this the rest of my life*. I felt blessed to have worked with Steven, who did a private screening for me of his and George's movies after I was done with the movie—and then I realized, *Wow, I was part of this big thing*."

Temple was nominated for Music and Visual Effects Academy Awards, and won for the latter. Along with Dennis Muren, George Gibbs, and Micheal McAlister, Lorne Peterson was one of the recipients: "Fortunately, I had said to Dennis at one particular time, 'If we can make this happen, and it's really model-intensive and the models work in the action shots without compositing, then if it ever comes down to Academy Award time, you oughta throw my name in the hat.' Lo and behold, the time came along later, and Dennis must have remembered. I think he appreciated that the show had really been very model-intensive."

Another celebration of the film had occurred earlier on May 16, 1984. "Part of the campaign for *Temple of Doom* was to enshrine George's and Steven's footprints in the cement at Grauman's Chinese Theatre," says Ganis. "Steven was here in Los Angeles and George was up north in Marin, so arrangements were made for George to come down on a private plane. But he was late, it was late, everything was late. And by this time both George and Steven were pretty famous guys, so the press was out there in really huge numbers—and we waited and waited and waited and finally George arrived and the ceremony went on. It was a great moment, those two guys side by side at Grauman's signing their autographs."

"I look back and I say, 'Well, the greatest thing that I got out of that movie was I met Kate Capshaw,'" Spielberg notes. "We were married years later and that to me was the reason I was fated to make *Temple of Doom*."

THE MONKEY KING

JULY 1984 TO MAY 1988

Even before *Indiana Jones and the Temple of Doom* was released, Spielberg, Lucas, and Ford had embarked on their several projects going their different ways. Spielberg would direct *The Color Purple* (1985) and *Empire of the Sun* (1987) while producing many other films and TV series. Lucas continued his retirement from directing, executive-producing *Mishima* (1985), *Labyrinth* (1986), *Tucker: The Man and His Dream* (1988), and *Willow* (1988), among others. Ford would star in several films, including *Witness* (1985) and *The Mosquito Coast* (1986).

But *Indy III* was always present in their minds. Less than six months after *Temple* came out, in September 1984, Lucas finished an eight-page typed story treatment titled *Indiana Jones and the Monkey King*. Though conceptually very far from the final film, it contains several elements that he would play with over the next few years (a couple of which were formulated in the first *Raiders* story conference): a foreboding castle (in Scotland); a boat chase; a female archaeologist; a key package in the mail at Indy's college; the return of Marcus Brody; a fight with a German tank to liberate its prisoner; and the possibility of eternal life.

The quest for immortality was an idea inspired by the ripples of a MacGuffin—the Holy Grail—which Lucas had been trying to work into the story without success. A memo from Debbie Fine dated September 13, 1984, shows that Lucas was trying to establish a link between Scotland and the Grail.

"The Holy Grail had been an early idea as one of the artifacts," Lucas says. "I think it was one of the original ideas around *Temple of Doom*, but Steven didn't like it. I brought it up before *The Monkey King*, but again he said, 'I just don't get it.' I had given the Grail some supernatural powers—healing and fountain-of-youth powers—and those ideas were put into the *Monkey King* scripts, but the original idea was the Holy Grail, and it just kept getting kiboshed."

Lucas followed up his treatment with a more detailed but undated 11-page typed outline. He then hired Chris Columbus, who'd recently written the Spielberg-executive-produced *Gremlins* (1984), to turn his story into a first-draft screenplay. Columbus signed his contract with Lucasfilm on October 1, 1984. He finished his first draft on May 3, 1985. Notes on June 21 from Debbie Fine to Columbus gave the writer more background on

"spirits and ghosts, Chinese," particularly on the subject of the "kuei—evil spirits, ghosts, demons… Hungry ghosts are one kind of kuei"—and he finished a second draft on August 6, 1985, titled *Indiana Jones and the Lost City of Sun Wu Kung* (another name for the Monkey King). Both scripts begin with a prelude adventure that takes place in a cursed castle occupied by a savage ghost (see sidebar, page 188).

"I salvaged the whole haunted-castle-in-Scotland idea because it wasn't used in the second film," Lucas says. "We took it and made it the opening of the third film—but it got kiboshed a second time. It really came down to the issue of the supernatural, with Steven and I going back and forth about how believable it would have to be. The Monkey King had a lot of supernatural powers. Finally we just gave up and started over again. It was a really good screenplay. It was just a little less realistic than what we were used to."

THE SAGA OF THE SCRIPTS

Beyond Lucas's and Spielberg's love of the character and his adventures, good economic reasons justified continuing the franchise. The *Raiders* videocassette, released in November 1983, had broken the all-time record for home video sales by December 1984, surging past the one million mark (and displacing *Jane Fonda's Workout*, the perennial number one). By February 21, 1986, it had been on the top-40 chart for 99 weeks. Following its home video release, *Temple of Doom* was number one for five weeks. In short, these films had legs.

Not satisfied with the story so far, Lucas hired Spielberg recommendation Menno Meyjes on January 1, 1986. Meyjes had written the screenplay for *The Color Purple* and had helped on *Empire of the Sun*. Between writers, Lucas and Spielberg had regrouped and worked out a rough plan for how a new MacGuffin might function within a new framework.

"After *Monkey King*," Lucas recalls, "I said to Steven, 'I know we can make the Grail idea work,' and he said, 'Well, okay, try it and see what happens.'"

"I wanted to flesh out Indy's relationship with his father," Spielberg says. "I said, 'We can do a really good character study of who gave birth

LUCASFILM Ltd

INTER-OFFICE MEMO

To: George Lucas

From: Debbie Fine

Date: Sept. 13, 1984

Re: Grail, etc.

Debbie,
Pls note George's comments
below. Jane
9-21-84

Got the message from Jane to pursue the grail and a possible connection to Scotland (which by the way I think is easy to make), but I have a couple of other questions to facilitate all this research. I will list them here and either write quick replies next to them and return to me or give me a call.

1. There are pagan or other grail legends *(e.g. Celtic)* and then there is the Christian Holy Grail of medieval romances. Do you have a preference on which would end up in Scotland? Underline one you prefer, or say I'm interested in either or both.

2. Of the Christian grail legends, although there are multiple versions, the two most prominent:
   a. The grail supposedly brought to Glastonbury, England by Joseph of Arimatha in 70 A.D. (which we could say was taken to Scotland at some point).
   b. The grail brought to southern France by the Magdalen about the same time and speculated was guarded by either the Knights Templar or the Cathar heretic sect. At the time of the Inquisition when the Templars and the Cathars were both wiped out in France (about 1309), all their treasures disappeared. Shortly after some Templars appeared in Scotland to help the Scots fight against the British and they might have taken their treasures there.

   Question: do you have a preference of story a or b? *no*

3. As all the above is only for the teaser portion of Indy III in Scotland, I presume we still need something to search for in the African portion of the script. Should I look separately for an African object, or lost treasure, or lost city. Underline any preference here. Or will the search for the grail continue to Africa? *no*

   Christian object in africa

   Meanwhile I'll continue the grail reading and make a summary report for you as soon as I can.

4. Should I abandon search for other Christian artifact if you are only interested in the grail. Yes or (no)

Debbie

INDY III

By: Jeffrey Boam

FIRST DRAFT
Pages 1-83
September 15, 1987

+
pages 84-102
Sept. 30, 1987

to this guy.' And George asked, 'Well, is that going to be conducive to the Grail search?' I said, 'The search for the father is the search for the Holy Grail, which is heightened if they're estranged by bitterness or different ideologies and approaches to archaeology.'"

"I was also a strong proponent of bringing in Indiana Jones's father and showing some new aspects of my character," says Harrison Ford.

"Including Indy's father came about because we were trying to get some other hook," Lucas says. "Steven was very worried about the Holy Grail, just like he was about the Sankara stones, which had proved that we should put more focus on what Indy is going after. It was in a story conference where he brought up the idea."

On October 2 Meyjes delivered his first screenplay, based on a story by Lucas and Meyjes; a revised first draft followed on November 21 (see sidebar, page 188). These developments combined to introduce a plot driver unlike Indy's previous MacGuffins, with the Holy Grail intertwined with the character of Henry Jones Sr., who is an expert on the subject. It would, as Spielberg pointed out, eventually serve as a metaphor for the film's father-son relationship.

"I really wanted to bring back the spirit of the original *Raiders* and have some fun with it," Spielberg says. "I wanted to bring the cast back, which I'd missed in *Temple of Doom*, so Denholm Elliott came back, and Rhys-Davies as Sallah."

REUNION

Although the script was not quite where Lucas and Spielberg wanted it to be, the *Indiana Jones* filmmaking group began to re-form in early 1987. Harrison Ford officially signed up for a third movie on February 9.

"It was an interesting evolution," according to Kathy Kennedy, who also returned. "When we started with the series, we were all at early points in our careers. Harrison, by the time we got to the third *Indiana Jones*, had become an enormous star. Steven had made *E.T.* and a number of very successful movies, and had become an enormous star. George, with Lucasfilm now in full tilt, was an enormous star. But what was fascinating was the way in which everybody comes together—and none of that seemed to impact the dynamics of the moviemaking, because all of us had such a good time. It was always about the experience on that film. Oftentimes those kind of dynamics can be the very thing that rips things apart, but in this case I think those dynamics brought everybody even closer and closer together, which was really nice."

"Everybody" meant Spielberg, Lucas, Ford, Watts, Slocombe, Scott, Tomblin, Williams, Kahn, and of course Marshall and Kennedy, who had gotten married in 1987. However, a third writer was needed to write the third screenplay for the third film. "Jeff Boam had done two of the *Lethal Weapon* movies, and Steven had heard of him," Lucas says. "When he brought him up, I said, 'Well, he sounds good to me.'"

"Steven Spielberg called with the Holy Grail of writing gigs, so to speak," Jeffrey Boam says. "I forget what he said, but it was something like, 'You wanna get real rich?' and I said, 'Yeah, why?' and he said, 'I think you should do the next *Indiana Jones* movie.'"

After Lucas and Boam met, about two weeks were spent working on the story. "Lucas had ideas for the set pieces already in mind," says Boam.

"Jeff was very collaborative," Lucas says. "He'd try to include both Steven's ideas and my ideas, and tried to get what we wanted done."

As usual, following the story conference, Lucas wrote up a summary. Dated March 1987, his six-page typed "third story treatment," titled *Indiana Jones and the Last Crusade*, has much of the movie as it would appear on screen, and incorporates into the mix more ideas from the very first *Raiders*' story conference: a female Nazi double agent; rats; and Indy almost drowning in an ancient edifice (the problem of where the water would come from was solved by placing the action in Venice). The story opens with a set piece, a fight on a moving train, which had been moved from midway in Meyjes's script.

Boam signed his contract on April 14, 1987. His first draft was titled *Indy III* (for secrecy's sake) and dated September 15, 1987; a partial revision followed on September 30 (see sidebar, page 192).

THE NAME IS HENRY

Preproduction followed the pattern established by the two previous films, with storyboards, illustrations, recces, and so on. Robert Watts traveled to Spain in late October 1987, and Spielberg eventually chose that country as a stand-in for several locations.

"Almería in Spain has it all," Watts says. "It used to be a filmmaking center, and parts of *Lawrence of Arabia* were shot there, as well as many

OPPOSITE: The title page of Jeffrey Boam's *Indy III* script contains the color coding for Debbie Fine's breakdown copy: yellow for legal; pink for production. Fine would also check for historical accuracy. The list of recipients was: George Lucas; Lucasfilm president Gordon Radley; Steven Spielberg; Kathleen Kennedy; Frank Marshall; Robert Watts; Patricia Carr; Elliot Scott; and Jeffrey Boam.

BELOW: Construction continued in the early 1980s on Skywalker Ranch, where Lucas would move his offices as work on the *Indy III* scripts continued.

INDIANA JONES AND THE MONKEY KING

EARLY TREATMENTS AND SCRIPTS SUMMARY

SEPTEMBER 1984 TO NOVEMBER 1986

[Note: The following summaries go over several stories and scripts.]

TREATMENT & OUTLINE BY GEORGE LUCAS, FALL 1984

Indy is on a fishing trip in Scotland, but is interrupted by a police inspector who needs help solving a series of mysterious murders. The inspector takes Jones to "a haunted castle which sits on a forbidding hill."

After a series of adventures and additional killings, Indy discovers that the murderer is a ghost possessing the body of a dead man. Indy defeats the ghost after being attacked by two dogs and two empty suits of armor.

Upon returning to his college office, he finds in his mail a letter from his old friend Marcus Brody, who writes of a woman zoologist who has found "an odd race of pygmies" that may have discovered a lost Chinese civilization. Brody asks Indy to lead an expedition to the city, as she doesn't have enough experience. He starts at an unnamed colonial African port, which has already been taken over by Nazis, where Indy meets the zoologist, a "Katharine Hepburn type" who introduces him to a mysterious pygmy. He also teams up with a mystical African environmentalist. The pygmy is kidnapped by Nazis while Indy is in a bar. He chases them in a speedboat among the docks, and one of the boats is crushed between two bigger boats. They escape, but Indy pursues them across Africa.

He and the zoologist meet river pirates, and they join forces. Their desert camp, however, is broken up by a stampede of wildebeests, triggered by a Nazi tank. Indy jumps on the tank and fights the Nazis. He wins and, from inside the tank, rescues a pygmy who leads them into the mountains, with the Nazis in pursuit.

Eventually Indiana meets the Monkey King, a talking spider monkey, who explains that "he has magical powers and that he has been alive for a thousand years because of a fountain of youth that exists in the village."

The Nazis arrive but, with large gorillas helping him, the Monkey King uses magic to turn the bad guys into stone, and orders Indy to fight the chief Nazi one-on-one. Finally the Monkey King is killed and his gorillas go crazy, but Indy escapes with the zoologist.

In the undated outline, this story is changed and enhanced. As the villain of the castle is driven away in a police wagon, Indy sees "the killer light a cigarette. And only Indy sees the reflection of the match shining through the killer's body. The killer is a ghost."

The African country is identified as Mozambique. This time a female student who is madly in love with Indy follows him there as a stowaway. When he meets the older but beautiful zoologist, the two women vie for Indy's attention. After joining up with the pirate king, who is a "Toshiro Mifune" type, Indy and the girls wind up in an old Model T Ford driving across a desert. When Indy fights the tank, he is riding a rhino.

When they arrive in the Lost City, they learn that the pygmy is of royal blood, and his father is king. However, the chief Nazi, who has a mechanical gun-arm, kills the king.

Ultimately Indy leads gorillas and pygmies into a battle against the mechanized Nazi army for the Lost City, which contains the fountain of youth. The Nazis mine the city, and a fight takes place as the fuse is lit, extinguished, and relit. The chief Nazi escapes into the desert with vials from the fountain of youth after Indy has won the battle. But we learn that only the pygmies can drink from the fountain without dying—in the desert the Nazi eyes the vials with great thirst. Meanwhile the outline leaves Indy's fate open: He either goes home with the girls or the girls may stay in Africa and do research together.

INDY III FIRST DRAFT BY CHRIS COLUMBUS, MAY 3, 1985; SECOND DRAFT INDIANA JONES AND THE LOST CITY OF SUN WU KUNG, AUGUST 6, 1985: COMBINED SUMMARY

The first draft places the start of the story in "Scotland, 1937," and follows the outline closely. Indy is recruited by Inspector MacGowan after an eighth murder. The suspect is a rich nobleman named Baron Seamus Seagrove III. "Some say 'e walks the moors every midnight… Others claim 'e's been dead for years." They enter the castle with a few men, some of whom are killed, and Indy has several bizarre adventures; in one he has to swim underwater to escape, emerging from a fountain in the nobleman's vast dining room. During the ensuing fight with the possessed suits of armor, one of the knights slices up a roast pig for the old man as it tries to kill Indy (an idea cut from Indy's shortened bazaar duel in Raiders).

Back in the States after defeating Seamus the ghost, Professor Jones encounters several enraged academics and students:

REBECCA: Two-timing bastard! How could you?!?…
My own Mother?!?… In my own bed?!?…
(slaps him again)
I've had it with you! It's over!

Marcus Brody rescues Indy and tells him about a female archaeologist, Dr. Clare Clarke, who has found a mysterious pygmy named Tyki, who is over 200 years old. At first Indy refuses to lead her expedition because he's already spent two years looking for the Monkey King, but Marcus persuades him to go to Mozambique.

Before leaving he has a run-in with Betsy, another student madly in love with him, who tries to kill herself in comical ways as he packs.

Upon arriving in Africa, Jones meets Scraggy Brier, an old friend and guide who speaks hundreds of languages and drives a battered Model T. After he meets Clare, Indy discovers that Betsy has stowed away. Clare is not amused. Nazi sergeant Helmut Gutterbuhg spies on them, later reporting to his boss, Lieutenant Werner von Mephisto.

MEPHISTO: (German, English subtitles)
Ever since our battle for the Lost Ark…
The Führer has been very interested in the
adventures of Indiana Jones.

Indy meets Tyki, who reveals that his belt is actually a cloth scroll known as a "Pai Cho": "the sacred proverbs and writings of Sun Wu Kung." In "Dashiell's American Bar," Indy, Clare, Betsy, and Scraggy discuss their plans to follow the writings to the Lost City, taking the Zambesi River—but meanwhile the Nazis kidnap Tyki. A speedboat chase follows, with Indy using his whip at one point to water-ski. One bad-guy boat is crushed between two ocean liners, but the Nazis escape.

Indy and his friends then take a tattered 55-foot wooden boat called the *Adobo* upriver, towing the Model T on a raft. They meet up with pirates, whose chief is named Kezure, a violent, ambivalent character. The increasingly motley crew piles into the Model T and drives to a village of the Mongooboo tribe. After they're almost killed in a booby-trapped jungle, Indy is disappointed that Kezure's presumed friendship with the natives doesn't materialize:

INDIANA: Is this the Tribal Chief you told me about?... Your friend?...

KEZURE: (points to shrunken head) No. That is him.

Stampeding wildebeests then arrive, provoked by Nazis traveling in a 100-foot-long, three-story-high prototype tank loaded with machine guns and a massive turret. In his battle to free Tyki from the vehicle, Indy takes a headlight and jams the barrel of the main gun; it explodes when fired, killing several Nazis.

Reunited with his friends, Tyki leads them to the mountain city of Sun Wu Kung, which is protected by savage gorillas. A Nazi army remains in close pursuit. Gutterbuhg kills the king, but he is in turn outsmarted by Indy and replaced by Tyki just as the Nazi main army attacks.

Indy leads the defense of the city with shield, pistol, whip, and sword. He tricks Gutterbuhg into firing electrical bursts from his mechanical prosthetic into a lake, sizzling that Nazi—but Indiana Jones is in fact *killed* by Mephisto, shot in the chest, just before the lieutenant is crushed by a rolling bell.

The Nazis are defeated and Tyki takes the fallen into a secret garden of sacred immortal peach trees. There the half-human, half-monkey king comes back to life, his skeleton animated by the gorillas, each of which turns into a single hair and accumulates on his bones. Sun Wu Kung resuscitates the dead, including Indy, and gives the archaeologist, whose adventures he's observed from heaven, his golden-hooped rod, which can change forms. Indy is amazed as the Monkey King returns to his skeletal form. Kezure tries to take the rod but dies after eating one of the peaches, because he is not pure of heart.

As he boards an ocean liner for the States, Indy learns that Betsy is going to stay and study with Clare.

BETSY: But now, I'll think of you as the Father I never had.

INDIANA: (rolls his eyes) Terrific.

In Columbus's second draft, Betsy is gone, while a new character named Dash, the expat who owns the bar, is the chief villain, with the Nazis working for him. In the Lost City, Indy meets Sun Wu Kung, a not-very-nice simian Monkey King. Jones must play a game of chess against Dash using real people as the pieces; when someone is eliminated, Kung disintegrates them with his magic Golden Rod. After a series of confrontations, Kung brings the dead back to life to pursue Indy. They turn Dash into a ghost, but Indy breaks the rod, escapes, and marries Clare.

INDY III BY MENNO MEYJES, BASED ON A STORY BY LUCAS AND MEYJES: FIRST- AND REVISED FIRST-DRAFT SUMMARIES, OCTOBER 2 AND NOVEMBER 21, 1986

The first draft opens with a battle in Mexico between Indy and Banano, a crazed individual with a whip and a loyal band of gorillas. The object of the r dispute is the death mask of Montezuma. Indy manages to throw Banano off a cliff, and his gorillas go free.

No sooner is he back in the States than Indy has to depart for France to look for his father—who has disappeared while looking for the Holy Grail. With a friend named Maude he goes to Montsegur, where they meet a nun named Chantal and her relation De La War, who explains that they had found a map that led Indy's father to Venice. But Nazis, led by Baron Balder von Grimm, were hot on the trail of Indy's dad. Grimm has a hapless sidekick named Hans, whom he is always calling "Idiot!" and then throttling.

After adventures in Venice and on the *Orient Express* where they are disguised as royalty, Indy and Chantal arrive in Istanbul. Clues and escapades put them on a train to Petra, where they are soon fighting for their lives. Fortunately Indy's old friend Sallah arrives with two horses, which they mount. Sallah then leads them to a Bedouin on horseback—who turns out to be Indy's father. Together they find the Grail in Petra, within the City of the Dead. At the climax Grimm shows up, but when he touches the Grail, he explodes; when Henry Sr. touches the Grail, a stairway to heaven appears, which he ascends. The nun Chantal is tempted to take the stairs as well, urged on by Indy. But her love for Jones makes her stay.

In the revised first draft the Nazi villain is Greta Von Grimm. And this time Indy finds his father tied to a pillar in a crusader's castle called Krak Des Chevalier. He'd been forced to help the Nazis in their search for the Grail, but they'd left him to die when he was no longer useful. At the place of the Grail, Indy does battle with a fantastic demon creature, whom he defeats by stabbing it in the belly with a dagger inscribed with the words GOD IS KING. Bad girl Greta is vaporized by the Grail.

LEFT: An illustration of the castle that began as the location for a haunting—an elaborate opening sequence in early drafts of *Indy III*.

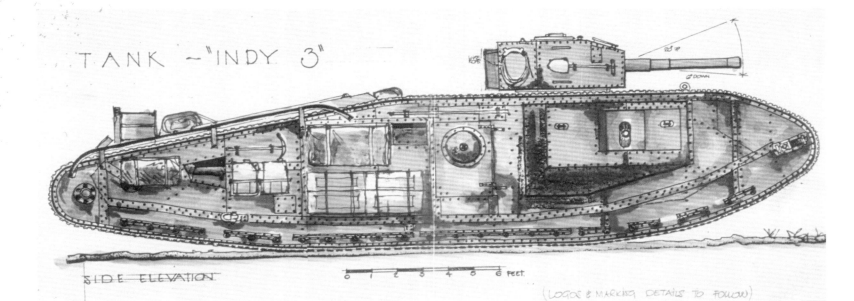

TANK ~ "INDY 3"

SIDE ELEVATION   0 1 2 3 4 5 6 FEET   (LOGOS & MARKING DETAILS TO FOLLOW)

TOP: Production designer Elliot Scott's illustration for the tank was based on reference photos (MIDDLE) and followed up with maquettes (BELOW); the first blueprint for the tank interior would be completed on November 24, 1987.

OPPOSITE: Recce photos taken of a temple façade in Petra, Jordan, and of the long canyon pathway leading to it.

spaghetti westerns. We found all the locations for the entire tank chase, the tunnel where the plane crashes, and the beach."

Of course during this time the real-life search for Indy's father had also begun. "As soon as Steven put the father out there, he had this thing in the back of his mind that he didn't tell any of us about at first—which was Sean Connery," Lucas says.

"When it came down to casting, I said to George there's only person who can play Indy's father and that's James Bond," Spielberg says. "The original and the greatest James Bond is Sean Connery."

"My reaction was no," Lucas says. "I said, 'He's James Bond. The audience is never going to think of him as anyone other than James Bond. He's a big movie star, and we don't need a big movie star.' Steven said, 'Yeah, but Indiana Jones is the spawn of James Bond.' I said, 'He'll want to take over a little bit.' But Steven said, 'No, no, I'll take care of it.'" And it did go that way, but Steven controlled it."

"Steven Spielberg contacted me and made an offer, and I was absolutely delighted," Sean Connery says. "I had a lot of notes, as usual, about the whole piece, so I had a meeting with George and Steven, which went very well."

"Sean had a lot of ideas for his character," Spielberg says. "He would come over to George and me, and say, 'Look, anything Indy does in the context of this story, I have done better. When he talks about sleeping with Elsa, you have to write in that I slept with her, too.' And it was Sean's idea that they should be tied back-to-back in a chair. Sean made major contributions to his character and to the story throughout the whole production."

"I had imagined an older gentleman, kind of a crazy, eccentric guy," Lucas says. "More of a professor but more of a British Laurence Olivier type, an Obi-Wan Kenobi type."

"Sean at first resisted the idea of playing my father, because he's only 12 years older than I," Ford says. "He also felt that the character was too thinly drawn. It turns out Sean is a great student of history, so he brought a lot of

INDIANA JONES AND THE LAST CRUSADE

LATER TREATMENT AND SCRIPTS SUMMARY

MARCH 1987 TO FEBRUARY 1988

INDIANA JONES AND THE LAST CRUSADE
TREATMENT BY GEORGE LUCAS, MARCH 1987

Indy rides with two friends into a "guarded outback town." They give a secret password and proceed to a cantina. On the bar are a lot of trinkets that the bandits have stolen, but Indy notices that one of them is a "pre-Columbian-looking idol." He winks at his companions; they start a fight in the cantina while Indy grabs the idol. They're pursued on horseback at first, but they hitch a ride on a train where, during a big fight, Indy defeats all the bad guys. Afterward much is like the final film. "Indy's father is a strong, Victorian-type teacher who has always been very strict with Indy, so their relationship is one of a strict schoolmaster and student, rather than a father and son." Nazis are again the chief adversaries. But between the Grail and the good guys, this time around, is an armored and mounted crusader knight, whom Indy defeats with his bullwhip.

INDY III BY JEFFREY BOAM, PAGES 1–83, SEPTEMBER 15, 1987; REVISED PAGES 84–102 (END), SEPTEMBER 30, 1987: FIRST-DRAFT

The story opens in Mexico 1939 with Indiana accompanied by two loyal friends, Astorga and Ponce, as he penetrates the hideout of a notorious Mexican bandit to retrieve a valuable statue of the Aztec Sun God. To create a diversion in the cantina, Indy turns to Astorga and says:

INDY: (improvising)
Go down to the end of the bar... count to
twenty, then grab it.

ASTORGA: But—

INDY: —do it.
(Astorga turns to go)
Wait. Better make it twenty-five.

Astorga nods, turns to go—but again, Indy
stops him.

INDY: Better yet—thirty. Count to thirty.

After a big chase on a circus train—where Indy encounters a lion, a gorilla, and so on—he succeeds in keeping the statue. He gives it to Astorga, who turns out to be a museum curator:

INDY: Dr. Astorga... I believe your museum is
the proper home for this.

Astorga takes the statue with a grateful
expression... then his look sours.

ASTORGA: Oh. You've scratched it.

Indy returns to his college and finds in his mail a shrunken head, sent to him, presumably, by an admirer. Brody's mail contains a book sent to him from Venice by Henry Jones Sr. Brody shows it to Indy when they discover that the house of his father has been ransacked. They also find in the yard a dead housekeeper, strangled with a clothesline.

When Indy arrives in Venice to find his father, Nazis—led by Vogel and a new villain, Kemal—are already waiting. They track Indy, Brody, and their contact, art historian Dr. Elsa Schneider, a woman with dark hair and dark eyes. Funded by the Chandler Foundation, she and Henry had been scouring Europe for the Grail when the latter disappeared in Venice. Indy is told by a café proprietor named Aldo that his last whereabouts were the catacombs. Their entrance is through a trapdoor in a library, the Biblioteca Nazionale.

Elsa and Indy find the tomb of a Grail knight, but Kemal tries to kill them first by fire in the catacombs and then with machine guns mounted in boats during a chase in the Grand Canal and the Venetian harbor. Indy outsmarts Kemal and learns, with an additional tip from Elsa, that he and his Ottoman agents are from the Republic of Hatay, the city of Iskenderun, which is built on the ruins of Alexandretta.

KEMAL: What you are after can never be yours!
It belongs in our land—to our people!

But Kemal confesses that the Nazis are holding Indy's father in Austria. So Brody goes to Iskenderun to search for the Grail, while Indy and Elsa voyage to Austria. When Indy finds his father in a castle, Henry Sr. smashes Indy over the head with a vase.

INDY: If I was one of them, would I have
broken in through a window?!

HENRY: (sarcastically)
Okay! I hit you 'cause you failed
trigonometry in high school!
(beat)
Jesus! We haven't talked in five years. We gonna
start off with an argument now?

In their escape they don't take the boats because it's been established that Indy is easily seasick and hates the water. They choose to go to Berlin because the Nazis won't look for them there. When they are shot at on the beach by a Nazi fighter plane, it's Indy who makes the seagulls bring down the last plane.

Inside the mountain temple, Kemal is about to force Elsa to brave the decapitation trap, having already killed all his retainers, when Indy, Henry, Brody, and Sallah arrive. Kemal shoots Henry Jones in order to make Indy do his bidding. Indy braves the traps and bests the crusader knight on horseback—"I am Lord de Bauvais, seigneur of St. Gobain and Folembray. Castellan de Cambri, Viscount of Savoy... known far and wide as William the Lion, Duke of Brittany."

Kemal drinks from the wrong chalice and dies. Indy tests the water from a simple earthenware jug—and his wounds heal. The knight then breaks off the outer vessel to reveal a radiant Grail hidden within the jug. Indy cures his dad, but Vogel grabs the Grail and is immediately crushed by a giant boulder. Elsa perishes, too, falling into infinite darkness; all Indy can see is the receding light of the Grail.

As they leave the mountain temple, the crusader rides out of a cloud of dust—but he and his horse are turned to stone, which then becomes sand and is blown away by the ensuing explosion that seals the cave.

INDY III, FEBRUARY 23, 1988: SECOND-REVISION

Much like the final film, the second revision begins with Indiana Jones as a teenager on a Boy Scout field trip in Colorado, 1912. When he races home with the Cross of Coronado, his dad is on a long-distance phone call concerning an important document. Indy's mother, Margaret, shoos Indy away.

A new character, only referred to in the previous draft, is rich philanthropist Walter Chandler, who tells the adult Indy: "Find the man and you will find the Grail." In Venice, Brody and Indy are introduced to a large Italian family, in whose house Elsa and his father were staying. The family provides comic relief and gives Indy a clue that leads him to the library. Elsa is more of a central character and an ambivalent figure. Her personality is more developed, with her distinguishing characteristic being that she is always eating or snacking on something.

Henry Sr.'s diary is more central to the story—everyone is trying to get it because it's the key to finding the Grail. Indy, Brody, and Elsa go to a basilica, where the priest tells them the library used to be an old church. Indy and Elsa fall through a trapdoor. As they make their way through the catacombs, we learn something new about Indy's father:

INDY: Ha! He never would have made it past the rats! He hates rats! He's scared to death of 'em!
(beat)
I know. We had one in the basement once. Guess who had to go down there and kill it? And I was only six!

When Indy and Elsa travel to Austria, there is more talking in the car, as they discuss food. The Nazi Vogel makes his first appearance at the castle. Chandler is also now in the castle. Indy escapes with his dad, and, on the road, Henry explains why it's so important to obtain the Grail and his diary, and hence go to Germany instead of rescuing Brody right away:

HENRY: There is an evil loose upon the world, son. Perhaps the greatest evil mankind has ever faced. The only thing that matters is the Grail… and who gets to it first.
(beat)
I had a lot of time to think while they were holding me in that castle. And I realized that this is why my search has taken so long… because now—at this exact moment in history— is the time to release the Grail's radiance upon the world. Now is the time to shed its light of goodness and wisdom. Of compassion and charity. Now is the time to share its power of healing and immortality.
(beat)
But if the Grail falls into Nazi hands, its light will be extinguished for all time… and it will be the armies of the Führer who live forever.

Once in Berlin, Indy crosses paths with the notorious Nazi filmmaker-propagandist Leni Riefenstahl, who is trying to shoot a documentary:

LENI: One step forward, please, Mein Führer.

Hitler takes a step back.

LENI: (sighing)
All right. That's fine. Everybody else… one step back as well.

They, instead, take one step forward. Leni wants to pull her hair out…

CREW MEMBER: (to Leni)
The Führer says, 'No double chin'!

Elsa is about to throw the Grail diary into the bonfire of forbidden texts, but Indy manages to switch books on her before she obliges Hitler and Riefenstahl's camera. Later, as father and son converse on the Zeppelin, Henry confesses that he slept with Elsa, too.

During Indy's fight with the Nazis in the desert, Chandler goes over the side of the cliff on the Nazi tank. He plunges to his death, but Indy—believed dead—has saved himself by cutting off part of his pants:

Indy carries the knife in one hand and his pants— which have been slit from the waist down—gather in a heap around his ankles…

HENRY: I would have missed you, Junior.

SALLAH: Junior?

Indy makes a face, tries to improvise a way of holding up his pants… Sallah laughs even louder—slapping Indy on the back—causing Indy's pants to drop around his ankles again.

Vogel is beheaded in the Grail trials. Then a big gun battle takes place as Kemal tries to blow everyone up so they can't retrieve the Grail; the fight is semi-comic as a trail of gunpowder is repeatedly lit and extinguished. Kemal and all his men are knocked out, with Sallah's help—but Elsa shoots Henry. After Indy locates the Grail room, it is Elsa who drinks from what she believes is the Grail cup—indeed, she is about to shoot Indy when she dies horribly. Henry and Indy cross over the seal with the Grail, provoking an earthquake. Henry almost falls to his death—but he lets the Grail go. The Grail Knight turns into a skeleton as they leave.

1.

FADE IN:

EXT. MEXICO - FOOTHILLS OF THE SIERRA MADRE - DAY

A mountain peak dominates the landscape. Three objects crawl across the bottom of the frame at the foot of this towering peak. It takes a moment to realize that they are THREE MEN ON HORSEBACK.

TITLE: MEXICO 1939

Mexican costume 1939

CLOSE ON THE THREE RIDERS

They wear ponchos and have their hat brims pulled down over their eyes to protect against the blowing sand. Still, one of them is instantly recognizable to us as INDIANA JONES.

The other two riders are Mexicans. ASTORGA is an archeologist like Indiana Jones. PONCE is their guide.

The very landscape itself communicates a sense of danger, offering perfect opportunities for an ambush. Indy takes the precaution of turning in his saddle to check the trail behind him.

Astorga glances up at the sheer canyon wall and nervously wets his lips, then exchanges an anxious look with Indy.

Ponce points ahead to a place where the canyon walls come together causing the trail to narrow down considerably. This natural bottleneck serves as:

EXT. ENTRANCE TO BANDIT VILLAGE

Indy, Astorga and Ponce are stopped by FOUR BANDITOS wearing serapes and waving Winchester rifles. Ponce makes some introductory remarks in SPANISH. *Costume*

The Banditos regard Astorga and Ponce with distrust, but they reserve their most suspicious and inhospitable expressions for the Gringo Indy -- who meets their looks with one of his own.

Ponce begins to ARGUE in SPANISH with the Banditos about -- we surmise -- entering the village. Finally, Indy terminates the debate with the utterance of one single name:

                    INDY
          Santiago Rivas. *Bandit*

The Banditos react to the name with fear and respect.

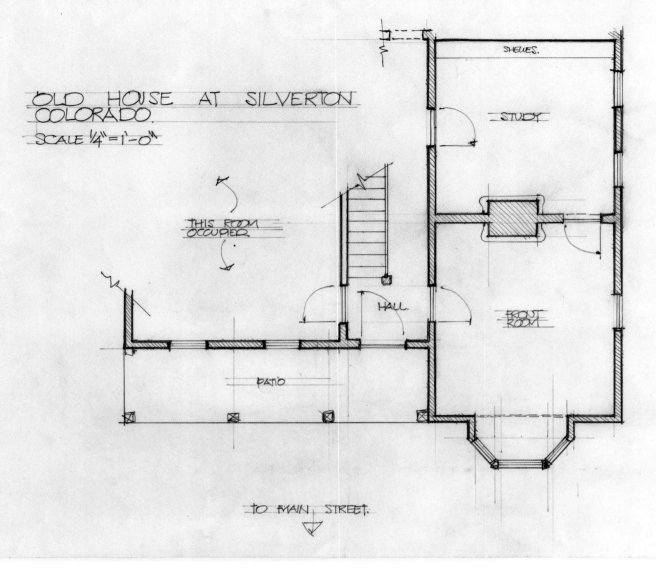

OLD HOUSE AT SILVERTON COLORADO.

SCALE ¼"=1'-0"

SHELVES.

STUDY

SIDE ROAD

THIS ROOM OCCUPIED

HALL

FRONT ROOM

PATIO

TO MAIN STREET.

RIGHT: A diagram shows the layout of the Jones house and its position relative to Main Street in Silverton, Colorado.

BELOW AND OPPOSITE: Circa January 1988, Elliot Scott started his production paintings for several scenes: (BELOW) Young Indy's room and Henry's study; (OPPOSITE) Indy's private office, Donovan's penthouse, Henry Sr.'s ransacked apartment, and the explosion and sinking of the *Coronado*.

DOORS FROM LIVING RM.

HENRY'S STUDY COLORADO

ideas that were incorporated into his character. He ended up less Yoda-like than originally intended and became quite a match to his son, including the fact that we both had a physical relationship with the leading lady."

"We were able to twist that particular idea into something funny and make it humorous rather than serious," Lucas says.

"One wanted the relationship between Indy and his father not to be so harmonious at the beginning," Connery says. "Sleeping with the same woman was a bit of anathema for George, but he eventually came around, because it was possible and funny. And we played up the fact that Indy told his father that he never took any notice of him when he was a kid. I reply, 'You weren't interesting until you were 19.' That was a terrific formula. It makes for good comedy."

All of these ideas and changes went into Boam's second revision of February 23, 1988 (see sidebar, page 192). "What I brought to it especially was this whole Sean Connery thing," Jeffrey Boam said. "The father character had never been evolved […], so that gave me a lot to work with."

This draft also contains another modification, with the train battle now a set piece for the first adventure of Indiana Jones as a teenager, during which the origins of several character traits are revealed. "I thought it would be fun to open the film with Indy as a young man," Lucas says. "Steven was a bit reluctant, but we explored the idea and he agreed it might give the story more depth."

THE TEMPTRESS AND THE VILLAIN

"I went for the audition thinking there was no possibility of me getting the part of Elsa," Alison Doody says. "I was 21 and Irish, and they were looking for a 29-year-old Austrian. I'd done some TV and a Bond film, *A View to a Kill* [1985], playing Jenny Flex. I think I was one of the first girls they saw. I met with Steven Spielberg, and then they asked me to come back to do a screen test. I vividly remember walking by one of the rooms in this studio and seeing another girl going for the part of Elsa. We just stared at each other. I remember thinking, *Oh God, will it be me?*"

Another key role to be cast was that of young Indy. "I loved River Phoenix's work, especially in *Stand by Me* [1986]," Spielberg says. "But I think that Harrison was the one who suggested River. He said, 'The guy who looks most like me when I was that age is this actor named River Phoenix.' They had done *The Mosquito Coast* together. I met River, thought he was great, and cast him."

Though not yet 20 years old, Phoenix was already a veteran and had recently been nominated for an Academy Award for a supporting role in *Running on Empty* (1988).

"I suppose it was my friendship with my next-door neighbor, Robert Watts, which got me the part of Donovan [formerly Chandler]," Julian Glover says. "I actually went up to be interviewed for the part of the German sergeant, for which I was eminently suitable, and I didn't get it. But the next day my agent called and said, 'They want you for Walter Donovan.' So I went back in with an American accent, had a 20-minute interview, and got the part. I couldn't believe it. It was one of the happiest experiences in my life. Then Robert Watts suggested that my wife in real life play my on-screen wife, and she was delighted to do it."

"They left me waiting for about four months," Alison Doody says. "And then I found out the good news and it all started. It was a bizarre time for me because I was quite young and naïve."

"Alison Doody played a part that many actresses played in 1930s movies, where femme fatales turned out to be more fatale than femme," Spielberg says. "That character was an homage to a lot of those Alan Ladd pictures where you never could trust a woman."

THE HOLY FATHER

In Boam's third draft, dated March 1, 1988, the only significant change is that, in keeping with Connery's development of his character, it is now Henry Sr. who thinks of using the seagulls to down the Nazi Messerschmitt. "There was so much humor to be mined in a father-son movie, especially when they haven't been getting along for 20 years," Spielberg says. "I loved the fact that Indy's dad keeps topping him, like when he uses his umbrella to make the seagulls bring down the enemy airplane."

Sean Connery signed his agreement on March 25, 1988.

Following an undated "Amblin" revision, a fourth revision with dialogue changes was completed by Barry Watson on May 8, 1988. Watson was the pen name for Tom Stoppard, in whose version Henry makes young Indy count to twenty in Greek; "Panama Hat," a bad guy

LEFT: Elliot Scott production paintings: A scene in an archives room from an early draft (this would be cut); the catacombs; the Grail room; and the Berlin airport (BOTTOM).

OPPOSITE, TOP LEFT: To play Indiana Jones's father, Henry Jones Sr., Spielberg chose Sean Connery. In the early 1960s Connery had become an international star when he originated the part of James Bond, whose character, created by author Ian Fleming, was part of the original inspiration for Indy. FAR LEFT: To play Dr. Elsa Schneider, Spielberg chose Alison Doody. RIGHT: Connery as Henry Jones Sr. with "Junior." "The big challenge was dressing Sean Connery as Harrison's father," says costume designer Anthony Powell. "And then I thought about my grandfather and, yes, those shirts and the little bow tie and fishing hat, tweed suits and things. It had to be right because the way the script was written, there was no chance for him to change clothes for the whole film. I also thought that it would be helpful for him to wear eyeglasses, but I didn't want to cover up any of that wonderful face. So the only thing was rimless glasses; but those couldn't be found anywhere in the world. We had to have them crafted specially."

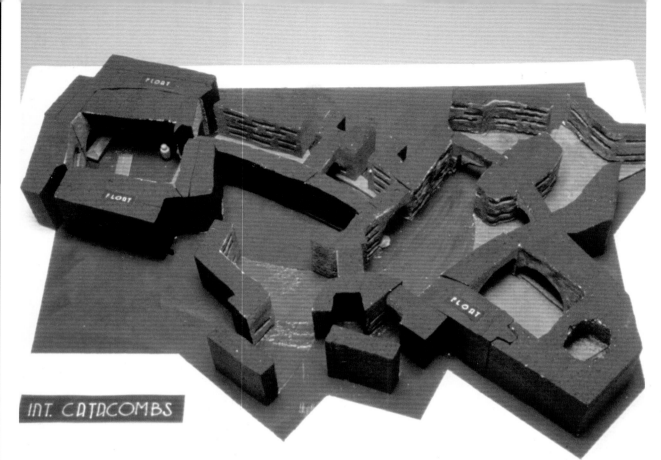

INT. CATACOMBS

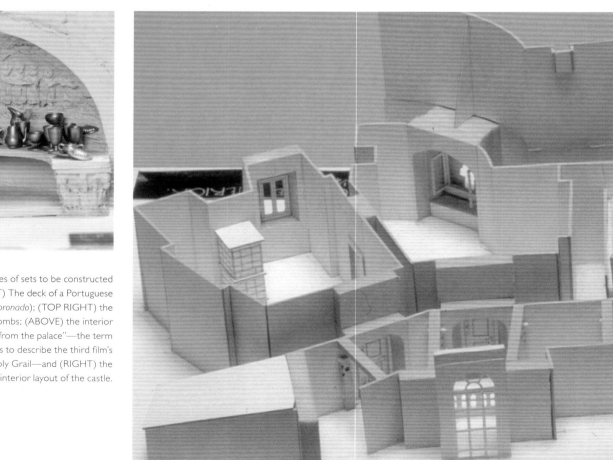

Production maquettes of sets to be constructed at Elstree: (TOP LEFT) The deck of a Portuguese cargo ship (the *Coronado*); (TOP RIGHT) the layout of the catacombs; (ABOVE) the interior for "the chalice from the palace"—the term often used by Lucas to describe the third film's MacGuffin, the Holy Grail—and (RIGHT) the interior layout of the castle.

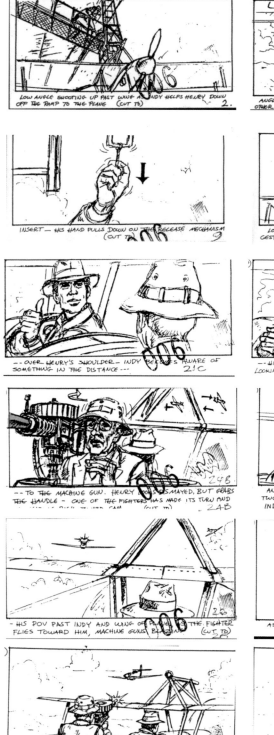

LOW ANGLE SHOOTING UP PAST WING AS INDY HELPS HENRY DOWN OFF THE RAMP TO THE PLANE (CUT TO) 2.

ANGLE ON PROP AND ENGINE COWLING OF INDY'S PLANE F.G. THE OTHER PLANE SEEN JUST PAST. THE ENGINE KICKS OVER, THE PROP 6.

THE OPPOSITE SIDE OF THE ZEPPELIN AS THE WORLD WAR I PILOT RATHER DRUNKENLY LURCHES DOWN THE RAMP, FOLLOWED BY THE GESTAPO AGENT.

AS HE REACHES FOREGROUND THE WORLD WAR LOOKS BACK 7B

INSERT - HIS HAND PULLS DOWN ON THE RELEASE MECHANISM (CUT TO) 9.

LOW ANGLE SHOOTING UP PAST SECOND BIPLANE, RUNG, THE GESTAPO MAN STARTS DOWN TO PLANE 12.

—ANGLE ON THE GESTAPO MAN AS HE SPLUTTERS, POINTS AND YELLS RE THE ACE'S OVERSIGHT, BUT THE WIND AND ZEPPELIN ENGINES AND ACE'S INSOBRIETY DROWN HIM OUT

INDY TURNS TOWARD HENRY, GIVES HIM THE THUMB UP SIGN, CAM DOLLYING RT ON INDY 21B.

—- OVER HENRY'S SHOULDER - INDY BECOMES AWARE OF SOMETHING IN THE DISTANCE --- 21C

—- HIS EYES WIDEN, HIS THUMB DROPS, HENRY WHIPS AROUND LOOKING IN THE DIRECTION INDICATED (CUT TO) 21D

— FOCUS —

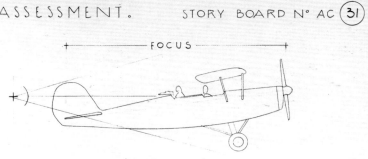

·ELEVATION·

—- TO THE MACHINE GUN. HENRY LOOKS DISMAYED, BUT GRABS THE HANDLE - ONE OF THE FIGHTERS HAS MADE ITS TURN AND HEADS BACK - WIDE CAM (CUT TO) 24B

ANGLE PAST HENRY'S SHOULDER - IN THE B.G. WE SEE THE TWO FIGHTERS TURN - INDY LOOKS BACK OVER HIS SHOULDER INDY FIRE THE MACHINE GUN! 24A

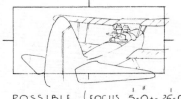

REVERSE ANGLE ON TAIL ASSEMBLY OF BIPLANE AS HENRY AND HIS MACHINE GUN RIP THROUGH THE STABILIZER, THEN THE RUDDER (CUT TO) 31

REQUIRED (FOCUS 4·0 to 10·0)   POSSIBLE (FOCUS 5·0 to 26·0)

- HIS POV PAST INDY AND WING OF PLANE - THE FIGHTER FLIES TOWARD HIM, MACHINE GUNS BLAZING (CUT TO)

AS IT FLIES PAST THE BIPLANE, HENRY FIRING HIS GUN 28B (CUT TO)

ANGLE PAST HENRY, CAM DOLLYING RIGHT AND PANNING W/ FIGHTER

CLOSE ON HENRY, THE GUN FIRES AT CAMERA, HENRY VIBRATING WITH MACHINE GUN (CUT TO)

ABOVE: Storyboards depict several moments in the German fighters' attack on the Joneses, and include the attempt of a World War I pilot to pursue them.

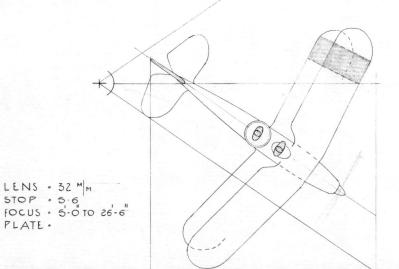

LENS · 32 M/M
STOP · 5·6
FOCUS · 5·0 TO 26·6"
PLATE ·

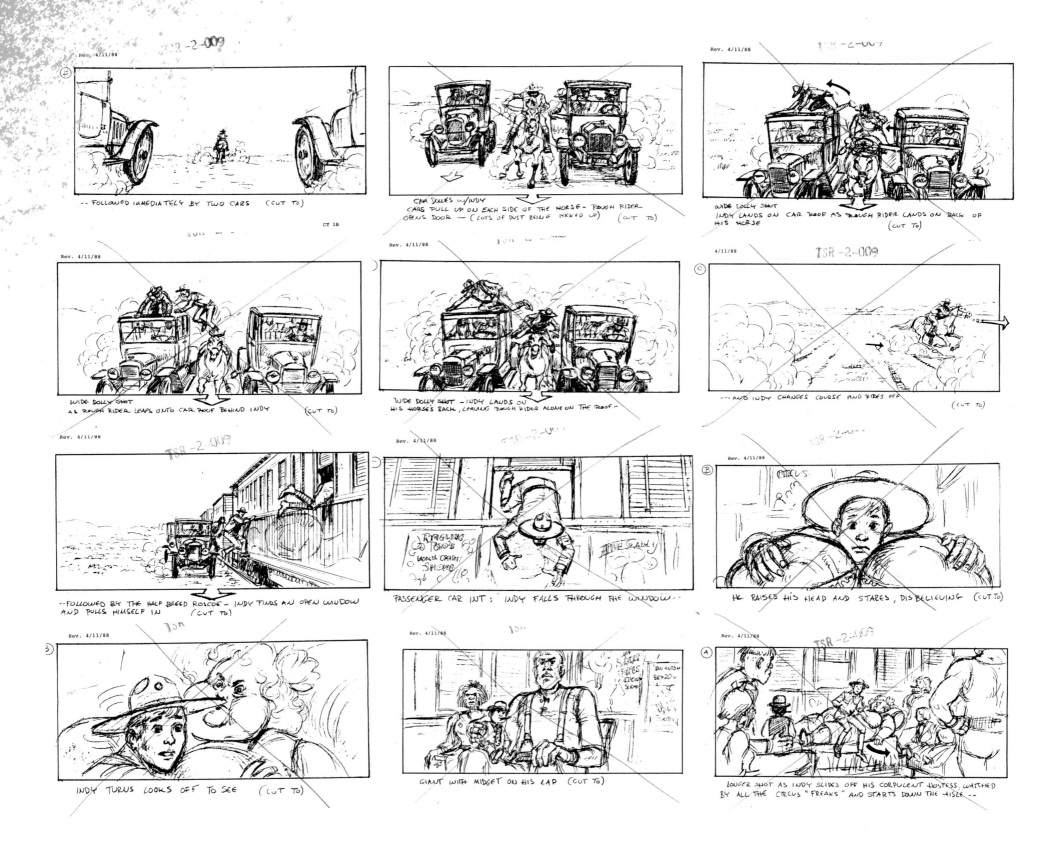

Rev. 4/11/88

-- FOLLOWED IMMEDIATELY BY TWO CARS   (CUT TO)

CT 1B

Rev. 4/11/88

CAM DOLLIES w/INDY
CARS PULL UP ON EACH SIDE OF THE HORSE- ROUGH RIDER
OPENS DOOR — (LOTS OF DUST BEING KICKED UP)   (CUT TO)

WIDE DOLLY SHOT
INDY LANDS ON CAR ROOF AS ROUGH RIDER LANDS ON BACK OF
HIS HORSE   (CUT TO)

Rev. 4/11/88

WIDE DOLLY SHOT
AS ROUGH RIDER LEAPS ONTO CAR ROOF BEHIND INDY   (CUT TO)

Rev. 4/11/88

WIDE DOLLY SHOT - INDY LANDS ON
HIS HORSE'S BACK, LEAVING ROUGH RIDER ALONE ON THE ROOF-

4/11/88

--AND INDY CHANGES COURSE AND RIDES OFF   (CUT TO)

Rev. 4/11/88

--FOLLOWED BY THE HALF BREED ROSCOE - INDY FINDS AN OPEN WINDOW
AND PULLS HIMSELF IN   (CUT TO)

Rev. 4/11/88

PASSENGER CAR INT: INDY FALLS THROUGH THE WINDOW--

Rev. 4/11/88

HE RAISES HIS HEAD AND STARES, DISBELIEVING   (CUT TO)

Rev. 4/11/88

INDY TURNS LOOKS OFF TO SEE   (CUT TO)

Rev. 4/11/88

GIANT WITH MIDGET ON HIS LAP   (CUT TO)

Rev. 4/11/88

LONGER SHOT AS INDY SLIDES OFF HIS CORPULENT HOSTESS, WATCHED
BY ALL THE CIRCUS "FREAKS" AND STARTS DOWN THE AISLE --

TSR-2-009

Rev. 4/11/88

INDY CLIMBS ONTO THE NEXT FLATCAR ALONGSIDE A LARGE CRATE TOWARD A STEAM CALLIOPE AS THE GANG STARTS DOWN THE LADDER -- (CUT TO)

Rev. 4/11/88

REVERSE ON INDY - PAST CALLIOPE PIPES - HE STOPS AT SMALL MECHANICAL CLOWN FIGURE, TURNS BACK TOWARD HIS PURSUERS (CUT TO)

Rev. 4/11/88

ANGLE-ON THE INDIAN AND OTHER THREE - WITH A GREAT BLAST OF STEAM AND A PIERCING SHRIEK, THE CALLIOPE GIVES FORTH, STOPPING THE PURSUERS IN THEIR TRACKS - (CUT TO)

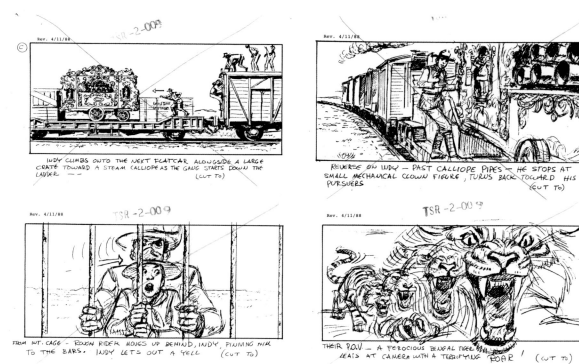

TSR-2-009

Rev. 4/11/88

FROM INT. CAGE - ROUGH RIDER MOVES UP BEHIND, INDY, PINNING HIM TO THE BARS. INDY LETS OUT A YELL (CUT TO)

TSR-2-009

Rev. 4/11/88

THEIR P.O.V. - A FEROCIOUS BENGAL TIGER LEAPS AT CAMERA WITH A TERRIFYING ROAR! (CUT TO)

Rev. 4/11/88

AS ROUGH RIDER STRUGGLES IN THE TIGER'S GRASP, INDY REACHES THE END OF THE CAGE, CAM CRANING AROUND --

-009

Rev. 4/11/88

NEW ANGLE SHOOTING BACK ON ROOF - AS INDY RISES TO HIS KNEES, ROSCOE DOES LIKEWISE, WHIPS BACK HIS KNIFE TO A THROWING POSITION, AND -- (CUT TO)

Rev. 4/11/88

ANGLE ON ROSCOE AS HE THROWS THE KNIFE PAST CAM (CUT TO)

CT 69

TSR-2-009

Rev. 4/11/88

-- WHEN ONE LAST TIME THE HORN BURSTS UP THROUGH THE ROOF, RIGHT IN FRONT OF INDY, MIRACULOUSLY INTERCEPTING THE BLADE! (CUT TO)

THONK!

RHHP

TSR-2-009

Rev. 4/11/88

ONE OF THE LIONS, GROWLING, STARTS TOWARD INDY, HEADING RIGHT FOR THE CROSS OF CORTEZ (CUT TO)

CT 87

-009

Rev. 4/11/88

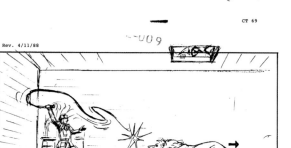

WIDE ANGLE AS THE WHIP CRACKS AGAIN - THE LION BACKING, INDY FOLLOWING (CUT TO)

CT 95

TSR-2-009

Rev. 4/11/88

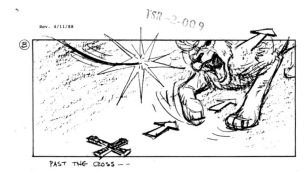

PAST THE CROSS --

CT 98B

OPPOSITE AND ABOVE: Deleted gags from the Young Indy train chase sequence, dated April 11, 1988.

RIGHT: Lucas and Spielberg meet with department heads to discuss the logistics of principal photography, spring 1988. BELOW: A production painting/prop, to be placed in the living room of Henry Jones, Sr., shows a Grail knight seemingly walking on air above a canyon. BOTTOM RIGHT: An Elliot Scott production painting of the "Castle Ext. Swinging Shot" was designed as a matte shot and as a "general idea only"; ultimately Spielberg would opt to shoot this on set and in-camera.

OPPOSITE: DP Douglas Slocombe (standing on left), production designer Elliot Scott (center), Spielberg, and Lucas examine the set maquettes.

who adds continuity to the early part of the film, appears; Elsa leads Indy and Brody straight to the library/ancient church, with all the Italian family scenes deleted; Kemal becomes Kazim; Chandler is named Donovan—and he, instead of Elsa, now shoots Henry Sr.

"It was a little tricky, and we were all a little nervous about that aspect of the story," Lucas says. "It kept evolving, but it seemed very logical to connect it that way and have the extra pressure of Indy having to get the Grail in order to save his father."

"When Donovan turns the gun on to Henry and shoots him right in the stomach, Indiana has a finite amount of time to discover the Grail," Spielberg says. "And that's when you know a story is working, when you have that kind of drama."

The Grail trials are also fully formed in this last version, which also has a moment where the Grail Knight attempts to figure out who will replace him:

```
KNIGHT: But now at last I am released to death with honor,
for this brave knight-errant has come to take my place.

INDY: (anxiously)
...there's a misunderstanding here...

HENRY: He is not a knight-errant, merely my errant
son who has led an impure life...

INDY: (agreeing)
...impure life...

KNIGHT: Is it you then, brother?

HENRY: Alas, I am only a scholar.
```

CHAPTER 10
THE PROFESSIONALS

MAY 1988 TO MAY 1989

Five days before principal photography began—on May 11, 1988—a shooting schedule was issued. Spielberg and crew's first destination was Spain, where they started the complex action scenes aboard the tank—which had not been easy to transport to such a desolate spot—and those scenes supposed to take place in the desert outside of Iskenduren. As Watts had planned, all the locations were near Almería: Rambla, Indalecio, Trujillo, Tesica Flat, Baños de Alfaro, and the Desierto de Tabernas.

"George wanted an old World War I tank," Spielberg says, "and I basically wrote the scene in storyboards."

"Originally it was just gonna be a small French tank," mechanical effects supervisor George Gibbs says. "We went to a museum and looked at these different tanks, but I thought to myself, *No, I'm gonna build it for real*. And I did: I built it using real steel. I made it look solid and heavy."

"We started shooting second unit two weeks before the main unit arrived in Spain, and the first sequence we tackled was the tank chase," says stunt coordinator Vic Armstrong. "One of the challenges was the fact that the tank could only go about ten, twelve miles an hour. So it was quite difficult to ride the horse and look as though you were going fast."

"Eventually, we had two tanks," Gibbs says. "We had one that weighed 28 tons and was like a real steel tank. And we had another tank on which we could mount cameras, and that was used for the close-ups of actors—and I must add that Harrison did all of his own stunts."

"Harrison is very tough and he wants to do everything himself," Armstrong says. "You've got to keep holding him back. He is physically fit enough to do it all, but he is the star and you can't risk anything happening to him. So it's a fine line that you have to walk, letting Harrison participate as much as you feel is physically safe for him."

"The notion that George and Steven had about putting my father in the tank and me having to stop it gave us the opportunity to come up with a lot of physical stunts and gags," Ford says. "As for the hat having to stay on, I'll tell you what helps a lot is a good sweat."

"The scenes on the tank were originally scheduled for something like two and a half days," Connery says. "And I think that we went until about eight or ten. But it didn't matter because a lot of inventions, a lot of ideas came out of the reality of it. Steven is always very confident and he really encourages you."

From late May through Wednesday, June 1, 1988, the director guided his crew through other sites in Almería: Bellas Artes ("the Sultan's Palace"); an Almería location ("Ext. Iskenderun Street"); Playa Monsul ("Ext. Beach and Seagulls"); Rodalquilar ("Ext. Road & Tunnel"); and Mojácar Airfield ("Ext. Airplane Chase House and Plane Crash"). On June 1 the company moved to Granada, and on June 2 Spielberg filmed the Iskenderun train station scenes at Guadix.

Of the beach sequence, Watts says: "Seagulls aren't trainable. So we put fake birds on the beach, and for when Sean Connery finally scares them off with his umbrella, we used white doves."

BELOW: Spielberg and Ford once again on location, this time in Almería, Spain.

LEFT: Spielberg directs Ford on horseback as Indy does battle with a tank, taking his battle with a truck one step forward from *Raiders*.

OPPOSITE, TOP LEFT: Michael Byrne (Nazi officer Vogel) was also on location for the tank sequences. "All those Nazi uniforms were genuine and were found in Eastern Europe," says costume designer Anthony Powell. "[Co-costume designer] Joanna Johnston was a wonderful organizer, and brilliant at handling large crowd scenes. I would give her research pictures, sketches and drawings, then she'd go out and find it all." BELOW: Spielberg with bullhorn, as Ford as Indy prepares to shoot several Nazis at once.

ELSTREE STUDIOS IS CRUMBLING

On Friday, June 3, 1988, production traveled to London to shoot once again on the stages of what had changed to *Cannon* Elstree Studios. On Shoot Day 17, Monday, June 5, on Stage 2, Spielberg started the castle interiors, which they finished on Wednesday, June 15, on Stage 10, appropriately burning down the set (as the story demanded).

"I had to act with an Austrian accent," Alison Doody says. "So I did a lot of work for that, and before I knew it I was on the set shooting with Harrison Ford, Sean Connery, Denholm Elliott, Steven Spielberg, George Lucas, and little Alison Doody, with an Austrian accent. I was really thrown in the deep end, I have to say."

"Playing with Harrison is great fun," Connery says. "Steven is always prepared and professional, and it was just a great crew. We had Dougie Slocombe, who's a wonderful old-school cameraman."

"We were a pretty well-oiled, fast-working, efficient group," Ford says, "which was good because it was probably the most complicated of the three films."

"Sean wants everybody to be very professional," Lucas says. "He doesn't want to be called to set and have to sit there doing nothing. He wants everyone involved to know what they're doing. Of course both Steven and Harrison are very professional, so it made for a fun experience."

"I like rehearsals, to work with all the actors or actresses before we start shooting," Connery says. "And that was no problem, because Steven was very certain of where he was going."

On Thursday, June 16, cast and crew made a short trip to the Royal Horticultural Halls and Conference Centre (Vincent Square, Westminster), for the Tempelhof Airport (Berlin) interiors, or the "Zeppelin queue." On Day 26, the next day, they were on the back lot for the brief motorcycle escape from the castle. Filming continued at Elstree until July 18, with a side trip on June 29 to Northweald Airfield for shots of Indy's departure in Donovan's airplane.

LEFT AND RIGHT PAGES: Behind the scenes and filming on several locations in Spain, with Ford, Sean Connery (Henry Jones Sr., on the beach at the Playa Monsul)—and the return of Denholm Elliott as Marcus Brody and John Rhys-Davies as Sallah (ABOVE). OPPOSITE, TOP RIGHT: Spielberg checks out a shot with DP Douglas Slocombe.

"After we came in with *Raiders*, Elstree Studios really became our second home for all three movies," Marshall says. "We couldn't imagine not shooting at Elstree. They had great stages, great craftsmen, great support systems, and we felt like they were really our lucky studio. It really saved us a lot of time and money.

"Unfortunately by that time, the economy of England and the economy of their movie business was really at a depressed stage," Marshall adds. "The studios weren't making enough money to keep going. But we knew that if they started disappearing, then the craftsmen and the film people would start disappearing, too. All of the experience that had been passed down over the ages would be lost.

"So we took our biggest hitter—that would be Steven—to Parliament

BELOW: At Elstree, Spielberg directs Alison Doody (Elsa) and Ford in the castle interiors. On Thursday, June 16, at the Royal Horticultural Halls and Conference Centre, Spielberg and company filmed the Tempelhof Airport Berlin interiors, with DP Slocombe in the visor (BELOW RIGHT).

TOP: Connery, Ford, and Spielberg shoot the burning interior castle shots. ABOVE: Frederick Jaeger was cast as the World War I flying ace who attempts to follow the Joneses from the zeppelin along with a crewman and a gestapo agent (Pat Roach); in the script he makes an error and his plane plummets like a stone to earth. LEFT: Spielberg directs Ford and Connery, seated in the biplane set.

LEFT & RIGHT PAGES: Spielberg, Lucas, Ford, and company during the scenes set in the Grail cave and cup room. Robert Eddison played the Grail Knight.

one day. We were shooting, but we put him in a car and raced him into London so he could appear in front of Parliament and make this plea in person. That was just part of our normal day [laughs]. We made a real plea to subsidize the studios and keep them alive and keep them going, and we saved a portion of it."

CHOOSING WISELY

A revised shooting schedule was issued July 19, which listed July 20–22 for scenes in the interior of the hidden temple: the pendulum, "Jehovah stones," and the abyss. Also included was the scene in the "small temple" of the Grail.

"Robert Eddison, who played the knight at the end, that extraordinary monk-like figure, was such a wonderful actor," Glover says. "Fantastic, wonderful, rolling voice. He had done TV and stage, but that was his first film ever, so he was understandably very nervous and excited. He kept asking me, *Am I doing it right, am I doing it right?* But at the same time, he was able to take that wonderful line, 'He chose poorly,' and do it in such a dry way that it was really funny."

"All through the movie, Dad only calls him Junior," Spielberg says. "The whole film he tortures him by calling him Junior. But for the first time, when his son is hanging on for his life, he says 'Indiana.' And that stops

Indy. Indy looks up at his father, and then takes his other hand, and is pulled to safety. That was the bonding moment between father and son."

"I didn't want to die at the end of the film," Doody says. "I remember suggesting, after they leave the cave, 'Let's show my hand coming out of the rubble.' And they kept saying, 'You're dead. You're dead.' So I was dead."

Monday and Tuesday, July 25–26, 1988, were reserved for a night shoot of Berlin, exterior street and square, which was filmed at Blenheim Palace, Woodstock, Oxfordshire. Wednesday was a rest day. From Thursday, July 28, to Friday, August 5, Spielberg shot the interior of the Biblioteca Nazionale, the deck of the Portuguese freighter, Indy's office, Professor Jones's house—and the catacombs.

"My job was to find thousands of rats," Marshall says. "So I found a couple of breeders and we bred rats!"

"Happily, rats don't bother me very much," Ford says. "When I was a young teenager I was a nature counselor, and, coincidentally, I did have as pets black hooded rats. First only two, and then pretty soon many, many, many more as they multiplied."

"The rats were great and, thankfully, they were not your average sewer rat," Alison Doody says. "It was something they brought up in the audition: They asked me whether I would have a problem with that scene and I said absolutely not."

"In order to have rats that aren't infected with some virus or disease, you have to basically cultivate them from birth," Spielberg says. "So our

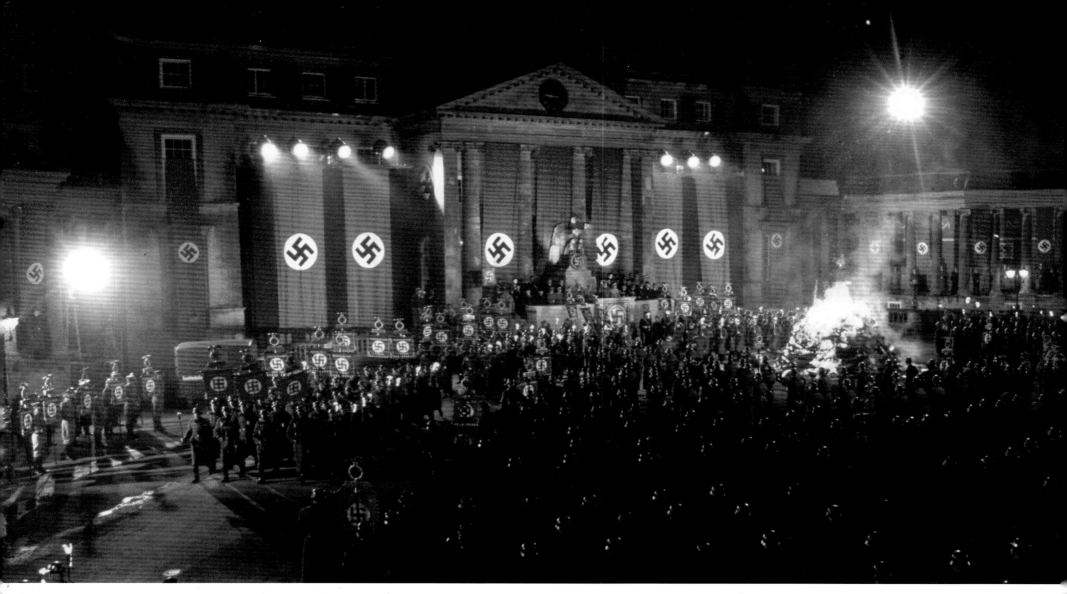

TOP: The Nazi book-burning rally was shot at Blenheim Palace, England, in late July 1988.
RIGHT: In a cameo appearance, Ronald Lacey, who played Toht in *Raiders*, played another Nazi,
Heinrich Himmler (with glasses), in *Last Crusade*. ABOVE LEFT: Spielberg talks things over with
executive producer Frank Marshall and producer Robert Watts. MIDDLE AND RIGHT: Scenes
aboard the *Coronado* were shot on a soundstage at Elstree with wind machines and fake rain.

LEFT: Ford and Alison Doody in the catacomb set—with real rats—but the torch in Doody's hand proved more dangerous. "I have an *Indiana Jones* scar on my hand from dripping wax," she says. BELOW: The giant propeller and sliced-up motorboat was filmed on Elstree's studio lake; here Ford, Alison Doody, and Kevork Malikyan (Kazim) laugh in the one boat to survive the chase.

animal handlers gave birth to something like 2,000 rats. I put snakes around Karen Allen's neck, I put bugs in Kate Capshaw's hair, and rats in Alison Doody's. I had no shame. We also had a lot of mechanical rats because we had to light them on fire. I may have no shame, but I do draw the line somewhere."

"In the catacombs when I was holding one of the torches, hot wax dripped down onto my hand," Doody says. "Harrison noticed and he quickly grabbed my hand and put it in water, but I got a scar."

England's Mill Hill stood in for the "American streets" outside Professor Jones's house, while on August 2 a flooded portion of the Elstree back lot stood in for the Venetian harbor.

"We were in what they call the studio lake," Spielberg says. "Elliot Scott and George Gibbs had built this tremendous propeller on the back of a boat. It rotated and was made of metal, so it was not safe to be anywhere near it. We did use stunt doubles for certain angles. I also used very long lenses to give you the sense that they were closer to the propeller than they were. We made the back of the motorboats a little bit longer so the propeller could have a lot more boat to eat up without putting the actors in harm's way."

On Thursday, August 4, Spielberg shot more Venice scenes at the Tilbury Docks in Essex. At the Royal Masonic School at Rickmansworth, as he had on *Raiders*, Spielberg shot interiors and exteriors for Indy's college, on August 5, wrapping principal photography in the United Kingdom on the last of 60 shooting days.

VENICE ON $100,000 A DAY

Without a letup, production traveled to Venice, Italy, where Spielberg met with Lucas on Monday, August 8, for one day of intense filming.

"I said going into this film, 'I don't want to go near Venice in the tourist season,'" Watts says. "Guess what? We were scheduled to go there in August. There was nothing I could do and it was really crowded. So I took a second assistant director out of Rome, who was Venetian-born, and I said, 'Show me every square that's got a canal on one side and a church in it—and then tell me which ones I can control in August.' So we went around, and we found one, and we managed to get control of the Grand Canal from, like, 7 AM to 1 PM for one day."

The plaza they were able to manage was the Campo San Barnaba. "Of course, when you're shooting period, suddenly you notice all these satellite dishes on the top of hotels on the other side of the Grand Canal," Watts says. "But Dougie said, 'It's all right. You won't see them.' I thought, *Thank God for that*."

"The whole piece in Venice where we're jumping onto the boat, I'm running in high heels and my shoes are giving way at this stage," Alison Doody says. "They're very wet and I'm jumping onto a wet boat—I cannot tell you how scared I was."

On Tuesday production traveled to Amman, Jordan, continuing the next day to Petra for the Canyon Temple scenes on Thursday and Friday.

"It was amazing to be able to shoot in Jordan," Spielberg says. "We stayed at the Royal Palace in Akaba and were guests of King Hussein and Queen Noor."

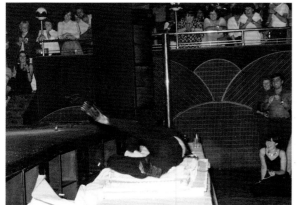

OPPOSITE AND ABOVE: In early August 1988 Spielberg, Ford, and Lucas returned to the Royal Masonic School at Rickmansworth, where they had shot Indy's college in *Raiders*, to film classroom scenes and Indy's office for *Last Crusade*.

LEFT: At the wrap party Frank Marshall performed as Dr. Fantasy—and threw himself into the cake once again.

"I ride horses. Badly," Rhys-Davies (Sallah) says. "I recall when we were going to ride out from the ruins of Petra, Sean's horse reared and spooked mine, just as I was getting on it; so mine just reared right up, too, and I had a rather undignified exit off the back of it."

Spielberg wrapped principal photography in Jordan on Friday, August 12. The following day they returned to London after 63 days of shooting.

"Connery elevated everybody's game," Ford says. "And it was maybe the most fun of all to make because it had so much physical action. It had great locations. It had a terrific leading lady, Alison Doody, and a real intriguing story to tell."

"Each film I've made has its own kind of place," Connery says. "But there are certain films that have a better taste, a better experience and souvenir. Others would be better forgotten. *Indiana Jones* is up there with the best of the films."

BACK IN THE USA

Michael Kahn had moved his cutting room from the United Kingdom to Amblin's offices in Los Angeles the week of August 7; intense editorial work then took place from Monday, August 22, through Friday, September 2.

The first unit was in the United States, in Colorado, by Monday, September 5, joining the second unit, which had already shot "horse transfers and opening mountain-troop-shot" from August 29 to September 3. Both units were now racing to complete on schedule the Young Indy opening for the film. The main unit began in Alamosa with the "Ext. Antonito/Train," "Indy dives in among freaks." On September 7, they moved to Pagosa Springs, Colorado, for the "Cumbres/Train (rhino horn)." On Saturday, September 10, it was Cortez for the "Lobato/Train" and the "water spout gag." On Monday, September 12, Spielberg shot the "long shot of troops approaching ruins" and exteriors.

"I only worked with River Phoenix [Young Indy] for a couple of weeks," Spielberg says. "But I really enjoyed it. He very seriously studied Harrison in all of his films, his vocal inflection and his physical style. He made the part his own, but incorporated enough of Harrison that you could really see a young Indiana Jones underneath the Boy Scout uniform." Spielberg would later remark that, "When I finally worked with Leonardo DiCaprio on *Catch Me If You Can* [2002], he reminded me of River. Not only do they look alike, their approach to acting, to their art, is very similar."

As an homage to Frank Marshall, one car of the train was named *Doctor Fantasy's Magic Caboose*. Earlier at Elstree, Dr. Fantasy had made a surprise appearance. "On the third movie, we were celebrating Amanda's birthday again," Marshall says. "The soldiers [Nazi extras] brought out this huge, long cake—and I had really prepared things. I had a little springboard, so I got tremendous air and plopped down in the cake in front of everyone—and, finally, everybody laughed. It was good."

The next stop was Los Angeles, where on September 14–16 soundstages were used to shoot Indy falling into the snake bin and holding off a lion.

Back on the road in mid-September 1988, cast and crew went to Green River, Utah, where they stayed at the Best Western River Terrace and the Greenwell Hotel, filming more of the film's opening in nearby Arches National Park.

BELOW: Spielberg sits with Connery in Petra, Jordan, where they stayed with King Hussein and Queen Noor, who came to the set and spoke with Ford, Spielberg, and Lucas (BOTTOM); Watts, Slocombe, Spielberg, Lucas, and Tomblin (BELOW RIGHT). "Looking back on the *Indiana Jones* trilogy, one sort of felt that it had quite a breadth of storytelling," Slocombe says. "And I'd like to say how much I enjoyed working with Steven, who was such a wonderful friend to me—a very warm companion, and such a brilliant director. Every setup came so naturally to him. Somehow he always seemed to know automatically where to focus his attention."

OPPOSITE: Lucas holds Connery's horse as they prepare and then shoot his scene with Rhys-Davies and Ford before the temple at Petra, Jordan, or the "Treasury" (El-Khazneh).

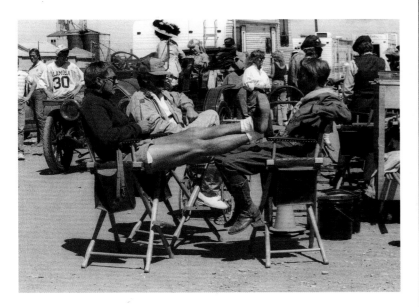

MOTORCYCLE ACTION

In late 1988 Spielberg and Lucas decided to add a motorcycle chase to the Jones's escape from the castle.

"That diary is like the Ark of the Covenant," Spielberg says. "First the good guys have it, then the bad guys have it, and then the good guys get it back. When I realized that the movie had become a chase movie, I felt it needed more action. So we thought up a good scene with the motorcycle sidecar, which we filmed near San Francisco, in the Bay Area, near where George lives."

"Not a terribly complicated sequence," Ian Bryce, at this point USA production manager, says. "We shot that in Fairfax [about 20 minutes from Skywalker Ranch]. We found some great country roads and did a stunt sequence in a week or two. We also went to Texas in early 1989 and did the final ride off into the sunset with the horses."

The selected dailies were given to Kahn, who edited them in. For his part Ben Burtt was editing in his usual assortment of creative effects. "I needed to make up sounds for what would be thousands and thousands of rats," he says. "And, oddly enough, I ended up using chickens. I put the sound on a keyboard and then played the highest notes. It sounded like rats to me, and I guess everybody else believed it.

"There's a scene at the end where Donovan shoots Indy's dad," Burtt adds. "I wanted to get a real echoey gunshot, so I took a revolver with some blanks in it and went into the parking garage underneath the Tech Building at Skywalker Ranch, because it's a very large, echoey space. Nobody was around, so I thought I'd be safe—and just as I fired the .357 magnum, George Lucas drove in to park his car."

Working quickly as usual, John Williams recorded the score during split sessions: from Monday, January 30, to Friday, February 3; then Tuesday, February 14, through Friday, February 17, 1989.

"I think the prelude sequence is actually about four minutes, and it's got something like 55 musical sync points for the snakes, for the lion, for the men jumping on top of the train," Williams says. "That sequence was

OPPOSITE: On location in Arches National Park, Utah, Spielberg shoots the mountain/Paramount logo and the Boy Scouts' approach to the caves, posing with them for a group shot (with J. J. Hardy as Herman and Larry Sanders as the scoutmaster, holding their flag on the far left). FAR LEFT: Spielberg with River Phoenix (Young Indy). OPPOSITE RIGHT: Also posing for a group shot are: Marc Miles (sheriff, left), Bradley Gregg (Roscoe), Jeff O'Haco (Half-Breed), Richard Young (Fedora, center), Vince Deadrick (Rough Rider), Tim Hiser (Young Panama Hat). TOP RIGHT: Lucas stands on the train in one of the several Colorado locations used during the train pursuit, and talks with Phoenix and Spielberg (ABOVE). TOP LEFT: Ford visits the set and chats with Spielberg and Phoenix.

TOP LEFT AND BELOW: Interiors of the train chase were shot on a soundstage in Los Angeles September 14–16, 1988, with a rhinoceros and Slocombe. FAR RIGHT: Spielberg also shot Richard Young (Fedora) and River Phoenix in the house interior near Arches on location. RIGHT: Alex Hyde-White portrayed Young Henry Sr., but in the film only his hands were actually shown.

OPPOSITE RIGHT: Ford filmed the step into the void on a section of set built at ILM, which was combined with a miniature and a matte painting (Paul Huston touches up the bridge, LEFT); Lucas and Ford examine the miniature fighter at ILM (BELOW).

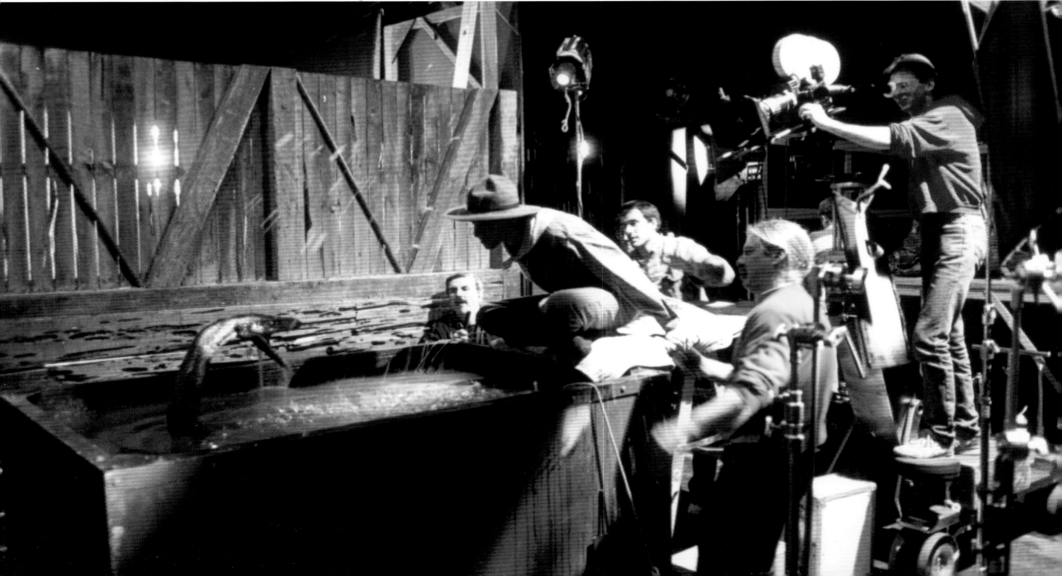

an indication that we were moving all the time. That was the spirit of the score."

"*Last Crusade*, thematically, is about personal leaps of faith," Spielberg says. "One of the greatest leaps of faith was the one where Indy has to step into nothingness and winds up stepping onto a forced perspective, onto an actual bridge made of rocks painted to look like what's below. That was one of the most interesting things ILM did."

"The leap-of-faith shot was probably the single most challenging concept in the movie," says ILM visual effects supervisor Micheal McAlister. "Nobody really knew how to do it. It was a combination of matte painting with a miniature set of the physical bridge. But the bridge blended into the background and was essentially invisible—then as soon as the camera would slide off axis, the illusion was revealed."

"In those days there was no such thing as digital fire," McAlister adds. "If you had a sequence that involved fire, you pretty much were limited to actually shooting it as a miniature set. Figuring out how to build the equipment so the camera and the plane could get through the tunnel, and

getting all the timing correct so that it exploded at the right place, was actually a pretty huge engineering feat."

With ILM finals due on Wednesday, April 5, 1989, and the Final Answer print scheduled for Friday, April 7, 1989, McAlister and crew had one other obstacle to overcome. "The death of Donovan was a severe challenge because morphing technology had barely been invented by then," he says. "So we created three different puppets in different stages of decay, knowing that we could eventually morph the three together."

Spielberg then finished editing the film with Kahn.

SUNSET, SUNRISE

Indiana Jones and the Last Crusade was released on May 24, 1989, on 2,327 screens, to great box office and mixed reviews, though the majors edged toward the positive. Andrew Sarris panned it in *The New York Observer*, as did David Denby in *New York* magazine, Stanley Kauffmann in *The New Republic*, and Georgia Brown in *The Village Voice*.

But *The Christian Science Monitor*'s David Sterritt gave it a begrudging thumbs-up, while Peter Travers wrote in *Rolling Stone*, "It's Spielberg's wide-eyed enthusiasm that turns *The Last Crusade* into the wildest and wittiest *Indy* of them all." Richard Corliss in *Time* lauded it, and David Ansen in

Newsweek praised it. Vincent Canby in *The New York Times* said, "It wobbles at a great rate of speed over a spectacularly bumpy course of adventure, like an old-fashioned touring car with one wheel slightly out of line, suddenly soars in the air with childlike delight and sometimes crashes, only to explode in laughter."

"What Steven and George did that really kept the movies alive was to put new elements in," Marshall says. "We had all the old elements—we had archaeology, we had fun, we had a lot of action, we had bugs or snakes or rats, that creepy element—all the things that the first movie promised were delivered in the second and then delivered to another level in the third movie. But with Sean Connery, that whole dynamic made it fresh and new."

Variety reviewer "Mac" agreed—"To say that Paramount's *Indiana Jones and the Last Crusade* may be the best film ever made for 12-year-olds is not a backhanded compliment"—while Duane Byrge in *The Hollywood Reporter* predicted that Ford would be unjustly ignored but that Connery could very well receive a supporting actor Oscar nomination: "Director Steven Spielberg's robustly articulate visualization, as well as the film's magnificently evocative effects, are, in Lucasfilm-speak, the ultimate Forces of Good here."

The film's box-office saga was entirely positive. While its final budget was $55,364,887, with ILM costs making up $3,485,901 of that sum, the first Saturday *Last Crusade* played it broke the single-day record with $11,181,429—the first time in the history of film that any movie had passed

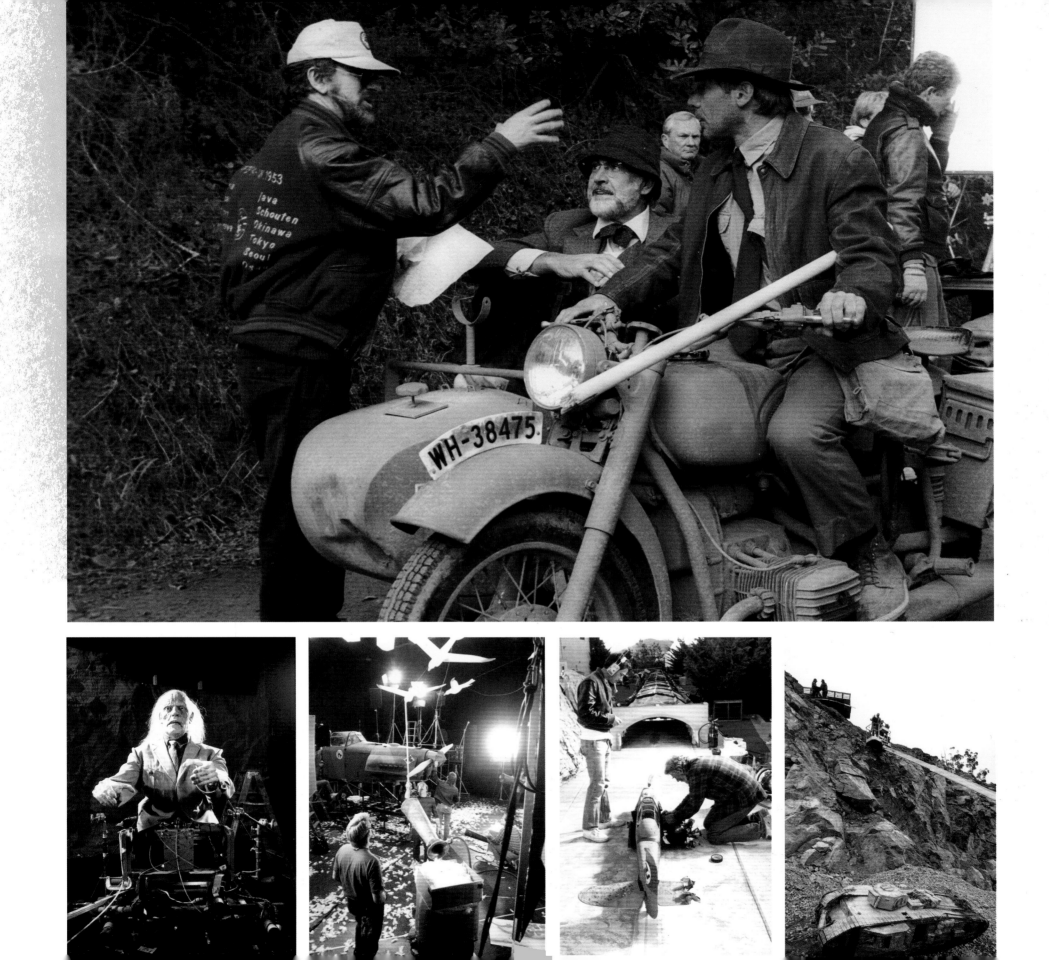

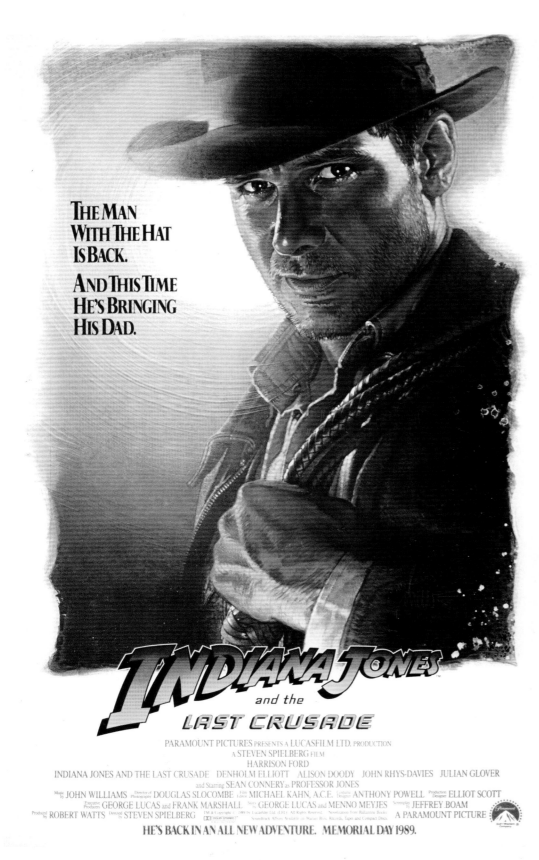

THE MAN
WITH THE HAT
IS BACK.

AND THIS TIME
HE'S BRINGING
HIS DAD.

INDIANA JONES
and the
LAST CRUSADE

PARAMOUNT PICTURES PRESENTS A LUCASFILM LTD. PRODUCTION
A STEVEN SPIELBERG FILM
HARRISON FORD
INDIANA JONES AND THE LAST CRUSADE   DENHOLM ELLIOTT   ALISON DOODY   JOHN RHYS-DAVIES   JULIAN GLOVER
and Starring SEAN CONNERY as PROFESSOR JONES
Music JOHN WILLIAMS   Director of Photography DOUGLAS SLOCOMBE   Film Editor MICHAEL KAHN, A.C.E.   Costumes ANTHONY POWELL   Production Designer ELLIOT SCOTT
Executive Producers GEORGE LUCAS and FRANK MARSHALL   Story GEORGE LUCAS and MENNO MEYJES   Screenplay JEFFREY BOAM
Produced by ROBERT WATTS   Directed by STEVEN SPIELBERG   A PARAMOUNT PICTURE

HE'S BACK IN AN ALL NEW ADVENTURE. MEMORIAL DAY 1989.

---

the $10 million mark. On June 1 Paramount took out an ad in *The Hollywood Reporter* to proclaim that its film now held the record for the best six days ever, with $46,931,772; *Variety* then reported in its headline that "Indy Races into Record Books," with $77 million in 12 days. *Crusade* took in $100 million in 19 days, another record. By end of year it had done $195.7 million; by March 1990, worldwide, more than $450 million.

While Byrge's prediction for Connery turned out to be incorrect, *Last Crusade* was nominated for Music, Sound, and Sound Effects Editing, with Ben Burtt and Richard Hymns winning the latter category in March 1990.

"We had an extraordinarily talented group of people," Lucas says. "From Dougie in the camera crew, and Ben Burtt in sound effects, to the art department. Michael Kahn is one of the most brilliant editors around. And, obviously, Johnny Williams. It just goes on and on. And it's always a thrill to see Harrison in that outfit. He becomes that character. You walk on the set and there he is. It's such an iconic image."

"I've enjoyed making the films because they are all about craft and collaboration," Spielberg says. "They've relied on the best that all the departments could give."

At the time, though *Last Crusade* was touted as the end of the trilogy, Richard B. Woodward wondered in *The New York Times*: "Is this *really* the end of Indiana Jones?"

"Of course the ending with them riding off into the sunset had all of us thinking that it was over," Marshall says. "But, you know, Sean taught us to say, 'Never say never'…"

LEFT: The teaser poster by Drew Struzan for *Last Crusade*.
ABOVE: Williams, Spielberg, and Lucas.

OPPOSITE BELOW LEFT: A note from Kiri Inomata alerts Paramount that the Japanese one-sheet (TOP RIGHT) would have additional photos of River Phoenix, Spielberg, and Lucas added to Struzan's artwork. BELOW RIGHT: The final shot of *Last Crusade* filmed in Texas, because the terrain was nice and flat, looked like the end of the series for Indy…

CHAPTER 11

ATOMIC ANTS FROM SPACE

BELOW: Some of the inspiration for *Indy IV* came from 1950s material like *The Man from Planet X* (1951), *Earth vs. the Flying Saucers* (1956), and *Weird Science* (cover art by Wally Wood, 1952).

Each *Indiana Jones* film following *Raiders* had gestated longer than its predecessor, and *Indy IV* would prove anything but the exception. "The short version is I thought we'd just barely got by in *Indy III* because the MacGuffin had always been the problem," Lucas says. "I felt we'd patched together something to make it seem interesting, if not compelling, but the story with the father carried the movie. So I said, 'I think we've played this thing out.' Steven was kind of interested in doing another one, Harrison was very interested in doing another one, but I was finished with it. I said, 'I'm the one who has to think up the stuff and I can't think up anything.'"

Content to let the matter lie for the moment—perhaps forever—once again Spielberg, Lucas, Ford, and the others went their separate ways. Spielberg directed *Hook* (1991) and executive-produced Frank Marshall's

directorial debut, *Arachnophobia* (1990), which Kathleen Kennedy produced, while Ford starred in *Presumed Innocent* (1990), *Regarding Henry* (1991), and *Patriot Games* (1992).

Lucas's work actually involved the character of Indiana Jones directly, as he embarked on a multiyear project executive-producing *The Young Indiana Jones Chronicles*, which debuted on ABC in March 1992. Produced by Rick McCallum, the hour-long TV shows featured Indy as a kid (Corey Carrier) and as a young man (Sean Patrick Flanery), traversing key events of the early twentieth century and meeting of many of its best-known protagonists. A few of the episodes were two-parters, such as the second season's "Chicago 1920" episode, which featured Harrison Ford as the adult Jones, who introduces and wraps up the story.

In December 1992 Lucas joined Ford for the two-day location shoot in snowy Jackson Hole, Wyoming. "Over the years I'd think about other MacGuffins and stories for *Indy IV*, but nothing really worked," Lucas says. "But when I was working on *Young Indy* with Harrison, the obvious suddenly dawned on me: If I did it when Indy was older, I could have it be in the 1950s. And if I did it in the '50s, maybe we could change that into a '50s movie—and what is the equivalent of a 1930s Saturday matinee serial in the '50s? Science-fiction B-movies. I thought, *Hey, that could be fun*. The obvious thing was Earth versus the Flying Saucers, so I thought, *That's the MacGuffin: aliens*. For God's sake, it can't miss.

"So I went to Harrison, out in the snow, and said, 'I came up with a MacGuffin and I think I could come up with another *Indiana Jones* movie.' He said, 'Oh, I'd love to do that.' I said, 'Well, wait until you hear what it is, because it's about aliens.' He then said, 'No, I don't want to do it.'"

"I didn't like it at all; I pitched it right back," Ford says. "There'd always been a mystical element in the stories about an archaeologist who wrestles with the mysteries of past cultures. But I felt this new angle didn't really take advantage of what we had done before."

"I said, 'But this is going to work. You've got to give me a chance,'" Lucas says. "Harrison said, 'Okay, you talk to Steven, see what he thinks about it.' I took it to Steven, and he said, 'I don't know. I've done a lot of these and I don't think we should mix genres.' I said, 'Steven, it's perfect. It's a B-science-fiction film. What could be more fun than that? And it fits Indy's age, because he'll be in his sixties.' But they were reluctant."

"All the *Indiana Jones* films have had paranormal concepts," Spielberg says. "So George came up with an idea that he wanted to do a paranormal story that would be a cross between psychic phenomena and the whole UFO craze. But I had done *E.T.*, I had done *Close Encounters*; I'd had my fill of extraterrestrials, so I resisted that for many years."

Lucas eventually convinced Spielberg and Ford to let him try an initial draft, and the first story conference notes for *Indy IV* are dated September 20–24, 1993. Additional notes from Lucas's phone conversation with writer Jeb Stuart are dated October 8. Following his modus operandi, Lucas had already come up with several set pieces, which he would recycle over the following years: Indy stumbles into a fake town on the grounds of an atomic-bomb testing facility and has to hide in a refrigerator to protect himself from the explosion; a fight on a rocket sled; aliens; extrasensory perception; Cold War Russians as bad guys; Indy married at the end; the CIA as helpers/hinderers; a CIA double agent; a sexy Russian woman.

"It was a lot about Indiana Jones being involved in Roswell," Lucas says. "And the alien was the MacGuffin."

Cowriter on *The Fugitive* (1993, which starred Ford) and *Die Hard* (1988), Stuart combined all these elements in his first draft titled *Indiana Jones and the Saucermen from Mars*, which he finished on May 24, 1994. In this version the story turns on an alien, whose life Indy tries to save, and Indy's relationship with a female archaeologist named Molly, whom he marries.

"With Jeb Stuart we did a draft and it did kind of work out," Lucas says. "It had the additional element of Indiana Jones getting married—that was going to bring the father into it. Indy meets this amazing woman who deciphers codes and studies ancient writings."

BELOW: The first concept artwork of red Siafu ants with enormous jaws, by Miles Teves. The aggressive flesh-eating ants, in particular, are an homage to *The Naked Jungle* (1954), in which Charlton Heston defends his plantation from the marauders.

AFI CONQUERS THE UNIVERSE

Just a few days before Stuart delivered the first draft, Lucas celebrated his birthday, which featured a surprise visit. "I thought that I should continue my tradition for George's fiftieth birthday," Frank Marshall says. "So I set it up with Robin Williams. We were the only two people who knew. As the cake came out—we had two cakes this time, because we knew that we'd have to replace the one cake—I came screaming out of the audience and crashed into George's cake. George loved it. It was good, it all worked—except that most people thought that I'd had too much to drink and had totally lost my mind. I heard all these stories afterward that I'd ruined the whole evening. So I've stopped doing that [laughs]."

More script discussions took place in August and September 1994, and Stuart turned in a revised draft on February 20, 1995. "I just didn't feel it was going to work," Lucas says, "and I started working with Jeff Boam." Jeffrey Boam ultimately produced three drafts, the last dated December 18, 1995, which was retyped in March 1996. At the time Boam said, "George is very happy with the script and Steven is happy with it, too, but the next step is to get Harrison on board." (Boam passed away in 2000.)

Then in July 1996 another movie came along that dealt with "saucermen." "When *Independence Day* was released and was this huge hit, Steven said, 'That was such a success I don't think we should do another one,'" Lucas says. "We had a script that I was happy with, *Indiana Jones and the Saucermen*. But Steven said, 'We're not doing a flying saucer movie, and that's it.' So I said, 'Okay, fine. But we're not going to do an *Indiana Jones* movie without aliens in it, because there's no point.' So I gave up and started doing *Star Wars* again."

"I didn't feel the scripts were worthy enough follow-ups to what some people think was arguably the best of the three, the one that Harrison did with Sean Connery," Spielberg says. "Harrison called me one day and said he was ready to make another one, but I wasn't. And I think George was very involved with his company and the future of his *Star Wars* legacy. So I kind of wrote it off because I was preoccupied with other topics, other subjects, other ideas."

Lucas returned in fact to the director's chair, embarking on a new *Star Wars* trilogy that debuted in 1999 with Episode I *The Phantom Menace*. For his part Spielberg had directed *Jurassic Park* (1993) and *Schindler's List* (1993); he went on to do *The Lost World: Jurassic Park* (1997), *Amistad* (1997), and *Saving Private Ryan* (1998). Ford starred in *Clear and Present Danger* (1994) and *Air Force One* (1997), among others. However, though *Indiana Jones IV* went into hibernation for nearly four years, rumors of another movie persisted.

"I don't care what movie I've made since 1990," Kennedy says, "every time I'm in an interview or talking to the press, whether it's in the United States or internationally, a journalist always asks me, 'When is there going to be a fourth *Indiana Jones*?'"

"There was a lot of pressure from the fans and even from the studio to do a fourth movie," Marshall says. "But everybody went their way to make other movies. And then we all went to Harrison Ford's tribute at the AFI [American Film Institute, in February 2000]. The whole group was backstage reminiscing and we realized how much fun it was to work together. We hadn't all been in the same room for a long time, so the idea was floated by George, 'Why don't we do another one?' In the euphoria of the moment, we all said, 'Yeah! Okay! Great! Let's do it!' And then, you know, reality set in."

ABOVE: Harrison Ford and George Lucas while shooting *Young Indy* in December 1992. BELOW: Over the years *Indiana Jones* anniversaries have been celebrated many times: after 10 years in *Lucasfilm Fan Club Magazine* (fall 1990); after 20 years in the French fanzine, *Star Wars Lucasfilm Magazine* (July–August 2001); and after 25 years in the United Kingdom movie magazine *Empire* (special subscriber cover featuring Richard Amsel art, August 2006).

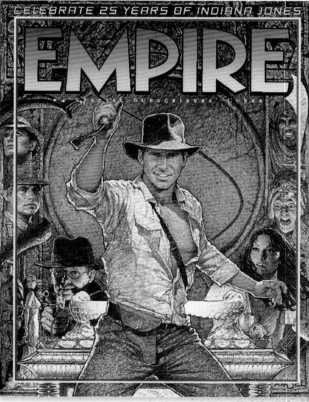

"At the awards dinner Harrison again asked, 'How is *Indy IV* coming?'" Spielberg says. "By that point George and I had put a couple of ideas into the works, we had toyed around with a couple of conceptual notions, but we hadn't really thrown ourselves body and soul into the process. Since the first time Harrison had asked about doing it and the next time, we were not completely committed, but Harrison continued to be our voice of conscience."

The "reality" Marshall mentioned was of course that they needed a script everyone wanted to film. Toward that end Lucas, Spielberg, and Ford met two months after the AFI tribute for a story conference, on April 12, 2000.

"There was a period of maybe five or six years where nobody anticipated doing another," Ford says. "And then we began, each of us in our way, to think about the potential, the possibility of doing another. Having been out in the world making all kinds of other movies, I was happy to do another *Indiana Jones* film just because they're so much damn fun to do. But we hadn't quite come up with the right story. The three of us never agreed on one of the notions that were advanced over the years."

"Steven and I sat down and said, 'Is there any way we can salvage this?'" Lucas says. "Because Harrison came back and said, 'I really want to do one of these things.' This is when the joint conversation came and they said, 'Can't we do it with Nazis hiding in Argentina?' I said, 'Look, I won't do it without aliens. That's the only thing that's going to work. And I won't do it unless we're doing it as a 1950s movie.' But I went off and thought about it …"

"Working with George is still the same," Spielberg says. "We still argue, we still compromise, and we still deal with each other like the brothers that we are."

Over the next two years, Lucas pondered; he held a story conference with Spielberg in December 2001 and two others in June 2002. The upshot was a meeting of the minds on certain issues. "The compromise was, I won't have any flying saucers in this movie, but I'm going to have aliens," Lucas says. "That's when I came up with the *Lost City of the Gods*, with a crystal skull as the MacGuffin. That's really what the whole thing has evolved from.

"We'd actually written an episode for *Young Indiana Jones* about a crystal skull, which was found in Guatemala," Lucas adds. "The series ended, so the script got put on the shelf, but we had done all this research on it. I thought it was kind of cool, because it's a supernatural object. So we started to say, 'Well, what if it was an alien skull? And instead of having calcium bones, they have crystal bones?'"

"I had heard about the crystal skulls," Spielberg says. "Whether you believe that the crystal skull was carved by humans or is an entity beyond the human race is the stuff that legends are made of. But there are enough speculations about the crystal skull from both the skeptics and the believers in the skull having paranormal properties that it was the perfect MacGuffin for the fourth *Indiana Jones* movie."

Frank Darabont became the next screenwriter. He discussed the story with Spielberg, and with Lucas on the phone several times in July 2002. Lucas wrote up an outline on July 31. Darabont completed the first draft of *Indiana Jones and the City of the Gods* about ten months later, on May 27, 2003.

"The idea was, the aliens came here hundreds of thousands of years ago and set up the human race," Lucas says. "Then we came up with a twist: The aliens didn't come from outer space but from another dimension. It's an antigravity issue to get them from dimension to dimension, or at least that's the theory. Then I combined that with the Nazca Indians. The idea was this

BOTTOM: In 2004 very early Lost City concept art was created by Erik Tiemens, who was simultaneously working as concept design supervisor on *Star Wars: Episode III Revenge of the Sith.*
BELOW: The crystal skull was also in the forefront of Lucas's thinking when it came to amusement park rides. *Indiana Jones Adventure: Temple of the Crystal Skull* opened in Tokyo Disneyland, Japan, on September 4, 2001.

RIGHT: Tiemens also did an early crystal skull painting, which was later modified by Miles Teves in this first concept sketch of the mysterious object (ABOVE).

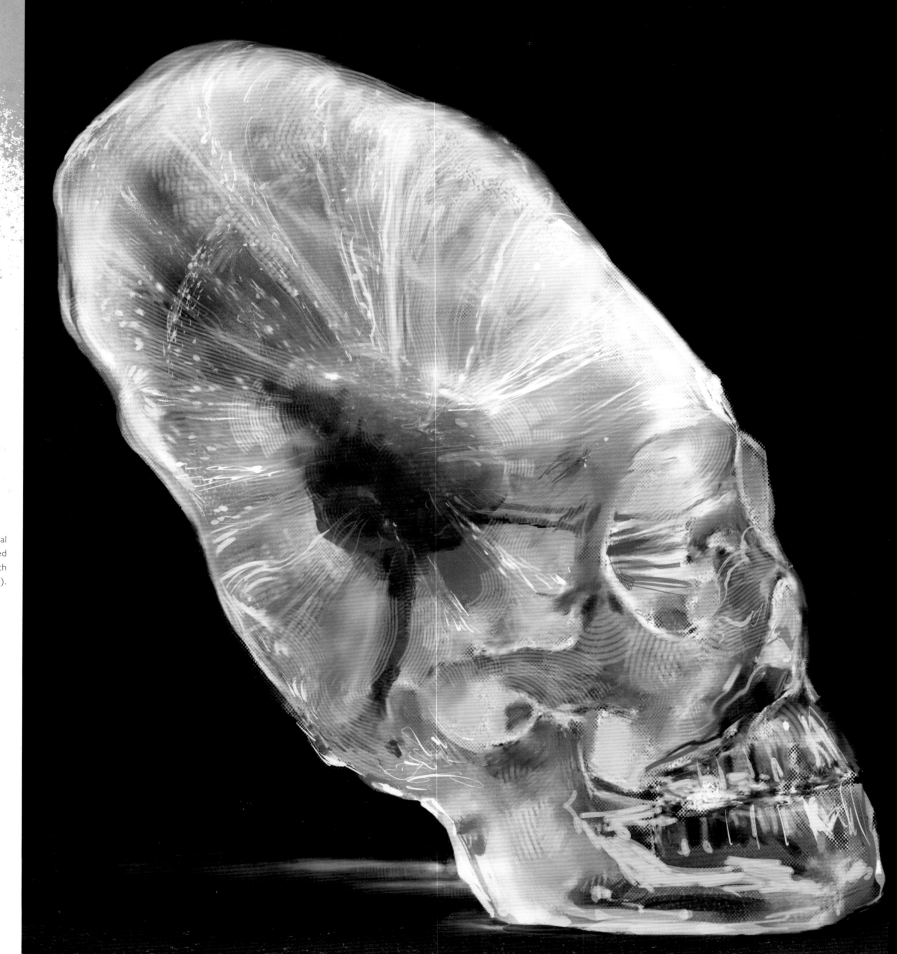

whole cult was built around these aliens that existed in this lost city on the Amazon, which was called at one point El Dorado, the city of gold. But the gold that they were talking about is the knowledge that the aliens created the human race."

After further conversations and a second draft, Darabont turned in a third draft on November 4, 2003, but Lucas felt it needed work. "After more than a year of working closely with Steven Spielberg developing the story, I had completed a screenplay that Steven loved and was hoping to shoot," Frank Darabont said at the 2004 Santa Barbara Film Festival. "However, George Lucas had issues with the script and slammed on the brakes in order to rework the material himself."

TURNAROUND CRYSTAL

By 2003–2004 the world was starting to wonder if *Indy IV* would ever materialize. Even within Lucasfilm the rumor mill was turning. "It's too early to tell," said Howard Roffman, president of Lucas Licensing. "We're sitting here desperately waiting for word on *Indiana Jones*, which we won't

have until probably late this year [2003] or the beginning of next year."

"Each time George and Steven were considering the project we would know because there would be a flurry of research requests," says Lucasfilm research librarian Jo Donaldson, who followed in the footsteps of Debbie Fine (who actually started *Indy IV* research before departing). "We'd do the research, write the reports, and then hear nothing for a couple of years."

"Each time one movie is a success, it raises the bar for the next," Kennedy says. "I think, if anything, that's what makes the process more difficult: You know you have a tremendous amount to live up to. And you've got a lot of people with the ability to now do lots of different kinds of movies, so there's much more demand on everybody's time. There was a huge demand on George's time when he decided to do another trilogy of *Star Wars* movies. Steven went on to do many, many more movies. Harrison has done many, many more movies. So now it's become a process of just figuring out everybody's schedules in addition to getting a good screenplay. That's really been the challenge more than anything."

"I heard rumors that this film was in the works for years and years and years," Karen Allen says. "Then it was, 'No, they don't like the script,' or 'There's a new script.' But when I was in Los Angeles with Kate Capshaw

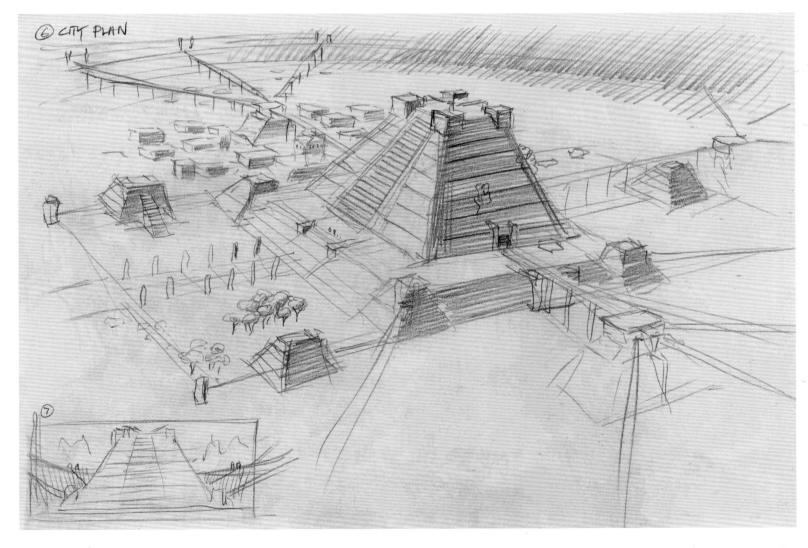

LEFT: The first concept artwork by production designer Guy Hendrix Dyas was a pencil sketch of the temple exterior and "city plan" (circa February 2007). "This was a gut reaction to what Akator should look like," he says. "But the raised aqueducts I later thought looked too modern, too Roman."

and Alison Doody, when they brought the three of us together for the 'Women of Indiana Jones' segment at the American Film Institute, there was more talk about a fourth one. Everybody was being very mysterious, but wink, wink, wink."

In the interim Spielberg directed *A.I. Artificial Intelligence* (2001), *Minority Report* (2002), and *Catch Me If You Can* (2002); Ford starred in several films, including *Six Days Seven Nights* (1998) and *K-19: The Widowmaker* (2002); Lucas directed Episode II *Attack of the Clones* (2002) and was in postproduction on Episode III *Revenge of the Sith* as he revised Darabont's scripts in the first half of 2004, changing the title to *Indiana Jones and the Phantom City of the Gods*.

As he finished pickups for Episode III (actually recording the last image of the *Star Wars* saga on the portion of Elstree that had been saved during the *Last Crusade* shoot), Lucas and Spielberg also began working with *Indy IV*'s fourth writer, Jeff Nathanson. Following story conferences in August 2004 and May 2005, Nathanson, who had written Spielberg's *Catch Me If You Can* and co-written *The Terminal* (2004), produced drafts in November and December 2005; the third draft bore the title *Indiana Jones and the Atomic Ants*.

"We brought on Jeff Nathanson to actually turn my script into one that Steven would be happy with," Lucas says. "He turned in his script and I did some rewrites on that, but Jeff was kind of caught between Steven and me: He'd do my draft, then he'd go back to Steven and do Steven's draft."

"There is a mutual respect and affinity between the two of them for the kinds of ideas that we engage here in *Indiana Jones*, the kind of filmmaking that we do," Ford says. "The process is not without contest, but it's a positive, constructive contest."

"So then we got David Koepp, and he said, 'I'm not going to be between you guys,'" Lucas says. "From that point, I would tell Steven what I wanted to happen and Steven then told David, so there was this hybrid, which was basically me telling Steven and Steven deciding what he wanted to tell David, and then David trying to interpret Steven."

"Finally I approached an old friend and collaborator who had written brilliantly for me, beginning with *Jurassic Park*—that would be David Koepp," Spielberg says. "I considered him to be more than likely our 'closer'—our best bet to get this leviathan onto thousands of movie screens."

"I worked primarily with Steven," David Koepp says. "I had some meetings with George, but mostly George talked to Steven about his ideas, then Steven and I would work together."

"It's all about the characters," Kennedy says. "David has a unique ability to create these three-dimensional, very funny but very credible characters, so he was the perfect choice to bring into the process."

"Harrison Ford *is* Indiana Jones," Koepp says. "There's no way you can separate in your mind the actor from the part. When I started writing the script I found a good picture of him looking at the camera and I made that my screen saver. That lasted about a day. I found the look too accusing."

"David is in touch with the humanity of things, but David is also in touch with the art of movies," Spielberg says. "He speaks the language of moviegoers and he had the rhythm of the *Indiana Jones* movie series. He brought that with him on his first draft. It just sounded, tasted, and looked like an *Indiana Jones* movie. It was perfect casting."

BELOW: Presentation art by Rodolfo Damaggio of the masquerading Russian convoy's entrance through the gateway to Hangar 51, early 2007. The air force vehicles are blue; army vehicles are green. This artwork was created by photographing a detailed model and then coloring it.

WEIRD TIME TRAVELING

"This is all backstory, but originally the Roswell aliens had come back to find the missing crystal skull that the conquistadores had taken from the original aliens, because they can't get back to their dimension without the skull," Lucas says. "The Roswell aliens are like emergency vehicle guys, but they crashed. The other part of it is that time in the other dimension is different from ours, so an hour to them is like a hundred or a thousand years to us. From their point of view in the other dimension, the conquistador invasion and their return to Roswell all happened rather quickly."

"George is a fountain of ideas," Koepp says. "He knows so completely the backstory of where those ideas came from, because his research is so thorough; he reads widely and he's interested in a lot of things. So you can have a meeting, start talking, and go for about an hour into just the background before page one—which is great, because you can't really do anything until you know what happened before."

Koepp combined several of the previous drafts with new material into *Indiana Jones and the Destroyer of Worlds*, dated July 28, 2006. "It's the fourth time I've written a movie for Steven," Koepp says (after the first two *Jurassic Park*s, and *War of the Worlds*, 2005). "Every time is different. In this case I tried to be aware of the history of the project. They had worked on a number of scripts over the years, with a number of writers, so I tried to be mindful of what worked and what didn't."

"George being George, he is tenacious, if not downright relentless, and he never blinked," Spielberg says. "I blinked to the point where George thought there was something wrong with my right eye. But George said,

absolutely and down the line, 'It's gotta be psychic phenomenon and this craze about flying saucers since it takes place in the 1950s.' And in a sense it took David Koepp, who was the final writer, to make that palatable for me."

One plot element that had been circulating for a while involved the return of Marion Ravenwood, and Koepp's script confirmed what everyone had felt would be a great surprise. "Bringing back Karen Allen was a great idea," Kennedy says. "Marion has clearly been one of the favorite characters, so everybody felt that was going to be a very important ingredient."

"When Frank Darabont did his draft for me, he introduced the idea of bringing Marion back," Spielberg says. "I accepted it and Frank put it in the script. When David Koepp came in, Marion was one of the ideas I tenaciously held on to, that I wouldn't let go of. I insisted it be carried through."

"Marion has a great sense of humor but she's strong, she's up to Indiana, and you believe that she can put him in his place," Lucas says. "They're a real team, so that's always a fun relationship."

"In *Raiders* you fell desperately in love with Marion," Koepp says. "The fact that they ended up not getting together beyond *Raiders* was maddening. So, in this one, Marion is the focus of the search; Indy doesn't know it, but she is what he's been searching for during the last 20 years."

"Marion remains as feisty, independent, and strong as she ever was, so the relationship is not without some degree of contest between them," Ford says. "His relationship with Marion, I think, most clearly describes his trouble with women in general. A lot of comic fodder comes out of their relationship and out of the process of the revelation of his fatherhood."

"Once we put Marion in the movie and knew they were being reunited, we first thought there should be a daughter Indy didn't know about," Lucas

ABOVE: Keyframe concept art of the rocket sled and tunnel by Collin Grant (pencils and inks)/Rodolfo Damaggio (colors) was intended to help ILM with its lighting. "In the art department we are absolutely fanatical about *Indiana Jones*," Dyas says. "And Steven was an absolute gentleman—so unspoiled—and such an approachable guy." Grant and Damaggio often worked as a team in the art department under the supervision of Dyas, with the former working manually with pencil and ink; after the artwork was scanned, Damaggio would color it digitally. "I wanted the illustrations to have a comic-book sensibility," Dyas says, "which is right for *Indiana Jones*. So we even used that discipline's methodology, having one person pencil and another add the color. 'It's a B-movie,' George kept saying, and that informed our technique, which Steven really responded to."

ABOVE: Early color-concept keyframe art by Grant/Damaggio of Indiana Jones and Mutt astride the latter's motorcycle as they traverse Marshall College—moments before the cycle goes on its side.

says. "She was going to be 13, a little spitfire. But Steven said, 'I've done that in *The Lost World*.' Eventually David Koepp revisited the idea with a son and it worked, though their idea was to make him a nerd. I said, 'That isn't going to work. He needs to be like Marlon Brando in *The Wild One* [1953]. He needs to be what Indiana Jones's father thought of Indiana Jones—the curse returns in the form of his own son—he's everything a father can't stand. But then they work their relationship back together again."

"Mutt comes out of movies of that era and *The Wild One* in particular," Koepp says. "It seemed obvious to me that his name is a reference to a dog, as Indy took his nickname from his dog. What I really enjoyed was writing a relationship between a father and son who don't know they're father and son. To write them again after they make that discovery was great."

"I was just ruminating on names and I thought, *That's what he is, he's the mutt*," Lucas says. "We had to keep up the tradition."

In October 2006 Koepp made revisions. "When Harrison reads the script, he certainly lets you know when he thinks stuff doesn't sound like him," Koepp says. "And of course he is always right because nobody has thought more about that character than he has."

"David Koepp has not only given us wonderful dialogue and scenes, but he's been able to get by one of the sticking points," Ford says, "which has always been these fantastic concepts that both Steven and George come up with. Wrestling those into scene-sense is sometimes difficult, but I think David has done a remarkable job. The hook for me was the script that Steven and George and David Koepp delivered."

By holiday season 2006 Ford, Lucas, and Spielberg were all happy enough with Koepp's script to announce to the world that *Indiana Jones IV* was officially a go-project.

"I was in my studio one day when Steven called," Karen Allen says. "There was something else that we'd been talking about doing together that had nothing to do with *Indy IV*, so I assumed the conversation was going to be about that—but Steven said, 'We just announced we're making the next *Indy* film and we really want you to be in it.' I was really, really wonderfully surprised. And then he told me what a major role he wanted my character to play in the film. That was another surprise, because I had imagined that it would be a little cameo."

Karen Allen wasn't the only one to get the call—as Spielberg swiftly contacted several other cast and crew. "There's a joke that British actors have," Jim Broadbent (Dean Stanton) says. "If a phone rings, a British actor will say, 'Oh, if it's Steven Spielberg, tell him I'll call him later.' So when you do get the call from him, it's an absolute thrill."

"Steven called and it was one of those calls I almost answer saying, 'Yeah, pull the other one,'" says John Hurt, speaking of when he was offered the part of Oxley. "But it was Steven and he said, 'I'm making an *Indiana Jones* film and would you like to come along with us?' He asked, 'Do you know *Treasure Island*? This is our version of Ben Gunn.' I said, 'That sounds like something I could get into.'"

"I sent him the script and said, 'Please, John, prejudice all your choices toward the Ben Gunn iconic image,'" Spielberg says.

"I was in Spain preparing for a film when I got a phone call," says production designer Guy Hendrix Dyas. "It was the phone call that you think is a joke: 'Can you hold for Steven Spielberg?' But I spoke to Steven on the phone and he had liked my work on *Superman Returns* [2006]. We talked about the aesthetic. He's a big fan of Norman Rockwell, of course, and I had used a lot of that. I've worked on large action-adventure films with a lot of practical effects, which Steven really wanted to have for *Indy IV*."

"I feel like I grew up on these films," says Cate Blanchett, who was tempted with the part of villainess Irina Spalko. "Everyone in my school class wanted to kiss Harrison Ford, but I actually wanted to be Harrison Ford, I wanted to be Indiana Jones. So when Steven asked me, it was one of those things you couldn't say no to."

"Cate Blanchett was my first choice," Spielberg says. "I didn't have a second choice. If she had turned me down, it would have been a long struggle to find someone to play Spalko. But Cate was game, though she had never really made a genre film before."

"Steven said, 'I'm going to be in New York in a couple of weeks and I want you to sit down and read the script," Karen Allen says. "I did that and, honestly, I was just very moved by it. The fact that Indy and Marion had created a child together and the wonderful repartee between them as they mend fences and come to realize that they still love each other was beautiful."

TRAINING AGAINST THE CLOCK

In a 1981 interview Harrison Ford had been asked, "What happens if this goes for two more movies?" "I'll get very, very sore," he answered. "I'll be 42 or 41 by the time I get the third one done. I don't know if I'll be able to do it. I think he's going to have to have a more sedentary life in the second and third films."

"I called Lucasfilm and got a pair of the original pants, a pair of boots, a shirt, a jacket, and a hat to try on; a whip, a gun belt, everything from the last film," says Bernie Pollack, costume designer for Harrison Ford. "I went over to Harrison's house and he said, 'Let's see if it fits.'"

"I hadn't worn the Indiana Jones costume for 18 years and, early in our production process, the costume was sent to my house for me to try on," Ford says. "I put it on and it fit like a glove. I felt really comfortable and ready to go."

On February 20, 2007, it was announced that Shia LaBeouf would play the role of Mutt Williams, the son of Indiana Jones. LaBeouf had already starred in several DreamWorks productions, and he was elated when he got the part.

"Steven right away wanted Shia in the movie," Kennedy says. "The minute he interviewed Shia for *Disturbia* [2007] and then in *Transformers* [2007], they just hit it off. Steven, I think, would put Shia in every movie he has if he could. He just sees a real talent there, so it's exciting to see him become a part of this franchise."

"I first met Steven Spielberg when we were doing *Disturbia*," Shia LaBeouf says. "He had just seen my audition tape; then I saw him again toward the end of that shoot and a third time when we were doing *Transformers* and a fourth time when this all happened. Steven just said,

BOTTOM: Digital concept art of Nazca Town by Rodolfo Damaggio. The art department had its own dedicated researcher in Dominique Arcadio, a specialist in history. "She really immerses herself," Dyas says. "One of her biggest discoveries was that South America, in the 1950s, would actually have looked like a place 10 to 20 years earlier." BELOW: Detailed pencil artwork by Nathan Schroeder of the sanitarium where Oxley was held. Mutt has just cleared the floor with a broom, and Indy stares at the floor where a map of the cemetery has now been revealed; the word RETURN covers the walls. "The lighting was very important to Janusz Kaminski, our DP," Dyas says.

'Welcome to *Indiana Jones*.' He wrote a little note on my script that said, 'Okay, now it's time to transform yourself into Mutt, signed Steven.' And he gave me three movies to watch: *Blackboard Jungle* [1955], *Rebel Without a Cause* [1955], and *The Wild One*."

On February 27, 2007, at the Governors Ball following the Academy Awards, Spielberg revealed that the start of principal photography would be June 18, with a release date of May 22, 2008.

"My reaction to the script was absolute excitement," says Dyas, who had the responsibility of designing the physical sets (and who actually began his career in the early 1990s working for Akio Morita, chairman of Sony, and then segued over to ILM before going freelance: "It was like film school," he says of his tenure at the visual effects house). "I went into Steven's office to read it, and my hands were literally shaking as I opened the first page. Between that first phone call and my first meeting with Steven I had literally 14 days. Based on the notes I took while carefully reading the script, I then did about 50 sketches; no phones were answered, I ate and lived at my desk.

"I wasn't sure how accessible Steven would be, but he proved to be incredibly easygoing and responsive," Dyas says of their March meeting. "But it was frightening when I heard the dates that we were supposed to be shooting for. I had an incredibly short prep time for a film of this scale, so I was very, very nervous. But the team around Steven all know him so well that they can sort of read his mind, which was very helpful."

One small department had already done quite a bit of work, which was particularly helpful for Dyas and his team at the outset. "We had written hundreds of pages of story reports for George on a wide variety of topics: myths and legends, historical events, locations, and animals," says Lucasfilm librarian Jo Donaldson. "We also drew on the large collection of historical material in the old Paramount Studios research library, which we acquired in the late 1980s—it was invaluable when we started the second stage of our research, providing visual reference to George, Steven, and the *Indy IV* art department during preproduction. Guy Dyas had an incredibly short prep time."

"When I arrived on the scene I expected that there would be maybe a few ideas from George or Steven about what they wanted to do," says Dyas.

RIGHT: Guy Hendrix Dyas did detailed drawings of the "Ext. Chauchilla Cemetery" on February 23, 2007, and (OPPOSITE) "Mutt Clings to Orellana's Skeleton" (beneath the cliff are the famous Nazca lines), February 19, 2007. "Steven decided that an archaeological dig on a huge plateau would be a brilliant place for stunt coordinator Gary Powell to stage a fight," Dyas says. "Originally the cemetery overlooked the sea, in the script, but I suggested that it overhang the Nazca lines—and Steven liked it and decided to use it." (Later Spielberg simplified the scene.)

EXT. CHAUCHILLA CEMETARY

02.23.07

"I just wasn't prepared for the huge amount of research that they had already prepared. Most of the vehicles had been pre-picked by George and Steven, and Steven had a stack of research that he and George had collected of what they called their key favorite images."

On the morning of Tuesday, March 20, 2007, hair, makeup, and costume camera tests were conducted by director of photography Janusz Kaminski on Stage 42 at Universal Studios, with Harrison Ford donning the mantle of Indiana Jones once again. On the first "feature production report," the title of the film was listed only as "Genre"—the code name for *Indy IV* throughout production.

"For the very first test we did with makeup, hair [Karen Asano-Myers], and wardrobe [Bernie Pollack], Harrison walked into the trailer with the original outfit," says Bill Corso, makeup artist for Harrison Ford. "I darkened the stubble a little bit and made him kind of tanned. It was so phenomenal that once Janusz got through with lighting him and we shot it, and we looked at the film, he looked too good and too young. Even Harrison said, 'I'm not supposed to look like that. I'm supposed to look like an older guy.' So we pulled back a little."

By this time several new key department heads had been selected, because several of the previous generation had either retired, such as Douglas Slocombe, or, sadly, had passed away (Elliot Scott in 1993; David Tomblin in 2005). Of course one of the key elements to *Indy IV* would be the stunts.

"Gary Powell's family worked on the previous *Indiana Jones*," Spielberg says. "Not only that, but Gary worked as a stuntman on *Saving Private Ryan*. I first met him on our Irish 'Omaha Beach,' and he did some of the best stunts on that movie. But when I saw *Casino Royale*, I didn't associate a name with the tremendous stunt work on that movie; I just asked my producers to get me the guy who did the stunts for *Casino Royale*, and it turned out to be Gary Powell."

"My brother, my uncle, my dad all worked on *Temple of Doom*," Gary Powell says. "I never dreamed that one day I'd actually be working on one—then all of the sudden you get the phone call."

On Wednesday, May 16, another morning of tests was completed—with Harrison Ford, Shia LaBeouf, and Cate Blanchett now working with stunt coordinator Gary Powell and sword master/stuntman Thomas

MUTT CLINGS TO ORELLANAS SKELETON

DuPont. The latter began training "mean girl" (Spalko) in sword techniques; Mutt also received his first motorcycle training.

"Cate Blanchett is such a physical presence," Koepp says, "so we wanted to give her some physical abilities that would surprise us, which is where the fencing came from."

"When the element of the sword was introduced, I found that really exciting to incorporate," Blanchett says. "I didn't want it to become swashbuckling; it had to have a precision about it, because I wanted her to have almost an impenetrable steel-like quality, not a hair out of place no matter what she was doing."

"The bluish gray jumpsuit that Spalko wears in the jungle is from the Soviet Union," costume designer Mary Zophres says. "The military uniform that the Russian soldiers wear is the real thing, too. If you open up the jackets, there's a Soviet stamp inside."

"Cate didn't want to be vulnerable at all," says costume designer Jenny Eagan. "So her costume is pulled up tight. We didn't want to show any skin at all. We didn't want her to be sexy in any way. We wanted her to be very domineering."

"Cate continues to astound me," Marshall says. "Kathy and I just produced another film with her, *The Curious Case of Benjamin Button* [2008], where she played such a different character."

"This was a new kind of a movie for Cate," Spielberg says. "Her enthusiasm was childlike when she sat with me and talked for the first time about her playing this Russian villain. She had thousands of ideas, right down to her costume and haircut. She read the script and she knew what this character should sound like and should look like, and she basically told us what to do to make her into Irina Spalko."

Blanchett had come up with the idea of a Louise Brooks–style black wig, which her hair stylist Barbara Lorenz then worked on (Morag Ross was responsible for Blanchett's makeup). "I researched yearbooks of people's high school photos in America in the 1950s," Blanchett says. "I found a couple of pictures, one of a Russian girl and one of an American girl with an incredibly short fringe; I thought that really emphasized the eyes, so that's what we went with."

Training continued on May 17; Blanchett practiced stunts the morning of May 24, and the stunt unit rehearsed all day. On May 25 John Hurt (Oxley) had a fitting; Ray Winstone, who was to play Mac, had had a fitting a few days before. To darken the veil of secrecy it was decided that the names of the principals would never appear on Call Sheets or Progress Reports: Harrison Ford was "#"; Karen Allen, "Damsel"; Cate Blanchett, "Mean Girl"; and so on.

"I knew Ray Winstone from seeing him in *Sexy Beast* [2000]," says Spielberg. "When I saw that film, I said, 'I want to work with that actor.' I think he is one of the most brilliant actors around, and he was the first choice to play Mac."

"I had never worked twice with the same director," Karen Allen says. "What's delightful about this is there's already a wonderful familiarity: We've been through this before. I felt it when I first came to do just some camera tests. It was great to see Harrison—and there was Kathy and Frank and Steven and George. So it was jumping back in, instead of the awkward feeling you usually have at the beginning of a film when you're meeting all of these brand-new people at once."

A press release was circulated at Lucasfilm on June 7, 2007, and was soon sent out to news agencies: "The *Indiana Jones* Cast Expands: Several stars have thrown their hats into the ring to join Harrison Ford and Shia LaBeouf in *Indiana Jones*'s latest whip-cracking adventure: Cate Blanchett, Ray Winstone, and John Hurt."

Absent from the list of actors was Karen Allen—her participation would be revealed later—and Sean Connery, who, though retired, had been the subject of intense speculation: Would he return as the wily Henry Jones Sr.?

"I get asked the question so often, I thought it best to make an announcement," Sean Connery said in that same press release. "I thought

BOTTOM: Concept art of the Russian encampment and vehicles in the Amazon jungle, where Oxley dances around the fire, by Collin Grant. "Janusz wanted the tents to glow like lanterns," Dyas says. BELOW: A pencil-and-ink drawing with gray washes by Grant shows Indy, stuck in a sandpit, being tossed a snake as a rope.

BELOW: Attack of the Siafu ants concept
art by Damaggio; the convoy has come
into a clearing but disturbed the ants,
which come pouring out of their hole.
BOTTOM: A concept piece by Grant/
Damaggio shows another part of the
convoy adventure in which monkeys leap
into the vehicles.

long and hard about it, and if anything could have pulled me out of retirement it would have been an *Indiana Jones* film. I love working with Steven and George, and it goes without saying that it is an honor to have Harrison as my son. But in the end, retirement is just too damned much fun. I do, however, have one bit of advice for Junior: Demand that the critters be

digital, the cliffs be low, and, for goodness sake, keep that whip by your side at all times in case you need to escape from the stunt coordinator! This is a remarkable cast, and I can only say, 'Break a leg, everyone.' I'll see you on May 22, 2008, at the theater!"

MAKE IT REAL

"The first thing Steven said was he didn't want this to look like a slick action-adventure movie with digital backgrounds and effects or stunts that you couldn't do in reality," Kennedy says. "Part of an *Indiana Jones* story is that you want to believe that Indy—and consequently Harrison Ford—is doing his own stunts, that Shia's doing his own stunts, and that Cate Blanchett is doing her own stunts."

"This movie was not designed around digital visual effects," Lucas says. "The first line of defense was to do everything live. I came off *Star Wars* where most of the sets were digital, with mostly tiny sets and bluescreens, and Steven said, 'I don't want to do that. I want to do the real deal.' And we're doing it."

"I like the old-fashioned way of making films," Spielberg had said. "And I hope that when I make a fourth *Indiana Jones*, we can do most of it in the camera. Some stuff will have to be done in the computer. But I will build real sets on real soundstages."

"I certainly have, as Steven does, a taste for physical effects compared to those that are produced by computer," Ford says. "I love being on a physical set. I don't so much love being in front of a bluescreen."

"At that first meeting with George Lucas and Steven Spielberg, we took a look at the script and the scope of the work," visual effects supervisor

ABOVE: Screenwriter David Koepp with Spielberg. TOP: "Ext. Temple of Akator Concept" by Grant/Damaggio, circa early 2007; the steps are on the opposite side of the temple shown in an early sketch by Dyas of "Exit from cliff cave into Akator," February 9, 2007 (LEFT). "This drawing pinpointed how Steven saw Akator," Dyas says. "It also solved our problem of how to treat the aqueducts, as they flow between monolithic stelae. This is where Indy and the others emerge from a cave and are surprised to see, in a big reveal, a kind of Lost World." (The stelae/totem poles, however, were ultimately abandoned.)

EXIT FROM CLIFF CAVE INTO AKATOR

EXT. AKATOR CITY CONCEPT

02.09.07

Pablo Helman says. "Steven Spielberg said to George, 'You know, I get a lot out of being on the set with a jungle that surrounds me. I get a lot of ideas.' The contributions of ILM to the movie therefore have to do with making the story completely real. One of the things that Steven keeps saying to us every time we work with him is, 'I want the visual effects to be invisible.'"

In addition to Dyas and his team's immense preproduction work on the sets, other departments, such as costume, hair, makeup, and stunts, forged ahead—all operating within the confines of a rapidly diminishing time allotment. "When I read the character of Mac, what I thought of was Ernest Hemingway," says costume designer Mary Zophres. "For Cate Blanchett's character, Spalko, it was Marlene Dietrich. Marion Ravenwood was definitely inspired by Amelia Earhart."

"Steven had the ideas and was working on the script, while his first AD Adam Somner was scheduling and we were doing sequences in 3-D on our computers," says pre-visualization supervisor Dan Gregoire. "Steven would draw rudimentary things for us, but the amazing part is that they all work. He'd sketch out a shot, and that's your framing; then he'll do A, B, and C positions, and you go into Maya, into the 3-D world, and it works. The lenses work, the framing works, the timing works. We'd do shots, edit it together, maybe put in a little bit of score, and then he would come back, look at it, make revisions, maybe cut out a shot, add a shot. It was this cyclical process that enabled us to do about an hour's worth of pre-viz for the film."

BELOW: The crystal skull at different stages at Stan Winston Studio.

OPPOSITE: John Rosengrant was able to manipulate the crystal skeletons on their thrones in the computer.

"One of the guys I work with on my team, Lee Morrison, is unbelievable on a motorbike," stunt coordinator Gary Powell says. "But Shia will do a lot of his own riding. We trained with him for six weeks, teaching him more each day; every time he got to a certain level, we'd push him further."

"Mutt had two main props. One was a switchblade, which is an Italian make, a very classic 1950s switchblade, and his comb," says Doug Harlocker. "We were with George Lucas and he said, 'Let me show you what a 1950s comb looks like,' and he pulled one out of his back pocket. So Mutt's comb etiquette came from George."

"Because Shia's character represents the youth of America, then and today, they wanted him to be hip and a bit of a bad boy," says hair department supervisor Kelvin Trahan. "So we went with a sort of greaser look, pompadour-ish, which took about forty minutes to do each day."

"The first time I saw Harrison in full regalia was during preproduction when we were training with the vehicles," Shia LaBeouf says. "We were on an air force base, and Harrison flew in on his helicopter. The door of the helicopter opens and, you know, it's Harrison. He gets out of the helicopter, takes about five steps, and he goes, 'Oh, wait,' and walks back to the helicopter, opens the door, and then reaches for something. He pulls out the whip, untangles it, greases it, and he holds it—and you're going, *This is so real.*"

"The whip came back pretty easily, too," Ford says. "I was surprised because it is a relatively uncommon skill and I wasn't terribly good at it, but

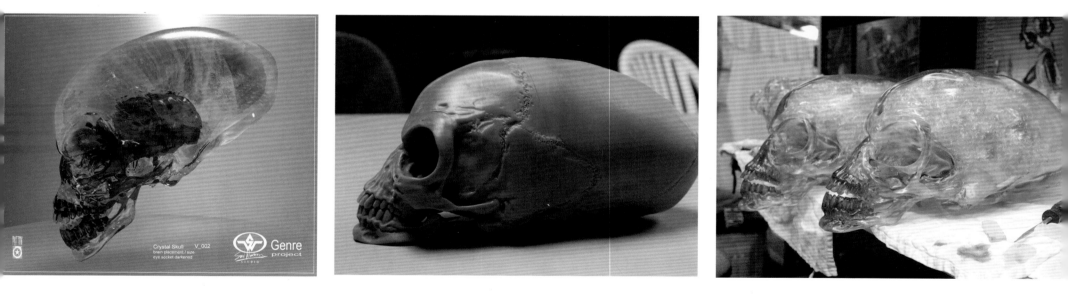

Crystal Skull V_002
brain placement / size
eye socket darkened

"This is my fourth picture with Frank Marshall and my third adventure with Steven," co-producer Denis Stewart says. "I did some work on *Amistad* as an AD, and some work on *Munich* [2005] as a production manager, so I knew how fast he is—but when I read the script and then went to my second meeting with him and he announced how many days he wanted to shoot this picture—yeah, I was surprised."

On June 4–6, 2007, Ford, Blanchett, LaBeouf, Allen, et al., rehearsed stunts for the jungle chase/convoy and the Marshall College pursuit, doing motorcycle work, fencing, and truck driving at California's Agua Dulce Airport.

I was good enough for show business when we did it 18 years ago. I'd lost touch with the first whip trainer that I'd used, so we had a new whip trainer, who had a different technique, and I was able to bring it back with a couple of weeks of pretty diligent application."

"The wonderful thing about a series of movies is that I was able to feel that little tickle of familiarity as soon as property master Doug Harlocker brought the whip and put it in front of me," says Spielberg. "And it was pretty amazing to watch how fast Harrison still was with the whip."

"I had never actually met Harrison," Blanchett says. "I knew him exclusively as an audience member as this character, or in the *Star Wars* films, so it seemed perfectly right that the first time I should meet him in real life should be in costume."

On Tuesday, June 12, a "MacGuffin Lighting/Camera Test" was shot for the crystal skull. "The first meeting we had with Steven was over at Amblin," says John Rosengrant, of Stan Winston Studio. "Scott Patton and I showed him all of the various skull designs, and he keyed in on a couple. We had also brought the computer program with us, so Steven was able to move things around right there on the spot. We ended up having to develop a way to make the crystal skulls out of water-clear urethane, which gave us a better turnaround time and more durability. The skulls ended up being cast hollow. They appear to be more solid because there's a little brain sculpted inside."

Preproduction was moving on several fronts now, with rehearsals at Universal; art department and pre-viz meetings at Amblin; fittings for extras in Deming, New Mexico, and in New Haven, Connecticut; and a scouting trip to Downey Studios and other facilities throughout the Los Angeles area. For the first time in eighteen years Harrison Ford, Steven Spielberg, George Lucas, Frank Marshall, Kathleen Kennedy—and Karen Allen as Marion—were about to embark on another great adventure in front of and behind the magical cameras shooting on celluloid.

"This whole series has defined our careers in a way," Kennedy says. "We were growing up together and we had such enormous success with the series that it became almost a badge of honor to be a part of the third—and I feel that the same feelings are going to carry over into the fourth."

"The film was not really a reunion in one respect, because I have worked with Kathy and Frank on so many other films in the intervening years," Spielberg says. "Working with them was business as usual."

"To be reunited with George, Steven, Kathy, and Frank, and many of the other people who were part of the original three films, is a great delight," Ford says. "Steven has created a small army of the finest craftsmen. Steven is so incredibly prolific that he's able to keep people busy from film to film. Many of these people have done ten or fifteen films with Steven, so they know what the goals are, they understand the man at the top and what needs to be done to satisfy his very stringent requirements."

"The speed with which Steven works is daunting for a lot of crews," Denis Stewart says. "But hiring a crew has never ever been this easy. People were lined up to do this movie. Everyone in Hollywood wanted to have a part of this film. It's a great piece of history. It's an amazing convergence of talent. After all these years all these guys got together, so we've got the best crew in Hollywood."

 Genre project

Crystal skeleton

V-001_001

INDIANA JONES IV

SCRIPT DRAFT BY DAVID KOEPP • SUMMARY AND COMMENTARY

APRIL 23, 2007

The backstory is that Indy served in the Army and worked for the Office of Strategic Services Society (OSS) during World War II. He went on many spy missions, liberating art and precious artifacts from the Nazis.

"Indy ended up a secret agent because he'd had all this experience in World War I in the Belgian army and as a spy; he was older, so he couldn't really fight," George Lucas says. "Afterward he got out of that, teaching and getting artifacts and selling them. So in terms of his personal life, he hasn't really done that much. He never got married, and his father gives him a really bad time about it—there are scripts where all this came out. His father wanted to have grandchildren, and he worries that Indy's not happy. Then his father dies, and Indy goes along in his rut."

"Indiana Jones has this dual nature that he's always had: part academic, part adventurer," Harrison Ford (Indiana Jones) says. "He's certainly older, if not wiser, but basically there's been no remarkable change between the Indiana Jones that we last saw some 18 years ago and the character who starts the adventure at the beginning of this film."

Indy IV opens on a lonely road in the Nevada desert, United States of America, 1957. A hot rod blasting music, with two boys and two girls, drives alongside a military convoy.

"It was important for me that Indiana age at least 18 years and that he move into the atomic age," Steven Spielberg says. "It was important not to put an older Indiana Jones into a younger era. We're letting the franchise mature as the hero has matured."

"I love the 1950s," Lucas says. "I grew up in the '50s, and in developing the screenplays I decided to open with Elvis Presley music—'Hound Dog.' It was a way of combining my love for the *American Graffiti* era and B-science-fiction movies with the genre of *Indiana Jones*."

The military convoy pulls off the road and up to a gate guarded by U.S. troops—who are gunned down by the convoy troops—who turn out to be Russian soldiers in disguise. They proceed to an enormous hangar, led by a mysterious dark-haired woman.

"Colonel Doctor Irina Spalko is our lead villain," screenwriter David Koepp says. "They called her 'Stalin's fair-haired girl' because she was running his psychic research program, which is based on real events. Stalin and the KGB were obsessed with the idea that there were psychic abilities in the world and that whatever government was able to harness them would be able to inflict a lot of mayhem on their enemies. They rounded up as many paranormal specialists as they could, and went around the world looking for artifacts that had supposedly paranormal powers. It's great because you get a villain who truly believes in what she's doing. She's not somebody's henchman—this is her passion, her life's work."

"In order to harness untapped powers of the mind they did huge amounts of experiments," Cate Blanchett (Irina Spalko) says. "Very secret experiments, where they would try to indoctrinate people and stretch the boundaries of the brain, which, if you think about it, does make sense. We really only use about five to seven percent of our brain power. I suppose the plan was that you could send telepathic messages to different parts of the army without having to send telegrams that could be intercepted."

"Like Hitler was a nut on the Ark of the Covenant and the Spear of Destiny, Stalin was a nut on the subject of psychic spying," Spielberg says. "So there was a historical precedent in involving the Communists in a search for a way into the consciousness of free nations and free individuals. And there was the fun of getting old-fashioned

Communist spies into our series, even though they had been the domain of the early 1960s *James Bond* movies."

Colonel Spalko orders a car trunk to be opened, and a disheveled, beat-up hostage is removed—Indiana Jones.

"We thought it would be fun to do the unexpected," Lucas says. "I thought it would be nice to have Indy appear just the opposite of the way he did in *Raiders*: Rather than this bold adventurer stepping into frame, cracking his whip, and getting rid of the villain, he's this poor guy trapped in the back of a car with another guy. He really is in a desperate situation."

"The first time we see Indy, he's dragged out of the trunk of a car," Koepp says. "I think that's great for a character who hasn't appeared on screen in 19 years—we've had him 'in mothballs.' He's been beaten to a pulp by nefarious bad guys who are after something."

The other guy in the trunk is George McHale, or 'Mac,' Indy's sidekick.

"Mac is a double agent who has forgotten he's a double agent," Ray Winstone (Mac) says. "He has switched sides so many times, he doesn't know who he's working for anymore. He is Indy's mate, but he can't help betraying him. For me, there's a bit of the Richard Burton character from the war thriller *Where Eagles Dare* [1968] in Mac."

"In 1957 a lot of popular literature was about spies, betrayals, sneaking around," Koepp says. "So the fun part about Mac is you never quite know whether to believe him or not. He tells lies throughout the movie to suit current circumstances. But he's charming, so we like him against our better instincts."

The Russians are looking for something in Hangar 51, which is located on a secret military base (that would later be called Area 51). They've kidnapped Indiana Jones because, in the backstory, Indy had been called in to investigate and had actually found one of the "little aliens" that had crashed in the desert of Roswell 10 years earlier. He'd turned the body over to the government—which then denied its existence. The Soviets therefore believe Indy can help them locate the alien artifact.

"Area 51 and that whole thing have always been a central part of this story," Lucas says.

"Right from page one," Koepp says, "we're

TOP OF AKATOR STONE TEMPLE·
OBELISK 2 SAND BOX PLATFORM.

02.11.07

pulling out some very specific iconography and American lore, which is that a lot of people believe that in 1947 a spacecraft crashed in Roswell, New Mexico; that the government found the remains of this crashed alien spaceship with intact and somewhat battered dead aliens in it; and that they spirited it away to a mysterious place called Area 51. So when you see the big number 51, you'll know exactly where you are and what kind of movie you're in for."

Spalko is an expert fencer and travels with an array of swords—in this case she uses one to force Indy into helping them find the

TOP: "Top of Akator Stone Temple, Obelisk 2 Sand Box Platform" by Dyas, February 11, 2007. ABOVE: "Ext. Temple of Akator Top Concept" by Grant/Damaggio.

OPPOSITE: Dr. Jones and Oxley run for their lives through a decrepit colonnade in another artwork by Grant/Damaggio.

RIGHT AND BELOW: Production concept art, "painted contact," by Nathan Schroeder represents five moments: Natives are worshipping the sun (RIGHT) when they are surprised that the sun becomes a strange being, with an elongated cranium, descending from the sky (FAR RIGHT); they are taught how to farm and build (BELOW LEFT) by the being (BELOW MIDDLE), who is a part of a group of 13 that unite in a circle (BELOW RIGHT). The artworks were created digitally, blown up, printed out as huge sheets, and applied like wallpaper to the actual sets. BOTTOM: Concept illustration by Grant/Damaggio of group traversing hallways illuminated by lights of ancient manufacture. "The script said 'lightbulbs,'" Dyas says. "So Steven gave us a challenge: 'What can we come up with that won't be laughable?' The answer was enormous crystals that may or may not be alien technology or which may be reflecting light coming from enormous shafts to the outside."

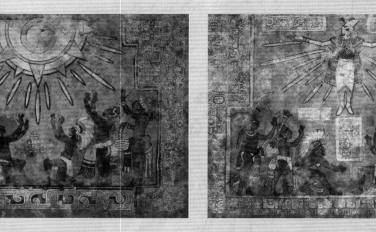

alien object. Indy manages to reverse the circumstances, and, after a wild chase in which several hidden objects briefly come to light—including the Ark of the Covenant—Indy fights a Russian henchman on a moving rocket sled, only to emerge in what he thinks is a suburban town—but which is really a test site for the A-bomb.

"Hangar 51 is revealed as the site where the Ark of the Covenant was entombed at the end of *Raiders*," Koepp says. "I think it's a great way to launch back into the series, nodding to the past but moving forward."

"The idea of actually testing atom bombs is so absurd, we now find it almost humorous that we were, as a country, so naïve," Kathleen Kennedy says. "But setting Indy right off the bat in a test area with an atomic explosion seemed like exactly the kind of thing an audience would want."

"We ended up putting the atom bomb scene that [screenwriter] Jeff Boam and I had in the middle at the head of the movie," Lucas says.

Miraculously Indy survives the blast by hiding in a steel-lined refrigerator.

"We're operating right on the cusp of believability here," Ford says. "By seeking shelter in a lead-lined refrigerator, and it goes on from there. On and on and on."

"In this film, the opening is a side story but still ties in to the main body of the plot," Spielberg says.

Dr. Jones is then interrogated by the CIA, who suspect him of being a double agent for the Russians. Indy is ultimately able to return to Marshall College where he still teaches, though his career is now threatened by his alleged links to the Soviets. As the archaeologist prepares to take a forced sabbatical, he is approached by 19-year-old Mutt Williams, a motorcycle-riding juvenile delinquent. His mother, Marion Ravenwood, and father-figure, Harold Oxley, have been kidnapped by the Russians (Mutt's "real" father died in WWII).

"I always liked the fact that his name is Mutt, because he has different father figures," Shia LaBeouf (Mutt) says. "Steven explained to me that he was a man-boy, this person who is trying to present himself as something he's really not. He says, 'I'm a man, look at this knife, look at this bike.' But he's kind of lost. It's basically about a bunch of people—Indy, Marion, Oxley, and Mutt—who are lost. Eventually, though, the unit becomes stronger."

"The backstory is that Indy and Marion had planned to be married, but he disappeared a week before the wedding without even telling her," Karen Allen (Marion) says. "Marion was crushed and, as it turned out, pregnant, which she may not have known at the time. She didn't know where Indy had gone or what to do, and decided to have the baby, which was quite a radical thing to do back in the 1940s. She married a colleague of theirs and I think probably lived fairly happily in an academic environment. But the man she married died when Mutt was just a child."

"Oxley really took some considerable umbrage at the way Indy treated Marion and lost contact with him," John Hurt (Oxley) says.

Seated in a malt shop, Mutt and Indy talk about Oxley, a friend of Indy's who is also the leading scholar on the ancient Lost City of Akator, also known as the City of Gold, built by an ancient indigenous culture around 2,000 years ago. He found the city but emerged a different man, no longer able to speak English, seemingly mad and carrying a mysterious crystal skull.

"The crystal skull of Akator was George's idea based on real crystal skull lore throughout history," Koepp says. "There are about twelve actual crystal skulls around the world. Their dating, carvings, how they were made, no one quite seems to know; they are without tool marks, no evidence of a lapidary wheel, no seams, no cracks. As a MacGuffin, the skull is great because it's compelling. We assume its powers have something to do with mind control, telepathy."

The Soviets have been tailing Indy and they try to nab him. Indy has Mutt start a fight between the greasers and the lettermen as a diversion, and the two escape on the younger man's motorcycle. A wild chase ensues through the town and through 1950s Americana. They blaze through the school library and across a football field [in one version of the script Indy catches the winning pass], and elude the Russians.

Indy and Mutt travel to South America and find clues to Oxley's whereabouts in a shady frontier town.

"The bulk of the story takes place in Peru, first on the Pacific coast and then on the Ucayali River in a place called the Iquitos, which I fell in love with when I was researching the film," Koepp says. "The Iquitos is referred to as the Gateway to the Amazon. It's the place where jungle and city meet—it just sounded like *Casablanca*—the perfect place for an *Indiana Jones* adventure to kick off."

Oxley had been locked up in an institution run by nuns. Indy and Mutt examine his cell and find the walls covered with paintings of a mysterious crystal skull and the word "Return." Indy deciphers clues that lead them to a cemetery where a conquistador is buried. (In the backstory, Oxley had found the crystal skull buried with the conquistador. The skull then instructed him to return it to its rightful place in the Lost City. Oxley found the Lost City but couldn't figure out how to get in and the Russians were on his tail. He hurried back to the gravesite, put the skull back where he found it, and then left the clues in his cell.)

"The Spanish conquistador Francisco de Orellana [circa 1490–1546] really went there and disappeared sailing up the Amazon," Lucas says. "So it's plausible."

Indy and Mutt are captured by the Russians after they find the skull where Oxley buried it, and are taken to a camp in the jungle where they meet up with Oxley and Marion. Oxley's mental abilities have been affected and he speaks only in an ancient native tongue. Indy is forced to look into the crystal skull, after which he can communicate with Oxley.

"Oxley is fun, because he's the Ben Gunn character from *Treasure Island*," Koepp says. "He's the guy who's gone off the deep end and says a lot of things that appear to be complete ramblings. He's the guy who originally found the crystal skull and gazed too long into its eyes. He has all this information, but it's coming out in such a jumbled way that he needs somebody clever to make sense of it, somebody like Indiana Jones."

"Oxley's madness is more like a possession, really," Hurt says. "Indy has a wonderful line to Oxley when he first sees him in this possessed state; he says, 'Come on, tell me you're just kidding. You were never this interesting.' It's my favorite line in the whole film."

Mutt leads Indy, Marion, and Oxley on a botched escape attempt, during which Indy and Marion sink into a sandpit. Mutt and Oxley run to get help, and, thinking they are about to die, Marion tells Indy that Mutt is his son. Mutt returns and throws Indy what he thinks is a vine, but which turns out to be a really long snake.

"Humor is also a vital ingredient in the *Indiana Jones* films, because there's so much suspense and so many cliff-hangers," Koepp says. "You've got to be able to laugh and release the tension a little bit."

They're recaptured, and the whole group then embarks through the thick Amazon jungle on their quest to find the Lost City, where Spalko hopes to find a treasure trove of psychic power. They have several adventures, which accumulate into a huge fight with Mutt taking on Spalko, blown-up cars, jungle mayhem—and oversized flesh-eating ants.

"The ant sequence has been there from the beginning," Lucas says.

"We have giant ants in this film, and they are another reference to 1950s-era moviemaking," Koepp says. "The way we explained it to ourselves was, we're up on a plateau that is previously unexplored, really high up, and the thing about plateaus is, as Sir Arthur Conan Doyle told us, they're cut off from normal evolution. So maybe the ants were that big when oxygen levels were higher on Earth."

"When I showed the first concept sketch of the ants to Steven he liked them because they were red," Guy Hendrix Dyas says. "He said,

'Great! Let's give them to Pablo,' and then ILM did some early tests."

"Koepp has this incredible ability to write action scenes," Kennedy says. "He understands the structure of how that works, how you build it up, so it's exciting and suspenseful."

"If you're lucky enough to be working with Steven Spielberg, you get an enormous amount of help," Koepp says. "I've always figured my job is to get the conversation started. Here's an idea of how it could happen, which spurs a lot of ideas on his part; then there's a back-and-forth, with whittling and changing and inventing."

Finally Indy and his group arrive at Akator Temple, heart of the Lost City, but to get inside they have to solve a physical riddle: how to raise a multiton obelisk into place.

"The idea of a large obelisk that has to be raised to vertical in order to open the temple is based on research," Koepp says. "The idea of placing it on the edge of a sandpit with plugs that kicked out derives from the way they used engineering in those days to accomplish things without more modern machines and tools."

After solving the puzzle, Indy and company make their way to a large stone throne room where they find 13 giant chairs in a circle, each with an alien crystal skeleton sitting on it—one of them is missing his head. The Russians have followed them there and Spalko places the crystal skull atop the skeleton—at that moment the room starts spinning like a spaceship about to take off. But rather than taking off, the "spaceship" fades into a parallel universe. The dimensional fissure and the spinning spaceship create a giant vortex that sucks in the entire city, as if it were disappearing into a black hole. Indy, Marion, Mutt, and Oxley are the only ones who escape.

Back home Indy and Marion are married.

OPPOSITE: Production illustration by Miles Teves of Indy entering the antechamber, which is filled with ancient relics and skeletons, and is dominated by a door leading to the heart of the temple. "I gave him a lot of time on this one," Dyas says. "Everything is very earth-colored up to this point in the film, with the exception of Doom Town—but suddenly we get color with these very red doors."

BELOW: In the heart of the temple, Mutt, Indy, and company are transfixed by the crystal skeletons atop their thrones in concept artwork by Grant/Damaggio. "I took this piece home every day for a month," Dyas says, "because I felt there was something wrong with it. Then I realized that the set should be bright red, like the door."

MR. JONES'S WILD RIDE

JUNE TO DECEMBER 2007

In June 2007 cast and crew moved into either the Hotel Santa Fe, Las Palomas, The Lodge, the Holiday Inn, or other hotels situated around *Genre*'s base camp at the Ghost Ranch Museum near Abiquiu, New Mexico. On Saturday, June 16, the second unit completed 15 shots, or 40 seconds, of the opening vehicle scenes on Route 84 in Abiquiu.

Another second-unit shot made use of a mound of dirt and a fake animal. "We actually transition from the Paramount logo to a gopher hole out in the desert, which is subsequently flattened by one of the vehicles," Dyas says of the film's opening shot. "On my hands and knees, I very carefully sculpted this gopher hole out of soil."

"The beginning is basically a prairie dog coming out of a mountain-shaped hole," visual effects supervisor Pablo Helman says. "Obviously there was no prairie dog, although we did have a stuffed one just for reference; that's something we'll be reproducing in the computer."

"We started in a place called Ghost Ranch," Dyas says, "which was found by the locations department, Mike Fantasia and his team. Steven wanted classic landscapes with beautiful background mountain ranges and all the orange colors of the soil. But there was only an old path here, so it was necessary to construct a mile-long road to accommodate the scenes of what we call the military convoy as it approaches the guard gates to Area 51."

TOP LEFT: On Route 84, Abiquiu, New Mexico, in mid-June 2007, Spielberg talks to executive producer Frank Marshall. MIDDLE LEFT: Steven Spielberg and George Lucas. ABOVE LEFT: Co-producer Denis Stewart talks with producer Kathleen Kennedy. "We make movies because people want to go see them," Kennedy says. "So if you're a part of something that people love, and want it to continue, then there's no better motivation to make a fourth Indiana Jones." RIGHT: Filming the American hot rod filled with teenagers (Adam Kirley, behind the wheel, T. Ryan Mooney, Helena Barrett, and Audi Resendez) as it races against a disguised Russian convoy.

LEFT: Spielberg behind the camera at Deming Municipal Airport, where production filmed exteriors of Hangar 51. BELOW: Spielberg and Ford. *Genre* was production's code name for *Indy IV*.

"For the opening scene, Steven early on said he wanted a *National Geographic*–quality location for the beginning of the movie," location manager Mike Fantasia says. "So I hired a fantastic scout in New Mexico and he searched for about a month and we just weren't finding it. But on *3:10 to Yuma* [2007], we had shot at the Ghost Ranch, so I pulled out some old photos and showed them to Guy and he really loved it. A bunch of us then hopped on a plane and flew to Albuquerque and drove two hours to the Ghost Ranch. As soon as we were driving there Janusz Kaminski was just going crazy: 'This is fantastic, this is beautiful, Steven's going to love it.'

"But when we got to the location, we realized that the road just wasn't high-enough quality to allow us to get the work done. So we met with an asphalt contractor and we basically paved one mile of an old highway. Then three or four days right before we shot, Guy Dyas and the greens men and some of the art department folks spent a weekend with a backhoe and two trucks full of dirt, and just spread dirt all over and aged it down."

DAY 1–8: MONDAY, JUNE 18–TUESDAY, JUNE 26, 2007
NEW MEXICO LOCATIONS: GHOST RANCH, ROUTE 84,
ABIQUIU—EXT. DESERT ROAD; DEMING MUNICIPAL AIRPORT—
INT./EXT. DESERT MILITARY HANGAR; DESERT "DOOM" TOWN;
FAIRGROUNDS—INT. DECONTAMINATION ROOM; CORRALITOS
ROAD, LAS CRUCES—EXT. DESERT MILITARY OUTPOST/ROCKET
SLED; DESERT/FRIDGE (GRAVEL PIT)

On Monday, June 18, 2007, Spielberg once again began principal photography on an *Indiana Jones* movie. A shooting schedule comprising the same number of days they had secretly scheduled for *Raiders*—73—was this time overtly planned, with an anticipated wrap date of October 1. Cast and crew call was for 5:30 AM, though a few were in makeup at 4:15 AM. On the first day, camera wrap was at 7:55 PM; "last man out" was listed at 10:48 PM. Ten vans and one "people-mover" ferried everyone from hotels to the locations.

ABOVE: Spielberg and his longtime director of photography Janusz Kaminski. "I have the best key grip Jim Kwiatkowski, who helps me tremendously with execution on very complicated shots," says Kaminski. "David Devlin is a great gaffer who can, independently of me, light complicated sets. Mitch Dubin is a fantastic operator, with whom I have worked on 10 films, and I have a great focus puller, Mark Spath." ABOVE RIGHT: Spielberg directs Cate Blanchett as Colonel Spalko. RIGHT: Ray Winstone (Mac), Harrison Ford, Spielberg, and first assistant director Adam Somner (who was third assistant director on *Last Crusade*). FAR RIGHT: Ford, Spielberg, and the car trunk.

On Day 2, after an early wrap at 1:30 PM, the two hundred people of production took a six-hour drive to Deming/Las Cruces, New Mexico. Another temporary HQ was established at Corralitos Ranch. "It was hot!" Spielberg says. "We were filming in New Mexico in the summer, but it was appropriate for the story. It was a tough schedule, but I had my family with me on location and on the set for the first third of the picture, and that helped a lot. Knowing that I could come home to them at night was great."

On Day 3 Harrison Ford had his first scene, as Indy and Mac are unceremoniously pulled from a trunk at Deming Municipal Airport, the stand-in for Hangar 51. As Spalko stands by, Indy's advent was prefaced with a new line: "Where's the professor?"

"When we started shooting in New Mexico and Harrison puts on the hat, that's when I first realized I was actually in an *Indiana Jones* film," Winstone says. "I watched the scene back on the monitor and I went, *Whoa.*

If you want to learn about what Indiana Jones is all about, you just watch Harrison. You get on the set and he can hit a fly on the wall with the whip. He can drive the vehicles. I've never seen nothing like it."

"It was a really strange moment on my first day of shooting, knowing myself as an audience member, the iconography of the films, and then having that moment of stepping into the frame," Blanchett says. "It was completely surreal and exciting."

"Harrison nailed Jones on the first shot, on the first take," Spielberg says. "He is at home in the skin of Indiana Jones. It's a character he helped to create. It's a character that he knows better than any other character he's ever

LEFT: Indiana Jones (Ford) outside Hangar 51. "*Raiders of the Lost Ark* was the first American movie I saw," says Pavel Lychnikoff (Russian "Hostile Soldier #2"). "It was in the days when Russia was the Soviet Union, and we weren't allowed to have VCRs. But whoever had a VCR would invite 15 to 20 people over; so imagine a little room with people cramped in there watching movies from the United States. That's how I saw *Raiders*. And I was blown away by it. We all were." BOTTOM: Spalko (Blanchett), Jones (Ford), and Mac (Winstone) inside Hangar 51.

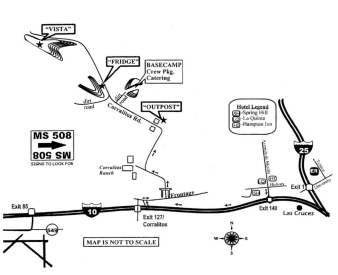

RIGHT: Spielberg directs Ford in a Doom Town exterior, also constructed on the grounds of Deming Airport. TOP LEFT: In a Doom Town interior, Indy looks for a safe place to hide; he will soon espy a very sturdy refrigerator (TOP MIDDLE). TOP RIGHT: A map attached to the Call Sheet indicates the location of the gravel pit where Indy would emerge from the fridge off Corralitos Road, Las Cruces, New Mexico. ABOVE LEFT: Spielberg inspects a mannequin.

OPPOSITE ABOVE: Ford as Indy, in the hills of New Mexico. BELOW: Ford in the refrigerator in the gravel pit.

ABOVE: Spielberg directs Ford in a partial re-creation of Indy's classroom from *Raiders* in June/early July 2007 (the original classroom was much bigger).

After two more days of shooting, production moved to Corralitos Road for rocket sled shots on Saturday, June 23. Sunday was an off day; Monday saw shooting in "Doom Town."

"Nearby the hangars, we were able to build Doom Town," Dyas says. "That was wonderful because we were actually building a fake town that was supposed to look like a fake town. We used extremely bright colors, period-correct to the 1950s, which gave the whole town a quirky flavor. I think the eeriest thing and the thing that caught Steven's imagination were the rather bizarre dummies all dressed in these wonderful period costumes; some of them had the most bizarre faces—they really looked spooky."

On Day 8 Spielberg filmed Ford as Indy emerging from the fridge after the atomic bomb explosion, at the gravel pit off Corralitos Road.

"On the outside of the fridge we had to create a fictitious name and then we had to match the interior color and tray configuration for the inside of the fridge," says property master Doug Harlocker. "We even had to put in period product so that Indy could pull out shelves and trays, and fit in there."

"Our set decorator, Larry Dias, found eight or so refrigerators, which we looked at and studied," Dyas says. "I don't think people know how much time goes into selecting something as simple as a fridge. You need one that's going to work in terms of Harrison being able to climb inside it, but it can't be anything too weird, and stylistically it has to be perfect. Then for legal purposes, we had to invent a new company for the chrome plaque on the refrigerator. Plus the back had to come off, and extensions were made so Harrison could go through the back and come out the front. It was actually quite a big character piece."

Wednesday, June 27, was a travel day to Connecticut.

SETUPS COMP: 161; SCS. COMP: 14/169; SCREEN TIME: 15:40

DAY 9-14: THURSDAY, JUNE 28-THURSDAY, JULY 5, 2007
NEW HAVEN, CONNECTICUT LOCATIONS: ROOM 113, HARKNESS
HALL, YALE UNIVERSITY—INT. HALL/CLASSROOM; GROVE,
ELM, HIGH, CHAPEL, COLLEGE STREETS—CHASE SEQUENCE;
THE VALLEY RAILROAD COMPANY, ESSEX—EXT. TRAIN STATION

"We had established a lot of locations in the first movies: where Indy lived and where he taught," Frank Marshall says. "In *Raiders* we'd shot parts of the exterior of the university and Indy's house in Northern California, but we had a lot more exteriors to do in this movie, so Yale became a natural place for us to go. We went about getting permission from the film commission in Connecticut and it was fantastic."

"From New Mexico we went to New Haven, Connecticut," Dyas says. "Yale was a foregone conclusion for Steven. I think he's a big fan of the architecture, as I am. We really wanted to romanticize this college where Indy teaches and we just couldn't find buildings that had that sort of majesty here in California."

"We worked very closely with the people that govern the city of New Haven, and the people at Yale University," says location manager Mike Fantasia. "We all worked together to make this whole puzzle work. We had public notifications well in advance of our arrival, so people knew we were going to be closing certain streets at certain times. We set up detours, put up a lot of traffic signs, blinking signs, that kind of thing, notifications in newspapers, on TV, on the radio, to try to encourage people to stay away from the downtown area if they didn't have to come."

played. And it's a character that I was really happy to see him recovering on that first day."

"The requirement for the film was to find a period-correct hangar, which was really a challenge," Dyas says. "Hangars become derelict buildings and are torn down, but Steven really needed a hangar that worked for the re-creation of the storage space that we see in *Raiders* at the end of the film. Our locations department found the perfect spot and led us to Deming. The local people were terrific, but it was the middle of nowhere."

"It was difficult for me to start filming on locations, because I knew it would be intense to step in front of the *Indy* camera for the first time," says LaBeouf, who had his first scenes in New Haven. "I kind of wished I could have been able to go back home at night, just to recharge, to return to something familiar. But I started in New Haven and then Hawaii. The good thing was that we all bonded. And I already knew the stunt team because I had been training for several months. But I have to say, the first half of the film, while we were on location, was very physical."

"It took me a couple of days to figure out a style for a fourth installment of *Indiana Jones*," Spielberg says. "It took me awhile to nail my contribution to the story. It took probably a whole week to figure out how to be a little lighter on my feet with the camera. What was hard for me was taking the subject matter seriously in a lighter way, because I've been making so many movies that have dealt with moments from history, not all of them playful, some of them deadly serious [*Schindler's List, Saving Private Ryan, Munich*], and I wanted this movie to jitterbug its way through our narrative legend and not be too somber.

"So it took me awhile to understand that I couldn't do any camera tricks, even though that's how a lot of 1950s filmmakers told their stories," Spielberg adds. "I wanted to stay true to the 1930s style of the first three and let the 1950s speak through the costume design, hairstyles, and Elvis Presley songs."

Spielberg and company shot in seven locations in and around Yale University. The anti-Communist rally was situated on the old quad, where production also installed a statue of Marcus Brody in homage to Denholm Elliott (who passed away in 1992). Interiors of the study hall were filmed in the University Commons, Woolsey Hall, where Jones answers a student's question from the back of Mutt's motorcycle during a pause in their wild flight from pursuing Soviet agents.

"The bike was tough only when Harrison was riding on it with me, because he had to be animated," LaBeouf says. "The pressure of riding through the library with Harrison was hard because you don't want to lose control, and Harrison knew I had just learned to drive that bike about three months prior."

"There is a scene where Harrison jumps on the back of Shia's motorcycle and that's a good example of a rig that involves a lot of departments," says special effects coordinator Dan Sudick. "We built it and then Gary Powell came in with his wires. Later, ILM will remove the wires and the rig, and it will look like Harrison jumped off the motorcycle, slid his feet on the ground, and then jumped back on."

"That hall was in fact a dining hall," Dyas says. "We had to remove all of the dining furniture and then re-dress that space as our reading hall. It was a very involved set, which will be on screen for about two or three seconds, I think. We should mention that the college that Indy teaches at is Marshall College, named after our producer, Frank Marshall."

"When we originally shot the college scenes in *Raiders*, we never had to call it anything," Marshall says. "But when we went to do the novelization, they needed to call it something, so we came up with the incredibly inventive name of Marshall College. I had totally forgotten this until I started seeing MARSHALL everywhere up in Yale and realized that this is what we had to live with now, which was a bit embarrassing."

"While Steven was concentrating on the actors, Dan Bradley, our second-unit director, was concentrating on some of the action scenes," stunt coordinator Gary Powell says. "Obviously one of the difficulties in New

Haven is that it's a very old place. You've got historical buildings, so we can't be bashing into walls; instead we put false walls in some places. We also had dialogue with the locations department to make sure we could skid cars and put some lovely black lines all over the place, knowing that we would get rid of them afterward."

In fact, because much of the permit process was public record, hundreds of people had gathered in the town square of New Haven to celebrate "the circus coming to town," as Lynn Bartsch, director of business affairs and and production counsel at Lucasfilm, put it. They screened the *Indy* films,

ABOVE: Indiana (Ford) in a corridor with Dean Stanton (Jim Broadbent), on location at Yale University, New Haven, Connecticut. TOP: Spielberg and Ford on the grounds of Yale University.

MARSHALL
STAFF
COLLEGE
DEPARTMENT OF
ARCHAEOLOGY

TOP LEFT: On the quad of Yale University, production erected a statue dedicated to the memory of Marcus Brody (and actor Denholm Elliott, 1922–1992). ABOVE LEFT: Frank Marshall with three coeds on the grounds of the fictional college named after him. "A large number of younger filmmakers come up to me and say, 'Raiders of the Lost Ark is the reason I got in the movie business,'" Marshall says. "They explain how they watched it in film school and how they learned so much." TOP RIGHT: Although Indy is already aboard, Mutt (Shia LaBeouf) follows him on his motorcycle, on location in Essex, New Haven. BELOW RIGHT: Ford and crew inside the train.

OPPOSITE TOP-LEFT: Indy and Mutt on a motorcycle escaping Soviet thugs in a chase through streets on location in New Haven. TOP RIGHT: Spielberg, LaBeouf, and Ford. MIDDLE: The character and look of Mutt were inspired by Marlon Brando in The Wild One (1953). BELOW: The chase continues as Mutt and Indy traverse a study hall at Marshall College (actually a dining hall at Yale).

ate food named and modeled after the banquet scene in *Temple of Doom*, and, of course, they dressed up as the adventurer. There was even a bullwhip teacher who gave lessons to the attendees. On local morning news shows, the weathermen and women told residents where they could gather to watch Spielberg and company each day they were in town. And a lucky few who had been picked out of the four to five thousand people at the open casting call got to play in the New Haven scenes as extras. (All of this attention made it doubly hard to hide the presence of Karen Allen, who was on location for makeup tests before appearing on camera the following week.)

"It was a challenge because we were a very attractive nuisance," says Mike Fantasia. "A lot of people wanted to see what we were doing, especially after the first or second day when we had been shown on local television. It drew more and more people. So we had a team of about thirty production assistants and forty policemen and security people, who worked together to keep the area somewhat secure."

"We had to go into each store, talk to them, and have them give us permission to turn their store into something from 1957," Dyas says. "That takes some negotiating, and that work always goes unnoticed because the cars, motorcycles, and trucks are traveling so quickly through the frame, all you'll see is a blur in the background."

"I got every yearbook I could get my hands on from the Northeast, in particular, Yale's yearbook," says costume designer Mary Zophres. "When I read the script, I immediately thought of an autumnal color palette for the college, and that's what we did."

"The first time I used second unit was on *Raiders* with Micky Moore," Spielberg says. "I don't like giving away my second unit, but it's a tradition on the *Indy* films. I was very careful on this new film to not only storyboard but do pre-viz, so Dan Bradley had my shots and lenses in hand, on his laptop, when he went off and filmed second unit."

Meanwhile Spielberg continued shooting Marshall College interiors with his first unit. "We did my first bit of filming at Yale," Jim Broadbent (Dean Stanton) says. "Just being there set the whole tone for the character,

for his relationship with Indy."

"Jim Broadbent has a couple of small scenes, but he brings to the film a beautiful camaraderie, replacing the loss of Denholm Elliott as the new dean of the school," Spielberg says. "Jim wouldn't get lost in his own museum, but at the same time he has the same kind of humanity that Denholm lent to the character of Marcus Brody; that deep, deep friendship with Indiana Jones was very important."

"You can see when you're working with Steven exactly why he is who he is," Broadbent says. "The vision and the attention to detail and the knowledge of the filmmaking process. It's a real pleasure to be alongside him when he's making his creative decisions. It's a privilege."

"Steven has a great comic sense," says Dimitri Diatchenko (Russian bad guy Dimitri). "My character is supposed to be this heavy, but there's been several moments where Steven would come up and say, 'On this one I think it would be funny if you did this.' That's one of the things I really enjoy about working with him: He's very improvisatory, and he expects his actors to think quickly on the spot like he does—it's an exercise."

SETUPS COMP: 272; SCS. COMP: 28/169; SCREEN TIME: 22:55

DAY 15-22: WEDNESDAY, JULY 11-THURSDAY, JULY 19, 2007
HILO, HAWAII LOCATION: KEAAU RANCH ROAD—JUNGLE
EXTERIORS; INT. IQUITOS TENT

On Monday, July 9, production traveled to Hilo, Hawaii—with Karen Allen joining the cast for the first time on camera as Marion Ravenwood. After a day of prep, filming continued on July 11.

"The hardest thing for me was to keep this a secret," Karen Allen says. "When we were shooting in Hawaii, I was checked into the hotel under another name. And in LA, each time I bumped into someone I knew, I had to pretend I was there for another reason."

"Having Karen on this movie was a blessing," Spielberg says. "She is a beautiful source of energy and light. In her costume and hair, she brought Marion Ravenwood raging back into all of our lives—as if those 27 years had evaporated the second she walked onto the set!"

"There is a great spirit to Karen—the minute she smiles, we're right back in 1980 when we were shooting the first Indy," Kennedy says. "It's pretty interesting to think about two actors who are actually reprising two roles 30 years later; instead of having to introduce the characters, you can play with the accumulated baggage."

"When Karen walked on the set," Marshall says, "it was like going back in time."

"When we shot Karen Allen's first entry into the film, everyone just cheered at the end of the first take," Blanchett says. "She's just this extraordinary, liberated presence on screen. I remember seeing her for the first time in *Raiders* and just thinking there was no other heroine I'd ever seen as free and as feisty as that. She really created something that was utterly inspiring."

"It's like we stopped for six months and then started up again," says Lucas, who also joined the group on location. "Nobody would ever believe how much time has gone by between the third film and the fourth one. Other than the fact that this is a new era, the style is the same, the humor is the same, the characters are the same—everything is the same and we've been able to build on it. The relationships are stronger and even more fun than they were in the very first one. But we're careful not to try and top ourselves—which I think is the mistake that many filmmakers make when they do sequels. We are focused on the characters, we are focused on the plot, and trying to tell a really great story."

"I didn't try to top any of the action-adventure movies that have been made in the post–*Indiana Jones* era," Spielberg says. "Some of those action scenes are brilliant, and I think owe a little inspiration to the Indy films. But I wasn't redoubling my creative efforts to top the young Turks, I was trying to be true to the level of action and adventure that audiences have come to expect from what we created in the 1980s with *Indiana Jones*, not from the other action-adventure genres that sprang up in the wake of *Indiana Jones*."

In Hilo, as on any location, safety scenes of interiors were always ready as backup in case of inclement weather. "The location we found in Hawaii was fantastic," says Mike Fantasia. "It's 16,000 acres, private, relatively easy to control, and it had a mile-long road through some incredible jungle; the property owners also granted us the ability to cut some roads adjacent to the main road, so we could do our chase and run vehicles back and forth. You never could find that flexibility in a national park or a state park, or any other place that we ran across. The topography was right, the vegetation was right. Between first and second unit we filmed there for about four weeks."

In case of injuries each day's Call Sheet listed the longitude and latitude coordinates of the day's scenes for emergency medevac evacuation. Although nothing like that occurred, Spielberg filmed plenty of action in Hawaii as Indy, Marion, and Mutt battled Spalko and her henchmen among the convoy vehicles and jungle environment.

"I've done five movies with second-unit director Dan Bradley, and he is one of the smartest men I know in this business," Denis Stewart says. "He can read between the lines of a storyboard. He doesn't do action for action's sake. He is always concerned with how it moves the story forward. I've watched him extract from Steven what it was that he wanted through his words, but also what he needed to tell the story with the action—including little bonus shots, pieces of things that present themselves on the day, in the moment. Dan Bradley's brilliant at recognizing those things, so he gave those to Steven, and all indications are that it's working well."

"Particularly for the chase in Hawaii, like Micky Moore in Tunisia, using B and C cameras, Dan was able to make contributions that I hadn't imagined," Spielberg says, "which helped make the scenes even more exciting."

"Our last large location was in Hilo," Dyas says. "The chase scenes were a real logistical nightmare. Everybody wanted to achieve the amazing pre-viz that Steven had done with Dan Gregoire and his team, but you can do things in a video game that you can't do in real life. We had permission to cut paths through this piece of wasteland to create roads, so on more than one occasion I had a machete in my hand cutting paths through the jungle to accommodate changes or new ideas that came up on the spot."

"You've got to be ready for anything because Steven does change things up in the moment," Blanchett says. "We were doing the chase sequence through the jungle in Hawaii, and all of the sudden he wanted to introduce this karate chop sequence. So we quickly got it together in a few minutes. It's a great way to work, actually, because it means that everything you do is really fueled by adrenaline—focused adrenaline."

"Steven is very good at story," Ford says. "He's just a master mechanic with film and really brings passion and energy to every frame. He's attentive and very clear about what it is that he wants to get out of every moment— and he is relentless about pursuing it, so I feel extremely comfortable in his hands."

THE GOOD AND THE BAD

"I must admit that Indy's hat is the biggest pain in the backside," stunt coordinator Gary Powell says. "It comes off when it shouldn't come off and it stays on when it shouldn't stay on."

"The sword fight was by far the most challenging aspect of the physical side of my character," LaBeouf says. "We knew there was a sword fight and I started training for it, but it kept evolving and changing. Eventually part of the sword fight took place over two trucks in motion through the jungle. Just standing on the trucks was actually harder than the choreography of the fight. The sword choreography we got within the first couple weeks—it was the movement on the trucks that became difficult."

"Shia's character is actually a fencing champion, but he never mentions it to anyone, so it's a total surprise to Indy when all of the sudden this kid grabs hold of his sword and starts dueling with Spalko," Powell says. "With the fencing, Shia worked incredibly hard. And Steven wanted this specific fight, so we had to choreograph it over three vehicles—not just two vehicles driving alongside each other. They're actually zigzagging through the jungle, with all sorts of obstacles on a bumpy road."

BELOW LEFT: Spalko (Blanchett) mans one of the guns. BELOW RIGHT: Spielberg talks with the actress, while John Hurt (Oxley) looks on. BOTTOM RIGHT: Spielberg and Lucas in Hawaii—where they first joined forces in 1977.

ABOVE LEFT: Ford as Indy in action.
ABOVE RIGHT: Indy (Ford) belts Mac
(Winstone) after one of the latter's several
betrayals.

OPPOSITE ABOVE: Shia LaBeouf and
Cate Blanchett share a joke; Ford and
Karen Allen. BELOW: Spielberg and the
jungle cutter vehicle.

"Shia is a wonderful improviser," Blanchett says. "As a young actor, he really understands stakes. I think a lot of young actors get frightened of putting themselves out there or fear that it's going to tip over into melodrama, but he's able to really raise the stakes and keep them raised."

"For the period vehicles, we found individuals who collect them," Dyas says. "But to make them work properly, in some cases, we had to rebuild the engine to accommodate the speeds and the control that the stunt team needed."

"I'm from Moscow and I served in the Russian army," says Igor Jijikine (bad guy Dovchenko). "I was in special forces from 1982 to '84. That's mandatory for Russians. I think our military advisers did really good job here because it's so close to reality, even the clothes; it's just perfect."

"We cast real Russians to play Russians, except for Cate Blanchett—who is very convincing as a Russian, by the way," Spielberg says. "We brought in Igor Jijikine, who was a high-wire trapeze artist for Cirque du Soleil. When he came in to meet with me, I knew that he was very physical and I knew he could do all the stunts very well. But he also looked very intimidating. I had preconceived ideas, but he was a beautiful, sensitive,

kind, and warm human being. Yet he could turn on the icicles and become a perfect match for Indiana Jones."

"I do speak Russian," says Andrew Divoff, who would join the production later on as a Soviet villain (Divoff was also in the TV series *Lost*, 2006–2007). "My heritage on my father's side is Russian, and it's a very old noble family. Started out actually as a French knight who migrated to the Slavic lands—this was 1398—and from that time we were sort of Russian nobility. I had the very good fortune of working with Mr. Ford about ten years ago on *Air Force One* and in that I played another Russian character."

"Cate Blanchett is, I think, going to create an amazing villain," Karen Allen says. "In real life she's such a sweet, warm person, but she'll go from chatting casually to transforming herself instantly into Spalko. It's fantastic to watch."

"I think playing an out-and-out baddie is incredibly attractive," Blanchett says. "You're pushing moral boundaries and, in this case, you're playing opposite Indy, who is not a pure hero; he can get hurt, he is flawed, which is what makes him so wonderful."

On July 20 Spielberg and company wrapped the Hilo location and headed for the mainland.

SETUPS COMP: 386; SCS. COMP: 49/167; SCREEN TIME: 32:00

"It seemed we were in all hot locations," Marshall says. "It started in New Mexico, continued in New Haven and Hawaii, and now we're back in Los Angeles. Everywhere has been hot just like Tunisia."

On Thursday, July 26, Spielberg appeared with Ford, LaBeouf, and Winstone via a live video feed to a packed audience at the San Diego Comic Convention. To great applause Karen Allen then joined the group, and Spielberg announced that she was returning as Marion in *Indy IV* (to the relief of the actress, who no longer had to keep it secret).

"One of the first very funny questions that Shia asked me was, 'Do you think she's an alcoholic because of all that drinking in the first movie?'" Karen Allen says. "I said, no, that was just how she was making her living at the time."

"When we first met, it was immediate," LaBeouf says. "You get Karen right away and there aren't a lot of variables. She's giving you exactly who she is."

At Downey Studios the group then went back to work filming more of the chase through Hangar 51, during which Indy stumbles upon a few surprises and begins his high-speed fight on the rocket sled. "Among the most complex sequences we worked on was the Hangar 51 interior, because of the necessity for a huge environment that couldn't literally be built," says pre-visualization supervisor Dan Gregoire. "So pre-viz helped figure out the scope of what the art department had to build and design, and how to make that look like a gigantic environment within a constrained set."

"Downey Studios is an enormous space," Dyas says. "So we used it to simulate areas of the famous hangar from *Raiders*. Normally we would've re-created the Ark, but because George Lucas's archives are so exceptionally kept, they had the Ark from the original film. So that was sent down for its shots. We actually had guards standing around it all day, because it's such a sought-after piece of memorabilia."

"An art mover brought the Ark down," says property master Doug Harlocker. "It's very precious and Steven hadn't seen it in a long time, but he didn't look inside it; he apparently never did."

"The Ark has a cameo in the movie—I was determined to get that into the movie," Spielberg says. "But you never get to see inside of it."

"At one point in the warehouse sequence you'll also see the staff carried by Moses in *The Ten Commandments* (1956)," Harlocker adds. "We reproduced the one that was used in the Cecil B. DeMille epic starring Charlton Heston by studying images from the film."

"The rocket sled was based on reality," Dyas says. "Back in the '50s, they were quite comfortable strapping people to rockets in the desert and sending them a couple of hundred miles an hour down the track to see what would happen to them. That idea obviously captured Steven and George's imagination. Our rocket had to be very theatrical and had to incinerate half a dozen Russians, so it became a lot bigger. We shot the exterior parts where Indy fights with the heavy on the rocket in New Mexico, and the interiors at Downey."

"Harrison looks fantastic, and I've watched him do these fight scenes again and again and again, where he's punching this one, kicking that one,

OPPOSITE: Ford didn't take long to remaster the bullwhip, which he used for scenes filmed in Hangar 51 at Downey Studios. "We got from Lucasfilm Archives Indy's original haversacks and a couple of whips," says property master Doug Harlocker. "But we ended up making new whips. We had them made in Australia then we distressed them down, so they looked a little bit older than the original ones. We made eight-foot, ten-foot, and sixteen-foot whips with tech line out the end, for Harrison and the stunt guys to be able to swing from."

"To see Harrison walk on to the set, pick up the whip, snap it, and wrap it around a Kalashnikov [also known as the AK-47 machine gun] was pretty amazing," Spielberg says. "To be able to walk around the set and see his haversack and other props was a bit nostalgic for me, as we brought back this character and all his trappings."

ABOVE: The rocket sled built by the design and construction departments, also at Downey Studios.

RIGHT: Spalko (Blanchett) opens a mysterious box. "We made a military coffin that Steven wanted to see buried among the boxes in Hangar 51," says Harlocker. "Inside the coffin was an alien created by Stan Winston Studio. Steven had us add vents so we could get a little cryogenic cloud of mist coming out of it when it opened up. Dry ice was used to make that work." "In the big mystical warehouse at the beginning of the movie, our main characters actually find this little grey alien," says John Rosengrant of Stan Winston Studio. "It's more of a traditional grey alien and is based on accounts of Roswell mixed in with our imagination. It had a forensic quality to it, because it had to look like as if it had been in the Roswell crash, so we incorporated some of the damage to the skin. The actual puppet that we made had little bones inside, so it could move, and it had a fleshy silicone skin to make it look more organic."

ABOVE: Ford among the crates in the Hangar set.

OPPOSITE: Ford performs stunts.

elbowing this one," Karen Allen says. "They'll do take after take after take, and he's up for it completely."

"We do a lot of fights," says Jijikine. "I'm a pretty strong guy. I thought it would be very easy, but gosh, I have to tell you, it's very hard. And you have to do it like you learn dance: Every step, every move, you have to deliver. I also admire Harrison; he really gets in there and he wants the fights to look real."

"Harrison, I must say, is unbelievable to work with," stunt coordinator Gary Powell says. "He's in incredible condition, very eager to do all his own stuff, so it's me that has to say, 'You can't do this or that.' Harrison is also very clever and suggests things that I wouldn't have thought of—because he is Indiana Jones."

On August 5 Spielberg and the main unit filmed more Hangar 51 scenes, while the "Iguaçu/Plate Unit" started in Brazil, shooting aerial images for the jungle convoy in several locations, including Iguaçu National Park; they then traveled to Argentina and filmed the Devil's Throat and Three Musketeer Falls for waterfall background plates.

"There's a sequence where the principals actually go through three waterfalls," Pablo Helman says. "When we got to Argentina and Brazil to film, we took this helicopter and we were flying about sixty feet from the water, so we were able to get some incredible plates. But we also realized that there were actually 247 waterfalls. When we came back we said, 'This environment is a lot more complicated than written.' So funnily enough, Steven went to David Koepp and asked him to revise that aspect in the script."

"Steven, early on, said he wanted to make Iguaçu Falls a part of the waterfall sequence," Mike Fantasia says. "So we went down and photographed for about five days. Three days in a helicopter, with a camera slung sixty feet below, going along the water, the waterfalls, and the river. We spent a couple days with a camera on sticks [a tripod] and a day in a boat getting all the different shots, fifty or sixty shots that together will comprise the whole sequence."

[PER AUGUST 14 STATS:] SETUPS COMP: 644; SCS. COMP: 55/170; SCREEN TIME: 49:40

DAY 38–45: TUESDAY, AUGUST 14–AUGUST 23, 2007 UNIVERSAL STUDIOS, STAGE 27—EXT. CEMETERY; STAGE 29—INT. INDY'S HOUSE—BEDROOM; INT. SANITARIUM CELL/ HALLWAY; BACKLOT—EXT. TOWN [PERUVIAN VILLAGE] NEAR SANITARIUM; EXT. SANITARIUM; PARAMOUNT STUDIOS, BACKLOT—INT. DINER/EXT. DINER ALLEY

By Wednesday, August 15, production was three days behind schedule. Second-unit work continued at Downey, while the main unit shot at Universal and Paramount Studios during the next two weeks.

"We'll shoot on all but two of the major lots here in Los Angeles," Denis Stewart says. "We've built 23 large set pieces and I think we're going to use 13

soundstages, along with pieces of back lots all over town."

"Typically in the summer, stages get fairly busy with television pilots, and this year was a very busy year," says Mike Fantasia, "but we were able to secure the correct stages at the correct studios. We needed certain stages with tanks and certain stages had to be very large and some could be smaller for the different sets. As we progressed, after we'd made some of the stage deals, Steven would cut and paste sets together—so all of the sudden a stage was twice the size that we needed for a set, or half the size that we needed for a set. Consequently, between the art department and production and the various stages, we then had to move stages around, move sets around. We've been bouncing around."

"This has been a very, very challenging production," Dyas says. "We have the misfortune of being spread all over Los Angeles. We'll be shooting at Universal, Sony Studios, at Paramount, at Warner, and Downey. We are all over the place."

If those logistical headaches weren't enough, cockroaches were used for the sanitarium interiors; for the Nazca Town exteriors, two horses, one llama, two goats, four burros, and 24 chickens. "Nazca Town was something that we achieved, here on the Universal back lot, by reconstructing a street and giving it a completely new look," Dyas says.

"We actually sent a shopper to Peru, a friend of ours who has a background in textiles and speaks the language," costume designer Mary Zophres says. "She pulled all the textiles for us, the ponchos and the hats. We aged them and fit our 250 Los Angeles extras who were to be Peruvian natives." (Eagle-eyed viewers may spot veteran stuntman Ted Grossman; in addition to working on previous *Indy* and *Star Wars* films, he played the estuary victim who gets eaten by the shark in *Jaws*—whose leg famously, and graphically, sinks to the bottom.)

"The Peruvian street was really fun to do because we had pulled a tremendous amount of research and tried to come up with a little bit of a mix that felt very third world and very primitive," says set decorator Larry Dias.

OPPOSITE: Ford as Indy bullwhips an enemy.

ABOVE: Spielberg examines part of the cemetery set. "There was a big disk in one of the tunnels where Indy crawled, and we had it on a hydraulic mechanism," says special effects coordinator Dan Sudick. "We had a breakaway floor and trapdoors. We built hydraulic floors and pneumatic openings in the cemetery."

RIGHT: Indy and Mutt explore the cemetery. BELOW LEFT: On the cemetery interior built on Stage 27 at Universal, first AD Adam Somner stands by the camera as Ford, LaBeouf, and and a stuntman get into position for a take. "We decided in the beginning we had to try to keep Shia fresh-faced," says Felicity Bowring, makeup department supervisor. "That's one of the things that Steven and Janusz wanted." BELOW RIGHT: The crystal skull created by Stan Winston Studio, based on concept art and Spielberg's instructions.

ANCIENT WARRIORS

TOP LEFT: The look of the cemetery warriors was the result of concept art by Miles Teves and research for the film by Dominique Arcadio; these drawings were designed to nail down the look for Spielberg, because the costume designers came onto the film later. "For the purposes of the story, rather than just concentrate on the Incas, this film encompasses also the Aztec and Mayan cultures," Dyas says. "We've taken all three of the famous South American ancient cultures and merged them into a fantasy culture." "For the warriors, well, I have to say that was Guy Dyas and his team's wonderful artwork," says makeup department supervisor Felicity Bowring. "I was able to execute his artwork by using a prosthetics house and a prosthetics person by the name of Matthew Mungle, who made encapsulated keloids [a type of scar] for us." TOP RIGHT: Warriors with key hair stylist Trisha Almeida.

ABOVE LEFT: "We had the other warriors, who we call the mud warriors, which again was Guy's creation," says Felicity Bowring. "The mud was made out of nontoxic clay with a cement mixer; we had to get the right color so that thirty people could be absolutely covered from top to toe in clay. I must admit Mary Zophres was very wonderful with her team. They came in with all these … what I would call 'ear bobs.'

"We started off very early in the morning. I previously had asked the actors to shave their bodies, so they didn't have any hair. We then dirtied up their bodies because they would never be clean running around in the areas that they were. We colored their teeth; we'd actually stayed up the night before mixing spirit gum and tinted makeup colors so that it could be put on their teeth. Then I went and got cake decorating colors and mixed those together, so we could stain the inside of their mouths and their lips.

"And then we had Rick Stratton who had designed for us some tattooing. All of this took in the vicinity of six and a half hours, and that was with two people working on them at a time, so it was very, very hard work. It was very time consuming, but it was so worth it."

ABOVE MIDDLE LEFT: Concept art by Ed Natividad (pencils) and colorist Chris Kitisakkul. Natividad was assigned to create concepts for the film's hard-surface objects, such as weapons and vehicles. "We made weapons for the warriors protecting Akator," says property master Doug Harlocker. "They were made of rubber. We added horsehair, muddied them, and wrapped them with raffia. We made blowpipes, and we brought details to them with paint, raffia, and feathers."

ABOVE MIDDLE RIGHT: Concept art by Dyas, for an idea that would be abandoned, had a mask over the skull over the conquistador's face. "The head was going to drop forward and give the audience a scare," Dyas says. "But the sketch showed that the geography wouldn't really work in the gag."

ABOVE RIGHT: The conquistador was based on Spanish conquistador Francisco de Orellana [circa 1490–1546], whose cadaver is discovered by Jones in the cemetery. "The original conquistador mask looked like a Colombian or Aztec mask," says John Rosengrant of Stan Winston Studio. "But Steven thought it would be neat if some of his facial features reflected those of The Man from Planet X—a 1950s B-science-fiction movie that he'd never forgotten." "For the armor on the conquistadores, we looked everywhere," says Doug Harlocker. "We found a lovely man who still hand-makes some. Orellana's armor was made by Wetta [Peter Jackson's effects house]. We basically gave them some specific illustrations, and they produced four identical sets for us."

"We created tapestries, weavings, found things from Peru."

Additional interiors included a 1950s diner and Indy's home. "We filmed the scene where I visit Indy at his home on a stage at Universal," Jim Broadbent says. "I'd never actually worked on the lot of a major Hollywood studio before, so it was a thrill. The set design was wonderful. It was like a visual biography of Indiana. All the places he has visited, the archaeological digs he's been involved in, all the anthropological quests are all there, present in the shape of an object, a prop, or a photograph. It's a room anyone would love to live in."

"In talking to Steven, we both felt it would be good to overstuff Indy's apartment with artifacts he had found, hinting to the audience that he may have had many adventures," Dyas says. "That set is a very special one, I think, for Harrison Ford. We had him view it before he actually performed there, just to make sure everything was to his liking." (The apartment is not meant to be Indy's original home; it is simply the one from this period of his life—however, thanks to intricate work and research by set decorator Larry Dias and his team, it is stocked with mementos from Indy's earlier cliffhangers.)

"I'm always a little nervous about walking onto something that represents the character I'm playing," Ford says. "I always hope that it's going to mesh with the ambitions I have for the character—but I was delighted by what I saw. I actually had very little to say about it, because everything was so spot-on and so good."

"The diner is called Arnie's, which is named after Steven's father," Dyas says. "The way the back lot is organized is that you have shells of buildings, and basically you turn the shells into something. [To give it a history,] we started with a 1930s diner and then added layers to take us into the 1950s."

On August 23, still one day behind schedule, Kathy Kennedy wasn't at all worried. "We're 45 days into shooting and Steven is cutting right to camera, so a week after we're finished with shooting, Steven and Michael [Kahn] will have the movie cut. I'm always amazed at just how fast Michael is. He doesn't need to be cutting electronically because he's as fast as anybody cutting on Avid."

SETUPS COMP: 781; SCS. COMP: 70/170; SCREEN TIME: 74:14

DAY 46–66: FRIDAY, AUGUST 24–MONDAY, SEPTEMBER 24, 2007 DOWNEY STUDIOS, STAGE 1—INT. AKATOR CLIFF CAVE; CLIFF ROTUNDA; UNIVERSAL STUDIOS, FREEWAY PARK—EXT. AKATOR CLIFF CAVE ENTRANCE; STAGE 42—REAR OF VEHICLE/JUNGLE CONVOY; BACKLOT—EXT. AKATOR, TOP OF THE GREAT STONE TEMPLE, EXT. JUNGLE ANTS, EXT. AKATOR CLIFFS; SONY PICTURES STUDIOS, STAGE 27—INT. TEMPLE STAIRCASE; STAGE 30—INT. IQUITOS TENT, JUNGLE; EXT. HOSTILE ARMY CAMP

Given that Spielberg had his professional start at Universal Studios, and that he and the studio succeeded wildly, the lot has a street named after the director—Spielberg Drive—along with those named after other legends

ABOVE: Spielberg directs Ford and LaBeouf in Indy's home, built on Stage 29 of Universal Studios, whose closet (RIGHT) conceals his "secret" identity and souvenirs. "The hat was a challenge," says Bernie Pollack, costume designer for Harrison Ford. "I eventually got hold of a guy who lives in Mississippi. His name is Steven Dell. He's a retired cabinetmaker and his hobby is making hats. He has nobody working for him, and works out of the back of his house, which he's made into a hat shop; he handcrafts every single hat, and he's got back orders for six months. But we were able to get about six samples, and the sixth one was almost exactly what I wanted. So I asked, 'Are you up to making me 30 of them?' We did some tests, and Harrison liked it but I decided to tweak it a little bit," Pollack adds. "I used a local hat shop in Burbank and I tweaked a little difference into each one. We then tried them all on Harrison until we got the one that really enhanced his face, yet still kept the Indiana Jones look." Tony Novak re-created the jacket under the supervision of Bernie Pollack. He made 30 of them, along with 60 pairs of pants and about 70 shirts.

of cinema. For *Indy IV*, Spielberg returned to the place where he had once filmed episodes of *The Psychiatrist* and *Columbo*, back in 1971, to create several of his new movie's climactic moments.

"Universal's Freeway Park has a monstrous set," Dyas says. "Steven has preferred to go the practical route with this film wherever he can. I think that when it comes to a lot of the practical moving parts, he feels they need to be real in order for the audience to believe them."

Another large set—the disappearing staircase—was housed within Sony Studios, formerly Columbia. "The way that Guy created this cylinder in the center with the steps retracting was amazing," Karen Allen says. "But it was very, very difficult to work on, because there was a huge gap between each one of the steps, so you could easily drop through. As they started to retract, the steps got narrower, so that gap widened. Luckily we were all on wires, but still this was physically the hardest scene for me."

"For my first meeting with Steven I had filled a sketchbook, which was very helpful," Dyas says. "I showed him my first sketches for the retracting-staircase gag. I had felt that after solving the obelisk riddle, to satisfy the 12-year-old in me, Indy should encounter more danger. The idea was that you have to run down the stairs before the stairs disappear—if you don't you fall onto huge spikes at the bottom of the well.

"Steven started immediately expanding on the idea," Dyas adds. "We eventually built an enormous spiral staircase that runs around a large central gold column. For that particular set we had to combine forces with Dan Sudick and his special effects department, who make all the practical effects work. We built the set in two sections on the same stage; the first is the top of the staircase and the second is the bottom part with the spikes."

"They were 20-foot stairs that weighed about 3,000 pounds each," says Dan Sudick. "Once the actors started to run, we would start retracting the stairs. The problem was that we had 30 stairs that all had to travel at the exact same speed. We thought about it for a while and decided to go back to a strictly mechanical system, something that we knew would always be synchronized, would always work, and whose speed we could control. All of those stairs were therefore on tracks and cables and pistons, so if Steven wanted them to go a little faster or a little slower, we'd have a lot of leeway."

Besides working on the large set pieces, the actors were also interacting, as is always the case on an *Indiana Jones* film, with notable live elements. "I was saying to the snake wrangler [Jules Sylvester, who was also the animal trainer on *Jurassic Park*, and had worked on the circus train sequence in *Crusade*], it's amazing how much of my last 25 years has revolved around people asking me about snakes," Karen Allen says. "And we do have one in this film: a really beautiful 13-foot-long olive python from Papua New Guinea, which we spent an entire day working with. A rare snake. He had never been on film before, but he didn't attempt to bite any of us."

"We had the requisite snake, a snake beautiful to us but not to Indy, of course," Spielberg says. "It was a rather large python. The audience wouldn't forgive us if we didn't have at least one snake in the movie."

"The funniest thing about that whole thing was, Steven is behind the camera and he wants me to hit a mark with the snake's head," LaBeouf says. "It's a live snake, but he puts an x in the sand and says, 'We'll put the camera right here and you put the snake right here.' But it's a heavy snake, about 50 pounds, and you're trying to throw the snake onto the mark, but the snake is retracting, and you hear Steven going, 'No, no, no, Shia, not over here, right here on the x.' We eventually got it, but it took a couple takes."

"I've seen people who just cannot be on the set when we bring a snake on," Ford says. "They just can't physically allow themselves to suffer what's going on in their bodies and they remove themselves."

"We did animal breakdown in the beginning, when I first read the script, and one of the animals that stood out was the snake," says Doug Harlocker. "I found an eleven-foot python, which is good. Pythons don't like to eat humans and they're pretty easy to work with. We brought it to Stan Winston's shop, and had them photograph it, measure it, and they sculpted and molded two of them."

"The animal trainer brought in the real thing so we could take photo references," says John Rosengrant, of Stan Winston Studio. "It showed up in a small box, but when it was stretched out, it was almost 13 feet long! It had a neat color, a weird, slight iridescence that we incorporated into the paint, which made our fake snakes look realistic."

"We have another form of creepy-crawly in this picture and that was the giant Siafu, the flesh-eating ants that ILM will provide for us," Spielberg says. "We had to act without them on set, but when people see the movie, they'll think we had them by the hundreds of thousands. On this film I didn't have to say to Frank Marshall, *There's not enough ants, get me more!* Instead I got to talk to Pablo and say, 'Pablo, I need more ants!' The ants are realistic and are voracious. They eat trees, animals, and, if you get in their way, they eat people. We have acres of ants and they're on a rampage!"

A SECRET IS REVEALED

"I think already, just in what we've shot, there is a dynamic between Shia, Karen, and Harrison," Kennedy says. "A real family unit there has become very clear."

"I didn't know Shia at all when I heard that he was Steven's choice to play my son. I hadn't seen Shia's work," Ford says. "But I was comfortable with that because I have a degree of confidence in Steven and George. I had no predisposition about Shia and he has turned out to be not just a wonderful actor—an inventive, unique, original personality with real storytelling sensibilities—but also just a sweet guy."

"Shia is an extraordinary young man," Karen Allen says. "He has incredible resourcefulness as an actor."

"When I got involved, I knew I was going to be Indy's son, even before they told me," LaBeouf says. "I had been hearing rumors for years that perhaps Indy would have a son or a daughter. But when it is revealed in the story, it's great fun because the relationship between Mutt and Indy has already been set up; they don't know they're father and son, but when they

ABOVE AND RIGHT: Indy, Marion, and Mutt deal with a python being used as a rope (production used a real and a synthetic python).

INDIANA JONES™

and the
KINGDOM OF
THE CRYSTAL SKULL™

realize that, it offers a whole new perspective on their relationship. It's fun for Harrison and me to play with that aspect of the characters."

"As Harrison had to eat crow under Sean's critical gaze, so, too, does Shia's character," Spielberg says. "Shia is an amazing actor and not afraid to fall on his face—and then get up, brush himself off, and try to recover his pride. He is not afraid to eat crow on screen."

On Sunday, September 9, at the MTV Awards, Shia LaBeouf announced to the audience, viewers, and world the title of the film: *Indiana Jones and the Kingdom of the Crystal Skull.*

"We'd been trying to get something that has the appropriate B-movie title, but which still describes the story," Lucas says. "In the end Steven wanted it to be *Indiana Jones and the Kingdom of the Crystal Skull.* I wanted it to be *Kingdom of the Crystal Skulls.* Steven and I have both gotten more curmudgeonly as we've grown older, so went back and forth about that for a month before we finally ended up with *Skull.*"

"The title was a struggle," Spielberg says. "I came up with *Crystal Skull* and George came up with the word *Kingdom.* He just said, 'I don't care what you call it, just get the word kingdom in there somewhere.' So David Koepp and I were able to place it in the title, which pleased George to no end. But we had a lot of titles. David and I spent weeks throwing titles around. We had *Indiana Jones and the Destroyer of Worlds,* which was a quote from Oppenheimer [J. Robert, 1904–1967, scientific director of the Manhattan Project]. It was a title that David and I fancied for a few months, but we then decided that it was too heavy. We thought *Kingdom of the Crystal Skull* was more inviting."

On Wednesday, September 19, Spielberg received news that his first grandchild had been born. "When we made the first film, Steven had never been married, never had any children," Karen Allen says. "In many ways Steven is the same man, but he has also changed now that he has a family. The first time I worked with him, I saw the filmmaker; now I also see the man himself. During filming, he became a grandfather and it was just amazing watching him get that phone call."

"Steven is remarkable in many different ways, but the one that I think is less observed by most people is his incredible, truly incredible capacity for hard work," Ford says. "I don't think I've ever met anybody who works as hard as Steven does and as easily. He doesn't get upset, he doesn't get angry, he has the capacity to be specific and demanding without being hard on people, so he gets the best from the people who work with him. And they enjoy giving their best, I think. You feel it. You feel it on the set."

"It's turning out great," Lucas says. "Steven is doing a fantastic job of directing it."

"I think he's having a lot of fun making this film," Karen Allen says. "Comparing working on *Raiders* versus this new one, I would say, it feels a bit looser. Steven is trying new things and discarding things every day, and it feels a little bit more improvisational at times."

"When you work with Steven, there's a lot of freedom involved," LaBeouf says. "Way more than I ever expected, which was a bit scary to me. This whole process is the most terrifying and electrifying experience of my life."

SETUPS COMP: 1,182; SCS. COMP: 115/161; SCREEN TIME: 117:59

DAY 67–80: TUESDAY, SEPTEMBER 25–THURSDAY, OCTOBER 11, 2007; WARNER BROS. STUDIOS, STAGE 16—INT. AKATOR HEART OF TEMPLE, ANTECHAMBER, TURBINE STAIRS; DOWNEY STUDIOS, STAGE 1—INT. TEMPLE HEART, CONVOY & HANGAR PICKUPS (BLUESCREEN); UNIVERSAL BACKLOT, FALLS LAKE—EXT. JUNGLE CLIFF TREE RIG, AMAZON RIVER/DUCK, CENOTE BLUFF

On Tuesday, September 25, Spielberg and crew descended upon Warner Bros. Studio Facilities, where several sets had been built on Stage 16: the temple heart and antechamber, featuring an incredible temple door; and a giant stairway (the stairway just fit onto Stage 16, the tallest on the Warner Bros. lot, as it had been originally raised for the 1936 epic Cain and Mabel, starring Clark Gable and Marion Davies).

As he had on *Raiders* 27 years before, and as he does on all his films, Spielberg arrived ahead of the crew and walked the sets. "Steven is always like 15 minutes earlier than anyone else before the call, he's always looking at the set thinking," says visual effects supervisor Pablo Helman. "You can see the process that he's going through."

"He always turns up early and gets his quiet time," Dyas says. "I really learned something there, because Steven never visits the sets during construction—he wants to come to the set and be surprised."

"Each set to me was more of the same good-old fun stuff," Spielberg says. "I'd walk on the stage and think, I'm on the set of an *Indiana Jones* movie. I felt lucky to get to direct another one of these things, and lucky to be working not in a digital bluescreen environment, but in a three-dimensional reality, not that much different from the one on the first three films."

As usual on a crowded soundstage, cast and crew were squeezed tight between the several constructions. Little oases of chairs and food existed between dozens of bright lights, silk and canvas screens, ad hoc carpentry,

ABOVE LEFT: On Sunday, September 9, at the MTV Awards, Shia LaBeouf announced to the world the title of the film—*Indiana Jones and the Kingdom of the Crystal Skull.* A logo had been secretly in the works for some time, however. ABOVE: Winstone, Spielberg, Stan Winston, and Hurt.

and the giant Technocrane that cradled the A camera. Hundreds of wires snaked along the ground as Ford, dressed as Indy, serpentined his way to the set, followed by LaBeouf, Hurt, and Allen. The first setup of September 25 featured the awestruck group entering the heart of the temple—a large and fantastically ornate room consisting of huge crystal skeletons seated on their thrones.

"Guy Dyas has given us extraordinary sets," Ford says. "In forty years of doing this I have never seen such attention to detail; it absolutely blows my mind. Really, really makes me happy."

"If Steven and Harrison are anything to go by, I'm sure the audience will be in for a big surprise," Dyas says. "Because certainly when Harrison turns up every day, he gets excited about the sets he's working in. On this particular one I took a little risk and had it painted bright red, which is not

what had been approved, to match the door. But I was feeling fairly confident by then—and Steven turned up and absolutely loved it."

"Guy Dyas made an enormous contribution to this film, but, like Janusz, he tipped his cap to the production designers we had on the three previous films," Spielberg says. "He did not choose to make a name for himself by reinventing a franchise; he went along with what had inspired him as a young production illustrator and he took it a step further."

Keeping up with tradition, in fact, this particular set also had C-3PO and R2-D2 etched into one of the yellow tiles, and *E.T.* in another (they're also in *Temple* and *Last Crusade*, if you can find them). With the artists now on set Spielberg quickly blocked out the scene, which had Oxley with the crystal skull cautiously approaching the one alien skeleton that was missing its head.

BELOW: At Stan Winston Studio the crystal skeletons were fabricated along with glowing eyes. RIGHT: Concept art of nine-foot high skeleton on throne by Teves.

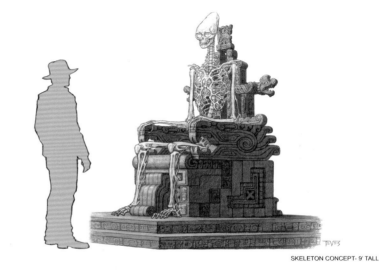

SKELETON CONCEPT- 9' TALL

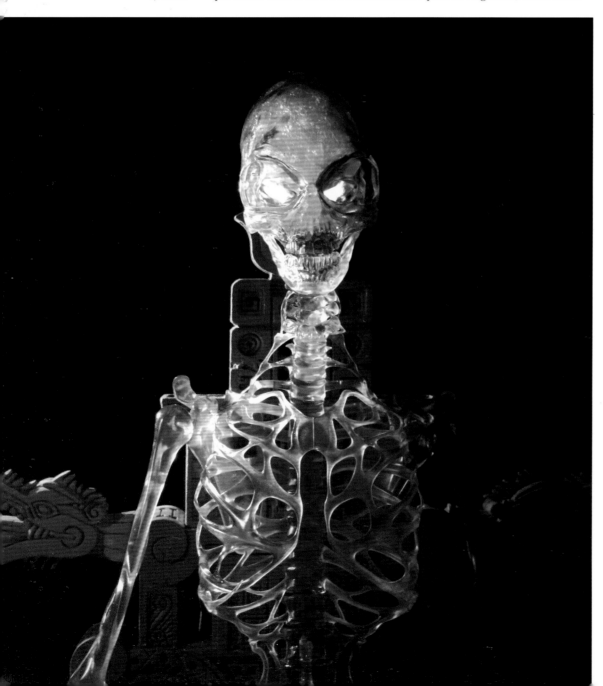

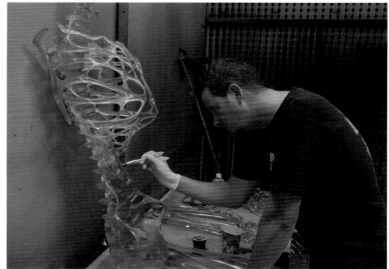

"The crystal skeletons were very difficult to create," John Rosengrant says. "We designed them first in the computer, and then we put them into a throne using a 3-D program, so that Steven could move around them almost as he would with a camera. We then did prototypes. There was also a special eye light on a rheostat, which could be adjusted to go brighter or darker."

"The skull was handed to us as an illustration, and, using that skull, we enlarged upon the rest of the body," Dyas says. "We started designing the chest, the legs, so everything came together as it should be. Steven wanted a very strange, lightweight skeleton. So we looked at all sorts of things, including bird bones, which are extremely lightweight and fragile. Imagine a human, but made of bird's bones."

"ILM is going to be working on the skull in different ways," Pablo Helman says. "We have a great piece that Stan Winston Studio did for the movie, so we'll be doing the animation part of it. There's a scene at the end in which we see one of the skeletons coming to life."

"You read it on paper, *crystal skulls*, but later you see what they have managed to come up with and how engaging it is visually," Ford says. "I've never been a fan of little green men and that sort of thing, but this is an intriguing new proposition about what might ensue from an extraterrestrial visit to an ancient culture."

After about seven takes Spielberg printed two or three and moved on. Toward the end of the morning George Lucas took a seat beside Spielberg— about 30 years after doing so for the first time in La Rochelle, France—and the two greeted each other warmly. Kathy Kennedy walked up behind them, while Frank Marshall was off to the side of the stage answering the day's questions.

"When I look back, I often think about a shot in *Raiders* where Harrison is in a plane and has a snake come into the cockpit; that took five of us holding this boa constrictor, feeding it into the cockpit of the plane so that Frank could get the shot," Kennedy says. "The interesting thing is that if we were doing a similar scene today and, if they needed help, I would jump in and do the same thing, so I really don't think much has changed."

Shortly after 1 PM cast and crew broke for lunch, lining up outside to choose among vegetable items, grilled salmon, chicken, and rib-eye steaks. As usual the food was substantial, for the work was exhausting. Crew then took their platters into a vacant soundstage where everyone was seated at long tables. Lucas joined Frank Marshall and Kristie Macosko, and they went over possible marketing blurbs, with Lucas suggesting, "How about, 'Remember when adventure had a name: *Indiana Jones* is back!'"

Back on the set Spielberg directed the second scene for the day, which consisted of Cate Blanchett as Spalko grabbing the skull from Oxley and approaching the same skeleton, only to see the skull fly out of her hands and take its place atop the alien—an effect that would be created digitally.

After one of the takes Spielberg said, "George liked that one best— print it!" Then while repositioning Blanchett for a new angle, Spielberg had to calm two overly enthusiastic PAs who had clambered into the scene with their marker tape, but obstructed his view. Lucas remarked to Spielberg that the next shot, in which Mac double-crosses Indy again, looked "operatic." During a break between takes Ford walked over to Spielberg and very quietly asked, "How about if I count on my fingers, one, two…" Spielberg immediately replied, "Great. Do it."

Ford stepped back into the scene and, after looking at Ray Winstone (Mac) in disbelief, counted on his fingers, "What are you a… one, two… a triple agent?"

After reloading the cameras, the team quickly finished the sequence, thanks in part to the dictates of first AD Adam Somner. "Aside from directing, the first assistant director has got the best job in the movie business," producer Denis Stewart says. "They are in the set, they are making the movie, they're in the director's head, they're with the actors, they feel the mood, they know the story, they know the nuance of the characters. Adam Somner is without a doubt one of the preeminent ADs in this business and he does an amazing job of not only keeping up, but staying ahead of Steven and Janusz Kaminski; he's very fast and demanding."

"My first job as assistant director was on *Last Crusade*," says Adam Somner. "That's when I first got my union card as an AD in England, working for David Tomblin, who was one of the great ADs, and Lee Cleary. They're the guys who trained me, so it's a very emotional kind of feeling to be back on the series that I trained on. David Tomblin was the greatest AD probably the world ever had, God rest his soul, because he passed away a couple of years ago. Comparing this experience to *Last Crusade*, it is a very

TOP RIGHT: Blanchett. ABOVE RIGHT: Ford and Lucas. LEFT: Spielberg directs his actors. FAR LEFT: Mutt (LaBeouf), Marion (Allen), Oxley (John Hurt), and Jones (Ford) prepare to return the crystal skull to its original place in the heart of Akator Temple, constructed on Stage 16 of Warner Bros. Studio Facilities. "For John Hurt, we studied photographs of homeless people and presented them to Steven, and he was quite in agreement," says makeup department supervisor Felicity Bowring. "The man has been out in the jungle. He's probably not bathed for quite some period of time. It was very nice to be able to ruddy his skin up by using layers of latex and green marble stickle, which shrunk the skin up even further and gave it a lot more texture." "I was very lucky, because John was in London where I had met an amazing wig maker named Alex Browse," says Kelvin Trahan, hair department supervisor. "So I sent him to her, and she made some fantastic wigs for him. Oxley's sort of gone crazy, so we had to make him look that way."

TOP: Stunt coordinator Gary Powell.
ABOVE AND RIGHT: Ford battles with a
Soviet bad guy (Dovchenko, Igor Jijikine).

similar pace. My perspective is obviously very different—I was not by the camera; I wasn't in the front lines as I am now—but Steven's always had that energy and that fast pace. He goes through the work very, very quick, very passionately."

"Janusz Kaminski's biggest challenge was to try to look at what Doug Slocombe had done with all the other movies and get nearly the same quality and look," Kennedy says. "It was very important to Steven that this look not exactly, but very close to what we had done. The interesting thing is technology has stepped in. There are lights that we use now that didn't exist when we did *Raiders*. We were still using arc lights, which give a golden, more yellow tone to the film; now we use HMIs [hydrargyrum medium-arc iodides, which are flicker-free], which give a bluer, slightly colder light. So we've actually had to use a lot more light on this movie in order to arrive at a look that is very similar to those early movies."

"There is a wonderful visual legacy of previous *Indiana Jones* films," says DP Janusz Kaminski. "So the style on the fourth film needed to be a continuation of the previous films: bright, very colorful, deep focus, and photographed with anamorphic lenses. Douglas Slocombe was the creator of that high-key lighting style. I must add that the new story takes place in

1957, almost twenty years later; I was thus able to modify the visual look of the film so it felt like 1957 and yet was more relevant for a 2007 audience."

"I sat with Janusz, and made him watch all three films on the big screen," Spielberg says. "I said, 'Look, we can't stray too far from the contributions and the look that Douglas Slocombe created. We don't want to suddenly invent a new look. We can maturate it somehow, because we're in the 1950s, but it's gotta have pretty much the same look.' And Janusz was also able to honor Doug Slocombe's contributions, respect them enough to create a similar lighting package. In fact Janusz had more lights on this movie than on any other film in his career."

"We have the best cinematographer and that's no disrespect to any of the great cinematographers I've been lucky enough to work with," Ford says. "I think Janusz is remarkable, and Janusz plus Steven is even more remarkable."

INTO THE DAWN

During the next few days Spielberg filmed his group approaching through the antechamber to the heart of the temple, out of continuity, as they solve

a puzzle to enter. The antechamber had been filled with reproductions of objects from many old civilizations. The cobwebbed pieces are essentially souvenirs of the aliens, lovingly created by Dyas and his team—right down to hundreds of coins artfully laid out in dark corners that the camera will only skim.

"The antechamber was a really great set to work on, as it features ancient artifacts, the Etruscan, Mesopotamian, and Egyptian eras," set decorator Larry Dias says. "But at some point it became a little bit overwhelming, and it started to look like a giant heap. So we had to start rearranging to create depth and strike a balance."

"The other day we shot a door," Ford says. "A door that we were able to open through a combination of our ingenuity and the psychic powers of the crystal skull—but the door itself was one of the most amazing things I've seen. It had physically about twenty elements that had to work together in order to open. A stone arrow descended onto two cylinders and pushed them apart to where they rolled off the edge and thumped down the sides, and then the door began to open in sections. It was incredible and it's a kind of throwaway in the middle of our adventure. It's just highly skilled work done by the effects and art departments."

"Originally the door was going to be a visual effect," Dyas says. "But Steven was getting really confident in our ability to design and build, so he called up one day, back when they were doing the hangar interiors at Downey, and said, 'Can you make this door work for real?'"

"We sat down as a group and watched the pre-viz with Dan Gregoire," says special effects coordinator Dan Sudick. "We talked about what we could do with it and then we built quite a mechanism. On the first take, after the doors opened, there was a round of applause at the cut."

Moving back to Downey Studios, Spielberg and cast had to film certain scenes against an all-bluescreen background. "Steven doesn't like bluescreen," Pablo Helman says. "I don't think Harrison Ford likes it much, either. I was apologizing to him when he came on set and he joked, just like

Indiana Jones would, 'Don't worry about it, pal. If it ends up looking real bad, it's going to be your problem.'"

On October 4, a confidential memorandum was circulated to cast and crew from Lynn Bartsch explaining that despite several thefts of movie information and images, honest people had contributed to the catching of the thieves and the prevention of secret images from appearing on the Internet and in the papers. A few days later, Spielberg invited some of those people to an informal meeting in order to thank them for their help.

On Friday, October 5, production moved to the Universal back lot of Falls Lake (off Spielberg Drive) for shots of the Duck vehicle dropping into a tree, waterfall shots, and the cenote bluff. On Thursday, October 11, checking in at 4:30 AM for the last day of principal photography, Spielberg, Ford, LaBeouf, and crew traveled on a one-hour charter flight from LAX to Fresno Yosemite International Airport. At nearby Chandler Airfield, they filmed parts of the travel montage, along with exteriors of the Mexico City Airport and an East Coast airport. After lunch they drove an hour to Eagle Field, outside Firebaugh, for shots of the desert airstrip in Peru and more travel montage.

"It wasn't an exhausting shoot for me, though it was the longest shoot I've had in a while," Spielberg says. "It was 80 days. *Last Crusade* was 78 days, *Doom* was 86 days, *Raiders* was 73 days—so it was within the realm of an *Indiana Jones* production."

"The physical environments that we've found right here in the United States are as fascinating and exciting to be in as the exotic places that we traveled long distances to shoot in before," Ford says.

"We were up in Fresno on the final day of shooting and Harrison came up to me and said, 'I'd like to give one of the hats to Shia at wrap. Do you have a felt pen, a silver one or a white one? Because I want to sign it,'" says Bernie Pollack, costume designer for Harrison Ford. "So we found one and he signed the sweatband inside the hat. He wrote something like, IT'S ALL YOURS, HARRISON FORD, and he handed it to Shia. Harrison was kind of grinning and then George Lucas walked over and Steven walked over, and it was just a very special moment."

"It was important that the baton be passed from father to son, as it had been when the audience realized that Indiana Jones could only have come from Henry Jones Sr., played so brilliantly by Sean Connery," Spielberg says. "There had to be a further passing of the baton to another generation of Joneses."

Principal photography wrapped around 8 PM, seven days over schedule but still very much on time for such a complex shoot.

"I've done a lot of big movies and still to this day I am amazed that Steven was able to do this picture in the number of days that he did," Denis Stewart says. "Maybe another director could have shot it in that many days, but it wouldn't have been as good as this one."

"We've put the cast through hell and back," Dyas says. "A lot of these sets are dirty, uncomfortable, smelly. They really are what they look like, but I haven't had a single complaint. Harrison is obviously a seasoned Indiana Jones who's done all this before, but we really came up with a few new things that put him through his paces."

"It has been great getting to work with Steven," Ray Winstone says. "What I appreciate about him is that he can do films like *Indiana Jones*, but

LEFT: The principals filmed in the Duck against bluescreen on the Universal back lot, Falls Lake. "One of the joys of acting, to me, is being able to create a character," says John Hurt (Oxley). "And I brought something to the character that wasn't on the page. I was visiting a friend in Ireland and he had been given in India some sort of musical instrument, which makes a very haunting kind of tune. I thought, *Wow, that would be a fantastic thing to have around the campfire when you first see Oxley.* My wife taped me playing with it and we sent it to Steven; he loved the idea so much that he sent his propman out to India to find one. They came back with a rather smaller one, but then made out of South American bamboo exactly the same instrument. And that is what I used in the film."

RIGHT: Spielberg directs Ford as Indy, who places the crystal skull in the elaborate red door designed by Dyas and built by Sudick and several departments. BELOW: The intrepid group approach the door.

also *Schindler's List*. There are directors who are very good with the technical part of things and others who are good with actors. Steven can do both."

[As of October 8] SETUPS COMP: 1,367; SCS. COMP: 150/158; SCREEN TIME: 131:14

THE POSTPRODUCTION SQUEEZE

By late October postproduction had already progressed rapidly in several areas. "We actually have a large crew, about 250 people," says ILM visual effects supervisor Pablo Helman.

"Before I even knew for sure that I was on the film I was getting calls

from people asking if they could be on this particular show," ILM producer Stephanie Hornish says. "When you're on a film like this, you feel like you're part of history in the making. There was a vibe on the set."

At this point in the schedule ILM had to finish 25 shots a week, having already completed 50. Everything was due by April 2008. "It's a challenging amount of work," Hornish continues. "We have about 570 shots, which is a lot for an action-adventure movie. It's very exciting and a bit terrifying. Fortunately Steven Spielberg has made it easier by delivering the sequences early in the process, giving us as much time as possible to do the work."

On the editorial side Michael Kahn and Spielberg, as always, had already finished their first assembly. Later in 2007 Spielberg and Lucas would go through their several cuts until they were both satisfied, as they had on the three previous films. "Motion means time," Lucas says. "The basic construct of time is rhythm, a beat, something that measures the time. So rhythm, structure, and intervals are very important in editing. Same thing in dance. That's all it comes down to."

"Michael Kahn and I still cut on film," Spielberg says. "We're very proud to say that we're the only ones still working that way."

"Steven is a sentimental sort of guy," Lucas says. "I'm not that sentimental, and I have a tendency to shortchange that part. So, between us, it comes out just right."

In fall 2007 Spielberg sat down with John Williams to spot the music, while sound design also began with Ben Burtt (who was also busy directing his own movie). "John Williams is obviously part of that family group that we've got going," Lucas says. "The scoring session is always a wonderful thing. He'll expand on the musical vocabulary he's created for the previous films, which is what we did with *Star Wars*."

"Overall the *Indiana Jones* scores have been very rich assignments musically," Williams says. "I have enjoyed them immensely and I have to say it's the result of Steven and George's personal predilections and feelings about music that's made it so gratifying. The *Indy* films have wall-to-wall music. It's wonderful for a composer when you have the opportunity to work on films that will hold that much music."

"I can't wait to sit in the recording studio when John Williams brings the baton down and 110 orchestra members start playing the *Indiana Jones* theme," Spielberg says. "I've heard it live at many concerts in the intervening years, but to be able to see the film using that music again eighteen years later is the moment that I've been looking forward to during the entire process of filming the fourth *Indiana Jones*. Everyone was humming the theme, and I was constantly playing it on the set."

Back at ILM, Helman and Hornish divided the team's work into three main areas: digital environments, such as jungle extensions, Akator wide shots, and interiors; particle work, a system for large-scale choreography of many small pieces that have to behave together as one; and creature work,

TOP LEFT AND ABOVE RIGHT: Allen, Ford, and LaBeouf did several scenes against bluescreen. TOP RIGHT: Blanchett as Spalko scales a cliff.

TOP LEFT: Spielberg in the church. "We begin the film in the fall and we end with the wedding in the spring, so it is a separate color palette, it is much lighter," Zophres says. "Marion wears a really great wedding suit that we built for her, and Karen looks fantastic in it. But it felt appropriate that she wouldn't be in a dress because she's a more mature woman; it's not her first marriage."

"For Karen's wedding outfit, Mary Zophres decided not to put her in a gown, and so a typical thing for a woman at that time was a suit," says costume designer Jenny Eagan. "A nice tailored suit; it's practical, but yet it's very sweet."

"For his wedding suit, I found a Donegal tweed fabric," says Bernie Pollack, costume designer for Harrison Ford. "It was a nice pastel shade and the only thing that I didn't like about it was that it was so hot. So we actually made doubles for it, because I thought he might sweat through it. We made shirts in a pale blue with a little tan stripe in them and then we picked a bow tie that incorporated the blue and the brown and it worked out very, very well."

MIDDLE LEFT: Lucas and Spielberg on the last day of principal photography. BELOW LEFT: Spielberg and Ford. "I was involved peripherally in the choices of the airplanes that transport Indy and Mutt to various places—you know, the red line on the map that shows our progress," Ford says. "And I found that the airplane they were planning on using seemed not to be the right one, and so I brought it up. I think we've sorted it out and we've got the right airplane." TOP RIGHT: Spielberg and Kristie Macosko. MIDDLE RIGHT: Allen and Ford join Spielberg in a celebratory toast. BOTTOM RIGHT: LaBeouf, Spielberg, and Ford

which included prairie dogs, monkeys, scorpions—and quite a few ants.

"We have a sequence that is full of ants, millions of ants," Helman says. "To do that we have a system to manage those assets where you tell the computer that these are the beings that live in this environment and they have a bunch of rules regulating interaction between them."

The monkeys had to be added digitally because the production wasn't allowed to bring its own animals to Hawaii. One shot in the script had Spalko callously knock a little guy off a cliff—but Spielberg later decided to show that the monkey survives his brush with the villainess.

"The hardest shots involve the spinning temple," Stephanie Hornish says, "because of what has to be simultaneously revealed and destroyed. It will keep developing as we work on it. It's a tricky concept and the big surprise in the movie depends on us getting that balance right visually."

"This show is very heavy on particle simulation," Helman says. "The last act of the film is basically taking the temple and converting it into particles, so we had to do a lot of research and development into that. It's not just particles that turn into water or dust or fire. They are behaving in a specific way and it has to be completely realistic."

"ILM's magic, as it has in the first three *Indiana Jones* films, will come in mainly toward the end of the story," Spielberg says. "They had their work cut out for them in the second act, but the magic will really pay off in the last ten minutes of *Kingdom of the Crystal Skull*."

COUNTDOWN

Another significant area of effects had ILM team up with Kerner Optical. The latter company was formed out of the ILM model shop when Lucasfilm, after moving its effects house to the Presidio in San Francisco, sold off its model shop and stages in 2006. Located on ILM's previous premises in San Rafael, on Kerner Boulevard, the company carries on the traditions honed over thirty years of making spectacular films. "They're among the best model makers in the business," Hornish says. "And it's great working with people we have a history with."

BELOW: Cast and crew production photo for *Indiana Jones and the Kingdom of the Crystal Skull.*

On Saturday, October 27, 2007, Pablo Helman and Stephanie Hornish spent the day outdoors at Kerner overseeing the explosion of an atomic bomb and the destruction of Doom Town.

"We won't see the beginning of the explosion," Helman says. "That event, which is a thermal detonation, will be done CG. Indy will see the tower from the town, and we'll zoom in on the bomb. Spielberg asked us to write on it, I LIKE IKE."

The vast miniature set consisted of roughly twenty one- and two-story houses built along a main street, with to-scale period cars, mannequins in costume, gardens, hoses, swings, and mailboxes. Everything had been built for certain camera angles; the whole took around seventy people approximately three months to build. Four cameras would film the explosion, running at different high speeds (60fps, 150fps), including a high-definition camera and a VistaVision significantly smaller than the one used by Richard Edlund three decades before.

"We took a look at the animatics that Steven had done with Dan Gregoire and his team," Helman says. "They had two cameras, so I suggested having a couple more. For research we studied a film made by Peter Kuran [who had started as an animator on the first *Star Wars* at ILM] called *Trinity and Beyond* [1995]."

The whole miniature set sat on a platform five feet off the ground, underneath which were the motors generating the air cannons, electricity, pyrotechnic controls, and so on. Every little bit of the miniature set had been detailed out, because the rule of thumb is: Whatever isn't appropriately finished will be the one thing blown directly at the camera.

To make sure the explosion worked visually, Helman had worked closely with model shop supervisor Brian Gernand. The two consulted on breakaway houses, pre-scored roofs, furniture, and houses stocked with debris that would be blown toward the cameras in a series of timed explosions set off back-to-front.

As is the case whenever something is about to be destroyed, the tension was palpable—there was no second chance. "Steven, Kathleen Kennedy, and Frank Marshall have been very trusting with Pablo and all of us," Hornish says.

As the moment of detonation neared, Pablo, DP Martin Rosenberg, and others took shelter in a equipment rental shed made out of steel. Additional crew and spectators retreated to a safe distance behind a fence; earplugs were handed out. Two guards out on the street stopped traffic where shards might land.

"Before you go hot, I'll yell 'All clear!'" Martin Rosenberg said. He then approached each crew member, asking, "Really clear to you what you're supposed to be doing? Really clear? Clear? When we're gonna start, I'm going to say, 'Ready'—but don't hit the damn button then."

Forklifts carrying huge fans moved into position. For eight days the wind had blown in one direction but now it was blowing in another, and they scrambled to get the logistics right. Time was running out.

"Pablo says shoot," one technician said.

"Oh, I'm starting to get so nervous," laughed one production assistant.

At the last moment more crew arrived to watch the explosion. John Goodman noted that it was unusual to be using air cannons with explosives. His lovingly detailed, miniature 1957 Chevy Bel Air was moved from up the street to a hero position in front of the carport camera. It had taken him forty hours to build, and it was so realistic that Gernand and Helman decided to use it instead of later compositing in a real car.

"What's your car going to do when it's hit by a ninety-mile-per-hour wind?" Gernand suddenly asked Goodman, who explained in detail all the inner structure of his model. "It'll work," he predicted.

Then, in what seemed like only a single second, the entire miniature set was blown to atoms. When it was found several dozen feet from the stage, Goodman's car was one of the few pieces relatively intact. Everything else had been reduced to shards or smaller. Immediately afterward, inside the shed, Rosenberg said to Helman, "The wide shot is good, then you cut to the other camera."

"It's important to remember that you see a lot more dust on the video than you will on film," Gernand said.

"Marty, all cameras ran," one technician reported.

"I think it's good," Helman said. "If there's a way to get a little less dust for the next one, I think we're okay." In two weeks they would complete a wider shot, adding new miniatures for a view with the sun at a different spot, because Spielberg wanted to give the audience the impression that the town was large.

THE GREAT UNKNOWN

On October 12, 2007, the Internet site MovieTickets.com, which had polled two thousand "active moviegoers" to find out which film over the next twelve months was the most anticipated, announced that "by a wide margin and across all demographic segments," it was *Indiana Jones and the Kingdom of the Crystal Skull*.

"The situation here is very much like what I had on *Star Wars* when I started it up again twenty years later," Lucas says. "There's a lot of anticipation on the part of the older audience because they loved the previous films, and hopefully they're going to want to take their kids to the new one. We're also trying to promote the film very heavily toward teenagers and young people, so they can discover this whole phenomenon for the first time."

LEFT: Seen from above, the Doom Town miniature built by Kerner Optical on the old ILM parking lot in San Rafael. TOP: Working with visual effects supervisor Pablo Helman (pictured) to finish the shots in time are: Richard Bluff, digimatte supervisor, also coordinating the Digital Artists Group in Singapore (another Lucasfilm company, consisting of about 10 people); Craig Hammack, who supervises the CG group and its particle work; Jeff White oversees the Digital Production group, writing codes to supervising rigid sims; and Steve Rawlins heads up the animation department, which focuses on creatures. ABOVE: The elaborate miniature is blown to smithereens, as one crew member plugs his ears against the very loud explosion.

"I want people to come to this movie and say, 'Oh, my old friends are back,'" Spielberg says. "And one of their friends will be the style in which we shot the previous films. I want audiences to come to this movie and make new friends, but rediscover that their old friends haven't changed all that much."

"We're excited to show it to an audience," Marshall says, "but there's tremendous pressure on everyone to live up to expectations. I think we all know what we're supposed to be doing and everybody's at the top of their game, so we just can't wait to show it."

"Because I know the other three films so well, I can already feel how this one is sliding into the canon," Cate Blanchett says. "It's really exciting to be part of something that you hope will really take off with a generation that doesn't necessarily know the franchise, but which also will last the test of time and sit in the little boxed set along with the other three films. I am completely and utterly stoked to be part of that legacy."

"The *Indiana Jones* films have inspired many directors. In fact, Michael Bay told me that the reason why he became a director was because of *Raiders*," Shia LaBeouf says. "The age span goes from 10 to 60. There's something for everyone in it, because Steven's mind works that way. He's built that way. Steven, more so than anyone I've ever known, understands the audience and understands how to make a joke for every single person, how to make a movie that appeals to as many people as possible."

"Both Steven and I adhere to the school of cinema as an emotional medium, and giving people an emotional experience is what we're trying to do," Lucas says. "We're not trying to write an essay on something. We're trying to do it in a nonverbal way, not in an intellectual way by reason and logic. *Indiana Jones* is very visual and it's very emotional, and that's why people like it."

"The *Indiana Jones* films truly are for the audience," Ford says. "They are visceral and emotional and surprising; it's a great ride. Part of it comes from a sense in Steven's mind that he is not separate and superior to his audience, that they are us."

"When I look back at the films, I have a lot of favorite scenes," Lucas says. "I love when Indy gets trapped in the cave with the spiked ceiling in *Doom*. I like the fight under the Flying Wing. But my favorite scene is the truck chase in *Raiders*—because that is really what got me thinking about the whole thing in the first place, that's how it got started."

"All the films I've done in the past 15 years have really been movies that have appealed to me," Spielberg says, "which I assumed wouldn't reach vast audiences on the levels of *Jurassic Park*, *E.T.*, or *Indiana Jones*. But this new film is for the audience; I had them in mind every waking hour: *What would they like to see, are we being too complex in our layering of clues, are they too far ahead of us, too far behind, are they going to laugh here, is this crazy enough, is it funny enough?* It was always for the audience!"

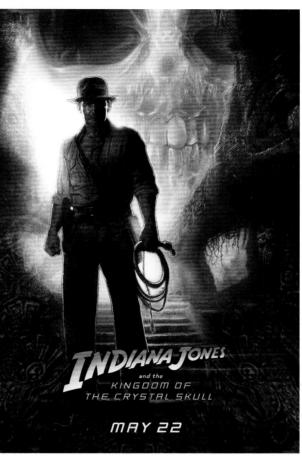

FAR LEFT: Concept art of the temple's disappearance into another dimension by Ed Natividad, which was further conceptualized at ILM. LEFT: Drew Struzan's teaser poster. BELOW: Concept art of Spalko's melting face by Alzman.

INDIANA JONES
and the
KINGDOM OF
THE CRYSTAL SKULL

MAY 22

BIBLIOGRAPHY

Ad Age, June 15, 1981.

Ain't It Cool News, www.aintitcool.com/display.cgi?id=17037, February 16, 2004.

Anonymous. "Finalists Selected for Student Film Festival." *Los Angeles Times*, January 17, 1968.

Ansen, David, with Martin Kasindorf. "A Cliffhanger Classic." *Newsweek*, June 15 and September 28, 1981.

Bandler, Michael J. "Kate Capshaw." *Moviegoer*, June 1984.

Broeske, Pat H. "How a Newcomer Became Indiana's Leading Lady." *San Francisco Examiner/Chronicle*, May 27, 1984.

Bruzenak, Ken. "Harrison Ford Battles Nazi Death." *Prevue Mediascene*, April–May 1981.

Burns, James H. "Lawrence Kasdan, Part 2: From Scripting 'The Empire Strikes Back' to Writing and Directing 'Body Heat.'" *Starlog*, October 1981.

Canby, Vincent. Review of *Indiana Jones and the Last Crusade*. *New York Times*, June 18, 1989.

"Chantal Interviews Kids Re: Violence in 'Indiana Jones.'" *Radio TV Reports, Inc.*, May 29, 1984.

Cohn, Lawrence. "Par Locking Up Firstrun Screens: 'Indiana Jones' Leads Off Summer Power." *Variety*, May 23, 1984.

Denby, David. "Movie of Champions." *New York*, June 15, 1981.

Elins, Merry, editor. "Steven Spielberg on Indiana Jones and the Temple of Doom." *American Cinematographer*, July 1984.

Ellison, Harlan. "An Edge in My Voice." *Future Life* 30 (November 1981).

Eon Magazine. Jeffrey Boam interview, 1996, reprinted February 2000.

Foster, Alan Dean. "Indiana Jones and the Temple of Doom." *Starlog*, November 1984.

Harmetz, Aljean. "Indiana Jones Stirs Rating Debate." *New York Times*, May 21, 1984.

Hearn, Marcus. *The Cinema of George Lucas* (New York: Abrams, 2005).

Holler, Ann, editor. *Raiders of the Lost Ark Collector's Album* (New York: George Fenmore Associates, 1981).

Jensen, Pennfield. "The Moving Image Interview: Michael Kahn: Film Editor at the Top." *Moving Image* (no date).

Kenyon, Nicholas. *New Yorker*, June 15, 1981.

Knight, Arthur. "Raiders of the Lost Ark." *Hollywood Reporter*, June 3, 1981.

Mann, Roderick. "Fluke Landing in 'Indiana.'" *News*, Philadelphia, June 9, 1984.

Marich, Bob. "Careful Promo Plan Pays Off on 'Raiders.'" *Ad Age*, June 15, 1981.

Maslin, Janet. "The Deadly Making of 'Raiders of the Lost Ark.'" *Los Angeles Evening and Sunday Herald Examiner*, June 6, 1981.

Pirani, Adam. "David Tomblin, A.D. to Indy Jones." *Starlog*, September 1984.

Pogache, Mark. "Indiana Jones and the Temple of Doom." *On Location*, June 1984.

Pollock, Dale. "Par Floating Lucasfilm's 'Ark.'" *Daily Variety*, November 30, 1979.

Rainer, Peter. "The Man Who Kept the Ark Afloat: Michael Kahn and the Fine Art of Film Editing." *Los Angeles Herald Examiner*, July 5, 1981.

Reilly, Sue. "Bio." *People Weekly*, July 20, 1981.

Reiss, David. "Raiders of the Lost Ark: An Interview with Steven Spielberg." *Filmmakers Monthly*, July–August 1981.

Rinzler, J. W. *The Making of Star Wars* (New York: Ballantine, 2007).

Sragow, Michael. "Raiders of the Lost Ark: The Ultimate Saturday Matinee." *Rolling Stone*, June 25, 1981.

Stewart, D. R. "Bruce Ramer, Hollywood Law Impact Report." Variety.com, March 28, 2007.

Tuchman, Mitch, and Anne Thompson. "I'm the Boss." *Film Comment*, July–August 1981.

Tusher, Will. "New PG-13 Rating Now Official." *Variety*, June 28, 1984.

Interviews by Laurent Bouzereau with the cast and crew of *Raiders of the Lost Ark*, *Indiana Jones and the Temple of Doom*, and *Indiana Jones and the Last Crusade* were conducted between January and June 2003.

Interviews by Laurent Bouzereau with the cast and crew of *Indiana Jones and the Kingdom of the Crystal Skull* were conducted between June and November 2007.

Special Note: Many quotes and some conversations are taken from Derek Taylor's *The Making of Raiders of the Lost Ark* (New York: Ballantine, 1981).

TRANSCRIPT SOURCES (CHRONOLOGICALLY)

Skywalker Ranch Library Archive Tapes (interviews by Derek Taylor and Phil Schuman):
George Lucas, circa July 1980
Steven Spielberg, July 14, 1980
Steven Spielberg, Well of Souls, July 18, 1980
Kit West and Paul Freeman, July 30, 1980
Frank Marshall, August 18, 1980
Howard Kazanjian, August 22, 1980
Steven Spielberg, August 26, 1980
Pamela Mann and Karen Allen, August 26, 1980
Steven Spielberg, August 28, 1980
Harrison Ford, September 5, 1980
George Lucas, September 5, 1980
Steven Spielberg, September 13, 1980
Steven Spielberg, September 14, 1980
Steven Spielberg, September 24, 1980
Doug Slocombe, October 5, 1980
Frank Marshall and Kathy Kennedy, December 2, 1980
Larry Kasdan, January 22, 1981
Steven Spielberg, February 5, 1981
Harrison Ford, February 12, 1981
Undated interviews, circa 1980–81: Steven Spielberg, Harrison Ford
Lunacon, April 13, 1984 (slide show presentation by Frank Marshall)
Omnibus interviews, circa 1999: Tom Pollock Steven Spielberg
History Project Transcripts, circa 2003 (all interviews by Pamela Glitenkamp): Ian Bryce, Ben Burtt, Sid Ganis, Steve Gawley, Howard Kazanjian, Kathleen Kennedy, Frank Marshall, Bruce Nicholson, Lorne Peterson, Ken Ralston, Howard Roffman, Tom Smith
J. W. Rinzler interview with George Lucas, August 14, 2007

PHOTO CREDITS